"To Ros,
I hope you enjoy the book.
Eddie

The Power
and
The Poverty

E. J. Colgate

George Mann Publications

Published by
George Mann Publications
Easton, Winchester,
Hampshire SO21 1ES
01962 779944

A CIP catalogue record for this book
is available from the British Library

ISBN 9780955241567

Printed in England

By the same author:
Falling Off a Horse in the Falkland Islands ~ ISBN: 0954163427

Further copies of this book may be obtained from:
E. Colgate, 7 Southview Terrace, Henfield, West Sussex BN5 9ES
Tel: 01273 494584

George Mann Publications

Contents

Illustrations

Other black and white illustrations are incorporated through the text as appropriate without captions. Apart from the colour portrait of Richard Davey and the pictures of Napoleon Bonaparte, no illustration is a presentation of a person named in the text.

Acknowledgements

Hurstpierpoint parish records items are published by courtesy of the late Rev. Michael Judge, as rector of Hurstpierpoint. For them and for the Cuckfield Union Guardians records, my acknowledgements go to the West Sussex Record Office and the County Archivist. East Sussex records are with acknowledgements to the East Sussex Record Office and the County Archivist. Census returns, transportation, the Hurst workhouse plan, Poor Law Commissioners' records and *Lloyds Shipping* are published with acknowledgements to the Public Records Office, Kew. For the Weekes family home life I am indebted to Mr. John M.T. Ford for his book *A Medical Student at St. Thomas's Hospital, 1801-1802*: London Wellcome Institute for the History of Medicine 1987. The colour print of Richard Davey is by kind permission of Rosalin Stenning, Hurstpierpoint. The prints of St. Lawrence Church & Holy Trinity Church (Quartermain collection) and the colour print of St. Lawrence Church by F. Earp are by kind permission of Barbican House Museum, Sussex Archaeological Society. The other colour plates are from *Brighton and its Coaches* by W.C.A. Blew M.A. published London 1894. The militia camp is from West Sussex Records Office; the New Inn and Archery at Danny are from Rev. Horsfield's *History of Sussex* 1835; Danny Mansion is from *The Worthies of Sussex* by M.A. Lower. The map of Hurst is based on the 1841 map by James Fisher at the West Sussex Record Office. The Yeakell and Gream map of 1795, plate 16 of M. Margary's '250 Years of Map Making in the County of Sussex 1575-1825', is reproduced with the permission of Phillimore & Co. Ltd. The sketches of country people and farming activities were drawn and etched by W.H. Pyne and are direct from prints published between 1802 and 1822. Wolstonbury Hill, the cottage and the National School are from the *Slight Sketch of the Village of Hurst, 1826*. The interior of St. Lawrence Church is an 'Inside View taken from the pulpit April 15th 1799 by William Hamper F.S.A' as copied for Mrs. Weekes of the Mansion House, Hurst, in 1845. Napoleon, and the man-of-war are from *The Life of Napoleon* by R. Horne: George Routledge & Son, 1875. The barque, capstan, reefing & treadmill are from *The Student's English Dictionary* 1895: Blackie & Son. The illustrations from 1830/40's *Sussex Advertiser, Brighton Gazette, Guardian* or *Herald* are with thanks to Brighton History Centre. For those from *The Illustrated London News* I am indebted to the British Library and to Hove Library. The top front cover illustration of the man seated with a book is by Marilyn Bechely.

Every effort has been made to trace and acknowledge each copyright holder. I apologize for any errors or omissions.

A sincere 'Thank You' to my publisher George Mann for his presentation of the text and his skilful enhancement of the 200 year old etchings used in the illustrations. Finally, 'Thank You' family for your wonderful patience.

Places in Sussex and Around Hurst

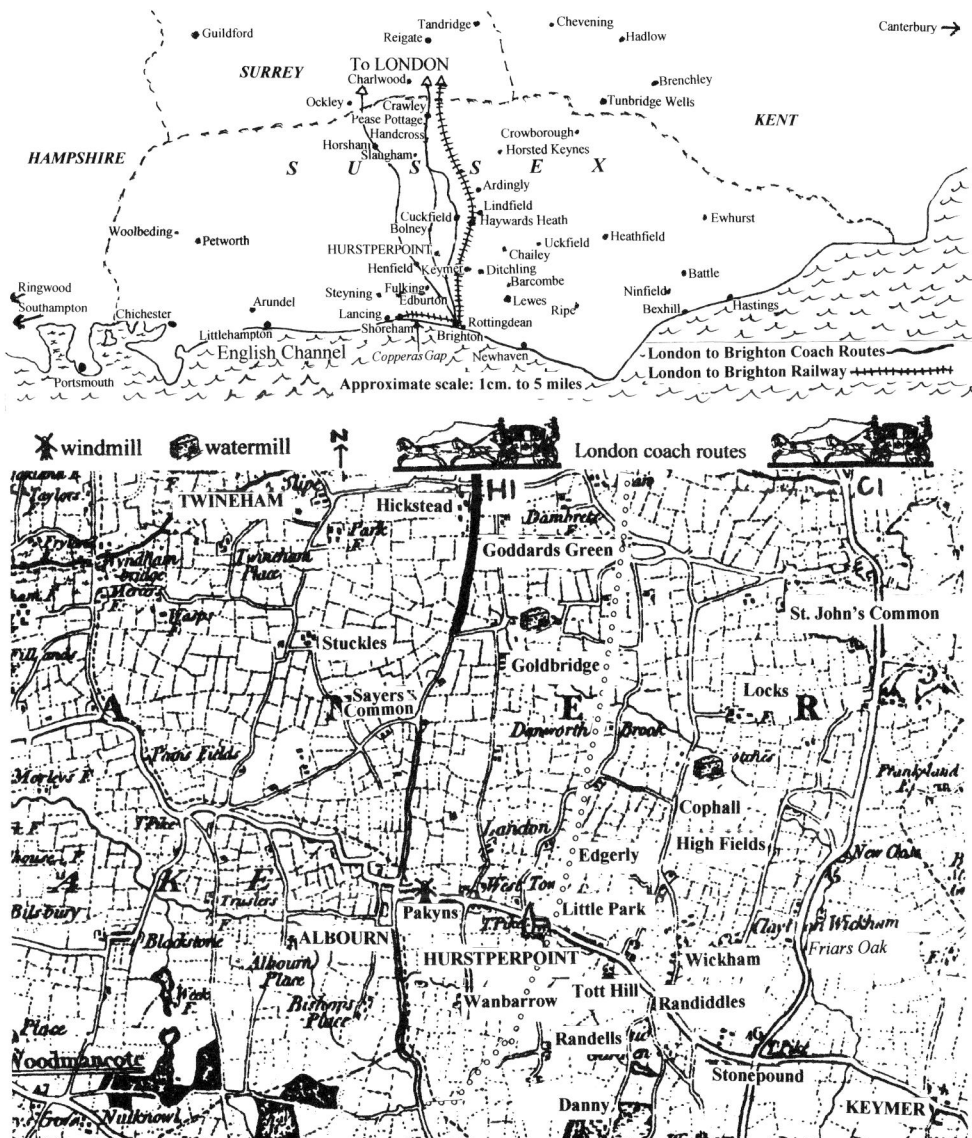

From Yeakell & Gream map of 1795 enlarged to scale approximately 1.2 cm = 1 mile
H1 & H2 = sections of new road 1808 from the 'Hickstead' route.   C1–C2 = route via Cuckfield & Clayton Hill
o o o o o o o o o = The 1835 toll roads south & north of Hurstpierpoint church.

Map of Hurstperpoint
based on the Fisher Map of 1841

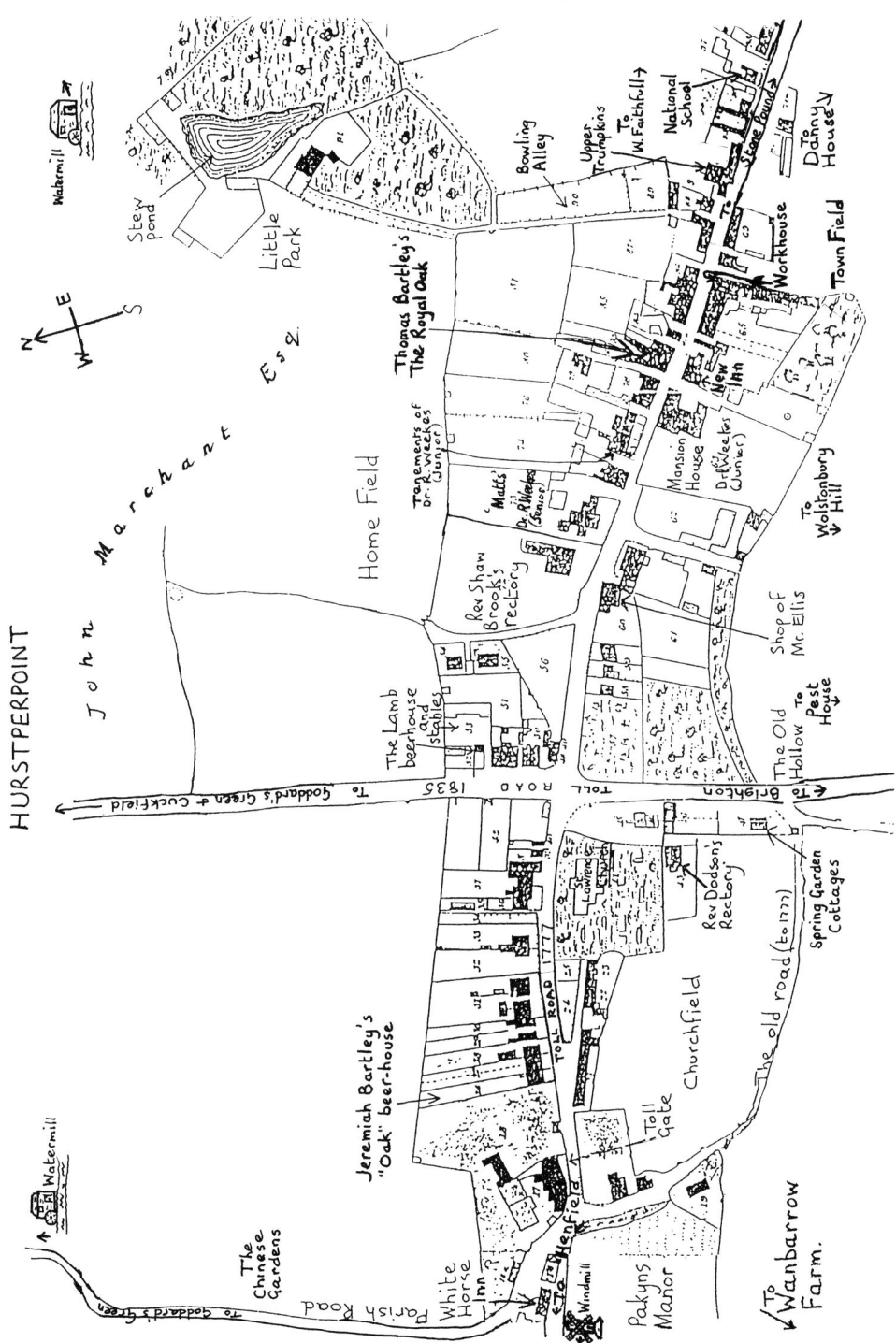

Wolstanbury Hill from the Church Yard J.Wells Del Hurst 1825

Introduction

This is a book about the people of a Sussex village, from 1790 to 1850, and how events elsewhere affected them.

The village, Hurstpierpoint, (Hurstperpoint in 1790 and for ease of tongue 'Hurst') lies some eight miles behind Brighton where the South Downs look out across the Sussex Weald. The southern landmark, the 600 foot bluff of Wolstonbury Hill, is in Pyecombe parish. From there, Hurst flows northward over a small sandy ridge onto heavy clay soils in a patchwork of fields and woodland merging with those round ancient Cuckfield. The easterly neighbour is Clayton, where the Brighton Railway's castellated tunnel plunges into the Downs beneath the Jack and Jill Windmills. The smaller parishes of Newtimber, Albourne, Twineham and Bolney complete the circle.

The pattern of life in England was slowly changing as agriculture and industry progressed. It was a progress that engendered sparks of unrest which occasionally flared until the law suppressed them.

Working days were long, and pleasures were few. Medical knowledge was restricted: death danced before everyone and gave no favours. Justice too gave short shrift. Since that was the way of things, people got on with life guided by their beliefs and prejudices. They worked, raised a family and found enjoyment where they could.

Property was held as freehold or copyhold of a manor, subject to the law and custom recorded on the manor roll.

The lord of the manor headed the parish hierarchy: a man of influence able, if need be, to sway the course of local affairs through the vestry committee. The rector enjoyed a special position with everyone – except the chapel-worshipping dissenters – as the guardian of souls. Landowner and farmer held sway over the shopkeeper and craftsman. Beneath them, came the farm labourer. All were superior to the pauper who by ill chance, idleness or loss of hope, depended on poor-law relief. Paupers were the bottom of the pile. Below it, were the law breakers.

Hurst's good times and bad are recorded in documents at County Records Offices and in contemporary newspapers which reveal pictures of parish life and the families living it. Their progress or failure evolves up or down a rigid social ladder set against a moving backdrop of war with France, burgeoning clubs and societies, religious rancour, village festivities, new voting rights and a transport revolution. Alongside is the ever beckoning door of the workhouse.

Several of the people in the book make a fleeting appearance. Others seem an integral part of the scene until they die or move away. A few are recorded on headstones in the churchyard, but anyone so poor as to need a 'parish' funeral lies in an unmarked plot somewhere beneath the levelled grass. When the churchyard grass is mown, who is being trampled on – Old Isaac Sayers perhaps, or Elizabeth Dunton's baby child, or the unknown vagrant from the barn?

At any rate, there they lie. Others who emigrated or were transported, who moved away or were sent 'Home' to their proper parish, all have a resting place somewhere because they too were real people living real lives – part of the power or the poverty of a Sussex village.

1790: The Village and The Gentry

At the western boundary of the parish, carpenter William Hamper erected a signpost beside the new toll road: TO HURSTPERPOINT.

Incoming travellers could already see the village windmill outlined against the Downs. Just beyond it, set back within spacious gardens, was West Town House – seat of William Borrer (senior), lord of Pakyns Manor. A little further on, St. Lawrence Church stood calmly aloof from the White Horse Inn which beckoned travellers across the road. Beyond there, the High Street began flanked to the north by the fields of Thomas Marchant's Little Park and to the south by Danny Estate land.

Danny was by far the wealthiest property with its glorious Elizabethan mansion, home of Henry Campion, at the foot of Wolstonbury Hill.

Danny House

The Campions were the pinnacle of Hurst society: selective in their guests; considerate and benevolent to the poor. Considerate as they were, they knew that each man, though no doubt equal before God, had his station in life. This had caused Mr. Campion great vexation when influential Sussex lords met at Lewes to petition Parliament for reform to allow every man the vote. He was adamant they were wrong and felt compelled to highlight the dangers through a letter to the Sussex Advertiser newspaper. He agreed that new towns should be represented and larger leaseholders enfranchised but never could the vote be given to the likes of butler, cobbler, tinker and chimneysweep. Bribery would be rife, corruption would become rampant. Only men entrusted with property, the providers of the nation's wealth, should decide England's Parliament. [1]

Although Mr. Campion occupied Hurst's grandest home and was the most influential person in the parish, he was still a tenant subject to his lord because Danny was in Hurst Manor, the main manor of the village, held by the Shaw family away at Eltham in Kent.

Another of the Hurst Manor properties, Wanbarrow Farm, was down a lane running south by the windmill: 92 acres (36 hectares) part arable and part meadowland. It was held by James Harmes, a sober industrious man. His main crops were wheat, barley, peas and beans. He ran a flock of sheep, a small herd of cows and some pigs. Poultry pecked around the barns. There were draught horses for farm work and a horse for himself. [2]

Horses, both draught and riding, had recently become taxable. Mr. Harmes already paid tithes on his animals and crops. The new tax was just one more with the land-tax, the poor-rate, the servants-tax, and the despised window-tax.

Only seven houses had more windows than his. Vast Danny contained 99 for which Mr. Campion paid £20 a year. It would take a labourer the best part of that time to earn such money. Many of the cottages with four or five windows were not taxed and their occupants were listed as 'Poor'. Throughout Hurst, 75 houses paid, 76 were exempt and one stood empty, 50% of the families officially declared poor. In parish terms, Mr. Harmes was a rich man. [3]

Wanbarrow farmhouse was sturdily built and provided plenty of room for the five Harmes children. Michael, the oldest, was 16 and well into his working life by the time his youngest brother, Edward, was born. All were baptized at St. Lawrence Church. Michael's baptism was recorded at the wrong place in the parish register resulting in the book's only illustration, a crudely drawn finger-pointing hand, suggesting that Michael should be elsewhere. The hand would hover over Michael throughout his life.

Mrs. Harmes was an astute housewife. When a parish officer visited London, she took the opportunity to order new gown material from there, her chance to parade a pattern not seen in the village. Locally bought coat, waistcoat and breeches for Michael cost just over £2. The vestry committee provided clothes for the workhouse girl sent out to Wanbarrow: shift, stockings, shoes, dress, coat and apron sufficient for a kitchen-maid. [4]

Mr. Harmes was a devout man acutely aware of the importance of status. He had already served his year on the vestry committee as overseer and had the hallmark of a future churchwarden. For £2, he had purchased prime front seats in the south gallery of the church, well worth the money. Church attendance was important. His family would pray, and be seen to pray. [5]

St. Lawrence Church was a solid landmark; stocky tower with shingle spire, nave, south aisle and two chancels – one for the church, one for the privacy of the master of Danny House. Only Mr. Campion and his entourage entered the Danny Chancel. There, unsullied by the general congregation, he made his devotions. The Danny Chancel was a bone of contention to some but no one was yet bold enough to voice objection. [6]

Each Sunday, the bells called the faithful to church. Gentry, farmer, tradesman, labourer or pauper, they quietly entered at the west door, its great oak panels forming the notice board for announcements of vestry meetings and Sussex Militia orders.

Inside, the church was hotchpotched and cumbersome. The old box pews reflected the status of the village families: Danny, wide and spacious, in the Danny Chancel; Little Park and Mansion House in the nave, standing higher and wider than those crammed around them. [7]

At the back, beneath the balustered west gallery, were the open pews of the artisans. There, too, sat the paupers from the workhouse who gathered each Sunday, by Workhouse Rule 4, to praise their Maker. Above the south aisle, the singers' gallery encompassed the thick-set pillars as if girding them together, and Gothic-arched windows filtered light onto whitewashed walls where sombre memorials frowned on all who dared admire William Hamper's nine decorative texts inscribed to brighten the gloom. [8]

The congregation occupied their allotted pews, chanted the allotted psalms, heard a lengthy sermon by their rector Rev. John Dodson and listened to the announcements of forthcoming parish business. Once a month and at Christmas, Easter and Whitsun, the service was followed by a celebration of the Holy Eucharist, the parish at peace with itself.

St. Lawrence Church

When Divine Service ended, the congregation scattered to their homes. Those living in the High Street walked the new toll road, following the hedge line along the Home Field pasture of Little Park Farm. Interspersed among the bigger properties were craftsmen's workshops – blacksmith, wheelwright, carpenter and shoemaker – but nowhere was the High Street crowded: plenty of space remained for future development.

Dr. Weekes was one of the first to reach home. His house stood on the north side of the road opposite the grocer and draper's shop of vestry clerk Charles Ellis. Dr. Weekes saw most parish children into the world and Mr. Ellis supplied many of their needs during life.

A few houses beyond the doctor's stood Widow Bartley's Royal Oak Inn, the 'Parish' inn. Of ancient heritage, it was the favoured spot where vestry committees met by inalienable right to transact their parish business.

Opposite the Royal Oak, Mansion House dominated the buildings. Mansion House was the home of Mrs. Beard, widow of Thomas who himself had once been dominant in parish life. Alongside it, was Mr. Courtness' shop with stables and outhouses. Mr. Courtness had obtained the vestry's permission and erected a vast wall between his garden and the next property, the place everyone shrank from – the parish workhouse with its paupers, simpletons and illegitimates.

After the Royal Oak, the High Street became a gentle hill dipping in front of Peter Wells' grocery to the Bowling Alley where 'Upper Trumpkins' stood four-square upon its hearth, barring the way and bidding the very road itself squeeze by as best it may. Finally, a little way beyond Trumpkins, were the slaughter house and butcher's shop of John Marshall.

The road continued eastward beyond the village: past the Randiddles Farmhouse at the corner of the Danny House lane, uphill by the mellow red-brick home of attorney Peter Morphee set within its orchard and meadowland, and on another mile to the Stonepound Toll-gate across the London/Brighton road where the Prince Regent's lordly coaches approached the grinding climb of Clayton Hill on their way to the pleasures of the sea.

The Workhouse and
The Vestry Committee

Campion and Borrer were relative newcomers to Hurst. William Borrer junior's children, William, as eldest son, John and Nathaniel were only the second generation there. The families filling the church registers from Tudor and Stuart days were mainly craftsmen's or labourers'. In past centuries they may have held property. By 1790 almost all were landless: Burtenshaw, Hazelgrove, Lewry, Sayers; Henty, Henley, Muzzell, French working a six day week on the farms for just 9s. 0d. (45p), and ensnared by Parliament's settlement laws which decreed that people belonged to the parish of their birth.

The exception was the baby born of a vagrant mother. That child was given its mother's settlement. A man's settlement predominated at marriage becoming his wife's as well. The indentured apprentice took the same settlement as his master.

People could move to another parish but their settlement did not change unless they purchased property there, occupied a house a full year for an annual rental of at least £10 or completed a year's employment contract. Few could hope to set aside more than £2 10s. 0d. (£2.50) for a year's rent. The majority stayed where they were, turning the same parish soil as their fathers and grandfathers.

The benefit of the parish settlement was that anyone utterly unable to provide for themselves could ask the vestry committee for help with food, fuel, clothing, rent or the doctor. Vestries were very aware that their responsibility was for bona fide parishioners only – and even then, not for a person owning property. Applicants with a doubtful settlement qualification were taken to the magistrates for questioning about their proper place. If the applicant could not prove the necessary settlement, the magistrates issued Removal Orders for a vestry officer to escort the person back to the correct parish.

James Hazelgrove discovered this when had to seek relief at Hadlow in Kent. They took him to the magistrates for examination. When his proper settlement turned out to be Hurst, the magistrates signed orders for his 'Removal Home from Hadlow to Hurst'. James and a Hadlow overseer set out.

When the pair arrived, a Hurst officer signed the order to acknowledge the completed removal and paid the expenses incurred. The overseer set off back to Hadlow. [2]

James was put into the workhouse. There he had to comply with the regimented plethora of petty restrictions that directed almost every minute of his day; up at six (sunrise in winter), prayers, breakfast eight o'clock, work, dinner hour at noon, work, supper, prayers and bed at eight (seven in winter).

The governess, Dame Gander, was allowed 2s. 0d. (10p) a week for each resident which gave her an income of about £2. With it, she shopped, cooked, made clothing and administered simple medicines although the vestry rejected her 1s. 0d. (5p) bill for 5 lbs (2½kg) of lard 'to cure the itch' – the excruciating soreness set up by scabies parasites tunnelling into the skin between the fingers and on the back of a sufferer's hands. Scratching the sores spread the scabies: entire households could be infested. Nobody wanted 'the itch' in the house but the vestry did not consider lard a potent remedy. [3]

Where possible, the workhouse was self sufficient. Vegetables were grown in the workhouse garden; potato, parsnip, turnip, onion, carrot and cabbage. Bread was baked in the kitchen. Pork and bacon came from the pigs kept in the backyard.

Butcher John Marshall supplied cheap cuts of beef, plus mutton for the sick. Charles Ellis provided groceries; tea, butter, Dutch cheese, salt, sugar, split peas, oatmeal, candles and best brown soap. [4]

The parish allowed half a bushel (18 litres) of malt a month for brewing. The brewhouse opened onto the yard and was the store for the wash-tubs and garden tools. Nothing interrupted the production of beer. A pot of beer was not only the main attraction at the pauper's meal but also essential refreshment for the washerwomen, the visiting carter and any craftsman doing maintenance work.

One rather unexpected item stood in the brewhouse – a bed. It was John Bodle's bed. With it were a chair and a hutch. They too were for John. The kitchen housed his pair of boots and the vestry room his best coat and kersey waistcoat. [5]

John's father had owned property in the village. In his will he had bequeathed everything to his wife with the condition that it should then pass directly to his daughter. Under no circumstances was his son to inherit anything. It was a wise provision because John was by no means a capable person, and a lunatic's property could be claimed as income for his support.

John was accepted at the workhouse. Dame Gander received 5 shillings (25p) a week for him and double price was charged for shaving him and cutting his hair. Occasionally he did unwittingly cause problems. When he had the misfortune to catch a particularly virulent bug, another workhouse man was given the unenviable task of 'cleaning Bodle' – a task that continued for three weeks. Generally, 'Mad John' was little trouble and remained quietly at the brewhouse to eat, sleep and pass the hours away. [6]

For the other residents, workhouse rules were strictly observed. Rule 3 stipulated that everyone was to go to breakfast, dinner and supper in the Dining Room where they sat at long deal tables, with benches for the able-bodied and chairs for the infirm. In reality it was the kitchen.

There, a black iron kettle hung from a pot-hook above a fire that kept an economic glow rather than a welcoming blaze. In the wall beside the fire was the oven. Poker, bellows and shovel leant against the fender. Overhead, part of the last pig-killing lay on the bacon rack. Along another wall, stood a leaf-table and an old dresser with the plates, the dishes, the candle box and candlesticks ready for the evening.

Water came from the well in the yard: a time consuming task. Each week the washerwomen spent two days scrubbing at the wash boards, starching and ironing. The well was cleaned at two shillings (10p) a time plus beer. The same rate applied for sweeping the chimney. The worst task was cleansing the privy: the one privy for everyone. The cleaners were allowed an extra perk of rum or gin, whichever they chose.

The rules demanded a standard of hygiene directing that 'The house and all the poor therein be kept clean and free from vermin.' Dame Gander gave the girls a thorough training in practical housewifery to keep the premises in good order. [7]

For some people, the workhouse was a temporary haven during difficult times. For many of the infirm and the elderly, and for eight illegitimate parish-children, it was their permanent home.

The infirm and the elderly were financed from the poor-rate. Payment for an illegitimate child came from the father. It was not a voluntary contribution. As soon as the vestry became aware of a single woman's pregnancy, she was taken to the magistrates. There she had to swear to the father of her child. The named man was summoned and he in turn stood before the magistrates to accept responsibility and undertake payment for his child's maintenance. It took a determined man to refute the charge and refuse to pay.

One of the illegitimates, Henry French, was just coming up to his fifth birthday. His mother had died when he was three. His father continued to pay the 2s. 0d.

(10p) a week maintenance charge. Along with the other children, Henry attended workhouse lessons where one of the paupers earned threepence (1¼p) per child per week teaching them to read from the Testament and to spell from 1s. 0d. (5p) spelling books supplied by William Courtness' shop next door. [8]

Across the road at the Royal Oak, the new vestry committee were gathering for the important Easter Week meeting. Their responsibilities covered much of parish life: the welfare of the poor, the upkeep of roads (except toll roads), health, local law and order, and the annual list of men eligible for service in the local militia.

The vestry was authorized partly by central government legislation and partly by justices of the peace at the quarter sessions court in Lewes. At the Easter Week meeting the vestry considered claims for Poor Law relief and set the poor-rate for the coming year to provide the necessary finance. The poor-rate was assessed on the value of property. It was paid by all land owners and by householders except those exempted because of poverty.

Parish relief targeted the most needy, the destitute poor – those too poor to maintain themselves. Simple poverty was no qualification. In normal times, the ordinary poor could guard against bad times by joining the Hurst Friendly Society which provided support for members during sickness or other need. In times of severe hardship, any labourer, and even the proud craftsman, might have to seek parish relief or dig flints with the unemployed on Wolstonbury Hill.

Vestry clerk Mr. Ellis was at the meeting to enter the committee's decisions into the minutes book. His knowledge gave the vestry officers (the churchwardens and overseers) essential guidance. The churchwardens were both experienced in vestry matters. The two overseers were just commencing their year of duty armed with the onerous directives received from the Lewes quarter sessions when their nominations were confirmed. The final directive warned that failure to give good account of expenditure could lead to court action. The vestry clerk's guidance was crucial.

The major item for the committee was determining the out-relief for people in their own home. First were the claims for weekly-pay, the money which kept families free of the workhouse. Mary Hole sent her claim by letter from Barcombe, ten miles away. She was 70 and had just been widowed. The vestry checked that she was a Hurst parishioner and granted her 1s. 6d. (7½p) a week. As long as she managed on the allowance, she could remain in her house: otherwise, she would be brought home to the workhouse.

Out-relief also covered the claims for fuel, flour and clothing. Through the year it would account for over £150 of poor-rate money. A further £80 was needed for the 33 families having rent partly or fully paid by the parish. Most of those families were still in Hurst. A few lived in other parishes safe in the knowledge that, for as long as Hurst remained their settlement parish, the vestry would provide their rent.

Finally, the butcher's contract for providing meat and the doctor's for attending the poor had to be completed. Mr. Marshall won the meat contract. Dr. Weekes became 'parish' doctor.

It all took time, plus a meal and drinks for the committee at parish expense. By the end, the poor-rate had been made at 5s. 0d. (25p) in the £ payable in summer and again in winter with the first money due in May.

Most ratepayers accepted payment as an unavoidable evil. A few withheld money until official last-reminders arrived from the parish solicitor. Anyone still not paying risked having possessions distrained by the bailiffs and auctioned to clear the debt.

The vestry had additional income from its cloth industry. Women were employed spinning woollen and linen thread. The weavers wove it into shirting or sheeting as needed at a rate of pay so low they had to weave over 50 ells (60 metres) to earn £1. Village dames earned precious pence bleaching the cloth. It then had to be carted eight miles to the fulling mill at Ardingly for finishing ready for market. Sales at the annual May Day Fair brought in £30 or more. Even better returns came just over the boundary at St. John's Common in Clayton, where 480 ells (600 metres) of cloth and 80 pairs of hose were sold for £50. It was valuable income. [9]

1791: Richard Pockney Buys a Horse

One of the regular paupers appearing at the monthly vestry meetings was Richard Pockney.

It was not that Richard shirked work. It was just that he depended for a living on his horse and a rather ancient cart. They formed his carriers business.

His equipment being what it was, he had to undercut rivals to gain trade. Occasionally he could earn as much as 6s. 0d. (30p) taking parish offenders to Lewes. Local work brought in only 1s. 6d. (7½p) a time for carting bricks, delivering coals and faggots or moving furniture when parish families were rehoused.

In November 1790, Richard qualified among the most needy parishioners given beef from a charity set up by 'Dog' Smith, a 17th century London merchant. He also figured on the list of ten poorest parishioners for a grant of 10s. 0d. (50p) from Hurst's own charity set up by past rector, Leonard Letchford. Richard's beef portion was a generous 28 lbs (14kg). His Letchford money was as good as an extra week's income.

Richard and his wife had brought up their six children in a rented cottage listed on the impoverished half of the window tax returns, '5 windows – poor'. The birth of the first child, another Richard, (now in service with the militia) had preceded the wedding by several weeks. The arrival of a child such a short time before its parents' marriage had not been newsworthy enough to arouse the serious village retribution reserved for those who gave birth to illegitimates.

The three sons had set out into the world as soon as they were old enough to earn sufficient to live independently. Just the eldest girl, Mary, remained at home. Mary, 31, was handicapped and unable to fend for herself. Second daughter, Charity, had been courted by day labourer, George Rowland, had married him at 18 and was now firm in poverty's grip with three small children to bring up. Youngest daughter, Elizabeth, had been away from home several years.

Both Mary and her mother contributed to the family income. Mrs. Pockney sat at her spinning wheel producing linen thread while Mary knitted worsted stockings. The vestry supplied the raw materials and bought the finished products for parish use. The family was still so poor they had to rely on vestry relief for their bread flour and the fuel to bake it.[1]

Fuel allowances were rigorously controlled. It was an ongoing expense for the vestry particularly during winter when cold weather brought greater demands from the labourers at precisely the time they were most likely to be laid off work. The largest households were allowed 200 faggots of wood or the equivalent in coal. A lone person's ration could be as low as six faggots. Mrs. Pockney had long ago learnt to use her fuel sparingly.

It was the vestry who provided the linsey-woolsey, baize, cambric and smidgen of lawn when Mary's coat became hopelessly threadbare. With the lining, the binding, tapes and a bonnet the cost was 17s. 0d. (75p) – far beyond the reach of Richard's purse. They also purchased new cord to support the mattress of his bedstead when a night's sleep became impossible.

During the winter cold of February, Richard's horse suddenly died. It was total disaster – his business as dead as his horse. Until the cart could move again, he would be dependent on his wife and daughter.

The vestry allowed him temporary relief of 2s. 0d. (10p) a week. At the next vestry meeting they lent him three guineas (£3.15) to buy another horse. He signed a promissory note undertaking to repay the money by a weekly shilling (5p). It would be tough going.

Richard was given the job of carting old Thomas Hazelgrove's possessions along the High Street to the workhouse when the vestry decided he could no longer maintain his home. There were few enough things for them all to be included in one load; bed, warming pan, chest, dresser, box, small table, chair, porridge pot, ladle, jug, tea kettle, teapot, gallon measure and a box iron with its stand – plus spade and mattock to recall past working days. Into the workhouse went Thomas and his belongings. If he could have a home again, everything would be returned. [2]

In the summer, the wheels of Richard's cart collapsed. Without it, he could earn nothing to repair it – a hopeless situation. Once more he had to ask the vestry for help. He was still paying them the weekly shilling (5p) for his horse but they decided his request was a reasonable one. They provided the wheels. Richard could breathe again. He was still an independent man. [3]

Independence seemed in jeopardy when the landlord gave three months notice for Richard to quit the house at Lady Day.

He appealed to the vestry for help. They promised to find another house at Michaelmas. Until then, the workhouse was available.

At the end of March, eviction day came. Richard, his wife and Mary had to move into the workhouse. They faced six grim months to Michaelmas.

The vestry accepted their responsibility for three Pockneys but were convinced the youngest daughter, Elizabeth, may try to join her family. Richard was warned that if any other member attempted to claim a place they would all be made to leave.

Life in the workhouse was the last thing on Elizabeth's mind. She was 19 and in love. Her suitor was William Burtenshaw, just two years older, a bricklayer although without steady employment. Their thoughts were on marriage.

Richard willingly consented. There was one difficulty, lack of money for the licence. The vestry overcame the problem by paying for both licence and ceremony. In April William and Elizabeth were married.

The parish had provided for the wedding out of poor-rate money: money that could only be expended on parishioners. As a single woman, Elizabeth had undoubtedly held a Hurst settlement. She now held her husband's. It seemed possible that Burtenshaw really belonged to Arundel. The vestry had to find out. They briefed attorney Morphee to investigate the matter. [4]

Mr. Morphee travelled to Arundel, Littlehampton and Steyning, a round trip of 50 miles, to subpoena witnesses who could help prove that Arundel was indeed Burtenshaw's parish.

William had to prove his Hurst settlement to the magistrates. His evidence was not accepted. Removal papers were prepared.

A Hurst overseer accompanied the newly wed pair the 20 miles to their legal home. There, he handed them over to an Arundel officer. The Arundel man reluctantly signed the Removal Order to acknowledge the Burtenshaws' safe arrival.

Both Arundel and the Burtenshaws considered themselves the victim of an injustice. For Hurst it was a closed case; they had acted as the law prescribed. If Arundel wished to dispute the findings they would have to do so through the quarter sessions at Lewes.

At the next quarter sessions, Arundel did appeal. The court found in their favour. Back came William and Elizabeth to continue their married life in Hurst. It was one more case of poor-rate money down the drain.

More money followed it when Thomas French was prosecuted for stealing an axe. Thomas was uncle to motherless little Henry French at the workhouse but had neither inclination nor money to befriend an illegitimate nephew. His own life provided more than enough problems.

One was the tedious obligation to attend periodic training camps with the Sussex Militia. When only 18, Thomas had been offered a chance to be the substitute for a man balloted to serve for Lancing Parish.

The militia had been reinstated in 1756 before the American war. Now, with revolution raging in France, a strong home defence force had become even more important. Each year, the vestry had to send the quarter sessions a list of all eligible men. A draw took place at Lewes to determine those who were to serve for their parish.

Those drawn for service had the option of obtaining a substitute to take their place. The substitute received an attractive bounty. It was enough to bait Thomas. What he failed to appreciate was how securely he was caught for training and actual service if needed over the next five years.

Thomas' next indiscretion was to court a young widow. Marriage became imperative. It was shortly afterwards that he was apprehended on suspicion of stealing the axe. The constable required blacksmith Herriot to help escort Thomas to Lewes and secure him in the house of correction.

The case was heard at the January quarter sessions. Thomas French was acquitted. Now he could unburden himself. Back he went to Hurstperpoint, to the White Horse Inn, known haunt of blacksmith Herriot. He burst open the door and confronted his man. Shaking his fist in the blacksmith's face, he vented his feelings: 'You are the rascal who helped carry me to the house of correction. Damn you! I'll take care you shall never do it no more for if I have an opportunity of catching you alone I'll do you. If I only had one at my side damn me if I would not do the whole house!'

Thomas French blustered back into the night. He had had his say and the blacksmith had better look out. [5]

Blacksmith Herriot did look out. Next morning he went to a justice of the peace to crave sureties against Thomas who was apprehended again and returned to prison.

At the summer sessions, Thomas French was ordered to provide a £50 recognizance and sureties to keep the peace for a year or to return to gaol. He was penniless and no one came forward on his behalf with £50. Thomas returned to gaol where he would remain until the money was produced.

He was still there three months later when the Michaelmas sessions were held. Up he came to court, listened to the same pronouncement about £50 with sureties and returned to his cell. [6]

Thomas never did provide the money. It was springtime before he saw Hurst again and that was just a fleeting glance because he was still a substitute required by the militia.

The militia camp was at Battle. Legislation granted a maintenance allowance for a militia man's family if they followed him to camp. Thomas took his wife and baby with him. Hurst paid them a weekly 2s. 6d. (12½p) and were then reimbursed by Lancing vestry because Thomas was serving for their man. The following April, Mrs. French had a second child and the allowance rose to 4s. 0d. (20p). [7]

Three months later, Thomas tired of the army and decided to quit. Lewes gaol had taken almost a year of his life, and the militia the next 15 months. Now he intended to be his own man. It was July – with long hours of daylight and the Lewes Navigation needing navvies: far better money in a far better environment. Thomas went.

He should have been well enough out of sight 10 miles away, yet a column in the Sussex Advertiser described six militia deserters and promised a £2 reward over and above the official rate for each apprehension. There among the descriptions was Thomas; his 5ft. 8ins. (1.7m) height, his fair freckled face, mob of red hair, grey eyes, his stout build, even his likely place of work. There too was the younger Richard Pockney, slightly shorter, grey eyed with light hair and a fresh complexion. [8]

The men were loose in Lewes, one-time home of infamous Thomas Paine who had sailed to France to champion 'The Revolution' and send back subversive ideas ripe for dispersal among disaffected Englishmen. For Hurst landowners, the desertion of Pockney and French was like men changing sides from protective militiamen to potential rebels spreading unrest and riot from across the Channel. Such dangers could not be ignored.

On Monday the 14th of January 1793, conscientious inhabitants of Hurstperpoint converged on Widow Bartley's Royal Oak Inn to form their 'Association for the support of the King and Constitution and the Protection of Liberty and Property against Republicans and Levellers.' It was an important meeting. [9]

The resolutions were read out. Everybody gave whole hearted support. They pledged their loyalty and determination to discover and punish any wicked persons holding illegal meetings to disturb the peace.

Rector John Dodson headed the signatories followed by Henry Campion, William Borrer, the lesser landowners, the farmers and the shopkeepers including William Courtness from his draper/grocer's opposite the inn. Although of advanced years, and far from firm on his legs, he was determined to show solidarity in the cause; duty to God, England and King George.

In turn they signed, or like unlettered William Sayers marked their X. The document was left at the Royal Oak for all those employed in labour and industry to sign as well and acknowledge their appreciation of the 'Blessings of that Establishment from which they received maintenance and Protection'. Few seemed willing to acknowledge their blessings.

A copy was forwarded for publication in the Sussex Advertiser. There it had to wait its turn with other loyal associations formed around the county.

On the 28th January, the Hurst pledge of loyalty was published. Just one column away was the paper's main story: 'EXECUTION OF LOUIS XVI'. The terrors of revolution were real. Four days later, France declared war. [10]

1793: Thomas Godman's Children Go in the Workhouse

In the summer of 1793, William Courtness passed away. His shop was put up for sale: 'An old accustomed Mercer's, Draper's and Grocer's Shop having large and convenient detached warehouse, stable, and other outbuildings, with a neat garden, walled in, the whole in good repair, and may be entered upon immediately.' [1]

The sale took place across the road at the Royal Oak. First William's stock (the Irish linen, hosiery, haberdashery and crockery) followed by the property. By evening, all had been sold, the bidders had gone and Widow Bartley could concentrate on providing good beer and wine for her customers.

For Thomas Godman, the opportunity to enjoy good beer did not arise. He was behind with his rent. This was dangerous practice with any landlord. It was particularly so for Thomas because his landlord was the younger Mr. Borrer who insisted that tenants who fell behind with their rent should look elsewhere for a house. Thomas knew he was in grave danger of losing his home.

The root cause of the difficulty was the vestry ending their undertaking to pay Thomas' rent. Although he had only two children, Mimay and William, his weekly wage could not cope with anything beyond day to day necessities. The responsibility for finding his own money was proving too great for him. He had been three months late in paying the Lady Day rent. September's Michaelmas payment was still outstanding in December.

Mr. Borrer felt he had been patient long enough. When Christmas passed without a sign of the latest rent, he decided it was time for action. £1 17s. 6d. (£1.87) was overdue. One way or another Thomas Godman would pay.

On the last day of the year Thomas had a visitor, bailiff Burchett with a letter in his hand. He showed it to Thomas: 'Take notice that by virtue of an Authority for that Purpose from Mr. William Borrer the Younger your Landlord I have this day seized and distrained -----.' Thomas had to stand aside as Burchett went through his whole house – the kitchen, the bedroom and the brewhouse – valuing his possessions ready for sale. Everything would go unless the rent was paid within four days. [2]

Thomas went to the vestry; it was them or lose his home. They took charge of the distraint notice and paid Mr. Borrer his money. The Godmans still had a home.

When the next rent day arrived Thomas asked for more vestry help. This time they made a condition: the two children must go into the workhouse.

There, they stood apart: two sore thumbs in ragged dress. Workhouse clothing was unmistakable, but not ragged, as befitted parish children destined to be farm boys or kitchen maids. People as far away as Brighton were keen to take them – along with a weekly shilling (5p) for keep and an annual guinea (£1.05) for clothes.

Although Mimay and William would not be put out to service, they were nevertheless provided with proper clothes. Shifts, petticoats, gown and tuck aprons were made for Mimay; regulation shirts and a round-frock for William. They would return home far better dressed as soon as their parents could manage to maintain them. [3]

For most women, making clothes was part and parcel of life. New technology in the cotton mills and the woollen industry meant greater choice of cloth. The draper's stock included calico, fustian, grogram, check and dyed cottons, brown Holland, blue baize, green prunella and diamond linsey with prices ranging from 1s. 0d. (5p) to 2s. 6d (12½p) per yard (0.9 metre). [4]

Such prices were beyond the reach of families on an annual income under £30. When the mother could not patch patched clothes any further or children had outgrown all the family possessed, the father had to ask help, hat in hand, at the next vestry meeting. And if the family managed to keep independent with clothing they would almost certainly need help with boots and shoes. On Thomas' money, Mrs. Godman had never stood a chance.

Mr. Borrer also had the frustration of being owed money by another of his labourers, George Rowland, husband of Richard Pockney's middle girl, Charity. Rent was never a problem for George because the vestry still paid it for him. His difficulty was the usual one of being stuck on an agricultural labourer's weekly wage with an increasing number of children to provide for. There was never any money.

Charity's own childhood had been fraught enough with her father's dependence on the parish hiring his horse and cart. She had known few of life's comforts and could offer no more to her children. The vestry gave her flour for bread, faggots for fuel and clothing for the children. Charity learnt not to think beyond essentials. Now she was in child again and, to crown everything, George had run up a £10 debt to Mr. Borrer.

Mr. Borrer waited for his money as long as his patience allowed. By December he had waited long enough. George was apprehended and taken to the debtors' gaol 15 miles away in Horsham. There he discovered a new depth to life.

Prison days were long, monotonous and seemingly endless. George could expect no visit by his pregnant wife, he was on his own. There he would languish, cold and forgotten, unless he could clear his debts or obtain favour under the Act for the Release of Insolvent Debtors.

The vestry provided for Mrs. Rowland. A further 25 faggots were delivered to her house and she was granted 3s. 6d. (17½p) in cash plus a weekly ration of half a bushel (18 litres) of flour from the miller and two ounces of 'threepence-an-ounce' (1p per 30g) tea from Mr. Ellis. She was given shoes for herself and linsey cloth to make clothes for the girls.

She settled to her needle and spinning-wheel. More blankets were provided for her children, her fuel stack was replenished. When April came and the baby's time approached, the vestry ordered the parish doctor. A parish girl was paid to sleep at the house. Dame Mary Jupp was detailed to attend at the birth.

It was in April that Mr. Ellis, as vestry clerk, received a letter from Horsham addressed to the 'Churchwardens and Overseers of the parish of hurst, Sussex.' He accepted it and paid the postboy: –

> 'Gentleman, With humble submission I take the liberty
> of addressing myself to you having sufford the calamities
> of a long confinement and not able to support my self I
> therfore most humbly implore that the gentlemen would be
> grashously pleased to interfere in my favour whereby I
> may be once more restored from the Dolesome walls of the
> prison warein I am confined that I may Do the best I can
> for my family a Gain. and by permission am Gentlemen
> your hmb srv George Rowland Horsham Gaol April 17th.' [5]

George's confinement had been four slow months, time enough for him to feel deserted and forgotten. Sending the letter raised his hopes but nothing happened to sustain them. In May, Mrs. Rowland had another daughter. She was christened Charity like her mother. George remained in gaol as unaware of baby Charity as she was of him.

George was equally unaware of a mid-May meeting at church where Mr. Borrer agreed to take him out of gaol on condition that a shilling (5p) a week was repaid until the debt was cleared. [6]

In June, George's great day arrived. The prison gate opened for him: freedom. Home he came to his new daughter – he was living again. In July, the vestry paid Mr. Borrer his £10 and began collecting the weekly shilling (5p) from George. The books would be clear in four years.

George continued his life labouring in the fields, unqualified, dependent on the farmer's needs and the weather, bound to poverty and his parish. His children's futures were as insecure as ever.

In William Borrer's opinion, poor-rate payments were squandered on families of men too idle to earn enough themselves. When the next demand was made, he studied it scrupulously. He objected to what he found. His own Pakyns Manor was fully rated but both Mr. Campion and Mr. Marchant had some of their property missed. Ordinary houses were not fully rated, some were not rated at all. The demand was partial and unjust. [7]

Mr. Borrer took his case to the quarter sessions at Lewes. The justices accepted his complaints and nullified the rate. Mr. Borrer was satisfied.

The vestry now had the major problem of setting a poor-rate that treated everyone the same. They were painstakingly careful. Every household was assessed. The new list included names which had never before appeared on it – cottagers so poor that they could easily slide into pauperism themselves. Where such people would find money to pay with, no one knew. However, the vestry had to pass a rate and it had to be accepted. [8]

William Borrer studied the new rate. He still considered himself wrongly assessed. He went to court again. The justices decided he and the vestry must arrange an intermediary to settle the issue.

It seemed impossible to achieve. At last it was agreed that Mr. Borrer would best ensure an equitable outcome by attending a special vestry meeting at which the poor-rate issues could be discussed and decided. The vote of that meeting would be binding.

At the next Sunday's Morning Service a vestry was called for the following Thursday. The minutes book was prepared in advance with the relevant resolutions set out: first the rate, at 5s. 0d. (25p) in the £, and second that the poor should be liable for payment.

The meeting took place.

The rate was passed unanimously. Next, the chairman announced that they had already met and decided the poor were not required to pay, thus the relevant resolution as set out in the book was null and void. The meeting concurred. The clerk scored through the entry and noted the chairman's remarks. Mr. Borrer had to accept. He was not a happy man. [9]

1794: Mr. Markwick Reaps
a Poor Harvest

The summer poor-rate of 1794 had to be set at 7s. 0d. (35p) in the £, a 40% increase. The vestry knew they had to be vigilant in curbing parish expenses. One area where they felt savings could be made was the workhouse. Dame Gander gave rise to no real complaint but was she running the place as efficiently as possible?

Dame Gander felt she was doing as well as the times permitted. She had even managed to cleanse young Mary French of the itch. When Dame French and her girl had entered the house the child had been full of it, her continual scratching threatening to spread the disease everywhere. Dame Gander knew her medication had ensured the general health of residents. [1]

The vestry were concerned with parish finance, not Dame Gander's medical prowess. She was replaced. It made little difference. Costs continued drifting upwards. Decisive action was needed.

One possible solution was to follow the example of parishes who inserted 'TO BE LETT,' adverts in the Sussex Advertiser inviting tenders from people for contracts to keep the parish poor. Besides terms for out-relief, the contractor would agree a price per head for providing good wholesome food and proper clothing for those in the workhouse and the terms for employing them in the woollen and linen manufactory.

Hurstperpoint were in luck. A Mr. J. Markwick showed interest in just such a proposition. The overseers and churchwardens met with him at the Royal Oak. There, it was agreed that for £70 a month James Markwick should maintain and employ the poor with the proviso that he need not attend the workhouse on Sundays. [2]

Mr. Markwick moved into the village. He would not demean himself by residing in the workhouse. He rented a place the other side of the street. He, James Markwick, was now the arbiter for pauper relief. His judgement would be final. [3]

It was August, the time of highest employment. Complete families were working in the fields although the bad harvest was restricting their earnings. With only 20 resident paupers and a handful of weekly-pays to provide for, the £70 would prove more than adequate.

Mr. Markwick ensured that everything was in order: the stocks of coal and faggots counted; the weekly-pay slips neatly scribed; the provisions order for Mr. Ellis carefully checked; the fuel, flour and clothing allowances authenticated.

The vestry ensured that everything was in order on their side. They charged £7 for the coal, £10 for the faggots and 1s. 0d. (5p) a pair for the 70 pairs of worsted hose in the workhouse. Mr. Markwick settled.

By the end of the month, he had fully rationalized the paupers' needs. Some living away from the workhouse had to accept a reduced allowance. Widow Hole out at Barcombe was informed she would in future receive no more than one shilling (5p) a week, a third of her money cut.

For his residents, Mr. Markwick had a well planned diet-sheet. Breakfast alternated between water gruel and broth. Dinner had one constant feature, a pot of beer. The food varied: soup one day; hot meat and hard pudding the next then cold meat and bread. Saturday was not so good depending on 'fragments' with bread and cheese. Everyone knew what supper would be: bread with butter or cheese and the redeeming pot of beer. [4]

People needing out-relief had to apply at the workhouse. When Mr. Markwick approved the request, he wrote an authorization note and sent the pauper up to Mr. Ellis for the requisite items. Mr. Wells' shop was nearer, just across the road, but Mr. Markwick knew the value of a good relationship with the vestry – the vestry clerk's shop was far preferable.

Paul Morris was one of the first to seek help. He took his note to Mr. Ellis' shop and was able to obtain his immediate needs. It provided for a few days but as no work was available he soon had to seek more help. Mr. Markwick knew that regular relief for the man was inevitable. The name was added to the list of weekly-pays. Paul Morris joined the group of parishioners turning up at the workhouse each week for the money to see them through to the next.

The weekly-pays were an unavoidable annoyance for Mr. Markwick, a constant demand on his resources. He knew he had to be on his guard against manipulative paupers: too many claimants were tarred with the same brush tacky enough to pick up whatever they came into contact with. Even people with a positive attitude to work needed to be assessed cautiously. Sometimes it was imperative for him to take the initiative. He did so when Dame Harland sent in a bill of 4s. 0d. (20p) for laying out one of Richard Wood's daughters. The woman's current claim may have to be accepted but it would be the last. He informed Mr. Ellis that future payments for laying out the dead would be reduced.

There was no doubting William White's honesty when he knocked at the workhouse door. His distress was obvious. His wife was seriously ill. She had to have nourishing food. He could not do it without extra money.

Although White had already received his two shillings (10p) for the week, Mr. Markwick agreed more was needed. The authorization was written, its limits carefully set. No more than five shillings (25p) was to be allowed. William White went home a happier man: he had food for his wife.

The next week White again needed extra money. Whilst Mr. Markwick knew he had to oblige, he made sure it could not continue:

> 'Mr Ellis Please to let W White have 4s. 0d. worth of goods and 2s. 0d. per week as usual from next Saturday JM.'

Henry Gander made his needs clear simply by being there – clothes. Nobody would willingly appear dressed the way Gander was. Mr. Markwick once again had little choice:

> 'Mr Ellis please to lett Henry Gander have 1 hatt
> 5 yds cloth for changes 2 pr hose about 16d or 18d
> each a new weistcoat Oct 23 1794 J Markwick.'

Gander's trousers would have to suffice.

Mr. Markwick was more wary when Charity Rowland claimed the vestry already knew about her request to do more spinning for the parish. Reluctantly he wrote Mr. Ellis a note expressing his concern but accepting that if necessary she should have it.

Mr. Ellis had no hesitation in supplying her. He knew Charity was trustworthy and capable, the mainstay of the family – so different from her incompetent husband.

Mr. Markwick did not argue. He was more concerned about the benefits of a better manufactory at the workhouse. It would enable him to ensure good yarn, good cloth and a bigger profit margin. He put his case to the vestry.

They allowed him £20 for building materials and took back £10 as part payment for the cloth he had received from the parish. Carpenter William Hamper supplied the wood and Mr. Markwick undertook the construction using the ample workforce at his disposal. He could look forward to increased productivity from spinners and weavers alike.

With the dark days of November, more candles were being used. Mr. Markwick accepted that decent candles were a necessity for work but elsewhere in the house rushlights would be sufficient. He decided his order:

> 'Mr Ellis 1lb (½kg) cotton twelves and 1lb small Rushlights JM'.

Thrift was as important in lighting as anywhere.

To add to difficulties, the early winter weather set in uncommonly cold making greater demands on his money. Extra economy was essential to ensure all genuine requests were met. His notes reflected his concern:

> 'Please to let dame Matthews have 8 yd of stuff to make a tick
> for a chaff bed Let it be cheap as any you have on account for
> Yr humble serv J. Markwick Dec 23rd 1794.'

It was the coldest winter for 50 years. Continuous frost froze the ground. Farmers stood more men down. They joined the band of weekly-pays at the workhouse door.

Mr. Markwick voiced his concern and sought further savings. There were 25 families on the weekly-pays list, a ridiculous number. No longer could he accept new names. He asked Mr. Ellis to reconsider them all and agree that in future the vestry should supply the money. The vestry did not agree.

Fuel expenses caused him further worry. True the weather was hard, but the fuel list was ludicrous; 3400 faggots distributed leaving him with a bill in excess of £40. Again he voiced his concern. The friendly relationship with the vestry was waning.

In February the two sides met to consider the disagreements. The vestry insisted they should have a written account of all monies received from them. Mr. Markwick gave it:

> 'Recd of Mr Wm Jenner the sum of four hundred and ninety
> pounds in full of all demands for the maintenance of the poor
> of the said parish £490 By me James Markwick.'

The vestry had no doubts about the matter. Markwick had entered into an agreement to provide for the parish poor and had been paid in full. He had enjoyed the harvest days of August; he must endure the frosts of February. Mr. Marwick had to accept.

Food prices, already high, rose higher. Workhouse-quality butter and sugar were at tenpence (4p) a pound (½kg) and cheese sixpence (2½p). Tea was 2½d (1p) an ounce (30grams).

On the threshing floors, the wheat yields proved less than expected.

Flour was up to 1s. 1½d. a gallon (6p for 4½ litres) or 9s. 0d. a bushel (45p for 36 litres). Wheat, barley, peas and beans were all scarce. Mr. Markwick had to turn to Mr. Ellis for help:

'Mr. Ellis, not having any flour in the house wish you could spare Dame Edwards 4 gals flour, I lb cheese, I lb butter, J. Markwick.'

Worse was to come. The miller failed to deliver an order and Mr. Markwick was without flour for the workhouse itself. He again turned to Mr. Ellis:

'Mr Ellis I should esteem it a favour if you Could Spare me 2 Bushels of Flower as the miller neglected some on Thursday JM.'

The grain crisis was so severe that the Government's new department, The Board of Agriculture, promoted potatoes as a commercial crop capable of providing sufficient nourishment if the summer's harvest failed. Their official guide recommended types to grow, methods of cultivation, safe storage and a recipe for potato bread. Farmers were encouraged to grow as many potatoes as possible. Best yields would be rewarded. [5]

Help from the potato remained a thing of the future. James Markwick needed help now. His £70 was no longer sufficient. He was broke.

When the weekly-pays arrived for their money, Mr. Markwick was even-handed with them – and utterly empty handed. He had no money for anyone. It was no use them saying he had to find some: there wasn't any. They would have to apply to the vestry.

The disgruntled labourers found the overseers and explained the position. Some had been on the list since August: most were out of work because of winter weather. Each had a wife and children at home expecting money for food, a total of 104 children. Where was their weekly pay?

An emergency meeting was called. The vestry sympathized with the labourers but would not provide money. That had to come from Mr. Markwick. Because he was refusing to pay, the men would have to appeal to the magistrates in Lewes.

Rev. Dodson agreed to support the appeal and speak for his parishioners. 25 Hurst labourers, accompanied by their rector, went the 10 miles to Lewes to claim their right to weekly pay; Hazelgrove, Pockney, Lewry, Gander, White, Sayers – names deeply etched in the list of parish poor. [6]

The magistrates heard each man and considered the rector's appraisal of their character. Just one man failed. He was sent away empty handed. The others each received an order for relief assessed on family commitments.

The men had a far happier journey home with magistrates' orders for their pay. Back in Hurst, they had the added surprise of being invited to the White Horse for beer at parish expense.

Mr. Markwick now had to meet his commitments and repay the parish the relief ordered by Lewes. Yet his debts were already so great with unpaid bills that a large part of his next salary was spoken for.

On the first of March, the vestry met again and authorized an emergency poor-rate at 3s. 0d. (15p) in the pound. It would finance the parish through the crisis to mid-April when the new churchwardens and overseers would set the next scheduled rate. [7]

Mr. Jenner wrote a note to Mr. Ellis authorizing him to let Markwick have essentials for the workhouse. Mr. Jenner himself would undertake payment.

For Mr. Markwick, it was a hopeless task. During March, the inmates chewed their way through 127 lbs (56kg) of cheese and 31 lbs (15kg) of butter washed down with copious pots of beer. Cleaning and lighting destroyed soap, brooms and candles. Cooking and heating swallowed faggots and coal. Richard Pockney took a weekly 6s. 0d. (30p) worth of goods. Charity Rowland had to be paid another 4s. 0d. (20p) for spinning. Henry Gander's breeches failed and their replacement cost 5s. 0d. (25p). Paul Morris, who had been among the first to seek Mr. Markwick's relief, had one final need – a 5s. 0d. shroud for his dead body. [8]

Mr. Markwick struggled on until the end of the financial year when accounts had to be drawn up. He prepared another statement:

> 'Recd of Mr Wm Jenner overseer of the poor of the above parish the
> sum of Seventy Pounds in full of all demands up to the above day
> This not being enough to Compleat the Month nor am I able to pay
> any further expense that may be incurred I hereby Indemnify the said
> Mr Wm Jenner from any Demand by me or in my name whatsoever
> Witness my hand James Markwick.'

Circumstances had beaten him. Whether it was the severe winter, poor management or the vestry luring him with £70 that seemed so much yet proved so little, Mr. Markwick was a broken man. He went. The vestry put Dame Gander back in charge.

For farmers, the spring was encouraging. Three weeks of dry weather helped everyone. The February frosts, so damaging to Mr. Markwick, had worked wonders on the soil.

Crops were now forward. Wheat fields were healthy and there was every promise of a plentiful harvest. Yet, until the wheat was safely gathered, the grain shortage would remain critical.

Foreign grain was preventing complete disaster but stocks were so low that rich and poor alike were called upon to refrain from eating white bread. Millers were told to produce only brown flour. 'A brown loaf is better than no loaf,' was the motto of the day.

The Prince of Wales set the example by allowing only brown bread at his table. Officers at the Brighton camp followed suit and reduced their ration to one pound a day using meat and vegetables to make up the deficiency.

The Hurst labourers wished they too could make up with meat instead of the rice suggested by Lord Sheffield as so wonderful an alternative. One pound of rice equalled eight of flour according to his lordship. Plain boiled rice with sweet or savoury sauce, rice puddings with milk, rice in bread, rice stew with a little bacon, rice with treacle, rice with apples. The combinations were endless. With rice at her finger-tips, what cottage wife need keep her family short of good nutritious food? And in a few months the new wheat harvest should again provide for all.

There was more encouragement for the cottagers when Henry Campion procured the lordship of Hurst Manor from the Shaws of Kent. They held on to the patronage of the church and would continue to appoint the rector but 'Lord of the Manor' was now Mr. Campion at Danny. He would not sit by and let his people suffer.

For the poor-rate payers, 1795 was a disaster. By the end of the year, payments had amounted to an incredible 23s. 8d. (118p) in the pound – a staggering increase imposed on landowners and farmers striving to feed a country at war.

1796: Henry Beazley Joins the Navy

The bad winter became a thing of the past but the fear of Republicans and Levellers and the war with France eroded civil liberties. Calls for Parliamentary reform ceased and habeas corpus was suspended. Greater powers were vested in justices of the peace. Public meetings were banned unless magistrates granted a licence.

The army and the navy were intent on finding recruits fit for fighting.

The navy was in dire need of men. The threat of the press-gang was very real but societies had been formed to raise money for extra bounties to encourage volunteers. The Campions at Danny did their bit for the cause by subscribing to the Lewes Society. [1]

Parliament decreed that parishes should supply men for the navy according to the number of houses rated. Hurst, with 80 houses rated, was part of a group having to provide three men. The only hope of achieving the task was to place an advertisement in the Sussex Advertiser:

VOLUNTEERS WANTED

THREE ABLE-BODIED SEA OR LANDMEN

BETWEEN THE AGE OF 16 AND 45 YEARS

TO SERVE IN HIS MAJESTY'S NAVY,

TWENTY GUINEAS BOUNTY

WILL BE GIVEN TO ANY SUCH, WILLING TO ENTER, BY APPLYING

TO THE CHURCHWARDENS OR OVERSEERS OF EITHER OF THE PARISHES

OF HURST, KEYMER, OR CLAYTON, OR THE HAMLET OF EAST-CHILTINGTON,

N.B. BY THE ACT, PERSONS ENROLLED ARE NOT LIABLE TO SERVE MORE THAN

ONE MONTH AFTER THE WAR, IF ARRIVED AT ANY PORT OF GREAT-BRITAIN. [2]

The Advertiser had a full column of parish adverts vying to attract navy volunteers. Some were full of advertisers' guile.

Steyning's offered opportunities to 'Four spirited young men, able and willing to serve their country, on board his Majesty's Royal Navy, and now on the point of sailing in quest of Spanish Galleons.... N.B. 4 only can be taken: – young Men, desirous of embracing this opportunity of making their fortune, may see a specimen of British Valour and Spanish Fighting by reading Captain Bower's letter, in Gazette of Tuesday last.'

Rottingdean saw no necessity to make any reference to valour. They felt confident enough to predict: 'Your purses shall be well laden with GOLD.'

Hurst's uninspiring advert did not attract a flood of applicants. Just two men responded; a 35 year old seaman from London, Henry Beazley, and Thomas Carpenter, a 16 year old who had wandered across from Wiltshire to Sussex and found work in Hurst as a labourer. He had to be provided with over a pound's worth of clothing to make him presentable. A £21 fine would represent the third man. [3]

Once both men were decently attired they were taken to Newhaven. The navy accepted them and they boarded ship. What Beazley and Carpenter would think of conditions at sea was of no concern to Hurst – but within four months the men of the Channel Fleet revealed their corporate opinion of the sailor's life by mutinying at Spithead.

Capstan   Man o' War   Reefing

Village lads were attracted by the drum and fife of the recruiting sergeant seeking soldiers for the regular regiments of the line. Vacancies were there for carters and drivers in His Majesty's Park of Artillery. Advertisements in the paper called on 'Spirited young fellows tired of following the dull plough,' to use their horse handling skills in the army where good clothing awaited them plus honour and pleasure. All they need do was turn up at Ditchling or Brighton and accept a handsome bounty. It was there for the taking. [4]

Richard Davey decided a soldier's life was the life for him. He took the bounty and became a King's man. He would prove a good soldier.

William Miles was attracted by the money paid to the militia substitute. He replaced a man drawn to serve for Woolbeding some 30 miles away. The camp was at Chichester. William's wife went too. Hurst sent her the allowance payable to militia wives. [5]

Militia Camp near Chichester 1790.

Mrs. Miles was expecting a baby. Nearer her time she returned to Hurst to await the birth. Dr. Weekes was booked to attend her. In late October a son, James, was born. The following summer, Mrs. Miles took baby James back with her to William, now encamped the other side of the county near Battle. Hurst increased her pay by 1s. 6d. (7½p) a week for James. With the extra money, life continued satisfactorily for almost a year until the baby's allowance failed to arrive.

William waited patiently but to no avail. At last he wrote asking Hurst to reinstate the money. He enclosed his service certificate proving him to be actually serving. [6]

The vestry considered it at the next meeting where they decided that the certificate had to be validated at the magistrates.

William sought the advice of the sergeant-major. The sergeant-major had no intention of allowing a parish to order the militia around. William was instructed to inform Hurst it was the vestry, not the militia, who should go to the magistrates and that his sergeant-major was the source of the information.

William wrote his letter. It was enough. The vestry took prompt action. Payments resumed and the family was able to cope.

Within a few months, Mrs. Miles had a second baby, Frances. The militia were now encamped back at Chichester. Increased parish payments arrived from Hurst weekly.

Family life went its normal course until an autumn fortnight passed without Mrs. Miles receiving her money. Penniless, she turned to Chichester vestry for help.

Chichester wrote to Hurst. Their letter was concise. If Hurst did not send money, Chichester would send the family.

Hurst chose to send money by return and were even more careful in making payments. Mrs. Miles could concentrate on raising her family.

The next year's baby was a girl, lovingly christened Barbara after her mother. Mrs. Miles found herself facing the winter with three children to feed, high prices and the cold intensifying. No longer able to cope, she took up her only weapon and wrote direct to Hurst vestry:

> 'sir we are all a starving for want of necessary provisions my husband has only 9½d. a day and i have only 6s.per week for myself and three children and rent and firing and everything to buy out of it i have no opportunity of earning a penny and my poor children are crying round me for bread when i have not to give them and i can't bear it sir if they will not send me some relief in the course of the next week my husband will get a furlow then he will come home with me and then i shall stop there for i think it is very hard to have no encouragement good gentlemen we want half a bushel of flour a week for our family where we have only a few potatoes and a draught of cold water... I can't say anymore so my good gentlemen if i don't hear from you next week i shall be at home the week after if it please god to enable me to get there from your most obedient servant Barbara Miles.' [7]

The vestry dealt with Mrs. Miles' letter by sending her another pound and continuing payments of just enough to keep the family away. Mrs. Miles expressed her gratitude. The vestry saw themselves as simply doing their best to keep expenses down.

Widow Mary Hole, struggling to maintain her home at Barcombe, was another one failing to cope. She feared the workhouse and was near to breaking. Although her allowance had been restored at the end of the Markwick days, life had become more and more difficult. In desperation she wrote to her son:

> 'Dear Anthony pray do for I am very poorly bag the gentlmen and overseers will be so good as to allow me a lettel more pay and let me not starve the lettl time I have to live for I of out live all my friends what shall I do a poor miserable widow Mary Hole.'

Her son forwarded the letter to Hurst. The vestry found it a discomforting case. Their own financial position was bad. Each expense had to be carefully weighed, every penny was crucial. They came to a hard decision. Widow Hole may have outlived her friends but it was scant reason for increasing her allowance. The workhouse was available.

Widow Hole was distraught. She wrote direct to Mr. Marchant:

> *'Sr I beg you will be so good as to lay this before the gentlemen and overseers at your meeting for I humbelly pray they will let me have Something more a week now in the time of this dreadfull dearth for I am old an cold an full of paine pray consider me and send sume relefe more whilst bread and everything is so very dear from a poor distresd widow Mary Hole.'* [8]

Mr. Marchant took it to the next vestry meeting. They agreed to increase her money by sixpence (2½p) to two shillings (10p) a week. With the extra sixpences, Widow Hole battled on.

The vestry turned their attention to another problem, Ann Grey, a parish-child in the workhouse who had strange mannerisms which made it difficult to place her as a servant. Thomas Bartley provided the solution by agreeing to take her at his saddler's shop beside the Royal Oak. The vestry allowed a guinea (£1.05) for Ann's clothes and paid Thomas the weekly shilling (5p) for her keep.

At first, Mrs. Bartley coped with the eccentricities. Gradually the bouts of strange behaviour increased until Ann was more a liability than a servant. Finally Mrs. Bartley could take no more. She refused to keep her any longer.

Ann was returned to Dame Gander who was allowed 8s. 0d. (40p) a week for the trouble incurred.

For a time, the 8s. 0d. seemed acceptable but Ann's behaviour continued to deteriorate until Dame Gander declared that she, too, could take no more. The girl was impossible.

After the Sunday morning service, Rev. Dodson called a special vestry meeting. Churchwarden William Jenner, overseer Henry Wickham and Dr. Thomas Marchant stayed with five members of the congregation, among them Michael Harmes, heir to Wanbarrow Farm, who was already accepting his social obligations. The agenda was Ann Grey. What should be done with her? [9]

There was general agreement that Ann was suffering some derangement of the mind although it did not warrant the expense of an asylum. They decided the practical solution was to put her in the Pest House.

Ann was taken to the Pest House under the care of pock-marked Mary Howard. The price for her keep rose to 10s. 0d. (50p) a week.

The arrangement had one glaring weakness. The Pest House was the isolated cottage rented from Mr. Campion as a safe place to put anyone with fever or smallpox. Ann Grey would be at risk next time smallpox broke out in the village.

The disease inevitably struck again. Ann, almost centre stage at the Pest House, fell victim.

Dr. Weekes still held the parish doctor contract so it was he who attended the pauper patients. Although smallpox sufferers were nursed back to health when possible, there was little hope of recovery if it was a virulent strain. The present outbreak was mild. Dr. Weekes' treatment was effective. His bill went to the vestry: 'Medicine & attendance on Ann Grey in the natural smallpox £3 3s. 0d.' (£3.15). [10]

When Matthew Martin and his wife went down with it, the vestry moved them and their four children into the Pest House. Dr. Weekes attended the parents and inoculated the children. Ann was nine, Catherine seven, Mary five and Thomas a two year old toddler. Because of their weak condition, they were allowed free regular meat, an unaccustomed luxury. [11]

For six weeks Mary Howard nursed the family. Mr. and Mrs. Martin slowly regained their health. The children suffered the discomforts of the mild disease but with it came the knowledge that they would be safe the next time an outbreak struck the village however virulent it proved.

Dr. Weekes' account for attending the family, almost £7, was paid out of poor-rate money. It would have taken Matthew three months to earn enough for the bill even if he had constant employment, months more to find sufficient to actually pay.

The vestry faced total smallpox expenses of £60 with another £50 for other illnesses. It was beyond anything they had budgeted for. The shortfall would be recouped in the next poor-rate.

Demands on their resources had become so great that the old land valuations on which the poor-rate was raised were no longer adequate. It was decided that the parish should be resurveyed for new valuations. The increases were accepted as inevitable.

A further task was demanded by Parliament. The French situation made it imperative that a true account of the inhabitants of Britain be compiled. The population was to be determined through a national census. It was to be carried out with all speed. The vestry complied. Hurstperpoint residents were counted and found to be 1104.

1801: Hampton Weekes
Attends Medical School

Dr. Weekes, whose inoculations helped families during the smallpox outbreak, had experienced sadness in his own family at the death of his wife when their four children were still young. For five years he had brought the children up on his own before marrying again. His two boys, Hampton and Richard, had later boarded at Merchant Taylors School in London. Both intended being doctors and helped their father as 'shopmen' preparing medication and assisting with patients. The girls too, Mary Ann and Grace, were knowledgeable in medical matters as well as the all important disciplines of fine needlework, etiquette and French. [1]

Their home, 'Matts', gave an uninterrupted view northwards across Mr. Marchant's Home Field to the Weald. The large walled garden was a delight to them. Fruit trees flourished: apple, pear, cherry, plum and a peach. There were grapes, an abundance of gooseberries and strawberries, and an array of flowers: snowdrops, aconites and crocuses in spring, Sweet Williams, pinks and roses in the summer and Michaelmas daisies to brighten the shortening autumn days. For daughter Grace, a tame robin bold enough to come for crumbs completed the picture, a pageant of colour and life. [2]

The family dined well with oysters from London, carp from the Little Park stewpond, Hurst mutton and their own garden vegetables. During the dark evenings of winter, dinner was often followed by cards. Hampton was in London for two years studying medicine at St. Thomas' Hospital so whist, the family favourite, gave way to quadrille where the girls were as skilled as anyone. Other evenings saw chess and backgammon, or Dr. Weekes enjoying a pipe with a friend whilst Mary Ann wrote to brother Hampton. No matter how insignificant the item – the rector off on holiday, Widow Gander turned out of the workhouse, Mansion House needing a tenant, the Watch calling that it was past nine o'clock – it kept Hampton in touch with village life, even when the social news from brother Richard was 'Hurst is as dull as ever.' [3]

Hurst's dull monotony had its moments. The Gunpowder Celebrations on November 5th were the chance for Richard to let his hair down with his contemporaries Nathaniel Borrer and William Ellis. They spent a full 12s. 6d. (62½p) on sky rockets – way in excess of the working man's weekly wage. At evening time they assembled on the church green. To the background noise of the bell ringers' Guy Fawkes peal, the rockets whooshed into the heavens, a thrill for launchers and celebratory villagers alike. [4]

Very occasionally a visit to London was possible. There was a reliable pair-horse coach service via Stonepound Crossroads. When Mary Ann was invited to stay with friends in London it was the perfect opportunity to see Hampton. Richard booked a seat for her to the Swan and Two Necks in Lads Lane. The journey would take a good eight hours. Hampton was told to be at Lads Lane by 4.30 to ensure he was there before the coach. Mary Ann would have no travelling companion. London was no place for a lady without an escort. [5]

Hampton made sure he was at the Swan and Two Necks in plenty of time, the responsible brother ensuring his younger sister's well-being.

With Hampton in London, it was simple to place town shopping orders. He was dutiful to his family whatever the request. Occasionally, a task involved a deal of searching. Finding a suitable wall to wall carpet for the best parlour proved difficult. The weave had to be close and the colour guaranteed not to show the dirt. The family wrote several times reminding Hampton of his task. He finally found a suitable one only a little too big and sent it down by Knowles' Wagon, the village's weekly link with the city. It proved an excellent choice.

Most requests were straight forward. London butter and London brewed porter were considered far superior to Hurst's. Hampton supplied both. When Dr. Weekes complained of the poor quality of Mr. Ellis' quill pens, 50 were sent with a pen-knife to repair them. When Mr. Randell, pre-eminent among the Hurst shoemakers, declined to make buck boots to Hampton's specifications, the order went to London. [6/7]

While the family could dictate their associations with the village traders, they were less able to influence their own standing with the Campions, the social summit of the village. The Campions consulted a different physician. It irked Dr. Weekes.

At last, common ground was found in Dr. Weekes' young horse, Bull, that caught the eye of Mr. William Campion, heir to the Danny Estate. Bull was inclined to shy and several times had thrown his rider. He had even bolted one dark evening at the sudden appearance of a group of labourers returning home from work. When Mr. Campion made enquiries, Bull's defects were discreetly avoided. A price was agreed and the sale was completed. Mr. Campion found Bull to his liking and rode him to the hunt. Both families were satisfied. [8]

An event of greater significance occurred when Dr. Weekes was called to Danny House to attend a sick visitor. After the consultation, Mrs. Campion expressed a wish to confer with the doctor, an honour indeed, and one so unexpected that Hampton was informed of it by the next post.

With the Borrer family, there was better rapport. Miss Sarah Borrer was known to accept the company of Hampton when down from his London studies. Such occasions were rare. Christmas was one of them. The seasonal round of balls at houses in the neighbouring villages included West Town. Hampton would not enjoy the 'Dash' there, the new dance of his London balls, but he would have the special pleasure of partnering Miss Sarah – and everyone enjoyed the match.

It was soon evident that Hampton would succeed at St. Thomas'. He was diligent in attending lectures, took careful notes at operations, and proved dexterous with scalpel and scissors in preparing body parts as anatomical specimens. Some of them, he parcelled carefully and sent down to Hurst with strict instructions for their preservation. At Matts, they were placed in a cage by one of the out buildings to bleach in the sun. In this respect, Hurst had the edge over St. Thomas' where the sooty London air engrimed everything. [9]

Hampton's pride and joy was his 'little female', four-feet two but no eyes of blue. She was a skeleton in her own specially prepared case. Hampton suggested that William Hamper should be asked to paint the case a mahogany colour to help seal the cracks and keep the dust out. Even so, the skeleton would still need to be taken out for the occasional airing and dusting. [10]

The dissecting room was one of the sights of London for friends visiting Hampton. Some could not break through the odour barrier surrounding the room. Some found one look more than enough. Others were fascinated beyond measure.

Dr. Weekes urged Hampton to be careful in his habit of allowing visitors in. They invariably talked of their experiences which caused unnecessary comment around the village about cutting up human bodies. The stubbornness of public opinion on so delicate a matter could damage the contribution his studies made to the family practice. [11]

Hampton's letters highlighted medical progress; the precision of surgery minimizing the patient's dreadful suffering, the efficacy of new medicines, the latest splints and treatment of fractures. Dr. Weekes considered each claim carefully before deciding its reliability and use in Hurst. [12]

He seized on the new powder for an ointment to keep open the induced blisters that were so important in drawing deep seated contagion. Also acceptable, was the amazing adhesive plaster for spreading on linen cloth to bind deep cuts, even a partially severed finger. With such up to date treatment, Dr. Weekes gained yet greater trust and respect throughout the neighbourhood.

In due time, Richard would have his turn at a London hospital. He could already undertake most of the everyday cases. Patients needing to be bled had full confidence in his treatment; cleansing the area, placing the leeches correctly and carefully removing them once sufficient blood was taken. He was skillful too at pulling teeth, an art gratefully accepted by those undergoing the agonies of toothache. His professional manner was appreciated at childbirth. Labour could be long. For much of the time, the doctor could do little more than help the woman keep her spirits up, often a none too easy task. [13]

Dr. Weekes' obligation to attend parish-contract women at childbirth, took him into the meanest of tenements. It sometimes entailed a journey of eight or ten miles when he had to attend a Hurst woman in one of the surrounding parishes. The only recompense was the generous travelling expenses he could claim from the vestry.

One of his workhouse deliveries was a son to young Barbara Manners. Rumour had it the child was sired by a neighbourhood doctor. Soon afterwards, the vestry received one of their occasional anonymous letters. It came from Lewes:

> *'Gentlemen, As a caution to you being an old parish officer myself I think a word of advise will not be taken amiss the affair you are in some way better acquainted than myself some time since Barbara Manners was Brought to Bed of a child in your parish the reputed father Dr. Verrall of – hs you must not by any means take Verrall's Security alone as his circumstances are not very good he has left his farm and mortgaged it for nearly the real value and more than that he bids you difyance to bring the woman to Justice. A Old Parish Officer I wish you to keep this to yourselves and you may depend on the truth of it.'* [14]

By this time, the baby had been baptized. He was now Henry of the workhouse, another squalling parish boy. The letter produced few long faces at the vestry meeting. They had already accepted a security from Dr. Verrall to prevent the child being a burden on the parish. Provided payment was maintained they were content.

Family trouble was mounting in Dr. Weekes' home. His second wife had been in poor health for years with a bad chest. She was a woman of calm courage but her hollow cough was getting steadily worse. Her wan body seemed consumed by illness. Dr. Weekes decided a gig was essential so that she could take the air.

Hampton was given the task of finding a good second-hand one in London. Luckily, there was a knowledgeable friend to assist. A suitable vehicle was found. It was strongly built, wide enough to seat three and the iron work showed no sign of rust. The driving box was removable and there was a travel trunk as well. [15]

The gig was carefully covered with matting ready for dispatch. A clear address label was sewn on. Knowles the carrier took it down to Hurst quite unaware that the travel-trunk was packed full of dissected body pieces carefully injected and varnished.

Everything arrived in good order. The specimens were placed in the surgery cabinet. The gig was thoroughly washed ready for the coach house. The doctor hired Thomas Bartley's cart from the Royal Oak and used it to train his horse to work between shafts.

For a few months, Mrs. Weekes could take the air again.

Dr. Weekes had done his best but medication and fresh air could not prevent the disease progressing. For a second time, he mourned the death of his wife. His sons supported their father without the same grief.

Hampton's studying and family errands still left time enough for leisure and interests; theatre, politics, scientific advancement and industrial progress. At Drury Lane, he enjoyed traditional Shakespeare in Hamlet and Othello. At Covent Garden, he gained equal pleasure from Sheridan's contemporary 'School for Scandel'. In more serious vein, he listened to five hours of debate on Ireland and the nation's finances at the House of Commons. [16]

In July, an ascent by hot-air balloon was advertised. Hampton and his friend went to watch. The place was packed. Hampton climbed on a coach for a good view. Two aeronauts were going up: a strange and wonderful spectacle of men like birds in the freedom of the sky. Whether their return to earth would be so wonderful was a matter of some concern.

At a chemistry demonstration, he marvelled at the power in a spark made of electricity. It was to have ignited hydrogen with oxygen to form water inside glass apparatus but so fast was the spark it cracked the glass which completely ruined the experiment.

Later, at a friend's foundry, he watched a lathe cutting cast iron. It was driven by a steam powered engine with the strength of ten horses. He was able to collect some of the chippings to send for Richard's ever extending museum. Anything strange or interesting was being added to widen the collection of fossilized rocks.

Hampton's pleasure seeking was not so rewarding. His determination to learn billiards entailed candle-lit evening lessons at 2s. 6d. (12½p) an hour. Expenses soon mounted. Cards were a pleasant episode when an hour's 'vingt-et-une' followed social tea. At other times, losses were reaching up to six shillings (30p) an evening. [17]

The family at Hurst urged him to desist and concentrate on his studies because the final examination was at hand and success was imperative. Richard would then continue in London, and Hampton would rediscover the true nature of the doctor's life; a five mile trudge through mud to treat a patient and come away with just five shillings (25p).

Richard's clothing for town wear was already purchased to accord with Hampton's suggestions. Although their father declared that in Hurst it didn't signify a farthing what you wore, Hampton insisted that it was important to dress as a genteel young man for 'Grandeur commands respect'. So Richard's wardrobe included a special blue coat, a pair of blue pantaloons and an orange waistcoat of twilled wool striped with black. To complete the picture, he grew his hair long in order to have it turned and combed back. Richard would cut a dash among the young men of London. [18]

1803: Napoleon Bonaparte Threatens Invasion

Official complaints were coming from Lewes quarter sessions that Hurst was giving too much flour to its parish poor. A substitute food had to be found immediately. Neighbouring parishes were giving herrings, rice and barley. The vestry decided they could best comply by a concentrated effort with beef.

For a change, the poor indulged the luxury of beef, and reduced their staple bread and hard-pudding. The vestry achieved a 25% saving in wheat, and Lewes were satisfied.

The flour was needed for the army. After eight years of war, matters were still unresolved between England and France. Sussex had become a front-line county with a vast influx of soldiers to provision. Times were uncertain. A spectre haunted everyone; Napoleon Bonaparte. Nelson had scuppered the French at the River Nile so Britannia ruled the sea – but Bonaparte seemed invincible on land. Britain's position was uncomfortable. No wonder the southern counties swarmed with military personnel.

Brighton, with a normal population of 7500, was awash with vigourous young soldiers. Hurst had a detachment of His Majesty's Artillery stationed with guns and 200 horses on Mr. Borrer's land by the windmill.

Illustrated London News 14-10-1843 Copyright The British Library Board. All Rights Reserved

The soldiers became prime suspects when one of the village carpenters had his saw stolen whilst he was working at West Town. At the end of the day, he had hidden the saw securely in an outhouse. By morning it had gone. He searched high and low to no avail. Two months later, he discovered it being used by the artillery blacksmith.

The blacksmith was tried by the magistrates. Although they found him guilty, his punishment was light, 14 days in the house of correction. He then resumed as blacksmith by the windmill. England at war needed every available soldier, and needed them fit for action.

For the army, disease was still a greater hazard than the bullet. Typhus and smallpox still rampaged the regiments. Although Dr. Jenner had perfected his cowpox vaccine, the army authorities were slow to accept its benefits – slower than Bonaparte's Committee in Paris.

Dr. Weekes did appreciate the vaccine's potential although he sometimes had trouble obtaining a sample and could not guarantee its effectiveness. The difficulty was that it had to be obtained at the right stage and had to be used fresh.

When Hurst suffered another smallpox outbreak, it was a more virulent strain. People were anxious for protection. Dr. Weekes vaccinated a group of the Danny servants. They waited a week for the swelling to appear. Nothing happened; the vaccine had been too old. Dr. Weekes wrote to Hampton in London seeking his help. [1]

Hampton managed to purchase enough for two people. He sent it by the first coach. At Danny, Dr. Weekes gently heated the vaccine and treated two servants. It was now a question of waiting.

On the eighth day, he inspected his patients. On their arms were ripe pustules at the ideal stage to provide fresh vaccine for the other servants. It was another triumph for Dr. Weekes.

The war news was good too. England and France were arranging a peace. Many people were sceptical but negotiations continued and at last came the announcement that Bonaparte agreed the preliminary terms. Relief was countrywide.

In Hurst, nearly all the higher echelons of society celebrated the event. They illuminated their houses with candles at every window. The young bloods of the village fired off guns. Rockets zoomed skywards. The street populace joined the celebrations and noticed Rev. Dodson had a still dark rectory. They felt shame at their rector's failure to mark the occasion. One of them heaved a brick through his window. In marked contrast to the rector's restrained reaction, Mr. Campion and Mr. Borrer both gave their delighted estate workers a dinner at the Royal Oak. [2]

Rev. Dodson may well have been awaiting the formal signing of a piece of paper peace. That took a further five months. It signalled another round of rejoicing. Mr.

Campion had faggots carted to the top of Wolstonbury Hill. Strong beer, bread and ten large cheeses followed. An open invitation was extended for any villager to gather on the hill that evening and celebrate. Up they went. The faggots were lit. As they blazed high, the night sky beamed the fire's glow across the weald. Bread and cheese were distributed, the beer flowed. Hurst was rejoicing and everyone could know. And if they were not on the hill, there was still beer and bread ready for the poor at West Town, for Mr. Borrer too was celebrating in hospitable style. [3]

The declaration of peace meant a relaxation of the troop concentrations around Sussex villages. The artillery by the windmill limbered their guns and marched away. Only a patchwork pattern where the tents once were and tumbled mounds of blackened fire bricks marked the soldiers' camp. Hurst reverted to its dull routine.

The vestry were not quite clear of military matters. Mrs. Miles wrote from Chichester stating that she and her four children, baby Esau being the latest, were out of money and would be starving by inches if no pay came. Her husband was now in the last year of his service so she hoped the vestry's kindness would continue.

It did – but two months later there was further trouble. The militia moved camp and marched the whole length of the county back to Battle. Mrs. Miles, following with her children on the baggage wagons, missed the vestry's pound note on its way to her at Chichester. William Miles waited in vain for the money to reach Battle. At last he asked his drum major's help. Another military letter was sent to Hurst explaining the distress. Another pound was sent by Hurst. For the final few months of William's service, his family's allowance arrived on time. [4]

By the end of the year, William was back in civilian life with his family at Hurst. Woolbeding parish repaid the money Hurst had paid to William during his militia service but he was now out of work and needed more help from the vestry; fuel, flour, clothes – even a bedstead. The extra costs caused careful scrutiny. The poor-rate was an exacting ten shillings (50p) in the pound. Out-relief was running at almost £2000 providing assistance for 190 Hurst paupers with over 350 dependent children. Was Miles really one of them? [5]

The overseers could not afford to be charitable to anyone with as doubtful a Hurst qualification as William's. He was taken for examination before the magistrates who concluded that he belonged to Clayton. Removal orders were issued. William and his family were conducted across the parish boundary. Clayton disputed the findings at the next quarter sessions but lost. The Miles family was no longer Hurst's problem. [6]

There was still plenty to contend with. Smuggling, although never a major problem in the village, was undeniably occurring. While life for most men went its steady course, for some there were occasional trips across the hills running contraband from France.

The excise-men were relentless in their efforts to stop the smugglers. They encouraged anybody who would report suspicious movements in the area.

Thomas Bartley, now landlord of the Royal Oak, knew full well how smugglers worked the vicinity and their contribution to his profits. He knew, too, the effect that informers could have.

In late September, Thomas and eldest son, also Thomas, set off on a journey. With them were four friends; Richard Chandler and 'Black' George Hards from Hurst, John Stoner from Henfield and Thomas Hollingdale from Brighton who arrived complete with shepherd's crook as if setting out for a lost sheep. [7]

They made their way through Keymer to Ditchling. There, they found Robert Bignall, nobody's friend, the reputed 'excise-man's nark'. Bignall was about to be taught a lesson. He was surrounded and jostled. The Hurst men made abusive accusations. Bignall heard himself damned and was afraid.

Ditchling pond was close by. Bignall was destined for the water. He lashed out. Hollingdale swung his crook. There was a crunch. Bignall's jaw sagged. He spat blood and a tooth.

Events were out of hand. Idling bystanders roused to action. Bignall had a sudden crowd of supporters.

Thomas Bartley's gang left hurriedly. They had made their point.

It was not the end of the affair. Action was taken to bring Bignall's assailants to account. Three days later, they appeared before a J.P. and acknowledged £50 sureties to assure their appearance at the next quarter sessions to face charges of assault.

The next month, they were in court. Robert Bignall swore to his accusation that they had fractured his jaw, knocked a tooth out and tried to throw him in the duck pond. For Thomas Bartley and his friends, it was a nerve-racking experience made little better when their case was respited to the January sessions. It meant three more months of nail-biting worry while Bignall blithely carried on 'informer' to the excise-man.

It did mean they were free to join the village Guy Fawkes celebrations where the grown sons of gentlemen let off more rockets, the grown sons of labourers quaffed strong beer, and the bell ringers pealed for everyone whether they wanted it or not. For that evening the Royal Oak was a happy place again.

The family with the greatest smuggling reputation among their neighbours were the Webbers of Locks Farm. The old Mr. Marchant of Little Park had enjoyed Locks brandy with the rector. Young John Webber made trips towards the coast that were rumoured to finish at Copperas Gap and other off-beat spots. Locks labourers lived-in at the farmhouse so a strong company could be counted on.

One Tuesday shortly before Christmas, John Webber and his friends made a journey towards Brighton. Unknown to them, they were being watched. When they returned, they were suddenly confronted by the excise-man – and with him was Robert Bignall. [8]

There was a violent argument and a single shot. John Webber slumped in the saddle, blood spurting from a stomach wound. Robert Bignall held a gun.

The parties split; Bignall and the excise-man disappearing at speed, Webber being helped towards the Stonepound Toll-gate.

Dr. Weekes was summoned. The shot had entered the body above the hip and passed through the colon. The doctor did what he could and sewed up the wound.

They got Webber home, where they comforted him as best they may. Dr. Weekes called daily but the injuries were too great. John Webber suffered for a week and he died. The inquest returned a verdict of wilful murder.

In London, Hampton Weekes read about the case. He entertained only one outcome. Bignall should gain his just desserts and hang by the neck until dead. His body should then be taken to Hurst for dissection. A good skeleton was all the man was fit for. [9]

Bignall was caught at a bolt hole among the seashore rocks near Newhaven. He was lodged in Horsham gaol.

At the January quarter sessions in Lewes, Thomas Bartley and his gang were found not guilty of assault on Robert Bignall. Webber's death had given them freedom. [10]

At the spring assizes in Horsham, Bignall stood trial for murder. His cousin appeared for the prosecution. On the morning of the murder he had been at work stone-breaking by the roadside when Bignall had remarked:

'Yonder goes Jack Webber highly mounted but I'll dismount him before morning.' [11]

Thomas Stevens had also been working on the road and corroborated the story. Against this, the excise-man held that the smugglers were the aggressors.

The court listened to five hours of evidence and argument. At last, the jury were ready to deliver their verdict: 'Not guilty.'

Bignall walked free, and the quiet smugglers of Hurst knew they were beaten.

Bignall's freedom left a dirty taste in the mouth for many people but, though they lamented the death of John Webber, something else loomed so large that the death of just one man became nothing. The peace with France had collapsed. Even now, Bonaparte's troops were gathering on the French coast, poised for the invasion of England.

Napoleon at Boulogne, 1803

At home, everyone was on full alert. Volunteer companies were strengthened. 25 Hurst men joined Captain Roberts' company of infantry in the South Lewes Regiment. They were a fair cross-section of the village; farmer William Jenner, the rector's son John Dodson, the vestry clerk's son William Ellis, parish clerk William Giles and day labourer James Flint, who in difficult times numbered among the paupers queuing for parish relief. William Bartley, the ostler son from the Royal Oak, and gardener Henry Muzzell volunteered to the South Bramber Corps. [12]

Another 25 volunteered as pioneers, all with a tool of some sort; axe, prong, handbill or spade. They had one thing in common; service with the volunteers exempted them from the ballot for militia companies.

The overseers had to ensure the parish militia returns were exact. Every man within the age limits was detailed showing occupation, number of children, and any grounds for exemption. Landowners and paupers were all included. Yet, such was the range of exemptions that less then a quarter actually entered the ballot. [13]

Butcher Luke Humphrey was too short. Francis Jenner was deaf and dumb. Isaac Sayers, like many day labourers with a large family, was excluded by poverty. Even when a man was drawn for service, he still had the escape clause of finding a substitute to take his place. But once in service the men drilled with urgency, England's freedom was at stake.

Detailed plans had also been made for the evacuation of southern villages. If Bonaparte invaded, farmers were to destroy their crops, round up all animals ready for drovers to take away, and provide wagons to convey people to the north of the county.

William Ellis visited each farm to compile an account of live-stock, from poor man's pig to Mr. Campion's mare. Hurst had 500 cattle, 1600 sheep, 300 pigs, 130 farm horses, 44 saddle horses – and two goats. [14]

Mr. Borrer had overall responsibility for organizing transport for people. Seven of the wealthier families had suitable vehicles and would be independent. For the rest, 27 wagons were needed. Farmers had to label each wagon clearly with the number given it, fit a tilt-cover and install seating plus tools and communal cooking utensils. Provisions were provided for ten days.

Most wagons were horse drawn, four to a team. A few had oxen. Richard Pockney's cart had been listed among the light carts but was not considered roadworthy enough.

The old, the infirm and mothers with young children were allocated places according to the part of the parish they lived in. Each had a printed ticket showing the location and wagon number. Other mothers, servants and older children would walk. Personal belongings were strictly limited; one blanket and a half-share of a corn sack to carry clothing. [15]

Mr. Borrer endeavoured to ensure that everyone in a wagon was of the same class. It was not always possible. The 19 allotted to James Harmes' wagon formed two incompatible groups. One comprised Mrs. Harmes and her four children with two other farmers' wives and children. The other was Richard Pockney, his wife, daughter Mary, Widow Standing from the workhouse and her two strange girls who made Mary's difficulties seem as nothing.

Mrs. Harmes was obliged to accept the situation. In normal times it would be too bizarre to consider. Bonaparte's threat made anything possible. If the evacuation did take place, the farming families could keep to one end of the wagon: no contact need be made with the paupers.

Michael Harmes had a specific task as one of the cattle drovers. As such, he, the heir to Wanbarrow Farm, would have to keep company with the likes of Isaac Sayers and sawyer Henry Henty. Michael would definitely be mixing with those below his status.

Although the norms of society could not always be upheld, one person was given individual attention. A two-horse cart was specially requisitioned with a carter appointed as driver. His designated passenger was John Bodle of the workhouse brewery. 'Mad John' would travel in splendid isolation safely couched in his hutch.

Mr. Borrer's plans were completed and forwarded to Lewes, nerve centre for the operation. There, crucial decisions were made and orders issued. To speed communications with parishes, a new cross-county post was introduced to supplement the cumbersome thrice weekly delivery via Brighton. Copious commands and counter commands flooded the parish vestries. The country was on a knife edge.

Millers were ordered to return forms stating how much flour they could produce in 24 hours. Estimates were received from the two watermills but Mr. Peskett at the windmill sent a blank return. Maybe he knew the vagaries of the wind too well.

If the wind brought Bonaparte's invasion fleet, beacons would be lit. There were 14 across the county, each about ten feet high of faggots and straw with a guard of soldiers on constant watch. Hurst had one close by on Wolstonbury Hill. Lighting the beacon would trigger the evacuation and local defence. While the evacuees moved north, the volunteer infantry and pioneers would muster their weapons. [16]

People waited and watched. Invasion days passed but no enemy appeared. Everyday life carried on.

1805: John Marchant Inherits Little Park

There was an upset in the daily life of 13 families at the death of William Sayers whose illiterate but loyal 'X' had once signified his support for King and Constitution on the Royal Oak resolution. William had farmed leasehold and copyhold land out at Goddards Green along the old parish road that wound northwards from the White Horse Inn, across fields of heavy clay, over the steep banked streams that powered the watermills, and out into the Sussex Weald. Now his land was to be divided among his children – his nine sons and four daughters.

To share the property equally was well nigh impossible. 11 of them were left £100 each, from which most had to defray £10 to £45 for outstanding debts to the estate. William left the leasehold land to his oldest son. The copyhold property went to Isaac as the youngest son because Hurst Manor followed the Borough English tradition of inheritance. [2]

Isaac's acute poverty, aggravated by his own growing family, had kept him dependent on the parish. With land of his own Isaac could envisage himself free from the ignominy of seeking vestry relief.

He attended the next manor court, was admitted to his holding and paid the entry fine of 6d. (2½p) Then, instead of swearing fealty to his lord, he surrendered the land to his brother, Richard, who paid another entry fine and became occupier. Isaac's brief moment of land tenure was over. It was almost as if he preferred the role of parish pauper.

John Marchant also came into an inheritance at the death of his father. Old Thomas Marchant had been returning from the Lewes races when his chaise overturned. He suffered fatal head injuries and died four days later. The inheritance was Little Park Estate valued in thousands of pounds.

Little Park, too, was part of Hurst Manor. At the death of Thomas, the reeve seized a pair of red oxen as the heriot required by the law of the manor. John redeemed his oxen for £37.

Like Isaac Sayers, John had to attend the next manor court. Whereas Isaac's fine at entry was 6d. (2½p), John's was £136. Unlike Isaac, he did swear fealty to his lord.

John Marchant already had a leading role in vestry matters. A complex issue on their hands was the increasing number of paupers needing the workhouse. The old building fronting the street was no longer big enough.

The vestry decided the best place to build an extension would be the corner of Mr. Campion's Town Field immediately behind the workhouse yard. They would first have to seek his approval. Mr. Campion gave his assent. The scheme could go ahead. [3]

A list was opened to raise a loan. The subscriptions reflected the parish wealth; Mr. Campion £200, Mr. Borrer and Mr. Marchant £100, Dr. Weekes £50, Mr. Jenner £25. At the vestry's 10% interest rate, they had secured a profitable investment. [4]

Detailed plans were prepared. The ground floor was to include a Wool Room for preparing raw flax and wool, a Work Shop for spinning and weaving, and a Dye Room with new copper and dyeing equipment. The first floor and garrets would be bedrooms.

It was agreed that as an acknowledgement of Mr. Campion giving up part of his property for the new building, his tenant on the Town Field, William Jenner, should have all the ashes and dung made at the workhouse.

James White won the building contract. Work on the house began in the summer of 1805. The new extension would open in September.

Mr. Borrer and Mr. Marchant provided much of the timber from within the parish and supplied a limited number of bricks although most came from the brickworks on St. John's Common. Mr. Chandler shaped ironwork at his forge. The numerous nails had to be carted from London on Knowles' wagon.

It soon became obvious there was no hope of the place being completed on time. While Admiral Nelson's ships patrolled the seas and fought Trafalgar, James White's men stolidly laid bricks. Work continued throughout the autumn.

A modern range and new cooking pans were purchased for the kitchen. The old copper boiler in the brewhouse was replaced. For the sleeping rooms, wooden framed beds were specially made with a lattice of nailed sacking lengths to support the bedding. Mr. Ellis provided the chaff mattress, pair of sheets, two blankets and a coarse wool rug coverlet for each bed.

Hurst shopkeepers competed to supply Waterford butter, small Dutch cheeses, yellow soap and candles. The established grocers were caught out by an enterprising new rival, Clement Lempriere, who undercut them for everything except candles.

Clement Lempriere was hard working with a keen eye for business. He was also a devout dissenter. The rituals of the parish church were not for him. He took his family five miles to Ditchling each Sunday to worship at the General Baptist Meeting House.

A Henfield man's bid to supply flour was matched by a combined one from Hurst millers, Anthony Ede and Thomas Uwins, at the watermills. The vestry accepted the local men as better placed to honour the contract. The details were entered in the minutes book: 'Messrs Ede & Uwins, 40 Sacks Flour, 50s per Sack,' and signed – first by churchwarden Anthony Ede and than by overseer Thomas Uwins. The supply of workhouse flour was theirs. Nobody questioned the deal. No one batted an eyelid. [5]

The building pace of James White's men remained slow. In the end the vestry sent an ultimatum: 'Finish or else…'. The men kept steadily on.

In January, they finished. The extension was at last complete.

On Monday 20th January, the manufactory started production. In the Wool Room, the women and girls prepared the raw wool with hand cards and a wool-carding machine to provide the spinners in the Work Shop. There, pride of place went to a pair of frames each holding six spinning wheels – the carders could not be idle. Another four wheels produced the linen thread. The thread fed a warping machine and that fed the weaving loom. The hum and clatter of Hurst's woollen industry had begun again. [6]

Over 50 of Hurst's inhabitants needed the comforts of the workhouse; the elderly forced there by age, widows with their children, John May whose mind had been voided by fever, the illegitimate teenage sisters Mary and Elizabeth Standing barely able to comprehend events around them, and Henry French with his fellow 'parish' children being trained to a life of servitude as farm boys or kitchen maids.

Richard Pockney was facing up to the realities of permanent workhouse life. Now 76 with deteriorating health, he had been forced to give up his carting business. It was the end of independence. He and his wife had seen it happen to others. It was happening to them; irreversible poverty, inability to maintain their home and the final defeat, entry into the workhouse. The Pockneys knew its shortcomings from their experience 15 years before. Then it had been for only a few months. Now it was to be for ever, to the end of their days. With them went Mary, shackled to her parents by her handicap.

With ample facilities available in the new building, the vestry economized on their out-relief by withdrawing payments for children aged 7 upward. If parents could not look after their offspring without vestry relief, the older children would have to go into the workhouse. For some families, there was no alternative.

The Pockney's son-in-law, George Rowland, had to send two of his boys. Things had never been easy since his release from the debtors' gaol. He had continued enlarging his family although never having sufficient means to provide for them. Try as he may, he could not make ends meet. Once more the family was broken apart. 8 year old John and 7 year old George followed their Aunt Mary to the workhouse.

The Martins were also hit. During the smallpox epidemic the vestry had paid for the family to be nursed in the pest house. Now, the three youngest were taken from home. Ann avoided it. She was 16 and in service. Catherine could have kept her independence if given encouragement. She had been a familiar sight in the hayfields working as hard as anyone. Now 14, she went inside with Mary, 12, and Thomas, 9.

Widow Henley had to take her family in. John, 15, was lame. He continued his apprenticeship with shoemaker Mr. Randell. 9 year old David joined the workhouse boys on the farms. Susannah, 7, was old enough to do her share of housework duties. Little Ann, barely 4, stayed with her mother.

Parents were still allowed daily access to their children during the midday visiting hour. To help maintain routine and discipline, the vestry resolved that victuals should be withheld from any pauper leaving the house without permission. It was an effective ruling. The boys sent out to the farms each morning could consider themselves lucky.

The Rowland brothers scared birds at 3d (1p) a day. Henry French, now 11, picked flints from ploughed fields at 8d (3p) a day. They cleared weeds, pulled acres of turnips, turned hay and helped at harvest. One thing they did not do – have the thrill of receiving wages. They were parish boys. Their days of employ were carefully recorded by the vestry. Their earnings went straight from the farmer to the parish purse.

Because the number of children younger than 10 had trebled, one of the new residents, 60 year old Richard Burchett, was detailed to 'teach school'. Richard was experienced. He had been teacher at the free school (now taught by gardener

Henry Muzzell) and, less significantly, collector of dog taxes. Those days were all times of the past. No longer financially able to keep himself, Richard was resigned to workhouse life. He could still feel of use.

For one man, things stayed much the same. 'Mad John' Bodle remained at the brewhouse passing his hours away into the summer when he quietly died.

John Still made the coffin and sent in his account:

> *'for a coffin for James Parker 15s. 0d.*
> *for a coffin for John Bodle 17s. 6d.'*

William Attree dug the grave:

> *'For Bering of Nat Goble 2s. 6d.*
> *For Bering of John Bodle 3s. 0d.'*

Even in death, 'Mad John' provided a little extra for those attending him.

1807: Catherine Martin
Tries Freedom

There was nothing extra for those looking after Ann Grey at the Pest House – except that her outbursts had so intensified they threatened to overwhelm everyone. At times she appeared totally out of control. Finally, the vestry accepted that the parish could no longer look after her. A place had to be found in an asylum.

Mr. Ellis wrote to Bethlehem Hospital. Changes were taking place there. One half of the old Bedlam had been pulled down. No vestry patients were being accepted.

He next tried another London asylum, Hoxton House, where Hurst already had a parishioner, Sarah Dunton, accommodated. Hoxton agreed to assess Ann at their St. Luke's Hospital and take her in if necessary.

Thomas Bartley, who had found Ann too difficult as a servant girl at his saddler's shop, took her the first part of the journey from the Royal Oak to Thomas Hitchener's Friars Oak half a mile (800m) the London side of Stonepound Toll-gate. There she was transferred to a chaise to carry her up to St. Luke's. [1]

St. Luke's diagnosed Ann as deranged. It was agreed she should have a place in the asylum at the same price as Sarah Dunton.

Hoxton's next half-yearly account to Hurst was a single bill for both women with comments on their condition: 'They both are in good bodily health, as to their minds they are much deranged.' [2]

Sarah Dunton certainly seemed deranged. The bills for her treatment had always included a complete set of new clothing and the use of a strait-waistcoat. Ann Grey's needs were far fewer, mainly shoes and mending. Among the Hoxton House inhabitants her behaviour was mild.

The accounts were paid promptly and the vestry were satisfied the pair were in the best place until a letter arrived stating that provisions in London had become so expensive the asylum were obliged to raise their fees by a shilling a week.

Their next bill showed the effect only too clearly, 18 weeks at 9s. 0d. (45p) followed by eight weeks at 10s. 0d. (50p). A bill for £24 with an extra £4 for Sarah Dunton's clothing. It had to be paid. Mr. Ellis sent off the half notes of £28. When he received Hoxton's letter acknowledging receipt, he posted the counterparts. [1]

The vestry discussed the increased costs. They decided their two lunatics could perhaps be as well provided for in Hurst. None of Ann Grey's reports suggested violence. Sarah Dunton's need for strait-waistcoats indicated greater difficulties but funds were tight and economies had to be made.

Hoxton House were informed of the decision. The women were collected and taken back to the Pest House. If they proved too difficult, they could be returned to the asylum.

The essential thing was to keep expenses to a minimum.

The Royal Oak also became involved in May's general election for the two Sussex M.P.s. Charles Wyndham, the candidate for the west of the county, was assured his seat but the other was far from safe.

John Fuller, the sitting member for the east, had sworn at the Speaker in the House of Commons and thereby incurred a public reprimand. The reason for the outburst was his intense opposition to legislation that destroyed the value of overseas property in the West Indies – Wilberforce's bill for the abolition of slavery. Fuller owned a plantation in Jamaica. He had voted for slavery.

His actions incensed many of the Sussex electorate, particularly the dissenters. People wanted Fuller out. Colonel Sergisson of Cuckfield was persuaded to stand against him.

Fuller may have offended many but he still had plenty of support, much of it from outside the county. Everyone knew the contest would be fierce: the freeholders of Sussex against the commercial interest of plantations.

A campaign song appeared:

> 'In Sergisson's cause, who is the friend of the Slave,
> May we boldly subdue ev'ry place-hunting Knave,
> State Robbers to Justice let's bring short and tall,
> So success to our cause – INDEPENDENCE for all!'.

Fuller's men sang from a different sheet: the chorus of the sugar lobby.

The election took place at Lewes. At the end of the candidates' speeches the returning officer called for the show of hands. The winner was announced: Colonel Sergisson. Great was the rejoicing until Fuller challenged the result. It meant 13 days of recorded votes, the first time it had been needed in Lewes for a hundred years.

Although county men were almost 100% for Sergisson, eligible voters were arriving from London and beyond. For twelve days the outcome seemed uncertain. The final day left a gap of 52 in favour of Fuller; 2530 against 2478. Sergisson was convinced he had been cheated. He demanded a scrutiny of the votes. The result was declared fair.

Sergisson had to accept. He still advertised his planned celebration although it would no longer be a victory salute: 'A match of cricket to be played at Hurstperpoint on Thursday 4th day of June next (being His Majesty's Birthday) between 22 Freeholders of the County of Sussex (all friends of Col Sergisson). The 11 winners to be entitled to a new bat each, in remembrance of the grand Contested Election. N.B. a good ordinary at two o'clock. By the Public's most obedient servant T. Bartley.' [3]

So the Royal Oak played its part. Not bribery beforehand but reward for loyalty to Colonel Sergisson and the abolition of slavery. Thomas Bartley was a happy contributor.

The village experienced a sad event when on the first of July the rector died. It was the end of a dynasty, of a hundred years of Reverends Dodson – grandfather, father and son. There was an heir, Dr. John Dodson, but the appointment of the new rector was in the hands of Sir Edward Winnington who temporarily held the patronage from Sir John Shaw in Kent. Sir Edward carefully considered the credentials of each potential incumbent to ensure he appointed the most suitable man. His final choice was made with full confidence. Hurst's rector would be the Rev. J. Shaw-Brooke from Eltham.

Although having been Shaw-Brooke for 10 years, the new rector was by birth plain John Shaw, the appendage being a legal accompaniment necessary from the time of his succession to the property of Joseph Brooke in Kent.

It was certainly a change to have someone from outside the parish but the full significance of the appointment was rather a shock. The Rev. Shaw-Brooke was already vicar of Eltham and he had no intention of deserting his Kent parishioners. A curate would be put in charge of his Sussex flock at a comfortable salary of £100. [4]

Rev. Shaw-Brooke would endeavour to visit Hurstperpoint whenever possible. He hoped to meet people at the annual dinner he would give for all tithe payers. He wished God's blessing on his new parishioners and looked forward to many years with them.

The parish settled to the new regime. The working year continued as before accruing gleanings of some £500 in tithes for the Rev. Shaw-Brooke.

It was money going to an absentee rector. Some voiced their disapproval, others kept quiet, and many who had no tithes to pay were little enough concerned. The day to day vagaries of life bounded their thoughts.

Catherine Martin was seeking an acceptable quality of life. It was two years since she had been forced to the workhouse by the vestry's new ruling about children whose parents could not maintain them. Other families were back together again, the Rowlands and the Henleys. She was still trapped inside with her brother and sister.

The vestry placed Catherine out as servant girl to a house in Ditchling. It did nothing to widen her horizons. She was fed, clothed and put to work – little else apart from a few hours sleep each night.

At the end of the agreement, she returned to Hurst workhouse. The vestry placed her out again. After five weeks she was back in the workhouse for failing to give satisfaction. Something had to be done.

Catherine did it. She resolved to shake herself free from the shackles of the vestry and leave Hurst behind her. She was 16 and ready for freedom.

Freedom was not something to be rushed. By the end of June, Catherine was only as far as Lewes enjoying life on the streets by day and finding outhouses for her night's rest.

On the 29th of June freedom came to a sudden end. She was apprehended and committed to the house of correction as a vagrant. She remained there a fortnight until the quarter sessions were held. At the sessions she was given another week's sentence as a rogue and vagabond. At the end of it, she was passed home to Hurst workhouse.

A girl with less spirit might have accepted her position. Catherine did not. She left the workhouse, walked the Downs to Lewes again and remained free until mid-August.

Once more she was committed for vagrancy and had to remain in Lewes house of correction until the October quarter sessions. Her sentence was another 14 days followed by the journey back to Hurst.

Catherine learnt her lesson. Next time she went south to Brighton and found lodgings in the alehouses. It was mid-February before the authorities caught up with her. She spent March and April back in the house of correction and appeared again at the May sessions. She was given a further three months. [5]

They took her back to Hurst in August. At last she made the workhouse her home. There, she saw the summer out.

At the end of October, the workhouse governor had to accept a woman brought home from Rottingdean. It was Elizabeth Dunton, wife of Thomas Dunton. Why she was apart from her husband nobody commented but her pregnancy was obvious. She entered the building, was issued with official clothing and became a pauper working for her keep until the baby's birth.

Five weeks later, in the workhouse cold of an early December day, Elizabeth gave birth; a girl so small and weakly that her survival was doubtful. On the 19th, she was privately baptized – Mary. On Christmas Day, baby Mary was buried. Elizabeth grieved. The workhouse had killed her baby, leaving nothing but a buried coffin and brief words in the church register.

Both Elizabeth and Catherine remained in the workhouse through winter into spring until the longer, warmer days of May when they walked out of the gates and away, free spirits seeking the companionship of other wanderers in the wider world of Sussex.

Elizabeth's place was soon filled. A Twineham overseer arrived with a mother and her baby son. Her husband, John White, was 300 miles away at South Shields by the mouth of the River Tyne serving for Hurst in the Sussex Regiment of Militia. Twineham had no wish to maintain the man's family so had obtained a removal order and taken them over the parish boundary into Hurst. [6]

Hurst acknowledged John White as being their militia man but not that he held a Hurst settlement. They began enquiries.

John White's father was questioned. He informed them his son had worked for some considerable time at Tandridge in Surrey.

The vestry were interested. They called in attorney Thomas Morgan and instructed him to ascertain the true story.

It seemed that John White's Tandridge employment had been with a Mr. Tyler. Mr. Morgan wrote to him hoping for proof that the employment had been for more than a year. The reply was that Mr. Tyler had moved further east across the Kent border to Chevening.

Mr. Morgan hired a chaise and set off to Chevening. He found Mr. Tyler and had a long and satisfactory talk about White's employment. He returned home the next day confident that Hurst could safely appeal against Twineham's removal.

His next task was to write to the commanding officer in South Shields explaining the position and enclosing a subpoena requiring John White to proceed home forthwith ready to appear in person at the quarter sessions. £6 was enclosed to cover the travelling expenses.

When John White received his orders to return to Hurst, he could hardly believe his ears. He was being sent home to his wife and child. What more could a man ask?

Whilst White made his way slowly south, subpoenas were served on his father and Mr. Tyler.

John White eventually arrived in Hurst thrilled to be seeing his family again. First, he was questioned about his time in Tandridge to confirm the case for the appeal. That done, he could enjoy a few days of home life – a welcome respite from militia training.

When the time came for the Epiphany sessions, the necessary people assembled at Lewes. Mr. Morgan presented Hurst's case. There was little counter evidence and the court had no hesitation in quashing Twineham's order.

White had to say goodbye to his wife and child. £5 was given him for his return journey. He started back to South Shields. As he no longer belonged to Hurst, his family was put back into Twineham which was where Mrs. White wanted to be. If Twineham considered they could turn the family over to Tandridge, that would be their affair.

Mrs. White was happy enough with the facilities of Twineham financed by the weekly 4s. 0d. (20p) Hurst had to pay while her husband was in actual service.

For Hurst it was an inevitable expense. Worse was to come. An unforeseen outcome occurred in the autumn; Mrs. White had a baby. This meant she should have extra payment. Twineham were determined Mrs. White would have her money. They took her before the justices where she swore a solemn oath that she was not receiving the proper allowance from Hurst for her new child. The justices agreed. They stipulated she should have a further 2s. 0d. (10p) a week in line with the daily rate for agricultural labourers which was what the militia allowance was based on. The J. P.s assured Hurst they could claim the money from the county. When application was made, it was refused because John White was the balloted man for the parish.

It was John himself who ended Hurst's commitment when he volunteered to the line. He could now be called upon to serve abroad and fight Bonaparte at the country's expense.

Another piece of inter-county co-operation came to fruition when John Wickham's house across the parish boundary in Albourne was robbed. His most valued possessions were stolen. A few days later he had the joy of his things being returned. The robbers had been caught. [7]

What a catch it proved. One of them was Robert Bignall, gun-man and excise-informer.

For the authorities, it was the conclusion of an investigation ranging from Somerset to Kent. Since the Stonepound smugglers confrontation, Bignall had moved west, robbed in Bristol, fled back across southern England and been captured in Kent. Imprisoned at Rochester, he had escaped, returned to his home area and robbed Wickham's house. Now he was back in prison, securely fettered in irons.

Bignall once again appeared at the Horsham Assizes. This time the verdict was 'Guilty' and the sentence 'Death'. When the assizes finished, the judge made ready to move on and he prepared his list of prisoners to be reprieved. Robert Bignall was not among them. [8]

During the next fortnight, Bignall repented his past and prepared for death. On his final evening, he wrote to his minister and family. The next day at noon, he was taken from his cell. He mounted the cart and sat with his coffin to be taken to the gallows on Horsham common where 3000 spectators awaited his arrival. There he exhorted them to avoid temptations, and he hanged. Smuggler John Webber was avenged.

1811: Thomas Bartley Pawns
The Royal Oak

Richard Davey, who 16 years previously had followed the recruiting sergeant's drum and fife into the Royal Artillery Drivers, had proved himself competent and reliable from the start. Through the years, he had been promoted; first to corporal and then sergeant.

Sergeant Davey was a devoted husband and father. Wherever the regiment went, Mrs. Davey followed. The two children, Sarah and Richard, had a secure life with their parents. For many years, the parish sent an allowance for the children until the family was quartered in Plymouth. There, family life came to a sudden end: the Drivers were detailed to Portugal to help Wellington harass Bonaparte. [1]

In January 1811, Sergeant Davey embarked for Lisbon. Mrs. Davey took her children back to Hurst. Young Sarah, now almost 13, was found a place as kitchen-maid. Nine year old Richard went to the free-school under the guiding hand of Henry Muzzell.

The Drivers had an uncomfortable two weeks sailing to Lisbon. The Bay of Biscay was storm-torn, and during a night of exceptionally bad weather a neighbouring vessel crashed alongside Davey's ship with a force that nearly knocked the men from their bunks. One of the smaller ships simply disappeared.

When they landed at Lisbon, they were kept busy from morning to night fetching fodder, checking horses and equipment, and cleaning harness fittings.

At last, Sergeant Davey found time to renew his link with home. The posting had severed him from his family. He determined to bridge the gap with letters to give his news and receive news from Hurst. Now he was able to write his first letter. Mrs. Davey would have to find someone to write the replies but that would not matter. The main thing was to know of his family's health and happiness.

He sent a shawl for Mrs. Davey to collect from the Blue Coach Office in Brighton. He told how he wished they could share the beef steak he was enjoying for his dinner. He promised presents for the children if they were good, and he stressed how Mrs. Davey should pay great attention to bringing them up in the fear and love of God.

Mrs. Davey received both letter and shawl. She wrote back anxious for Richard's safety and longing for his return. For her part, she was working hard, the children were both well and none of them was going to be a burden on the Hurstperpoint vestry.

That year, William Jenner was High Constable of the Hundred of Buttinghill. As such, he was local organizer for the second national census. Mr. Marchant and Mr. Ellis carried out the count. The parish had changed very little, an increase of just 80 during the decade. Henry Campion had died, so his son, William, was now master of Danny and lord of the manor. [2]

At the Royal Oak, Thomas Bartley was finding that being master of property could cause a deal of worry. In the days of relative prosperity, the Oak had comfortably supported his large family. Now, although only his younger children were dependent on him, he never had sufficient money.

When he had taken over at the death of his mother, the future had seemed bright. Soldiers were billeted with him and people on parish business lodged there. It was the venue for property auctions, the monthly vestry committees and the big Easter Monday meeting which still concluded with the parish funded dinner. His wagon was hired to convey parishioners being taken to the Lewes magistrates. Beer for parish assisted funerals came from his barrel and he provided the bread and wine for the church.

Almost imperceptibly, trade had slackened. It was not that the labourers drank less. It was the better customers who stopped coming; those who took supper and stayed overnight. The vestry continued their monthly meetings and the trustees of the new Brighton Road just west of the village (the Prince Regent's direct 'Hickstead' route from London) gathered there to auction their toll-gates. Yet general trade was down. Parish lodgers were few and far between – too often the vestry put them up at the White Horse. [3]

Thomas had been part of the Royal Oak all his life; born and bred there, helping his mother after the death of his father and bringing his own family up in the saddler's shop beside the inn. Yet, of his own children, only William seemed willing to share the load – and as ostler he took wages out of the Oak's falling income.

The oldest four had all benefited under their grandmother's will with bequests towards their education. She had stressed its importance and how without it the children would be denied many opportunities of advancement in life.

George had made the most of his schooling. He had then set off for London convinced his education would bring its rewards as grandmother had so often told him – but nothing came home from him although he had made fine promises of how he would remember those left behind in Hurst. Tom was down on the coast somewhere still getting into scrapes with the law like the Ditchling Pond scuffle with Bignall and being far too independent to think of helping his father. Charles was away labouring for a living. Barbara, as good a daughter as she was about the place, did not contribute financially and young John, who had just left school without learning to write, gave virtually nothing. James, Jane and Jeremiah, the baby of the family, were still a drain on resources.

Thomas knew his income was stretched to breaking point. The less his trade, the less he could repair his premises. The less he repaired them, the greater the faults and the bigger the eventual bills would be. At last, he had to accept that his money could never go far enough. He made a grim decision: mortgage the Royal Oak. With the money, he could carry out repairs, attract more customers and regain his slipped reputation.

Mr. Rickman, a financier in Lewes, saw the premises as a safe venture. He agreed terms with Thomas. The Royal Oak was in pawn. [4]

Thomas decided his best course was to concentrate on the saddlery and trust the Royal Oak to a landlord whose income would depend on sales. He installed John Tobutt. The future was immediately brighter.

Opposite the Royal Oak, the one-time shop of William Courtness had just gone on the market again. With its stable, outbuildings and walled garden it made an attractive investment. It was soon sold.

The new owner set about renovating the place. He was obviously a man for modernization. Gradually the old timber facade disappeared within thick plaster scribed as quasi-stonework with deep-set windows and a new imposing doorway. Rooms were altered. Stabling was improved, and standing for carriages prepared.

Thomas watched with growing apprehension as the alterations were completed and furnishings arrived; too many beds for even a large family, too much wine and spirits for any private cellar.

Finally it was there; William Courtness' old shop in shining new paint and a staring sign-board, THE NEW INN, bang opposite the down-at-heel Royal Oak.

It was no real secret. People in the village had been taking sides; Thomas Bartley's or the new place? In September, the justices had two applications for licences; John Tobutt as landlord of the Royal Oak, James Edwards for the New Inn. Both were granted.

On October 14th, Mr. Edwards had a front page advertisement in the Sussex Weekly Advertiser extolling the clean and well aired rooms and beds of The New Inn, assuring clients of his greatest attention to their comfort and listing his best wines and 'spiritous' liquors, London porter, beer, cyder etc with good stabling and standing for carriages.

John Tobutt acted promptly. He put his own piece in the next week's Advertiser, although he could afford only an inside column. He begged to inform the public in general that he had taken that old-established house known by the name of the Royal Oak Inn, it being well adapted for the business and with large convenient stables. He assured them that every attention would be paid to merit their favours. He had neat wines etc. [5]

The New Inn's advert still sported the front page, and again the following week. The Royal Oak's was a once only. John Tobutt knew he could not compete in advertising. He determined to compensate by his attention to his clients. He provided entertainment for them, relaxed his hours and encouraged a cheerful bonhomie.

Although the innovations attracted a handful of critics, most drinkers enjoyed the brighter atmosphere. Lost custom returned. Thomas knew he had installed the right man.

The Royal Oak had always been a tempting location for Isaac Sayers on the few occasions when he came into the village. Mainly, it was on his visit to the vestry to collect out-relief. Isaac had as great a taste for beer as anyone. He liked nothing better than to pop into the Oak for a quick drink or two and a chat before he went home. Sadly, with growing children to support, his chats could not be as regular as he wished.

If it were not for his gun, Isaac would have been in a far worse position. Living out at Goddards Green had one great advantage. With few people around he could go out with his dog and gun without the constant fear of being caught. At least he was able to provide meat for his family.

Even that proved to have its limitations. On one of his shooting mornings, he obtained his meat within too close earshot range of a disgruntled farmer. It meant trouble. He should not have had a dog or a gun. He was not qualified to kill or destroy game.

Isaac had to appear before the magistrates. They convicted him of unlawfully killing game and imposed a fine of £5. He tried to explain that he had no such sum of money. To the magistrates, it was the familiar story of a defendant refusing to pay his fine. The alternative would apply – time in Lewes house of correction.

In he went. Isaac Sayers: age 36, height 5 feet 2 inches (1.5 metres), complexion fair, build slender, hair light, eyes grey, labourer, Sussex: poaching. It would be three dry months before Isaac enjoyed another beer. [6]

The Royal Oak also made a deep impression on High Constable, William Jenner. He wondered at the new atmosphere being engendered there. The stark contrast between the Oak and the New Inn was staggering; the jollity of the one almost invading the solemnity of the other. The long hours landlord Tobutt seemed willing to work and the festive behaviour of his customers were amazing. How could a landlord achieve such transformation?

In January, John Tobutt was summoned to attend the justices. There were misgivings about his hospitality. William Jenner provided the facts and figures: 'John Tobutt did on the 19th of October 1811 and on various other days permit and allow diverse riotous and disorderly persons to be and continue in his said house the Royal Oak and therein to make and commit diverse great noises, riots and disturbances and did supply them with beer and other liquor and further allow such persons at unreasonable hours from 12 to 3 in the night time to continue drinking, tippling and dancing.' In short, he was keeping a disorderly and ill governed house. [7]

The justices considered they had no alternative but to forfeit John Tobutt's £10 surety entered into when he was granted his licence. They also banned him from holding a licence for three years.

Thomas Bartley's anger and frustration were intense. He had turned the Royal Oak around only for the parish vestry to ruin everything. Instead of a profitable inn, there was nothing but a mortgage debt.

He kept his saddler's business going in his shop beside the empty inn and nursed his wounds. Mrs. Bartley tightened the family belt. With three young children still on her hands her housewifery skills would be pressed harder than ever.

Through the winter the Royal Oak's increasing deterioration was obvious. By the summer Mr. Rickman knew he could no longer wait for his money: the unoccupied premises were going to ruin. He wrote to the vestry explaining that he was willing to lose a considerable sum if a mortgage agreement could be drawn up with them to enable Bartley to continue at the Royal Oak. [8]

The vestry prevaricated before at last making an offer of £24 per annum. It was ridiculously low. Mr. Rickman decided not to enter into further drawn out bargaining. He concluded a private sale with Clement Lempriere, the enterprising grocer who had once undercut Mr. Ellis for the workhouse contracts.

The sale was bad news for Royal Oak supporters. Clement Lempriere – the avowed General Baptist who travelled five miles each Sunday to worship in a chapel. Who could imagine him with a beer? They knew the last Oak drink had been drawn.

The vestry found a place for the Bartleys. Thomas felt the loss of his home deeply and was bitter that nothing had been done to help him hold on to it. From being owner of the Royal Oak, he had become under-tenant in one end of a shared house. How could his wife bring up children decently in such circumstances? It was akin to being a pauper.

From the parish point of view, Bartley had held the means of making a living. His failure was of his own doing. Their aid was for people unable to help themselves. As a property owner, the man had not qualified. Now that he owned nothing, they would pay rent for him as they did for other paupers.

In November Thomas had the humiliation of receiving meat from the Dog Smith charity. In February he received 10s. 0d. (50p) from the Leonard Letchford charity.

1812: David Batchelor Tramps the London Docks

Whilst Thomas Bartley was left to lament the loss of the Royal Oak, Michael Harmes was taking over the family farm at Wanbarrow following the death of his father. James Harmes had been ill throughout the winter. When the farm had become too much for him he had met with the steward of Hurst Manor to negotiate its return to Mr. Campion.

The one remaining Harmes property, Hatches, with its orchard and acre of land just up the lane from the farm, was inherited by Edward as the youngest son through the Manor English inheritance law although during his mother's life it would be hers, her 'Widow's Bench'. She moved in and wisely sublet part of the house to provide income. Wanbarrow Farmhouse would now be home for Michael's young family.[1]

His only regret was being a tenant of Mr. Campion without the security of the land being his own. With the war preventing the import of European wheat, it was a time of prosperity for farmers with more and more land under the plough. Wanbarrow was productive, market prices were high and profits up.

Michael also had greater social responsibility on that year's vestry committee as overseer. He was proving himself an efficient official. As such, his immediate concern was with a cooper, David Batchelor, his wife and two small children who had just arrived from Lewes. The whole family had been ill with fever. Batchelor had been unable to work, failed to pay his rent and had been evicted. [2]

Michael Harmes had no hesitation. His duty was to direct them straight to the workhouse. He did so.

Reluctantly, Batchelor took his family inside. They were parish paupers.

The workhouse was demeaning. Strange faces peered at strange newcomers in a sombre muddle of rooms leading by dark stairways to more dark rooms lined with beds – and, everywhere, a virtual silence devoid of hope.

It was certainly no longer the busy place of recent years. The bustle and clatter of the manufactory was missing. The parish cloth industry had declined until the vestry decided to close it. They ordered the governor to dispose of all material in the chest except 40 yards (36 metres) of linsey. Of all the cloth makers' years of endeavour, just the 40 yard length of linsey would remain: a hidden tribute to the parish spinners and weavers. [3]

The Batchelors had to spend October in the workhouse. David had no intention of becoming institutionalized. He had the pride and determination of the craftsman. Somewhere a cooper was needed. He would find that place. To trail small children around would be a handicap. In any case, his wife was pregnant: she could not traipse the streets. The family would have to stay in Hurst workhouse whilst he searched.

On the second of November, he set off. He tramped November away and by early December was doggedly trying the London Docks. There, by the Thames at Deptford, he found work making barrels for ships' stores. It was a far cry from Lewes with its few small vessels on the River Ouse.

London Docks
Illustrated London News 27-9-1845 Copyright The British Library Board. All Rights Reserved

Ships stretched each way along the Thames. A forest of masts marked the Surrey Docks. Across the river on the Isle of Dogs was another forest, the West India Docks. Deptford was shipping – shipping was work. Work meant long hours from five in the morning until seven at night but 14 hours of Thames-side slog was nothing compared with the stigma of the workhouse. David wrote the good news to his wife: she could be free.

The vestry gave Mrs. Batchelor £5. With the money she would travel by coach as far as the Elephant and Castle and then by carriage across to Deptford. She and the children set off.

David had rented suitable rooms and found a pawnbroker who, for £7 payable at 5s. 0d. (25p) a week, supplied furniture for the home. Mrs. Batchelor arrived with the children. They were a family again.

The weekly 5s. 0d. (25p) went to the pawnbroker: the furniture gradually became their own. Mrs. Batchelor's baby was born (David, after his father). The days of Lewes poverty dimmed. [4]

Through the summer and into the autumn, work was plentiful. Then, in November, the management decided they had too many on Day Work. David was given the option of leaving the yard or buying a set of tools and doing piece-work on 'The Block' making casks at 3s. 6d. (17½p) each. David himself was over a barrel. Winter was setting in early and cold. He had to spend nearly £3 on tools. His hours were restricted, only 8 a.m. to 4 p.m. Life was once more uncertain.

After Christmas, the cold intensified. Ice edged the river, inching out each day until nothing could be shipped from the shore. Men were laid off. Over 100 ships, loaded and ready for sailing, were frozen in the West India Docks.

It was a year of such intense cold that the Thames froze its width from London Bridge to Blackfriars. The ice set so solid and deep they held a Frost Fair on the river. Booths were erected and bedecked with streamers. Swing-boats provided rides for revellers. Ninepin skittle-alleys flourished, hot food and drink vendors were in abundance. Anyone not content to slip and slide could hazard themselves on donkeys that ferried from bank to bank. Merriment was on the Thames but despair lurked in the tenements beside it.

Coals cost a scandalous 3s. 0d. (15p) a bushel (36 litres). With food and provisions so dear, David's independence was threatened. He wrote to Hurst pleading for aid, using the timeless ploy: 'I must send my family home.' The message did its trick. Off went the money, the just enough to keep the family away, but the charm of Deptford had gone. [5]

The winter cold did see the return of one Hurst parishioner. Elizabeth Dunton arrived unannounced; a bundle of clothing on her back and a young child in her arms, her son.

Elizabeth was assigned to the workhouse. She had to give up her clothing, put on institutional dress and merge with the pancake faces of pauperism in regimented days of subservience. She had bitter memories of the workhouse and the death of her baby Mary there. The experience was ingrained in her mind. Hurst workhouse was no fit place for anybody, let alone a mother with an infant child. It would be shelter during winter's cold, nothing more. She was determined her boy would not be subjected to workhouse life.

Elizabeth made freedom her sole aim in life. In the end, the vestry decided she could leave. Indeed, they were not going to keep her any longer. She would be granted 4s. 0d. (20p) a week and go. If she dared to come back to the workhouse she could expect to be sent to prison. Elizabeth's clothes were returned to her. With her son in her arms, she made herself scarce.

Another of Hurst's wanderers, Catherine Martin, had been making her way slowly back to the parish. She was 19 and heavily pregnant: her days of freedom were over.

When she arrived, she too was assigned to the workhouse. There Catherine gave birth, another sickly baby whose chance in life seemed slim.

The baby died. Unlike Elizabeth Dunton's little Mary, Catherine's child had not received the blessings of baptism. George Cripps billed the parish 2s. 6d. (12½p) 'for a coffin for Martin's child.' William Giles charged 3s. 0d. (15p) 'for Catherine Martin's child's funeral'. Nobody recorded the baby's life in the parish register.

Catherine remained at the workhouse for a few weeks then she was away again. She seemed set in her ways and went no further than Lewes, enjoying the open air and, when circumstance dictated, finding lodgings in alehouses. By the next summer she was in good health again, her dark brown hair framing a face tanned by the weather, her hazel eyes alive with the glint of freedom. [7]

This time her freedom was ended by an alert parish officer who asked her to account for her movements. Catherine did the best she could. It was not enough. She was apprehended and sent to the house of correction, a place she knew only too well. [7]

At the quarter sessions, they accused her of 'Having no visible means of gaining a livelihood but by prostitution'. They sentenced her to another month in prison. At its end she was returned home yet again to Hurst workhouse. She fretted a few weeks there and then walked out again to resume her chosen way of life, the freedom of vagrancy.

Mrs. Davey, who had travelled the country so many years with the Royal Artillery Drivers, was content with life in Hurst. Her great wish was to see her husband's safe return from Spain. His letters continued to arrive. Each was read time and again. Each was saved. She still shuddered at his descriptions of the awful horrors of battle.

For Sergeant Davey, the privations of winter were almost as bad: men marching ankle-deep in mud during 14 days of rain, at times receiving no rations so having to boil acorns and imagine they tasted of potato; soldiers collapsing as they marched, exhausted by hunger and fatigue; 4000 men dying.

At last the Drivers made their base beside a small village. Snug quarters with good beds soon saw them in better spirits able to laugh at past hardships and exchange jokes over a pint of wine. If they had known how Bonaparte's decimated army was retreating from Moscow through the snow of a Russian winter losing

132000 men to hunger and cold, they would have danced round their fires.

The campaign in Spain lay dormant until better weather allowed more movement. Another summer of battles saw Wellington's army at the Pyrenees. In the February of 1814, Sergeant Davey and his drivers crossed the mountains into France – horses in mud to the knees, three days with no food but a handful of potatoes – and were then forced to retreat back into the hills. When they advanced again, it was to discover deserted villages. Tables and chairs in the abandoned houses became fuel for the soldiers' fires.

In April, Davey wrote home of the victory at Toulouse, the wonderful news of peace and the downfall of Bonaparte. At last he could think of his homeward journey. [8]

News of Bonaparte's abdication reached Hurst well ahead of the sergeant's letter. The reaction was spontaneous rejoicing. Plans were drawn up for the village's participation in the national thanksgiving: a celebratory banquet – by invitation – for Hurst families, a money subscription to provide a special meal for the parish poor and a signal banner of victory to be flown from the church. [9]

No adequate flag was available but somebody knew the ideal substitute, 40 yards (36 metres) of white linsey deposited in a workhouse chest when the cloth manufactory had closed. What grander signal could there be? The linsey was found, split to make a double length and flown from the church spire. In the blustery wind it was an inspiring sight.

The appropriate families dined at the New Inn and gave generously to the collection for the poor. It amounted to a wonderful £20. And at Pakyns Manor the poor thoroughly enjoyed their treat; food, drink, song and dance – and down the drain with Boney. Let him lead the dance on his own Mediterranean Island, the Emperor of Elba.

Mrs. Davey had to continue without her husband. Staff-sergeant Davey's hopes of returning home were dashed when his corps was shipped to America to join in the war against the United States. There, the Royal Artillery saw more action at Platsburg and then went to winter quarters in Montreal – deep snow everywhere. The transport was novel. People and produce all travelled on slides. What Davey did not enjoy was the bitter cold. When the soldiers' boots began to freeze on their feet, they found the Indians at the market place and bought beef-skin shoes made from a single piece of leather.

The place was not without its blessings. He had a nice little room in a public house and ate with the family, all for only £2 a month. It was so comfortable, he wished his family could be with him because he saw little likelihood of returning home as the war seemed set to last a great while. All he could do was urge Mrs. Davey to bring the children up as well as she could: above all, to encourage them to learn a trade. [10]

1815: Susannah Almon Goes to Prison

Hurst also had a visiting soldier, newly married Peter Almon, a private in the 45th Regiment of Foot. His bride was Susannah, a Hurst girl who had been away in service several years. As soon as Almon spoke, everybody knew where he came from – Ireland, the land without a Poor Law. If anything went wrong, Susannah might still qualify for relief from the vestry. They were determined to avoid such expense.

Almon was taken to the magistrates for examination. He claimed to have made his way through England without obtaining any settlement. It was a fact only too obvious to the magistrates: a fact that Hurst was obliged to accept.

The couple showed not the slightest concern. At the end of the hearing they went off happily to the regimental camp.

For a year and more nothing was heard of them. Then Susannah reappeared in the village. The overseers were perturbed. Here was a heavily pregnant wife, yet there was no husband. Room was made for her at the workhouse to await the child's birth. She was questioned but had nothing useful to say. Married bliss had lasted only a short time. When the 45th marched north, she had not followed.

Susannah had a son. He was baptized, David, in St. Lawrence Church. The register left a blank for the father's name.

The vestry were convinced her husband was not the father. Rigidly upheld, the law laid down imprisonment as a punishment for women who bore illegitimate children. The woman had such a child. Hers was as wicked an offence as that of being an unmarried mother. They consulted solicitor Mr. Kell at Lewes and decided the law should be upheld.

Susannah was taken to the magistrates. Her explanations about the child were ignored and she was sentenced to 12 months in the house of correction. Baby David went with her. [2]

The prison surgeon ordered milk to be provided for David. Susannah had to survive on the daily ration of bread. She found imprisonment tough.

It was not long before the meagre rations and hard environment took their toll. Susannah's health began to deteriorate. The doctor decided medication was necessary. She was prescribed liniments, mixtures and gargles every few days. Life was a struggle.

Six months later Hurst had another unwelcome visitor. Elizabeth Dunton turned up. The vestry were not amused. She had left the workhouse the previous year on the clear understanding that if she showed her face again she would be committed to the house of correction. Now she was in the village with not only her toddler boy but also a baby girl. She had some explaining to do.

Elizabeth told how she had given birth to her daughter at Slaugham. They had moved her on as soon as she regained her strength. She had nowhere else to go to otherwise she would not have come back to Hurst.

The vestry decided to deal with her return once they had sorted two priorities. First was the baptism. Elizabeth chose to name her baby Louisa. Next, a claim was made for Slaugham to pay for the child's maintenance whilst in Hurst.

That done, they considered their next course of action. Richard Davies, a tenant farmer on the Danny Estate, was the current overseer. He was instructed to ride over to Lewes and ask Mr. Kell to take steps to have Elizabeth committed. Mr. Kell began the legal process. Elizabeth appeared at the next quarter sessions. She too was sentenced to a year's imprisonment. [3]

With Susannah Almon already in prison for immorality, Elizabeth's commitment would mean two Hurst mothers in gaol. Such measures, although a commendable example of retribution to sinful women, were not without weaknesses. One was the women's health, another the upkeep of the older Dunton child.

The vestry knew Dunton could well suffer the same way as Almon: prison was unlikely to improve poor health. They decided to ask for Susannah's release. She must have learnt her lesson. [4]

The magistrates gave their agreement dependent on the woman's prison record. The gaoler's certificate recorded her behaviour as 'Good' so she was released.

Surprised and delighted, Susannah took baby David off to Hurst whilst Elizabeth, heart-broken at the separation from her son, took baby Louisa into prison. The vestry put the boy into the workhouse.

Two other Hurst women were sentenced at the sessions. Catherine Martin had been apprehended in Brighton during the cold weather of February along with her sister Mary and three other women. All were charged, as ever, with 'Lodging in alehouses, the open air and elsewhere and not giving a good account of themselves.' They were confined in Lewes house of correction to await trial. Catherine was in such poor health, she was prescribed lotions and mixtures with which she coughed her way towards the warmer days of spring. [5]

At the Easter Sessions, they were all adjudged rogues and vagabonds. Mary had to endure a further week in prison. She was then returned home to Hurst.

Catherine was a hardened sinner. Because of her previous record, she received a four month sentence.

Gone was the tanned and healthy Catherine of the previous summer. Now, dark hair framed a wan, drawn face. Her hazel eyes had the dull glaze of sickness. Imprisonment deprived her of both freedom and the chance to restore her health. The future was bleak.

But somebody had gained freedom to face the world anew and restore past glories. The village and nation were a-buzz with the news. Bonaparte had escaped from Elba. His triumphal progress north through France, and his rapturous reception in Paris, were noted with increasing concern. Wellington was assembling a force to accost him.

For Sarah Davey, the news caused no immediate worry. Although the war with America had ended, her husband was still stationed the other side of the Atlantic safely out of the way.

For Mrs. Carter and Mrs. Godman, it was an anxious time. Mrs. Carter's husband was with Wellington's men in Belgium. Mrs. Godman's was at Woolwich with the 1st Battalion Royal Artillery under orders to sail for a foreign land.

The parish authorities shared the women's anxiety. Both mothers had children to bring up. If the men should die, who would provide for their families? The vestry knew they might unless they did something about it.

Mrs. Carter had a watertight settlement but William Godman had lived away in Henfield long enough to qualify for a settlement there. It was enough. The Godmans belonged to Henfield. Removal proceedings would begin.

On the 17th of June 1815, orders of removal were signed by the magistrates. On the 19th, Isabella Godman and her children were taken from Hurst and delivered to the overseer at Henfield. In time of war the vestry had to be decisive. [6]

There was one crucial item of information none of them knew about. On the intervening day, Napoleon Bonaparte and Wellington had fought the decisive Battle of Waterloo. Bonaparte was fleeing for Paris.

When the news of Wellington's glorious victory reached the village, everyone rejoiced. The scourge of Europe was at last laid low.

Only later did definite

word of casualties arrive. For Mrs. Carter, it brought an aftermath of sorrow. Her husband was dead, a hero of Waterloo. His memorial would be a small weekly allowance to Mrs. Carter for her children's upkeep.

William Godman had never left Woolwich. He was released from the artillery on the understanding he was liable to recall at any time. He settled down again in Hurst and his family was able to return from Henfield.

Staff-sergeant Davey was also en route for England. His corps sailed from America in late June. After 33 days crossing the Atlantic, they came up Channel as far as the Isle of Wight and anchored off Portsmouth. He disembarked to tread his native soil again after five hard years abroad. Elation bubbled – and was abruptly flattened; they were ordered to sail at two for Flanders. Davey just had time to buy some roast beef and porter. [7]

With that he had to be satisfied. Portsmouth, the Isle of Wight, the Sussex coast were lost to view. Staff-sergeant Davey would not yet be home.

Elizabeth Dunton was still shut away in Lewes house of correction serving her sentence for immorality. No one would sing her praises but she was a conscientious mother. Her great difficulty was her growing baby's need of warm clothing. Elizabeth had no intention of allowing her child to suffer. She sent the overseers a carefully worded letter:

> *'Mr. Davey I hope no offence in writing these few lines to you to inform you that my child is very bare of clothes and I should be very glad if you ould be so kind as to grant me a little for it whant a pare of shose and a night gown and a coat and a frock and I should be glad if you ould grant me a pare of stockings and a upper petticoat and a apron but I humbly beg that you ould forgive me and consider me for the sake of my children I hope to do better for the time to come and will do the best that lays in my power to help bring the children up please God they live for it is a very hard case to be shut away from a child and never to hear from him I beg your pardon in being so bold but I hope no offence from your humble servant Elizabeth Dunton Lewes Prison'* [8]

The letter was put before the vestry. They resolved that four yards (3.6m) of calico and four of flannel should be allowed. A man was sent over to Lewes with it. Elizabeth was able to make her baby's clothes.

In the spring, she wrote again explaining how the growing baby needed more clothing. The vestry sent a second parish parcel complete with tape and thread. Elizabeth was thankful, but she had another worry. She had heard that her son was ill. She wrote asking for news of him and begging them to allow her shoes, shift and apron because she had been confined so long her clothes were worn out. The vestry did not wish to supply more clothes until her release. They did set her mind at rest over the boy; he was in good health.

Barbara Bartley was in difficulty too. Unlike Elizabeth, she had no wish to confide in the vestry. Times had been hard since the family's eviction from the Royal Oak (now a grocer-cum-draper's shop). She had managed to keep body and soul together pretty well until a visitor from Reigate in Surrey blighted her prospects.

Barbara was able to keep things to herself at first. Eventually the vestry had to become involved. They decided to refer the matter to the Lewes magistrates. Barbara stated upon oath to them that the man responsible for her condition was named Marshal Wortley. [9]

As a result, Marshal Wortley was apprehended as the named father of a child being carried by Barbara Bartley. At the Lewes magistrates he was made liable for the expenses of her lying-in and the upkeep of the child. He did not dispute the facts.

Barbara had little fear of punishment for her erring ways. The vestry did not zealously commit every unmarried mother, only those who seemed set in the ways of dishonour.

When her time came, she gave birth to a son. She named him Marshal Wortley as a tribute to his father, and as such he was christened. Father Marshal Wortley paid the first instalment on his child. He would be tied to them for many years.

Up in Deptford, David Batchelor faced an insecure future. He had survived the big Thames freeze-up but with work again slack and with four children dependent on him he had to accept defeat. He could no longer keep his home. Only one course seemed open to him: return to Hurstperpoint. [10]

The family arrived in January 1816. Soon they had a quiet and heart-warming celebration in St. Lawrence Church when three year old David, who had been privately baptized at Deptford, was admitted into the church family. His sister, Susan, was baptized.

The welcome at the church was the most encouraging part of the family's return. Employment prospects for a cooper were anything but heart-warming. Work was almost as short in Hurst as in Deptford. David Batchelor had intermittent employ making tubs and hoops, mainly for the parish. There was never enough to allow him complete independence. For his rent, he had to rely on vestry aid.

He kept his business going until a summer fever laid him low. The fever was severe. Dr. Weekes was called in. He applied poultices to draw out the contagion. He positioned leeches to cleanse the blood. He prescribed pills and emetics. His treatment could not be faulted, yet it was not enough. For two months, David fought a losing battle as he weakened and died.

The vestry offered their sympathy and assured Widow Batchelor there was suitable accommodation available in the workhouse. She took her children to relations in Brighton.

One death caused more than condolences. For some time, Henry Henty had suffered from increasing stomach cramps. The attacks came without warning at home, in the garden or at work, the pain leaving him gasping for breath. Those at work took him worst for he was a sawyer, the underdog cramped in the confines of the narrow pit. When his stomach cramped, he was forced to stop till the spasms settled.

Then came an attack at home worse than any he had known. His wife, son and daughter-in-law were with him but could not ease his distress. There was no way to help, no easing the pain. Henry sank into unconsciousness and died.

It was some days after the funeral that the vestry received a letter from the county coroner. He took the parish officers to task for having neglected to report the sudden death of Henry Henty which should have been subjected to a coroner's enquiry. The neglect meant the officers would have to appear at the next assizes where they would be liable to a fine for default.

The vestry were astonished and alarmed. They quickly arranged a special meeting. There, Widow Henty reiterated what she had already told them about her late husband's health. Her son, Henry, confirmed her statement. The vestry instructed Mr. Ellis to send a letter explaining why the officers had not considered the case one for a coroner's inquest. The explanation was accepted and no fines ensued, but they had learnt a lesson about snares in the parish officer's path. [11]

They also found themselves at odds with Dr. Weekes over the contract for attending the parish poor. Costs, as elsewhere, had risen. Attendance on a woman in labour with her first child was £1, vaccinations were 5s. 0d. (25p). The dispute arose when Dr. Weekes charged an extra 15s. 6d. (77p) for attending a woman living near the plantations which he considered as not coming within the contract. The plantations were in reality part of the woodland on the Danny Estate. They were not as easily accessible as most places but they did lie within the doctor's contract area. The vestry rejected the extra charge.

Shortly afterwards, they sent Thomas Pierce to Dr. Weekes with a letter. It explained that because Pierce had received parish relief that month the vestry considered him a fit person to apply to them for medical assistance. They asked the doctor to attend Mrs. Pierce under the parish agreement.

Dr. Weekes quite enjoyed the letter. It enabled him to reply that if the vestry reconsidered their refusal to pay the 15s. 6d. (77p) for attending Knight's wife near the plantations he would attend Pierce's wife in her confinement, but not otherwise.

It settled the immediate issue. The vestry decided to pay the disputed charge. In August, Dr. Weekes attended Mrs. Pierce for 15s. 0d. (75p) but when the medical tender came up for renewal the following April, Dr. Weekes refused it. [12]

The vestry advertised in the Sussex Advertiser.

A doctor offered terms. They were attractive. An annual charge £10 cheaper with vaccinations costing only 2s. 6d. (12½p). Perhaps less attractive was the man himself, Dr. Verrall of Ditchling – the doctor who had sired 'Henry of the workhouse', Barbara Manner's illegitimate child. [13]

The terms were accepted. The vestry now had a parish doctor with an offspring in the workhouse as a possible patient. It was a tricky situation. The son was 18. It was high time he showed those important attributes – independence and a will to succeed.

Henry, too, seemed aware of things. He left Hurst and set off into the world. Dr. Verrall and the vestry could relax.

A few weeks later, the vestry of All Saints, Lewes, had to deal with a youth who had become a nuisance in their parish by seeking sustenance. It was Henry. They took him before the magistrates, obtained orders of removal and escorted him home to Hurst. His first attempt at independence had failed.

Henry had to be accepted back at the workhouse.

The vestry wasted no time. If the youth was incapable of maintaining himself, his father should be involved. Arrangements were made for Dr. Verrall to meet with the overseers and Henry at the New Inn. There, the doctor signed a terse five-line contract hiring Henry for one year at a shilling (5p) a week. Henry added his signature, the landlord witnessed it and Henry went home as his father's hired servant. It was indeed the perfect solution. The vestry could feel satisfied. [14]

Another Hurst man was on his way home. The Royal Artillery Drivers had finally returned to Woolwich from Flanders. At last, staff-sergeant Davey was poised for demobilization.

Mrs. Davey felt great excitement. At the same time, she was strangely uneasy. She carried out her husband's instructions to buy a bed and the other things she felt necessary. She folded the final letter from him and tucked it with the rest safely kept from the days long ago when Richard had sailed away to Lisbon. Now he was to be back in triumph, riding his own horse – a day of pride to her and an eye-opener for the village: the once drink-loving soldier, now staff-sergeant, upright in bearing, God fearing and worthy of respect. Hurstperpoint would see a real man. [15]

1817: William Buckman Seeks Help in Harwich

Mr. Long, landlord of the King and Queen Inn at Brighton, was quizzing visiting traders from Hurst about the attributes of their parish officials. His brother-in-law, a carpenter at Harwich with a wife and six children to support, wanted to know the best person to approach for help over the embarrassment of seeking assistance. The traders gave most plaudits to Mr. Marchant. Mr. Long informed his brother-in-law.

Mr. Marchant was the eventual recipient of the Harwich letter. It came from a William Buckman. He was convinced he was the first in his father's family ever to seek parish relief but it was not through idleness or drunkenness, just the hardness of the times preventing him from bringing in a single penny for a bit of bread to put in his children's mouths. He had been born in Clayton but when he was 14 his father had placed him apprentice with carpenter Jasper Still at Hurst where he lived-in at the shop, dependent on his master for everything except clothing. After seven years he had gained his apprenticeship indenture and with it his Hurst settlement qualification.

For several months he worked as a journeyman carpenter in the village. Then he set out east and eventually found work a hundred miles away in Suffolk at Woodbridge where they were building a military barracks almost entirely of wood. When the barracks closed down work became hard to find. He had a wife and family but he had never hired a house for more than £8 a year so had not gained a new settlement. Because of the scarcity of work he now had to ask for a few pounds to be sent to him via the Post Office or he would be brought home to Hurst under removal orders.

The vestry were unimpressed. None of their money was going a hundred miles to anybody unless under a legal obligation. They informed Buckman he would have to attend the Harwich Magistrates and be examined about his settlement. If it was judged to be Hurstperpoint, he should send proof.

William Buckman went to the magistrates. They listened to his evidence and determined his settlement. It was Hurstperpoint.

There was a delay before the findings could be sent because the mayor was taken ill and his signature was needed. Three weeks later, a copy was on its way to Mr. Ellis.

When Mr. Ellis showed it to the vestry, their faces fell: a two sheet document detailing the man's apprenticeship, his employment at the Woodbridge Military Barracks, his marriage and his children – Mary Ann, aged 13; William, 9; George, 7; John, 5; Charles, 2 and Hannah 9 months. It concluded with the definitive statement: 'That he hath never done any subsequent act whereby to gain a settlement in any other parish than appears by this examination. Before us this 30th July 1817 Hy Deane Mayor, John Hopkins.' [1]

The vestry instructed Mr. Ellis to file the copy. If the man really needed relief, he could write again.

What the examination failed to explain was William Buckman's slide into poverty. For 12 years he had enjoyed constant employment, first in the erection of Woodbridge Barracks and then in keeping them in good repair. The barracks accommodated 5000 men with stables for 100 horses. Carpenters were in high demand.

At Bonaparte's abdication everything changed. Army numbers decreased. Early in 1815 the barracks was declared surplus to requirements and closed. The workforce was suddenly redundant.

The flood of surplus carpenters on the market made it impossible to obtain sufficient work. William Buckman decided to move. He took his family south and found a place just over the Essex border near Harwich at Dovercourt.

Regular employment was still hard to find. With only intermittent work, he was powerless to stop his family's living standard drift. Gradually the tell-tale marks of poverty showed; shabbier clothes, smaller fires, scant food and drawn features. Finally he felt forced to seek poor-relief. Ahead of him was the chasm of pauperism. He was about to be pitched into it. His shame was acute.

Although despondent, William felt confident. His Hurst settlement was legally secure. It had the backing of the magistrates. Hurst vestry could not ignore it. He patiently awaited his relief.

It was a long wait. In October he wrote again. To him, the gentlemen seemed unfeeling in not sending anything. His troubles had become worse. He had been out of work during August because his employer had been very ill. When the rent became due, he had to pawn some of his furniture to raise the cash. He also had the poor-rate to pay. His earnings simply were not enough. If Hurst vestry wanted a reference about his character, they could write to either his employer or the overseers of Dovercourt. The only alternative to money was removal to Hurstperpoint workhouse.

This time the vestry accepted their position. Removal proceedings could be costly. They decided to send £2.

William was thankful for the money. It paid the rent and kept the family intact for another six months.

When the next rent became due, he was again without money. He wrote to the vestry explaining that whilst he earned more in cash than the Hurst paupers they gained by having food, flour and rent assistance. His wife was spending 14s. 0d. (70p) a week for bread and flour alone which left just 5s. 6d. (27½p) to cover everything else. It meant his children going almost bare foot for want of shoes. Then there was his wife's health. It had been bad since the birth of their baby daughter. His money just did not stretch to clothing and certainly did not allow for rent. With work slack, he was having a hard struggle to earn a living wage. Now the landlord was threatening to take the few pieces of furniture they still had. Just £2 was needed.

The letter missed the vestry meeting so had to wait. Unaware of this, William called at the post office each day expecting to find a reply. With nothing arriving, he had to keep asking his landlord to wait one more day, and one more, until the exasperated landlord finally declared he would not be trifled with any more. In desperation, William wrote again assuring the vestry he would have to keep writing until he gained an answer.

By now the vestry had considered the letter. They agreed to send the money. William was saved again.

He wrote more letters when the landlord's next two dates came. The vestry responded with £2 each time. [2]

William Buckman had quietly installed a regular six monthly income for rent to keep a roof over his family but his failure to provide for his children properly was beginning to tell on him.

The vestry were satisfied that the expenditure was no greater. They had other matters to deal with.

A letter from Kell, the Lewes solicitor, kept them on their toes:

> *'One Susan Almon was committed to the House of Correction here as a vagrant yesterday. You will remember her. She is to be confined only seven days or until she gets well. I write to you for any information as to her settlement, by her husband or husbands, lest if that cannot be ascertained the magistrates should send her to Hurstperpoint.'*

Susannah. The vestry remembered her well, their Irish soldier's wife, and how they had been so forgiving in arranging her early release from prison with her young child.

Since then she had apparently married again, one Samuel Provett, although nobody was convinced that the first husband was actually dead. Her present imprisonment was because she could not give a satisfactory account of the second husband's settlement. She could only say he was across Kent way, hop-picking in Ewhurst.

The second marriage now appeared as precarious as the first. Hurst certainly did not want the woman back. They instructed Kell to enquire further. He questioned Mr. Provett senior who stated that Samuel had served an apprenticeship at Lewknor in Oxfordshire.

This was excellent news: the way was clear. Apprenticeship was a settlement qualification. If William Buckman could use it to advantage, so could Hurst. Samuel Provett must have a settlement in Lewknor. His wife must share it. Removal orders were obtained.

Meanwhile, Susannah remained in the house of correction. The prison doctor prescribed pills. It did not need his practiced eye to notice Susannah's greatest need, nourishment. Food was provided by the gaoler. He was generous to the young mother with such a small baby. Milk, vegetables, wine, beer, tea, butter and cakes to the value of 19s. 10½d. (99p) supplemented the prison bread. Never had Susannah been able to spend so much on food in one week. Prison life had its compensations. [3]

When Susannah finished her week, she was taken to Hurst. The overseers were surprised by the baby: the birth had not been announced. It was of no moment because the next day Susannah started her journey to Lewknor.

She and her baby were safely handed over. All that the Hurst overseer now had to do was attend the Midsummer quarter sessions at Lewes and go through the formalities of recording the removal.

The next month when the overseer attended the sessions, there was news of an appeal. Lewknor were preparing a case ready for the Michaelmas Sessions. They intended challenging Samuel's apprenticeship, the baby's birth settlement and the legality of the marriage. Susannah was not so safely out of the way. To stave off her return, Hurst would have to ascertain that Peter Almon was dead. Otherwise the second marriage was invalid.

Kell wrote to the War Office asking if Private Peter Almon was still alive. Reply came that he was currently in Ireland with the 45th Regiment of Foot at Cork. It was sobering news. If Lewknor got to know of it, the case was as good as lost. Mr. Kell made discreet enquiries and discovered that Lewknor did indeed know. [4]

The inevitable happened. Susannah and her baby returned to Hurst. The vestry could no longer dispute whether Susannah was theirs, but surely the baby was not. They questioned Susannah. She knew she had been just over the border of Kent, at Brenchley, when the baby was born.

The vestry had no hesitation in writing to Brenchley demanding payment for the child's upkeep. Brenchley, too, were well versed in the law and declined on the grounds that, as the mother was a vagrant when she gave birth, the child had her settlement, Hurstperpoint.

Hurst had no intention of accepting Brenchley's ruling so another court case ensued. Hurst lost again. Susannah's baby was theirs.

The vestry's frustration over Susannah and her baby was calmed a little by the news of a much happier event in Hurst, the wedding of Thomas Harris and Widow Carter. Since her husband's death at Waterloo, life had been a constant struggle on her meagre pension from the army subscription; £10 a year with 5s. 0d. (25p) a week to support her two children, plus clothing when adjudged necessary. Thomas Harris' wage at the chalk-pit was not good, but together they would provide a secure and loving home for the children independent of parish aid.

George Bartley at last felt financially secure enough to offer help to his brothers and sisters. He had set off from Hurst confident in his grandmother's promises about reward for good education. It had taken a long time to materialize but he had eventually established himself a few miles short of London among the fruit fields and market gardens of Hammersmith.

George knew his father's shortcomings, his unreliability and the bitterness felt towards the parish over the loss of the Royal Oak. He knew, too, that little could be done for the older members of the family. He had completely lost touch with Tom. Charles, now in Brighton and married with four children, was already in poverty's grasp. William was doing his best to maintain independence as a gardener. He had a determined streak in him and was not afraid of hard work. He also had the expense of a young family which made it much harder to survive without asking for vestry relief. George felt most sorry for Barbara whose baby had so surprised the family. Of the younger ones, James could be helped.

James went to live with George and was fully supported by him for food, clothing and even pocket money. George obtained a place for him at a firm of drapers, Elling and Andrews, in Canterbury. They were so impressed by the boy's industry and aptitude that they agreed to take him as an apprentice for five years. George bore the major part of the cost of binding him, £25, and Hurst vestry gave £5 as their commitment to James as a Hurst parishioner. At the successful completion of his apprenticeship he would become a freeman of the City of Canterbury with every prospect of being a draper in his own right.

George insisted that the youngest members should not incur more misfortune than their father's reduced circumstances had already caused. He entreated his father to keep Jeremiah and Jane at school to give them a chance to receive a proper education which could help them find good positions in London.

Thomas Bartley was still having to share a house and suffer the indignity of pauperism. It was as well he knew nothing of the anonymous letter being penned to the vestry:

> *'Sir I hope you will Exques my boldness but I am one that am Ablige to pay the poor rate Thirefore I take the lebety to inform you that the daughter of Thomas Bartlee it is sayd is in the Family way Again it is har mother that as Sayd it And She as got one Child that the parrish is Ablig to keep and the child is at tulley at randidels and the Garl is on Takeing the child Away to put it to Sum Other woman ware you moust gaive 4 Shillings and the woman that as it at this time offers to keep it For 3 shilling per week before Shee will leve it and If you can Save one shilling per week it is Necassary it Should Stay ware it is and I heard Mr. Wells say it ware Exsceeding well don for thirefore It is all right it Should Stay and not be removed And it is your place to See the garl to know how Curcumstancess Stands and not for the parrish to have Such heavey burdens brought on them by A parsal of wores*
> *I am your Humb Sarvt S S'* [6]

There was no doubting S S's views on Barbara. Nor was there any doubt by January of her condition. She was again taken to Lewes to swear a father. This time she named Francis Newnham. The baby was a girl, christened Barbara. Francis Newnham accepted fatherhood and paid £20 to free him from any further expense in the maintenance of the child. [7]

On the other hand, Marshal Wortley, the father of Barbara's two year old son, was causing concern over his payments. As he lived in Reigate, his only contact was by letter. To one he added a P.S. 'I hope the child is in good health and the mother likewise.' After that, he showed less concern for them and more for his own position. His payments became overdue. He regretted it was not in his power to pay at once. He would do so as soon as possible.

Eventually Wortley sent word that he had arranged payment through Reigate Bank. The vestry waited and waited but received no money. They wrote to the bank asking for confirmation of the payment. The bank's reply confirmed the vestry's misgivings; no payment had been made by Wortley. [8]

Solicitors Kell were consulted. They sent their clerk to Reigate. He made enquiries explaining who he wanted and the nature of his business until he managed to locate Wortley.

Marshal Wortley realized he was the topic of Reigate gossip. Infuriated, he wrote to the vestry complaining of being brandished as the man who had ruined a girl in Hurst. He pointed out that it was not a pleasing thing to hear from a customer and that it was hurtful to his father's business in times that were not good.

The vestry instructed Mr. Ellis to reply that the matter was now out of their hands. Solicitor Mr. Christopher Kell would contact him again in due course.

The solicitors wrote to Wortley explaining yet again the legal implications and urging him to find security for payment of the debt. They even offered him a considerable time in which to pay. It was to no avail, he did not reply. [9]

The case was brought against him. William Ellis rode across to Mr. Kell to ensure they both agreed on the facts and how they were to conduct the case.

They both gave evidence at the hearing. The court favoured the parish. Wortley had to face facts. With costs, his debt grew by nearly £40. [10]

The next task was to obtain payment. It was perhaps short-sighted of Hurst vestry not to have anticipated that if Wortley was not paying the original money there was little chance of any coming for the additional costs.

The solicitors put the matter in the hands of the Sheriff's Officer who issued a distraint on Wortley's possessions in order to sell them and raise the necessary money. The officer made out the papers and went to Wortley's shop in Reigate. There he was told bluntly that the shop was the property of Widow Wortley. Marshall was journeyman to her. Nothing in the shop belonged to him, nor would it until his mother died. He had no property for anybody to distrain. The papers were useless. [11]

Word was sent to the solicitors. They considered their options. They could stay proceedings against Wortley and await his mother's death or imprison him for debt. Mr. Kell asked Hurst for instructions.

The vestry were in a difficult position. They could not wait indefinitely, yet if they imprisoned Wortley would they be any nearer recovering the money?

They instructed Mr. Kell to stay proceedings for the present.

1820: Michael Harmes Falls into Debt

Isaac Sayers was struggling to safeguard his out-relief. He had become thoroughly disillusioned with the vestry. For 20 years they had directed his life and he had quietly acquiesced. In Isaac's eyes, he had never had more than he was entitled to as a pauper; rent, fuel, flour, his weekly cash and occasional clothing. He had been denied his dog. He had been denied his gun. The wonder was that he had coped so well, for indeed he had. His family was a credit to anyone. The eight children still at home were all healthy and strong, and his wife kept the house, or their half of it, in good order.

Isaac's crisis came when the vestry suddenly reduced the flour allowance so that only three of his children were eligible. His ration dropped from eight gallons to only three (36 litres to 13). He accepted the reduction one week. When he stood before the vestry the following week to find his allowance still only three gallons, he refused to accept it and declared he would not go home to his family. Nor did he. He disappeared. Mrs. Sayers with her eight children, from 14 year old George down to six-month Emma, were taken into the workhouse.

The vestry placed one of their advertisements in the Sussex Advertiser:

'ABSCONDED AND LEFT HIS WIFE AND FAMILY CHARGEABLE TO THE PARISH OF HURSTPERPOINT. ISAAC SAYERS A MAN OF SHORT STATURE ABOUT 45 YEARS OF AGE, GENERALLY WEARS HIS BEARD VERY LONG. TWO GUINEAS REWARD.'

It was effective. Isaac was apprehended and taken before the magistrates. The vestry wished to make an example of him: as idle and wayward a man as any on the parish books. They catalogued all the aid he had received during the past three years. They pressed for a severe sentence.

The magistrates found him guilty of leaving his family chargeable to the parish: sentence six months hard labour at Lewes. The vestry were satisfied. [1]

Isaac changed into gaol dress and began his prison routine. Every day, weather permitting, he had an hour in the 'airing-yard'. Whenever there was Divine Service, the whole company gathered together in the chapel.

Isaac did have the satisfaction of earning money by his labour. Half a prisoner's earnings went towards his prison keep. The rest was the man's – unless his crime was to run from his family. In such cases, the parish first claimed their expenses in maintaining the family. Poor Isaac; the family would take all he earned and more besides. Isaac settled to enduring his six months.

Hurst vestry had their own problem, a worrying disturbance in the spiritual life of the parish. A Methodist Chapel was nearing completion at the eastern end of the High Street. It fronted the road as if cocking a snook at St. Lawrence Church and its absentee rector.

The erection of the chapel had been watched with misgivings. Too many people were deserting the established faith to follow their own interpretation of Christ's teachings. What could be done to counter the threat?

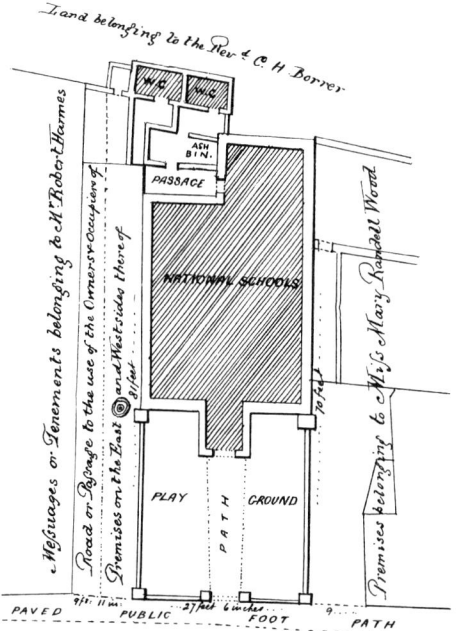

When the vestry discussed the problem, they realized the position had potential. The parish had five schools offering education for appropriate families but it was in sore need of a suitable building to accommodate the free school for lower class children. If the chapel could be purchased, it would be killing two birds with one stone; a Dissenting Chapel gone and a National Schoolroom gained.

Negotiations were begun. The owner of the chapel agreed to sell for £460. [2]

Dr. Weekes provided most of the money at a low rate to put with £130 from the National Society for the Education of the Poor. The purchase was made. Dissenters were granted a licence to worship in a room of a private house in the north of the parish.

By the time Isaac finished his prison sentence, an extra floor had been inserted in the chapel to form separate boys and girls schools, each with a room 30 feet by 24 (9 metres by 7) able to accommodate 100 children.

Water came from the communal well for a row of labourers' cottages that lined the trackway beside the building. At the back, they dug the privies. All was simple, cost effective and adequate.

Isaac passed the new school on his way to collect his family from the workhouse – except for George who had already left to find his own living. He walked them home to their half house at Goddards Green. Whether or not his children would ever walk back into the village to gain the benefits of National Society education was extremely doubtful.

Staffing the Boys School was a straightforward affair. The ideal man was already there at the Free School, Henry Muzzell. He had directed the boys aged 5 to 10 in reading and writing skills. The girls from 6 to 11, under the watchful eye of their mistress, had also learnt to be proficient in needlework.

Although Henry had a second income as a gardener, he remained embarrassingly poor. Yet he had ambition. He wrote a fair hand and was quietly learning the most rewarding ways of behaviour towards those who held the purse strings. He was diligent in carrying out his duties and showing respect for those in authority. He took care not to blot his copybook.

Recruiting a suitable person for the girls proved more difficult. An advertisement was placed in the Sussex Advertiser:

'A MIDDLE AGED, ACTIVE WOMAN TO UNDERTAKE MANAGEMENT OF THE HURST NATIONAL SCHOOL FOR GIRLS. ONE ALREADY INSTRUCTED IN THE NATIONAL SYSTEM OF TEACHING WOULD BE PREFERRED. FOR PARTICULARS APPLY TO THE REV. EDWARD TURNER, HURST.' [3]

When the school opened, the curate could feel inward satisfaction. About 60 boys and 60 girls attended – most of the labourers' boys and well over half of the girls. Dr. Weekes knew he had invested his money in a worthy cause.

The National Society provided a carefully planned education in reading and writing. The girls also continued learning the all important skills of needlework. Selected tracts from the Society for the Promotion of Christian Knowledge formed an integral part of the reading matter. Pupils were instructed in the liturgy and catechism and they attended Divine Service in St. Lawrence Church on the Lord's Day. Such were the advantages of National School education that the vestry agreed to allow the 5s. 6d. (27½p) quarterly payment to enable four children out of the workhouse to attend. [4]

It was a little ironic that whilst the gentlemen of Hurst were providing for the education of labourers' girls, the eminent school for their own girls was suddenly closing. The two Miss Crundens who had achieved so much at their Hurst Academy were now moving to Henfield. For the Miss Crundens the move was not without misgivings but the chance to have a larger school could not be missed. They hoped for continued support and emphasized the scope of their tuition; English Grammar, History ancient and modern, Geography and the use of the globe, Plain and Ornamental Needle Work, with Writing, Arithmetic, French, Music, Dancing and Drawing. [5]

Nathaniel Borrer had no misgivings about the education of his son, Carey, who learnt his Latin with the curate. Although Carey's destiny was not fixed, it would involve Eton and Oxford.

Carey enjoyed a secure home life free from excesses. He learnt the thrills and spills of horse riding, he stoically stomached the stench of hot camomile tea whenever he caught a chill, he endured the cold of Brighton's sea at the merciless hands of bulbous Martha Gunn and he encountered the sadness of losing a loved one when his sister died. His father inculcated in him a charitable regard for the hardships of the poor and instilled a sense of service to the village that would be repaid in respect and obedience.

The agricultural labourers were certainly facing hardship as farmers laid off men for the winter. The vestry had increasing difficulty finding work for them. As many as possible were sent flint digging on Wolstonbury Hill. Somehow, work had to be found for the rest until April when the farmers would take men on again. It was resolved that the unemployed should be put digging, grubbing roots or mudding out ditches. Payment would be per completed measurement with the cost shared 50-50 between vestry and farmer. It solved the immediate problem.

Stephen Mills took full advantage of the scheme to see him through the winter months. At its end in April, he was out of work, money and food. He traipsed the south of the parish and had a fruitless morning. About dinner time, he was heading north at Mr. Hider's Cophall Farm. The answer about work was the usual: 'No'. Then he asked for a bite to eat. To his delight, they obliged – a heartening event for one who had eaten no breakfast. He gratefully accepted his dinner and set off again, a happier man.

Just past the next cottage, he came across something which made him happier still. Strewn across the hedge in the afternoon sun, was an array of men's hose. Many were darned and threadbare. One pair looked almost new. They were ribbed worsted; far too good to be left on a hedge. Stephen took them and continued on his way.

Shortly afterwards, there was a commotion from the cottage area – a lady's strident voice, men shouting and a figure pounding along the lane towards Stephen. There was little point in Stephen hurrying too. He walked on. When the runner, Mr. Hider's nephew, caught up with him and mentioned a theft of stockings, he did not bother to resist.

They took him to a J.P. who committed him to Lewes house of correction to await trial at the next quarter sessions due the following month. There he received six weeks for petty larceny. [6]

Farmers themselves were experiencing financial difficulties. In the days of peace since Bonaparte's defeat, income seemed on a downward spiral whilst the poor-rate went up and up. Many of the landowners blamed weaknesses in the new Corn Laws introduced at the end of the war despite opposition by biased northern industrialists. The laws were meant to provide protection against cheap imports: they were failing. Market pressures were so great that producers had to accept whatever price the purchaser dictated.

Michael Harmes was encountering particularly tough times at Wanbarrow. He had six children to provide for, task enough without the slack prices of recent markets. He had found it impossible to produce his last poor-rate money on time. Not until the vestry had gone to the extent of issuing a distress warrant had he at last scraped together enough to pay.

By April, Michael had amassed a debt of £51 to the parish. The vestry referred the matter to the solicitors. Michael was faced with another distress warrant.

May Day was no time of celebration for him. The evening was spent trying to explain his predicament at the vestry meeting. The members were considerate to a fellow farmer in difficulties. They declared that £25 of his debt should be paid in a fortnight, the remainder at the June meeting.

Michael made the best he could of the respite. He put all his energy into raising cash, even carting coals for the parish. It enabled him to pay off £38. Just £13 was needed. [7]

He did everything he could to clear the debt. The task was beyond him. At the June meeting, he had nothing more to offer. He was sorry for causing inconvenience again but he had paid all the ready money available. If they could postpone the deadline a short time his books would be in good order. He had potatoes, peas and beans for ready cash as soon as they could be cropped, as well as 30 acres (12 hectares) of wheat and oats. The money was there, maturing in the ground. It just needed a few weeks for harvesting. [8]

To the rest of the committee, the matter was not that simple. It was well known in vestry circles that Mr. Campion's bailiff had just made a report on the farm. Wanbarrow's fields and hedges were far from the pristine condition they had been in during the days of James Harmes. Michael Harmes was not the farmer his father had been. Mr. Campion wanted Wanbarrow in the hands of a reliable tenant.

The vestry had to act independently. They decided to abide by their resolution that the outstanding money should be paid at that meeting. Michael Harmes had not yet produced the £13. The matter would have to be referred back to the solicitors who would advise the correct course of action.

The solicitors gave their findings. The consequences were dire.

Mr. Campion took the farm back, the bailiffs took household effects enough for the debt and Michael had to take his family up to the village, homeless and broke, with his remaining possessions piled on a cart. The tenancy of Wanbarrow Farm passed to Thomas Wickham, a farmer of good repute.

Michael felt the bitterness of the dispossessed. For want of £13 they had taken his farm and his home. Where was justice? Who was on his side? He would not recall his own sentiments of eight years past when he had been parish overseer.

Not even his mother could offer him anything. She already rented her spare rooms to Michael's brother and another family. Her home was full. Michael would now have to make his own way in the world as a hired hand.

Michael was in difficulties throughout the summer. Even with the higher earnings of harvest he was still struggling. He attended the September vestry to ask a little help.

The previous September he had been there by right as a rate-paying parishioner. Now he had to show deferential meekness to the men who only a year ago had been his fellow farmers. It was hard for Michael. Even harder was the vestry's refusal. Michael tried to reason. Nobody would listen. No longer did he have the right to promote his point of view. He was an applicant for relief. They had heard his case and refused him. He must go.

Michael left, thwarted yet determined. They may humiliate him in Hurst but he still held Lewes in his hand. He walked across the Downs and explained his case to the magistrates. He chose his words carefully: clarity and detail were important; there would be no second chance.

His description of events was effective. The magistrates had no hesitation in deciding Hurst should come to some agreement with him or attend the next week's sitting when both sides could explain their position. [9]

The vestry chose to contest the issue. At the hearing, Michael again spoke to good effect and was granted 5s. 0d. (25p) a week assistance. It was a personal victory. He walked home in far better spirits.

If anyone felt an atom of sympathy for Michael Harmes it was John Marchant, owner of Little Park, East and West Edgerly, the Bowling Alley and numerous fields by the Hurst/Ditchling road. If the truth were known, John Marchant himself was in desperate straits: so much property, yet so little available finance. He, a respected member of Hurst establishment, must raise money or go under.

John Marchant had a hard decision to make. He could pretend his affairs would suddenly improve or he could seek help. There was no real choice. He had been pretending long enough. He must pocket his pride and go cap in hand to his old friend William Borrer whose financial affairs were known to be sound.

Mr. Borrer was an understanding friend and an astute gentleman; £1500 for a year at 5% with both East and West Edgerly as security and the deal to be entered at Mr. Campion's next Court Baron. John Marchant agreed. He would have no difficulty repaying the debt in full since his financial embarrassment was of a fleeting nature. [10]

Farmers across the parish felt themselves being sucked under by ever rising taxation. They gathered in force at the December vestry meeting determined to seek redress where they could. A reduction in tithes was the first step: nobody could deny they were unjustifiably high – and all were going to their absentee rector 40 or more miles away at Eltham. Mr. Ellis was instructed to write him a letter to explain their position and ask for a reduction. [11]

Rev. Shaw-Brooke gave the matter great thought before replying. He wished to be entirely fair. Whilst he fully appreciated the present low state of the market, he had to point out that the agreement over money payment of tithes had been made on a fair assessment of returns. In Hurst it had been agreed at 4s. 4d. (23p) per acre. In Eltham it was 10s. 0d. (50p). Would Hurst farmers match a reduction at bad markets with an increase in good times? He thought not. He felt unable to make any justifiable adjustment.

Mr. Ellis read the reply to the next vestry. The farmers had to accept. Tithes were paid but the sore remained.

The next harvest was poor. Another letter went to Eltham. Hurst farmers would not have money ready for the date of the proposed tithes dinner. Would the rector like to postpone it?

The rector happily concurred. He could accept a few weeks delay in collecting his money.

He was less happy with the letter from the Hurst farmer explaining that future tithes would be available in the traditional way – set out 'in kind' on the fields ready for the rector to collect. Church tithes was a prickly subject.

Jeremiah Bartley Sits in the Stocks

For the village, the great event of 1820 was the national drama sparked by the death of King George III which made the Prince Regent king in fact as well as function. As king, George IV determined to offer his royal-wife, cousin Caroline, an annuity of £50000. All she had to do was renounce the title of Queen and continue living on the continent.

Queen Caroline's reaction was to return to England. She was Queen. King George promptly inveigled the Government to produce a Bill of Pains and Penalties against Caroline. It would expose her infamous life-style and lead to a royal divorce.

In the eyes of the people, it was their profligate king who led an infamous life-style beneath the ornate domes of his Brighton Pavilion. They were for Queen Caroline.

Brighton Pavilion
Illustrated LondonNews 27-10-1842 Copyright The British Library Board. All Rights Reserved

Peers and bishops assembled at Westminster to hear charges of adultery against her. It was trial by innuendo. A bare majority of lords condemned her. The Government knew it was too small a margin. The Bill was withdrawn.

The Queen's victory was cause for countrywide celebration. Everywhere, illuminated transparencies were the order of the day. Michael Harmes could enjoy them in Hurst.

Pride of place went to Mr. Allen whose artistry and wit produced a semi-circular arch round an emblem of wisdom inscribed: 'Modesty and Decency'. Above the arch was an imperial crown and the bold motto: 'No Half Crowns'. [1]

Mr. Allen had made his mark. He was the focus of conversation at the celebratory dinner held at the New Inn: a time of excellent songs and unusual glee that showed how sensitive the people of Hurst were to their queen. She had their full support. They would not stand by and allow her to be ill-used. They stood for justice and the individual's liberty. Let no one doubt it, even the king.

Justice and liberty were not ready bedfellows for the wandering vagrant. One man's liberty took him to an outlying barn on Locks Farm. When Mr. Webber's men discovered him he was beyond moving himself. [2]

It was another case of ill health and starvation, the second in a fortnight but more acute. Food and 2s. 0d. (10p) from the vestry had helped the couple found at the watermill. This time Dr. Weekes had to be called. He advised a place at the workhouse.

The overseers were contacted. Admittance was authorized. Mr. Webber provided a cart, and the man was lifted aboard.

At the workhouse they put him on a bed. He lay listless as if in a stupor, unable to communicate. Where he came from or where he was bound for nobody knew. Nothing could be elicited from him that day and he showed no interest in food.

Next morning he was dead, an anonymous corpse. Two of the workhouse ladies laid him out. Mr. Ellis supplied a shroud and pall. The curate conducted the burial and recorded it in the register: '*Man, name unknown, age unknown.*' Dust to dust in an unmarked corner of the churchyard. [3]

Another arrival at the parish had no hesitation in announcing himself. He was John Gray, back home 200 miles from Cornwall on his own initiative with his wife and child.

The vestry gave the family temporary lodgings at the White Horse.

At the next vestry meeting, Gray's arrival was discussed. Doubts were raised about his home being Hurst. His parents had left the parish in 1793 when he was still a boy. It was almost inconceivable that he had never qualified for another settlement. The committee decided the man should be questioned by the magistrates.

Solicitor Kell arranged the hearing. The magistrates concluded that Gray was mistaken in thinking he had come home. His home was in Cornwall. He would have to go back there.

Although the vestry were gladdened by the news, they knew there were difficulties to face if they took out removal orders. First, one of the overseers would have to escort the family for part of the journey. Second, although Gray had not proved his Hurst settlement, there was no incontrovertible evidence that he had gained one elsewhere. The grounds for removing the family could well be disputed. If a receiving parish challenged Hurst in court, heavy expenses would be incurred.

The vestry agreed an alternative solution. They would finance the Grays to return on their own. That way expenses could be kept to a minimum.

Mr. Ellis was instructed to go to the White Horse with £5 and a ready written receipt acknowledging it as money for the family's return journey. John Gray accepted the money and marked his X on the receipt. Three weeks after their arrival, the Grays began the long trek back to Cornwall. [4]

The vestry turned their attention to complaints being made about the general behaviour of the village boys. They had become very tumultuous. People seemed unable to pass along the street without being insulted. There was only one practical way to deal with the trouble. The overseers ordered the headborough to take any offender into custody.

Thomas Bartley's youngest boy, Jeremiah, was out in the High Street with baker Taylor's son in the mood for laughs. They were blissfully unaware of the vestry's latest directive.

Mr. Borrer's bailiff approached. He was too good a target to let by – Mr. Bull! The boys thoroughly enjoyed themselves at Mr. Bull's expense. Mr. Bull continued his way without glancing in their direction. They gave a farewell 'moo' as he disappeared. He had been a good laugh.

It was not the end of the affair. Baker Taylor was informed of his son's escapade. He decided a lesson should be taught. His son was not going to insult members of the public. Certainly he would not offend somebody of the status of bailiff at Pakyns Manor. Mr. Taylor sent for headborough Penfold. He asked that his son be put in the stocks.

The headborough went one better and put both boys in. There they sat for all to see and comment on. They found out what it was like to receive ribaldry. They did not enjoy the experience.

After an hour, Penfold unlocked the stocks. Two very deflated boys scuttled home. The friend found no sympathy. Jeremiah did. Thomas Bartley was inflamed. His dormant wrath over losing the

Royal Oak exploded. His son had been put in the stocks without sufficient cause. Penfold would answer for it in court.

Thomas went to Lewes and commenced proceedings. Penfold was summoned to appear at the next sessions to answer charges.

The vestry consulted Kell the solicitor. They had instructed Penfold to take unruly boys into custody. He had not been empowered to determine punishment. Should they defend Penfold or leave him? Mr. Kell considered the matter. Bartley had surely acted in anger. Prosecutions were expensive. Could the man afford it?

A compromise was suggested. The sides should come to a mutual understanding without recourse to a court case.

For a time, such a move seemed beyond Thomas. In the end, common sense or poverty prevailed and the case was dropped. Mr. Bull, however, was ensured a peaceful walk through the village. [5]

Widow Batchelor was going through a trying time with one of her sons, George. Life had always been difficult since the big Thames freeze that had ruined her late husband's work at Deptford. Her move to a brother in Brighton had affected the children's behaviour. George had gone from bad to worse. Lying had given way to petty theft.

The boy was taken to one side. The uncle pointed out how Mrs. Batchelor had been almost driven to distraction. He described the consequences of thieving and telling stories. His nephew listened quietly.

Consequences seemed best avoided. George left home.

He did not have the run of the streets for long. A constable apprehended him as a young vagrant. Brighton passed him home to Hurst.

There, he was confined in the workhouse where he quickly discovered the governor kept rules that had to be obeyed. Discipline was strict. George had enough sense to adapt and behave himself. In six weeks Hurst sent him back to his mother – a reformed boy. [6]

The vestry knew that discipline was an important part of the workhouse child's upbringing; good training for their adult life. Discipline itself was a disciplined duty. They had become only too aware of intemperate behaviour towards parish-children when young Susan Henley was put out to a family in Albourne. Within two months there were stories of her being ill-treated.

A visit was made. The stories proved only too true. From all appearances, Susan had been beaten hard and often. The vestry immediately took her away and put her with a reliable family in Ditchling. More clothing was provided. In her new placement, she was treated as well as any parish-child. [7]

There was a far more delicate situation when Sarah Sayers fell out with her mistress. Sarah had been placed out as under-maid to a family in Brighton. She had created a favourable first impression but fell from grace and became depressed as her mistress increasingly found fault with her.

Sarah's difficulties came to a head on a hot July Sunday. The day began badly. First she was scolded for being dirty. After church she was forbidden to go out.

Sarah dwelt on her troubles. To be confined to the house for your Sunday free time was hard; on a glorious high-summer day it was worse. Coming on top of a scolding it was almost unbearably unfair. By evening, she knew she had put up with too much.

Early the next morning, she slipped out of the house and set off for Hurst carrying her belongings with her. She was well on her way before they missed her.

Her mistress was furious. The tales of the girl being the type who would tire of work as soon as she was fed and clothed had proved true. A letter to Hurst vestry was the only course to take.

Mr. Ellis received it by the next post. From the tone of the contents, he had no doubt the writer was extremely upset. More than a pound's worth of clothing had been spent on the child over and above what the vestry had provided. The stuff the girl must have taken with her would be proof indeed. She had never been ill-treated, her very appearance would testify to that. She had indeed aroused feelings of Christian sorrow in her mistress – yet the ingratitude, the selfish ingratitude of the girl should rightly be punished. [8]

The vestry agreed that children should behave themselves in a seemly manner but they had no intention of being harried by a hurried letter from an irate employer. Sarah would remain in Hurst workhouse.

1821: William Buckman Loses Hope

The fear of workhouse life had become a constant theme playing on the mind of William Buckman in Essex. The wartime days of work for carpenters at the huge Woodbridge Barracks had long gone. Now when he had employment his earnings were barely enough for daily needs. Far too often there were long spells when nothing came in. Money set aside for rent had to be spent on food. The threat of eviction and his family's removal to Hurst loomed ever larger. William was a caring father. His inability to provide for his family worried him: the less the work, the greater the worry.

Through the cold of January and February, William's worry became deep melancholy.

His wife was unable to raise his spirits. Finally, she called the doctor. He could find no apparent disease, just a case of dejection causing a loss of bodily energies. William was not ill enough to die – but he did.

Mrs. Buckman was distraught. The doctor wrote to Mr. Marchant for her:

> *'Sir*
>
> *I have attended in a medical capacity for the last two or three years a poor, industrious and exemplary man Wm Buckman whose death, to my great regret and to the regret of the neighbourhood took place on Monday evening last. He has left a wife and seven children who as you may suppose from the loss of an affectionate father are thrown into the greatest distress. The poor woman has requested me to make her misfortune known to you and to crave parish assistance.*
>
> *During his residence here (and which by the bye, has been in a house of mine) he has not had a sufficient hire to fix him on the parish of Dovercourt – the rates and taxes being paid by myself.*
>
> *The poor woman is desirous of continuing where she is at present having gained by her own and her husband's excellent conduct many friends by whose kind assistance she hopes to be able to provide for her numerous family but in this wish she must be guided by the quantum of help she receives from your parish. In the hopes of an early reply*
> *I remain Sir*
> *Very respectfully yours*
>
> *John Bailey.'*

Vestry clerk Mr. Ellis replied asking the doctor to inform them the exact position of the family. He did so. Widow Buckman earned up to 7s. 0d. (35p) a week by taking in washing. The oldest girl, Mary Ann, was 15 and now in service. 13 year old William was a bricklayer's labourer earning 1s. 0d. (5p) a day when in work. George, 12, was with his uncle the landlord of the Saracen's Head in Ipswich. The other four were all aged under eight. Neighbours were showing a lot of sympathy which, though a welcome help, would not go on for ever. Her landlord considered she needed about 2s. 0d. (10p) a week for each child that was not earning but he felt the parish officers of Dovercourt were better fitted to give advice.

Mr. Ellis laid the information before the vestry. Widow Buckman was certainly in a position none of them would wish upon her. However, they were legally obliged to distribute aid within clearly defined rules. William Buckman had held a Hurst settlement. The vestry had met their obligations to him as a parishioner. Now that he was dead they could not justifiably make an allowance to the widow unless it was shown that the family still belonged to Hurst.

Widow Buckman was informed. She went straight to the Dovercourt vestry who took her to their magistrates to be examined. She produced the crucial apprentice indenture, listed the times they had been relieved by Hurst and reiterated that her husband had never gained a new settlement since his apprenticeship. The magistrates confirmed she had a Hurstperpoint settlement.

Dovercourt vestry sent a copy to Hurst. They also made it clear that if Hurst were willing to make the widow an allowance Dovercourt would pay it to her weekly. If no allowance was being made, Dovercourt would take out orders and have the family removed home to Hurst.

Hurst had little option. All they could do was make terms to their best advantage. They offered 5s. 0d. (25p) a week and said how sure they were that the widow would be happily satisfied as prices of flour and provisions were so moderate. [1]

Widow Buckman accepted with as much good grace as she could muster. She could neither express honest satisfaction nor dare barter for more money.

The widow's troubles increased that winter when William caught typhus, the great scourge of the poor. When three more of her children went down with it, Widow Buckman had to stop taking work. The health of the children was of paramount importance; nursing took all her time. No money was coming in, expenses were rising. Again the rent money had to go on food, just as it had done before her husband died. [2]

For Widow Buckman, responsibility banished any thought of depression. Not until she was certain the children had safely passed the crisis stage of their disease did she resume work. William returned to the brickworks but the younger children did not throw off the effects of their illness until deep into summer

In September, William lost his work. In October, all the children caught scarlet fever. Widow Buckman was back nursing without even being able to think of recouping her losses.

In November she wrote to Hurst asking for help with her rent. She was humbly obliged to them for past favours and would not trouble them except she was a laundress and had to have a bit of garden to dry her linen. If she lived in the town it would be £7 for one room but it would be no use to her. The smallest cottage she could get was £9 a year. Also, Dovercourt widows with four children had as much as eight shillings (40p) a week. With the blessing of God, William would soon be learning a stone mason's art. She expected him to be apprenticed and that would be another of them off Hurst's hands.

The vestry decided it was unwise to provide rent money consistently. They explained how the money was her weekly allowance plus a gift because of her distressed condition.

When William's apprenticeship was arranged, he had a shock. £16 was needed to bind him. He followed his mother's example and wrote to Mr. Marchant for the money explaining how without it he would have to work three years before receiving any wages. He pointed out that his apprenticeship would gain him a Harwich settlement and he would not then be a drain on Hurst poor-rates. He trusted the gentlemen would grant the money.

The vestry had no hesitation: they could not think of doing it. They did take the opportunity to amend Widow Buckman's allowance. With the son off her hands, her allowance would be adjusted from five shillings to four.

Widow Buckman reminded the vestry of their decision when she wrote the following winter. When the Christmas rent had become due she had not had sufficient money. If the vestry had helped her son, he would have had money to help her. Her earnings were barely enough to feed the family. They were living on potatoes with very little else. If Hurst gentlemen would send £5, she could have her second son, George, apprenticed to a cabinet maker and get him off their parish. She needed £10 to bind him. Even then, she had to find him clothes and provisions for three years. A lady had advanced her £5 that she now had to work out. She was glad to say she was known for hard work and honesty which she considered to be all a poor person had to look up to. If they doubted her word, they could write to Mr. Warner, the Dovercourt overseer, because he lived next door to her.

The vestry noted Widow Buckman's remarks and decided she could have a gift of £3 to assist putting George apprentice. She should take it from the £10 they were forwarding to Mr. Warner for her allowance over the past year.

With Widow Buckman's apprenticeship difficulties sorted out, Hurst turned their attention to another problem. Barbara Bartley was in trouble again. Her children Marshal and Barbara, now four and two years old, should have been claim enough on her time but they were not. There had been time for men. Once more, the vestry had to take her to the magistrates to swear her coming child's father. She named her man, William Nicholls. Nicholls refuted the allegation.

In November, Barbara gave birth; another girl. She was baptized Eleanor.

Baby Eleanor made it three illegitimate children in six years. The vestry could not condone such behaviour. They decided to set Barbara before the magistrates as a lewd woman deserving imprisonment.

Barbara was taken to Lewes. Her immoral life-style was explained to the magistrates. They rebuked her but refused to impose imprisonment. A baby of so few weeks should not be separated from its mother, nor was prison a suitable home. The question should be left until the child was weaned. Barbara Bartley would nurse her baby in Hurst.

Meanwhile, William Nicholls had been on the move. The vestry traced him to lodgings in Brighton along Little Russell Street. He was ordered to pay £4 for the lying in and 2s. 6d. (12½p) a week for the upkeep of the child.

Nicholls was not going to be saddled with an extra-marital child. He was a literate man well able to put his thoughts to paper. He had no intention of paying a penny for a wretch he had never had any connection with except talk to as he went to and fro the stable at work. It had already cost him £1 a week through losing his job at Lewes. Since then his wife and children had been surviving on a single meal a day until the past three weeks when he had managed to find more work. He had two children of his own to keep and his lodgings took 2s. 6d (12½p) a week. His money was not there for another woman's child. If the vestry wanted to see him they could arrange it at Lewes because that way he would at least have gaol allowance. [3]

The vestry took him before the magistrates. They were not going to be put upon by the likes of Nicholls, particularly where it concerned the depraved life style of Barbara Bartley.

Still he did not accept fatherhood. The baby remained a parish expense.

1823: Michael Harmes Becomes Parish Beadle

Michael Harmes was opening a school. The vestry were delighted at the news. He was still receiving the weekly 5s. 0d. (25p) granted in the confrontation at Lewes magistrates. In April, he had asked for more help to provide faggots. The vestry had felt obliged to grant him £2. Now he seemed determined at last to live by his own endeavours. Once established, the school would provide a reliable income. [1]

Michael first had to overcome the difficulty of attracting pupils. Poorer families seemed content with the National School. Wealthier families already had their favoured schools. Scholars were slow to present themselves.

Short of money, Michael turned for help to his mother. Old Mrs. Harmes still rented out part of her house through the vestry to pauper families. Michael wrote a note for her: 'Sir, Please to pay the Bearer on my account my half years rent up to Lady Tide.' His mother added her signature and Michael presented the request at the next vestry meeting.

He went home a happier man by £3 10s. (£3.50). It helped for a few weeks but nothing brought him pupils. In the end he had to close his school. It had never really opened. He was back on the vestry's weekly relief.

In July, he decided to be a carrier. He just needed the vestry's help in providing a horse and cart to start him off. The vestry agreed and lent the necessary £2 capital towards costs. They would ensure repayment by withholding Michael's relief money for the next eight weeks. Michael bought his horse and cart. This time he was determined to succeed. [2]

Although there should have been ample local work, custom was hard to find. People seemed reluctant to trust their business to Michael Harmes. His initial enthusiasm dampened. In August he was back at the vestry asking help with his rent. They granted him £1. In October he asked for nine weeks pay in advance. Again they obliged.

The carrier's business needed something to bolster it; a steady coals contract from Southwick, or flint carting from Wolstonbury Hill. Nothing came Michael's way. Instead, he caught a fever. He was ill through December and January into February. His 'Carriers' business went the way of his school. He was an everyday pauper on the vestry's relief book again.

At that time, the vestry were very concerned over the trouble caused around the parish by vagrants. A dead one had been found in one of Mr. Sharp's barns near the Twineham boundary. The tragedy was that the man had more than enough money in his pocket to provide lodgings at an inn. There was no reason at all for him to seek shelter in a barn. Yet he had, and now they had to bury him. The man's money, £3 14s. 5¼d. (£3.72), was used to defray the cost of the inquest and funeral. He had at least been self sufficient in his burial. [3]

The major problem with vagrancy was the nuisance caused by begging. The vestry decided to appoint a beadle to apprehend or move on all undesirables. Apart from the cost of a uniform, it need not be a burden on the rates because a pauper could be appointed at 10s. 0d. (50p) a week. They had the ideal man on the parish books, Michael Harmes. He was anxious to regain a sense of status and independence, his year as overseer had shown him adept at upholding order and he was literate. Michael was appointed. As soon as his uniform was ready, he would be out on patrol.

Within a week, he was able to commence duty. His new uniform made him one of the most striking figures in the village; blue cloth coat with scarlet collar and cuffs, scarlet waistcoat, strong cord trousers, a cape for protection from the weather and a gold banded hat with gilt buckle. In his hand he held a painted staff varnished and inscribed with his official rank. Michael was a man of authority again. [4]

For six months he upheld the law with the full vigour of a parish officer. Vagrancy fell. With fewer intruders around, Michael could feel a sense of pride: thanks to his efficient control the parish was a far better place.

The vestry were not so convinced. A parish beadle should be on top of things the whole time. Harmes had not always been up to the mark. Another man, Matthew Miles, had just been taken into the workhouse. Miles had the makings of an efficient beadle – and as an inmate he would not need paying.

Michael Harmes was dismissed. His uniform and staff of office were withdrawn and issued to Matthew Miles. [5]

Michael did not dwell on the setback. He decided to move to Brighton where there were more openings for an educated man. It would need a little parish assistance by way of rent and transport costs. He felt confident the vestry would not stand in his way.

He was right. They granted him10s. 0d. (50p) to convey his goods, 4s. 0d. (20p) per week towards rent and £3 for general expenses. [6]

There was just one consideration. Michael was to keep his family with him and stay away for at least 13 months, a condition that hardly smacked of friendliness. Michael shrugged it off, collected his money and went. Both sides enjoyed the prospect. For the vestry, to have Michael Harmes off their hands would be wonderful. They saw him gaining his family a settlement in Brighton. Michael saw a new life free from the deprivations of Hurst.

Michael Harmes had hardly taken his family clear of the parish when a Brighton parish officer arrived with George Giles and his family. George was a Hurst man, a journeyman carpenter with a decent job and a basement home in Brighton until he incurred debts and failed to pay his rent. He then found himself on the street, forced to seek help from Brighton vestry. Their response had been the normal one of obtaining removal orders. [9]

Mrs. Giles and the three children were placed in Hurst workhouse. George was allowed to return to Brighton and try to settle his rent. He was a brother of the clerk at St. Lawrence Church so perhaps gained favour. Certainly his young crippled son aroused a modicum of sympathy.

Within a few days, George had sorted out his affairs. His wife and children could return home. The vestry's understanding action had borne fruit.

Far sooner than she had dared to expect, Mrs. Giles was once more stepping into her own house. What a home-coming it was. No table, no chair, no cradle or even the cripple boy's bed. Apart from one bed, everything had gone, including her husband.

Mrs. Giles appealed to Hurst vestry. It was obvious to them how George Giles must have sold the family furniture to clear his debts. They could deal with him once they had settled the immediate issue.

The family were given enough things to prevent them being put out on the street again. Mrs. Giles made the best she could of the situation. She declared she would try to earn enough for her children by taking in needlework. If Hurst would just grant her a weekly allowance, she could cope.

The vestry had no hesitation. The man had deserted his family, the wife was requesting relief. She could have 10s. 0d. (50p) a week.

Mrs. Giles accepted gratefully. She also accepted the attentions of a bricklayer's labourer who quickly became the new man of the family. This unconventional step necessitated a change of address. A room was found at a nearby house in St. John's Place.

Mrs. Giles and her man were settling in nicely when the couple lodging them discovered the true nature of things. Mrs. Giles was peremptorily put out on the street: cripple child or no, the laws of common decency must be upheld or what would the neighbours say? They were, in fact, saying quite a lot, and George Giles was not far off, hearing it all.

George had been making enquiries about his wife. Before the move with the bricklayer's labourer, Mrs. Giles had needed medical attention. George did not have first-hand knowledge but friends had been observing the movements of his wife and they kept him informed. They noted the doctor's arrival, it was Dr. Ivory. He descended the steps to the house. The friends noted the strange procedure that, as soon as he was in, he locked the door.

Mrs. Giles was in the bedroom. The curtains were drawn which should have permitted the doctor to attend his patient in strict privacy. The curtains did not fully meet. George's friends discreetly noted the consultation. Mrs. Giles lay on the bed. She was joined by Dr. Ivory. When the doctor arose, it was he who paid the patient. The watchful friends felt bound to give George a factual account, sobering as it may be.

George was angry though hardly shocked. His wife had been leading him a merry dance. He doubted the doctor was the first. He decided to place his affairs in the hands of the vestry. He wrote to his brother, asking him to show the letter to Mr. Ellis or the overseer. The letter opened their eyes. [10]

George declared he would have nothing more to do with the woman. He suggested a solution. He would pay 2s. 0d. (10p) per head for the family. If Mrs. Giles was dissatisfied she could sort it out with him at Brighton Town Hall or she could leave him the children. The vestry resolved that George should pay 10s. 0d. (50p). He was adamant he should not.

The affair had to be settled at the magistrates. Mr. Marchant was spokesman for the vestry. He argued that George should take his wife back. The magistrates were convinced the woman was profligate. They would not command George to have her. He was to pay 8s. 0d. (40p) a week until all debts were cleared and then 10s. 0d. (50p). The vestry had to agree.

Another problem awaited the vestry's attention. Dr. Caudle of Brighton had written explaining how he had been helping a young Hurstperpoint man who was suitably qualified to be a medical shopman except that he had neither instruments nor decent clothes. The doctor suggested that the Hurst vestry should now assist the man to equip himself and thereby become independent of parish aid. His name was Henry Manners. [11]

Henry Manners, the illegitimate boy sired so long ago by Dr. Verrall. Mr. Marchant could well remember Henry's birth in the workhouse and the anonymous letter about the doctor. No doubt Henry's training had begun when his father hired him for the year after the removal home from Lewes. It was a pity he had not remained with his father. Perhaps to do so would have been an embarrassment to the doctor.

Be that as it may, the vestry had to decide on a course of action. Before they could do so, another letter arrived, this time from Henry himself. Henry's letter explained his plight. He did have the necessary equipment, both instruments and clothes, but when he left his last place of work he found unexpected difficulty in procuring a new position. That had been four months ago. Having no money, he had been obliged to pawn first his instruments and then his clothes. Now he could have a place if only he could redeem his property. To this end, he was humbly asking a trifle from the vestry. The money would be repaid as soon as possible.

The letter arrived just too late for the vestry meeting. It lay amongst correspondence to be dealt with the following month.

Receiving no reply, Henry wrote again, addressing his letter to Mr. Marchant. This clarified matters. He had been unfortunate in the position he expected to obtain. The man who had been going to leave for a place on the hospital staff had not left after all. However, thanks to Dr. Caudle's friendship, Henry could have a room where he would doubtless get on – except if he could not redeem his things he would lose his lodgings. He was still unable to do any hard work or gain a living in any other way because his complaint was as bad as ever.

The bad complaint was news to Mr. Marchant, as was Henry's explanation that the trifle of money for the pawnbroker had to include sufficient to reach a shop somewhere in London: it was not in Brighton at all. Mr. Marchant scribbled a note at the foot of the letter and had it delivered to Mr. Marshall, his fellow overseer. It suggested obliging young Manners. Mr. Marshall agreed. 25s. 0d. (£1.25) was sent. [12]

Henry was delighted with the money. He set off for London. There he wrote another letter to Mr. Marchant explaining how he still lacked the cash to redeem his clothes and instruments. In truth, he was entirely destitute walking the streets by day seeking a position as medical shopman. He had great expectations of getting a situation within a week or two and hoped that in the meantime Mr. Marchant would not be averse to recommending the parish to send him something to subsist on. It should be addressed to H. Verrall Manners – an interesting development from his baptismal record of simple Henry Manners where his name made no reference to his father. [13]

Mr. Marchant was not stirred to action. Henry was living close to London's great Leadenhall Market. He should be able to procure almost an abundance of provisions if he was resourceful enough. He should also be able to find work if he would diversify his efforts a little. The vestry could not constantly send money to adult 'parish-children' simply because they were fussy in the work they undertook. Henry must walk on and find his expected position.

Henry did not appreciate the lack of reply to his letter. He wrote another, to the parish officers, and signed it Henry Manners Verrall. It helped his self-esteem if nothing else. He had been obliged to move into Whitechapel. Not that he actually had lodgings. No. He was in great distress, as ill as he could be, without money or funds to get him anything to eat or lodgings to rest in. The parish had to help him; he could not live on air. If something was not sent directly, he would have to set off for Hurst. Nor would he walk home; he could not. He would throw himself on a parish so that removal orders had to be made out. He would then be brought home by transport of some sort.

Henry awaited the reply. The vestry ignored his letter. They had a concern of far greater significance, the death of the parish doctor, old Dr. Weekes. He had been a true disciple of the medical profession and a respected member of the community, a progressive doctor keen to use any worthwhile development in medicine or surgery and wise enough not to discard his tried and trusted remedies hurriedly. The practice would be continued by his son, Richard.

'Young' Dr. Richard now resided on the south side of the street in Mansion House where he continued adding to his museum. The discovery and collection of items was a relaxing hobby. An ancient gold ring found in the churchyard, a new fossil, the bone of a huge monster unearthed by his friend Gideon Mantell of Lewes, all gave pleasure and furthered his knowledge of the hidden wonders of the world and human craftsmanship.

The medical practice was in capable hands. Richard had shared his father's work for many years. He was a skilled doctor but in the future there could be stressful occasions. Richard had ambition, vigour and the determination to achieve what he wanted – the converse of poor Henry Manners who eventually arrived back in Brighton, still the unemployed medical shopman lacking instruments.

1825: Henry Henty Walks the Treadwheel

Henry Henty, the son of the sawyer whose death had caused the vestry such trouble with the coroner, was now having to face the pitfalls of providing for his own children. Henry did not follow his father's profession. He stayed a day labourer hovering between poverty and pauperism. He depended for survival on a wealth of local knowledge about the best fields and woods for supplies – and which farms were best avoided.

Henry's immediate task was to obtain the family meat. He knew a field on the further edge of Danny Estate which normally proved good for hares. He quietly made his way there. It was Sunday. No labourer was at work in the field. No prying eyes were around.

In Henry's coat were 13 wires. Deftly he set them in the grass and continued on his way.

When he returned to inspect his wires, he took the usual precautions. Nobody was about.

The first wire was empty. No matter, he was not fool enough to expect a hare every time. He moved to the next. Empty again. He straightened his back and was grabbed hard and firm: gamekeeper Michael Marchant, damn him.

And that was that. Henry was forced to track along the rest of the wires. In one was a hare, his family's meat. Some Sunday this had turned out.

At the magistrate's he pleaded: 'Not guilty'. His word against Michael Marchant's and a dead hare. He might as well have said 'Guilty'. The fine was £5. Henry could not pay: he would do three months hard labour in Lewes house of correction. [1]

Since Isaac Sayers' six month stint there, a treadwheel had been installed to provide power for a corn-mill. So far, no Hurst man had trodden the wheel. Henry was about to change that although he would hardly enjoy the experience.

The first men on the wheel had soon found their 2lbs (1kg) of prison bread inadequate. The threat of further punishment did not deter them from asking for more: they could not survive without it.

They petitioned to be allowed extra rations, each man signing or putting his X beside his scribed name – no one was going to gain anything without risking the possible retribution. The prison doctor agreed an improved diet was necessary. The magistrates decreed that soup should be added.

The men's diet now appropriate, the mill-stone turned to the rhythm of their feet. [2]

When Henry arrived, he was the novice in the gang; 19 men to whom the walk was an everyday monotony, and Henry with it all to learn. They would not drain ill-nourished energy. Henry did. When he stuttered in walking the wheel, the wheel took over walking him and that was even worse. He experimented and adjusted until he found the knack. It did not take him long, self preservation saw to that.

Soon he was well and truly one of the gang. In unison they lifted their paceless feet, 7½ inches (200mm) every tread, 15 minutes 'on' and 5 minutes rest in a neat take-over technique to ensure no power was lost. A full 10 hours of synchronized energy transmitted by shaft to turn the grindstone. [3]

Lucky miller. Even in days of calmest drought his mill had power. Wheaten flour or hog feed, the men were there. Neither knowing nor caring, they lifted their 60 steps a minute and saw the treads revolve before their eyes until time said stop.

At last, Henry's day of release arrived, he was a free man once more. He returned to his poverty in Hurst. The vestry found him work with the road-gang.

The next day, Mr. Marchant was back at the solicitors in Lewes. Henry Henty had refused to do the work provided for him by the vestry. Once more he was before a magistrate as an idle and disorderly person refusing to work whereby his family became chargeable to the parish of Hurstperpoint. His sentence was a month's hard labour. He was one of the gang again getting nowhere on the treadwheel. [4]

Whilst the vestry were keeping a close eye on Henry Henty, a Parliamentary Select Committee was keeping an eye on parish vestries directing them to give a satisfactory account of their poor-law finances. Abuses in the use of poor-rate money were believed to be widespread. The committee's enquiry found that much of the evil lay in the annual appointment of new overseers whose main aim was to be rid of the office with as little trouble as possible. In general, the management of the poor had shown little improvement since the severe winter of 1795 when many parishes had begun using money from the poor-rate as contributions to healthy labourers in full employment.

A remedy would be to replace the annual churchwarden/overseer vestry by a permanent select-vestry. The vestry would draw up rules and regulations to be their parish law for the following year and would appoint a salaried assistant overseer to administer poor relief.

Hurst vestry debated the point. There had been difficult decisions to make but Hurst had made good progress since 1795 when the old rector had championed his parish labourers at the magistrates against the overbearing ways of Markwick the workhouse master. There had not been an administrative scandal since in 30 years.

Just after Christmas, the vestry met to decide their future. It was a well attended meeting; the new curate Rev. Tufnell, churchwardens Mr. Marchant and Mr. Jenner, William and Nathaniel Borrer, Drs. Richard and Hampton Weekes and a number of other farmers. When Rev. Tufnell called for the vote, members favoured the traditional annual vestry. The churchwardens and overseers had proved worthy servants in the past, they could continue to do so. Hurst did not need a select-vestry.

That summer, churchwardens Mr. Marchant and Mr. Jenner suddenly found themselves under suspicion. It was over an alleged accountability for the supply of parish flour.

Both the origins of the grain and the quality of the flour were in question. Doctor Weekes had decided to undertake an investigation when he noticed Mr. Jenner presenting a bill for parish wheat that was to be off-set against his poor-rate demand. The doctor copied the bill and consulted with Richard Davies who had been refused his requests to supply wheat for the parish from his farm on the Danny Estate. Why could vestry members like Jenner and Marchant be accommodated yet not others experiencing difficulty in finding cash for their poor-rate?

Dr. Weekes was convinced he should take legal action against the churchwardens under an Act from George III's time designed to prevent parish officers supplying a workhouse for their own profit. The issue would be decided in court.

When word of the forthcoming trial spread, there was immediate reaction. An extraordinary parish meeting was called for the express purpose of making known people's sentiments respecting the churchwardens' conduct for the previous two years. Rev. Tufnell took the chair. It was resolved unanimously that Hurst had nothing to allege against the churchwardens and fully approved their conduct as parish officers. The minute was witnessed by 83 supportive parishioners right across the spectrum of parish life. Everyone defended the good names of farmers Jenner and Marchant. [5]

The vestry spared no expense to confound the allegations, even surmounting religious differences to engage Hurst's most prominent dissenter, George Faithfull, as defence solicitor. George Faithfull, the preacher who thundered forth in his own Brighton chapel berating the Established Church for corrupting the tithes from being a fund for the poor to becoming a purse for the clergy. Now, he was to defend the Established Church over corruption in the provision of succour for the poor. It was indeed a strange twist. Yet, as a conscientious solicitor, George Faithfull could not deny a man the chance of a sound defence. Against them would be another local man, Mr. Hannington.

Mr. Jenner was the first defendant. It was alleged that on various occasions he had supplied the workhouse with wheat for his own profit, to the great detriment of the poor, who by reason of the quality of the wheat were obliged to eat inferior bread; and that when respectable farmers in the neighbourhood wished to serve the workhouse with flour they were refused.

Mr. Jenner explained that most farmers sent wheat to Mr. Uwins who also held the contract to supply workhouse flour. For 20 years, Mr. Jenner's wheat had gone to Mr. Uwins' mill but on no occasion had the miller said whether or not any would be ground for the use of the poor. The normal practice was to mix portions of various flours to provide the correct 'seconds' quality required.

Mr. Davies claimed that Mr. Jenner had actually admitted to supplying flour specifically for the poor and had said he would continue doing so. Mr. Jenner rejected the allegations and stated the parish records would prove his integrity on all occasions.

It turned out that no records were available: they were still locked inside the chest at Hurst. Solicitors Faithfull and Hannington disputed whether they had been told to have all parish papers available. They could not agree.

In the end, the non-appearance of the explanatory papers swung the case.

'Guilty,' was the verdict. The judge announced a £100 fine.

Visibly shaken, Mr. Jenner stepped down. His place was taken by Mr. Marchant. His trial was shorter but with the same outcome, £100 fine.

The verdict stunned curate Tufnell. The parish officers had been found guilty of dishonest practice. The church vestry had to make its position known. [6]

Another meeting was called. Two resolutions were made. Rev. Tufnell entered them in the book:

'Resolved, That as an expression at the late proceedings and as a mark of approbation of the general conduct of the Churchwardens, a subscription be now opened in aid of defraying the penalties inflicted on and the expenses incurred by them.

Resolved, That Books be opened for subscription and left at the New Inn and at the shop of Charles Ellis in this parish.'

Never had such insults been hurled. Never would they be countenanced while the Rev. Tufnell held office for the absent rector. The subscriptions would be an acknowledgement of the debt owing to the two churchwardens.

William Jenner's tenure as churchwarden ended and he was able to farm his land in peace. John Marchant again became entangled in law proceedings. It began in February when Frances Glazebrook confessed to being in child.

The father proved to be Daniel Jenner from Albourne, a pauper labourer dependent on parish support which meant the baby would become another Hurst parish-child. The vestry decided it would be better for everyone, particularly the baby, if the birth was to married parents. The marriage would have to be by licence. The vestry obtained one and accepted the cost since Daniel Jenner obviously had nothing to pay with. Similarly, the ring and church expenses had to be on the parish account.

All was prepared. On the first day of June, the pair were married. They soon had a son, James. The marriage also had the effect of giving Frances the same settlement as her husband, which also applied to baby James.

The vestry felt they had done their duty towards Daniel and Frances in marrying them. There was now a duty due to Hurst parish; that of removing the new family to their proper place.

Daniel Jenner was first taken to the magistrates for his examination which was straight forward enough except that his settlement parish proved to be not Albourne at all but Cuckfield.

The ruling was of no consequence. It simply entailed the Hurst overseer turning up at Cuckfield with the family, a slightly longer journey. There he stated his business. The Cuckfield overseer signed the removal order to acknowledge safe receipt of the family. They were now Cuckfield's problem.

It was at this point that John Marchant's troubles began. Cuckfield vestry were convinced they had been tricked. They should not be liable for Daniel Jenner's family. It was Hurst seeking to reduce their own expenses by forcibly marrying paupers in order to ship them off to other parishes. The more Cuckfield thought about it, the angrier they became. In the end they sought legal advice.

The advice supported their view. It was just as they had surmised, evil to the extreme. To remedy it, they determined to bring an action against the Hurst churchwardens, John Marchant and his new partner Henry Hider of Cophall

Farm, where a work-seeking pauper had once gathered ribbed worsted stockings from the hedgerow and paid with a six week prison sentence.

The charge against the churchwardens was far more serious and reflected ill on the characters of the two men. It was a complex accusation: 'In order to free the parish of Hurstperpoint from expense and to inflict it upon the parishioners of Cuckfield the Hurst churchwardens did with Force and Arms unlawfully and wickedly conspire, combine, confederate, agree and meet together with the wicked intent and purpose to persuade Daniel Jenner to marry Frances Glazebrook and did promise to pay all expenses to the great damage, oppression and grievance of the inhabitants of Cuckfield and against the peace of the King his Crown and Dignity.' [7]

Once again, John Marchant found himself in court. How could a conscientious churchwarden and parish officer find himself under such stress for a second time? Would justice be just? John Marchant could not help but feel the strain of this second trial.

Cuckfield knew they would have a deal to do once the Grand Jury had accepted there was a case to answer. It was certainly not a clear cut issue but it was essential to win and prevent such trickery being repeated. Cuckfield had no intention of taking in other people's dirty washing.

The court procedure began. The Grand Jury were sworn in. The charge was put. Was or was there not a case to answer?

'No Bill', declared the Grand Jury. Cuckfield were down and out at the first hurdle. John Marchant and Henry Hider could afford a smile of relief.

The case had again highlighted the way vestry members could be ensnared by the law. Fresh doubts arose in Hurst about the merits of the traditional vestry. Surely a select-vestry would be better.

In November 1825, the curate chaired the regular vestry. They resolved unanimously that in their opinion a select-vestry should be formed.

Just before Christmas, a further meeting was convened at the workhouse to implement the decision. The curate again took the chair. This time the room was full. Farmers were there in force including John Marchant and William Jenner, guilty of flour offences, along with Richard Davies whose wheat had been refused. Henry Hider was there too, the Cuckfield marriage case still fresh in his mind. [8]

The only notable omissions were Mr. Campion and the old rector's son, Dr. J. Dodson, whose daily life was centred in London. He still owned land in the parish but his local affairs were dealt with by an agent, none other than school-teacher Henry Muzzell. Henry Muzzell's social rank was steadily rising although he did not yet aspire to vestry status.

The curate brought the meeting to order and proposed the formation of a select-vestry. Less than a year after the rejection of the first attempt, they raised their hands in favour. Members present would have a place on a select-vestry 20 strong. Such unity would not only ensure efficient administration of the poor-law in the parish, it would also protect its members from vindictive court cases. It was time for change.

They resolved to appoint an assistant overseer with a dual responsibility as governor of the workhouse. He would have his own accommodation there and be answerable direct to the select-vestry.

It was also agreed that Ann Grey should be allowed twenty shillings for her good conduct and general service in the house. Ann Grey, the workhouse girl once so difficult she had been sent back from the Royal Oak because of her unacceptable behaviour as a servant, whose continued waywardness had obliged the vestry to move her from the workhouse to the Pest House and from there to London's Hoxton Asylum. Now she had completed her return. From Hoxton to Pest House, to workhouse and a reward for good conduct. If the select-vestry could reintegrate such as Ann Gray at their first meeting, the parish paupers in general should be able to benefit.

An advertisement for the post of assistant overseer and workhouse governor was placed in the papers. Of the several applicants, the select-vestry chose a Brighton man, James Rice.

They now had to decide upon a matron. Their choice was bold and controversial, Ann Grey. [9]

A sub-committee was appointed to audit the parish books each month. A copy of Burns Justice in five great volumes was purchased to assist with legal issues. Efficiency would be the watchword.

Hurst's select-vestry kept assiduously to their task throughout the winter. The needs of their parishioners took far more time than any of them had anticipated.

In April they met to appoint the members for the ensuing year. This time the curate was absent. Nathaniel Borrer took the chair. [10]

Members present had a lot on their minds. It was spring. Farm commitments were rising again; crops to be brought on, young animals to be nurtured. A day had few enough hours for life's essential tasks. It was time to concentrate effort. No longer did they have spare hours for parish business.

There was little need for an exchange of opinions; in depth discussions had already taken place. With a minimum of preamble, the question was put whether a select-vestry should be continued. The response was a unanimous: 'No'. Four months of select-vestry was enough, they had their own lives to lead. One facet would remain, the salaried assistant-overseer, who would undertake the more onerous tasks previously incumbent upon the annual overseers.

The select-vestry's last positive action was to legislate for a place of confinement for disorderly persons. Thomas Wadey undertook to provide one for £14. It measured 10 feet by 5 (3 metres by 1½) set in the angle between two walls at the workhouse.

The brickwork was soon finished. The blacksmith's work went to Joseph Chandler. He supplied 6 long bars for the windows, lengths of new chain, bolts, staples and padlocks. John Still fitted the heavy door and did the painting. Hurst now had a modern black hole as escape proof as any. [11]

1826: Michael Harmes Favours
Brighton

Hurst's black hole was of no concern to Michael Harmes. He now had comfortable accommodation in Brighton where he had managed to rent a house from Mr. Chalcroft in Gardener Street. Michael was also receiving 7s. 0d. (35p) a week for his family from Hurst vestry.

Mr. Chalcroft gradually learnt that his new tenant was slow to pay rent. Finally, the arrears had risen so much that he decided to write to Hurst vestry suggesting it was high time money was forthcoming.

Hurst agreed that they had undertaken to pay 4s. 0d. (20p) a week. They would do so as soon as Mr. Chalcroft cared to send a bill. He sent it at once explaining that the full rent was 7s. 6d. (37p) a week which meant Harmes owed £3 17s. 0d. (£3.85). Since the man obviously could not bear the sight of work, Mr. Chalcroft did not expect to receive a single shilling from him.

The parish paid the entire rent. They made it clear that they would not settle any further demands. Michael found his weekly relief from them reduced by 2s. 0d. (10p) a week which would continue until the vestry had recouped his rent arrears. [1]

Michael now had to find his own rent, which he did as if to disprove the comments about his attitude to work.

He persuaded one of the town butchers to provide him with sufficient meat to set himself up near the Brighton Level. The butcher's safeguard was that Michael first had to obtain written approval from Hurst vestry. Michael was positive he would have no difficulty.

Within a few days he was able to give the butcher a note-of-hand from Hurst stating they would be answerable for meat to the value of forty shillings (£2) for M. Harmes. The signature of Mr. Ellis formed the legal seal. The butcher kept his part of the deal and supplied the meat. Michael could now support his family and pay his own rent.

He succeeded until November when he again found it difficult to earn enough for his family's daily needs. Just before Christmas, Mr. Chalcroft asked for his rent. Michael explained how he did not have the money to hand immediately but Hurst vestry were making it available on the Monday. He would then pay immediately.

Mr. Chalcroft was not entirely happy: his tenant was verbally adroit with a seemingly inborn ability to present facts to his advantage, if not to entirely misquote. Reluctantly, he waited.

Michael did not feel waiting advisable. That evening, he gathered his family and goods together. During the night, they quietly moved house.

When Mr. Chalcroft called Monday morning, there was no answer to his knock. People hastened to tell him how the family had gone in the night. He knew at once, only too well, the man's promise to 'Do him' if he could.

Mr. Chalcroft returned home and took pen and paper. His letter was polite but forceful: Mr. Ellis was to inform him by return of post if Hurst vestry was paying Michael Harmes' back rent. He explained what had happened and stated his determination not to be done easily. Harmes had served several people the same. Mr. Chalcroft's greatest wish was to find the man a berth at the treadwheel.

Michael managed to evade everyone over Christmas. New Year's Day saw him detained in Brighton's own black hole. Mr. Chalcroft was in earnest.

Mrs. Harmes took the children back to her mother-in-law's in Hurst at the house near Wanbarrow Farm. Next day she attended the vestry meeting to collect her allowance for the family. She was refused. The vestry had a note-of-hand for 40s. 0d. worth of meat supplied to M. Harmes. When Mr. Ellis had seen it he had straightway pronounced it a forgery, the Ellis signature in no way resembled his own. Mrs. Harmes would certainly receive no relief and her husband would find himself in deeper trouble than ever. [2]

On the 5th January, Michael stood before the Brighton magistrates charged with having 'Surreptitiously removed his goods to put it out of the power of his landlord to pursue a summary process of recovering his rent.' Michael strove to explain his actions. He convinced nobody and was fined £5 with costs. [3]

A battered Michael crept back to Hurst and stumbled straight into the arms of the vestry who wished to prosecute him for gaining money under false pretences. On the 23rd, Mr. Rice took Michael to Lewes bent on painting as black a picture as possible. Michael would need to be at his persuasive best to deflect the charges. Somehow he did it.

The next month he was at the vestry, as buoyant as ever, requesting them to forward him 10s. 0d. (50p) to fetch his household goods from Brighton. It was granted. [4]

Michael was home again, one more man to be found employment. He was assigned to flint digging on Wolstonbury Hill watched over by brother Edward as superintendent.

Diggers needed a mattock and shovel. Michael had neither. He was given a vestry chit to take to blacksmith Chandler who shaped the tools at his forge. The vestry settled the bill and regained the money by docking a weekly 1s. 6d. (7½p) from Michael's pay. [5]

Once equipped, he was able to turn-to with the other diggers and the Pyecombe sheep on top of Wolstonbury. Well worn paths marked where the men climbed the steep face of the hill. Deep ruts in the chalk tracked the wagons carting the flints along the gentler slopes down to the village.

The rules lay down that flint diggers would work a twelve hour day with an hour for dinner. Eons of erosion had left the stones scattered in a mantle of clay-chalk debris on 600 feet (200 metres) of hill too old for any flint. It was grit and muscle piece-work at 3s. 0d. (15p) a load for small, road repair flints or 5s. 0d. (25p) for those large enough for house building. The digger's bushel (36 litres) measure had to be filled 60 times for a load – a lot of sweat by any man's brow.

The more the man sweated the more he earned. Two loads a week were expected. Earnings could be more. Isaac Sayers and his grown sons all turned in good scores. Michael Harmes found the effort too much, a load seemed his limit. Edward Harmes recorded the diggers' completed loads and noted the owners of wagons taking flints away.

Henry Henty was given a respite from work. Instead of being sent up the hill, he had to report at nine o'clock every day for a shilling (5p) relief. A daily shilling should reach his wife intact. A weekly allowance could lead to temptation. Henry accepted the terms; it was preferable to parish work. [6]

His respite was short lived. He was put on the road-gang chipping flints ready for resurfacing. One of the parish roads was in such a bad state that complaints had been made at the quarter sessions. They ordered its repair. The vestry immediately instructed the surveyor of Hurst highways to start work.

First need was broad-wheeled wagons to carry sand to be laid as a base for the flints. More wagons carted flints from Wolstonbury to be heaped by the roadside ready for the gang.

Henry had enough sense to work this time: his treadwheel experiences had taught him the folly of outright refusal. Hammer in hand, he sat at the roadside and chipped his flints. Others hammered too and their pile of chippings grew. Sadly, Henry's failed to keep pace. He was sacked.

Once more he was obliged to apply for vestry relief. The vestry knew of his efforts on the road and refused him. They told him to apply to the magistrates if he felt wrongly treated.

Henry would have gone to the magistrates if he had not begun to be troubled

1: 1790: Mr. Harmes had draught horses for work on Wanbarrow Farm and a riding horse for himself. All were taxed.

2: 1790: The church was a solid landmark. Headstones marked the resting place of past parishioners.
Paupers had the anonymity of their own area.

3: 1803: Soldiers were a common sight in Brighton.
Regular regiments and the militia were spread across southern England ready to repel Bonaparte.

4: 1805: Old Thomas Marchant of Little Park was involved in an accident whilst driving home
from a day at Lewes Races. He suffered fatal injuries.

5: 1807: Thomas Bartley took Ann Grey to the Friars Oak half a mile north of Stonepound Tollgate. From there a chaise would take her to Hoxton Asylum.

6: 1826: Henry Henty was set to work beside the highway chipping flints to the small size needed for road repairs. Passing vehicles rolled them in.

7: 1826: In Brighton, the London stage coaches set out from Castle Square by the Pavilion.
The route varied; via Cuckfield, Henfield or, quickest, Hickstead.

8: 1830: Mr. Ingalls wrote from London informing the vestry of a Nova Scotia bound emigrant ship
suitable for Mrs. Gorringe and her children.

by sweating. It was a hot, uncomfortable sensation, not the everyday sweat of work. When the shivers started, Henry worried. He felt horrible and knew he had the tell-tale symptoms everybody dreaded: he had a fever. Henry made for home and bed.

Mrs. Henty acted at once. She sent word of her husband's illness to Mr. Rice who immediately authorized a visit by Dr. Morgan of Henfield, the Hurst parish doctor for that year.

Next day, Dr. Morgan rode over and confirmed that Henry did indeed have a fever. He needed both medical attention and relief.

When the fever sweated itself out, Henry was too weak to do anything. Dr. Morgan prescribed mutton to nourish him. Mrs. Henty made him broth and he gradually regained a little of his strength. There was no question of him attempting work. Mrs. Henty collected vestry relief each week. [7]

The money did not stretch to anything like clothes or allow for rent. Nor did the landlord allow for anything. He sent the bailiffs in. Henry's scant belongings were seized. If the family were not prepared to pay rent for the house they would not be having furniture for the rooms. Those were the rules, and the landlord was playing by them.

Mrs. Henty also knew the game. She used the counter move, the appeal to the vestry. The vestry backed her with £1 16s. 0d. (£1.80) to clear the debt and free her furniture. In time, Henry would be fit for work. Whether he would actually do it remained doubtful. [8]

That summer, Samuel Goodman moved into the parish renting Stroods Farmhouse close by the Brighton Road just north of Sayers Common. The site was ideal as Mr. Goodman was a proprietor of the Red Coaches on the Brighton/ London run. Also convenient, was the newly built inn at Sayers Common with its stabling for coaches and its fleet of post-chaises for hire.

Mr. Goodman's Brighton coaching office was in Castle Square where both the Red and the rival Crossweller's Blue stage-coaches set off to join the other companies on their varied routes to London.

The old unsprung coach of the pair-horse days had gone. Proprietors stressed the comfort and elegance of their vehicles; good springs, fine lines and padded seating. The journey was much quicker, too.

Routes varied. Some kept west via Henfield and Dorking, some kept to the old Clayton Hill and Cuckfield route but the greatest rivalry was on the direct road through Hickstead where the fastest coaches vied for pre-eminence. It was a cut-throat business.

Mr. Goodman had a good name amongst the coaching fraternity. His coaches and horses were well turned-out and he had top rate drivers. He himself often drove the morning Times on the Hickstead road reaching London within six hours.

The Hickstead Road

Blue and Red coaches alike benefited from the great activity happening along the approach ways to Castle Square in Brighton. The town commissioners had voted for street lighting to be modernized. Trenches were dug and pipes laid. New gas standards rose to interlace the old oil lamps. When all was ready, oil gave way to gas, and night became day in a brilliant blaze welcoming incoming travellers and bidding cheerful farewell to those leaving.

Mr. Goodman's move coincided with the publication of a book about the village. Its production was quite an event. Thomas Wells, heir to Peter Wells' grocery, drew the illustrations. The printer was shoemaker William Randell. [9]

The author intended to remain anonymous, but when afternoon-tea turned to the 'Slight Sketch of a Picture of Hurst', the name that came onto everyone's lips was Miss Grace Weekes. The book was a lively subject, full of gossip pickings. Who were the people alluded to in its pages? The clues gave so many pointers. None more so than 'Mr. ----' who on his rare visits showed anger if people complained about the new rectory turning its back on the community and raising a high wall to keep out the street: 'Lest our look should pollute its sanctity'.

That the ever absent rector Shaw-Brooke filled the gap, no one could doubt. That Miss Weekes should take it upon herself to put such thoughts into print was more questionable.

The Home Field pasture with its horses and cows, its pigs and geese, and the row of old cherry trees framing the farmhouse just had to be Mr. Marchant's Little Park. How he would love the description.

The tale of happy-faced children on the lawn fishing for a sixpence, and strolls amongst the garden's jasmine, honey-suckle and roses would bring a smile to Mr. Borrer at Pakyns Manor.

To the writer, everything in Hurst was commendable; the paved pedestrian path through the street, the National School, the inn and even the workhouse. All were of the best. For Miss Weekes, Hurst was a village of kind, friendly and affectionate feelings.

Mr. Rice, as assistant overseer, was dubious about the extent of friendly feelings. He had rapidly become aware of the pitfalls and difficulties encountered in collecting poor-relief money from unwilling ratepayers. Among the present handful of defaulters was one gentleman, Mr. Pattenden, who for some reason was being particularly stubborn.

Although Mr. Pattenden was not a parishioner, he was normally punctual in paying rates for his Hurst land. That winter he had failed. Warning letters were ignored. Mr. Rice twice had to ride over to Lewes; first to obtain a summons and then for a warrant to distrain enough of Pattenden's goods to cover the assessment. For Mr. Rice, the trips themselves were rewarding with a day out and 5s. 0d. (25p) a time expenses. [10]

The distraint proved a difficult task, there was not even a load of old hay on the land. Fortunately, Mr. Rice was told of an alternative source: Mr. Pattenden also ran sheep on Wolstonbury as one of the tenantry farmers of Pyecombe.

Mr. Rice went up onto Wolstonbury Hill. It was late March. Frisky lambs were at play. He gathered 16 ewes with their lambs and drove them off the hill to the parish pound. He left the official distraint notice for Mr. Pattenden warning that, unless the full payment was made within four days, the sheep would be sold.

The seizure prompted a swift reply. It came in precise wording from a firm of Brighton solicitors. Unless the ewes and lambs were returned immediately, an action would be commenced by Mr. R. Tamplin and others of Brighton, the real owners of the sheep.

Mr. Rice moved with alacrity. The sheep were out of the pound and back through the village to the top of Wolstonbury just as fast as they would move. And in due course, solicitors paid the outstanding rate from the estate of their late departed client Mr. Pattenden.

The vestry were beginning to doubt the integrity of Mr. Rice. He was dealing with inmates at the workhouse well enough. Outside, he was not always as efficient: the failure against Michael Harmes in the counterfeit note of hand affair and now the ewes and lambs fiasco. Such incidents were annoyances that could perhaps be overlooked. The main concern could not: their assistant overseer's financial affairs were in a dubious state.

An internal audit of the parish accounts was begun. By the time it highlighted unaccountable anomalies, Mr. Rice had disappeared. [11]

Great care was taken over the appointment of a new assistant overseer and governor. The vestry chose Mr. James Penfold who came from Petworth with excellent references regarding his sobriety, honesty and industry. Total integrity in parish business was essential.

1828: John Talmey Enjoys the May Day Fair

The new governor was having a very quiet start at the workhouse apart from the rats. The place seemed infested with them to a degree that he had no intention of accepting. Rat catcher Peter King was called in. Peter King killed rats at two-pence a body. He set to and caught 21 at the workhouse – enough to earn himself 3s. 6d. (17½p). He signed his X to the receipt and went home a happy man.

Mr. Penfold was determined to run a quiet, efficient and healthy house. He included fish in the diet, herring or mackerel as in season from the Brighton fishermen, and had a gallon (4.5 litres) of milk each day from one of Mr. Borrer's farms. He purchased boxes of ointment and a stock of medicines for simple complaints; arrowroot, magnesia, sulphur and Friars balsam. He employed Sarah Pratt at 10d (4p) a day to do the needlework making and repairing inmates' clothes. [2]

On November 5th, the quiet ended. The bell ringers were ringing their special peal; song and companionship were to be had in the ale-houses. Celebrations were no different from other years but it was also the night of the vestry meeting.

John Talmey's wife turned up with her child to say her husband had cleared off. Room was found for them in the workhouse. Isaac Sayers turned up the worse for drink seeking his family's relief. He was sent packing without it; little or none would have reached home. [3]

Matthew Miles, arrayed in his scarlet and blue as parish beadle, neglected his duties and persuaded young Edward Oram to sneak out of the workhouse and celebrate with him. In the absence of the beadle, a group of four young paupers, George Rowland's son James among them, were so enjoying themselves in the High Street they constituted a riot. Their arrest was imperative. The vestry detailed Penfold to deal with the rioters and maintain the peace. He did so and deposited them in the black hole. The absent beadle would answer when he returned.

Edward Oram had a great evening that lasted all night. The morning light was a sombre grey, conducive to solemn thoughts. What would his reception be back at the workhouse? He was absent without leave. The workhouse code meant there would be no breakfast awaiting him, although there would be plenty else of an unappetizing nature. Edward decided his best interest lay in not returning to the workhouse.

Matthew Miles did dutifully return and was deprived of his office for a week. He was detailed to dig flints with the rest on Wolstonbury Hill.

Two days later, governor Penfold had Edward Oram safely back and being punished for going out without leave. Edward cooled off on even less food than usual.

At the end of the week, Matthew received his staff of office again and resumed duty as beadle. Isaac sadly turned up at the vestry 'In liquor'. He was refused relief. On the 19th it happened yet again. At the last meeting of the month he was cold sober. He received his full relief plus something for the previous week. Isaac was facing reality.

John Talmey discovered that he too had to face reality. A warrant was issued for his arrest. He was apprehended and taken to the magistrates who sentenced him to three months at Lewes for leaving his family chargeable to Hurst parish. He would spend his time walking the treadwheel. [4]

During December, Isaac Sayers worked hard. He kept it up into the new year then hurt his back. It was a genuine injury which entailed a visit by the doctor. A sickness certificate was issued. Isaac qualified for a weekly 10 shillings (50p) from the vestry.

By the end of the month, he was mobile enough to get out with his dog and gun. Life was worth living again. He was still not ready for work and had to present himself at the next vestry for his money. They refused him; he had been seen on one of his dog and gun excursions.

Isaac's back was still injured, he could not work and he had a wife and three children waiting at home for food. Where was food to come from if he had no money? Isaac knew the answer, it could not come and if the food was not coming to him he would have to go to the food.

The next day, he marched his family in from Goddards Green and presented them at the workhouse. There they were, a starving family for which he through illness could not provide. Since the vestry refused to give money, Mr. Penfold must take Mrs. Sayers and the children into the workhouse. On this Isaac was adamant.

Governor Penfold needed advice. The overseers gave it. Isaac was to be detained while governor Penfold rode to Lewes for a warrant. The next day, Isaac, too, went to Lewes. The magistrates considered him guilty of leaving his family and refusing to work under pretence of being ill. They sent Isaac 'inside' for a month on the treadwheel. It would sort his back out no end. Mrs. Sayers received parish relief. She went home with her children to await her husband's release. [5]

Isaac's son George looked after the dog. It gave him the ideal opportunity to go out with his mate Jesse Gorringe and give the animal a run in the peace and quiet of late evening – a practical way to finish their day.

Mr. Campion's Sand Field was the perfect place. They could decide a course, set it out and then let the dog off the leash. George and Jesse were keen participants; especially when the outcome was a rabbit or two.

One night, they were silently joined by a third man, John Jupp, underling to the gamekeeper. Their evening had gone badly wrong.

Jupp took George's marker, a long net, and recovered another from Jesse. He took the men as well and reported back to his boss, Michael Marchant.

Michael Marchant saw to the charges. The result was the £5 fine for violation of the game laws, the introduction to three months hard labour at Lewes. [6]

There, they learnt the art of walking the treadwheel and finding strength in prison soup and bread. At night, they retired to bed on straw-filled mattresses ready for the new 'same day'. They toiled on through boredom, Christmas and New Year towards the 6th of February, their day of release.

Whilst George and Jesse were safely lodged in gaol, the Hurst vestry received news that two more of their parishioners, Matthews and Botten, were in trouble as deserters from the militia. They were guilty of the old dodge of agreeing to act as substitutes, pocketing the first payment and then failing to attend for training. Their initial offence had occurred 18 months before. It had obviously been well planned.

They had gone off north together and offered themselves as replacements for men drawn in the Surrey Militia. Rather stupidly, they had given not only their names but also their parish. Although the Surrey Militia were interminably slow in tracing their men, they were at last doing so; desertion would never be allowed to go unchecked.

After such a time lapse, there were difficulties over identification. Nobody in the militia knew what the men looked like. It was hoped Hurst would attend to the identification so that a non-commissioned officer could travel down to have the deserters committed to prison.

The vestry agreed. Matthews and Botten were interrogated. Both claimed surprise at being detained. Both stubbornly denied their guilt. It was an awkward case for the vestry to handle. Neither man was known as a trouble-maker. 18 months was a long time to track back. Investigations would have to begin at the suspects' place of work.

Soon the facts became clear. Matthews and Botten had never left Hurst, their masters could verify it. All of which left the vestry in a bigger quandary than ever. Who were the phantom deserters? Were they men of Hurst at all?

It would perhaps have been as well to leave matters unresolved but country memories were long and first one name and then another was tipped as having been away at the relevant time. The two new names were even then away from the village. The vestry knew where to find them because the names were George Sayers and Jesse Gorringe, each with about a week of their game-laws sentence to serve.

The vestry sent assistant-overseer Penfold over to Lewes to arrange proceedings with solicitor Kell.

Word was sent to Surrey. A sergeant-major travelled down to have the men committed. The magistrates refused. The sergeant-major had to accept the decision but he had no intention of allowing deserters to go unpunished. He took them back to Surrey. George and Jesse were taken before magistrates at Reigate. They received six months hard labour in Brixton. If nothing more, they would be able to compare prisons. [7]

John Talmey had safely completed his three months on the Lewes treadwheel. He made a determined effort to succeed in life. His cause was helped by the forthcoming annual May Day Fair.

The fair was the big event of the village and attracted people from surrounding parishes. It was the one occasion when even the workhouse inmates were given a bit of spending money. Each adult received sixpence (2½p) and each child threepence (1¼p). [8]

John Talmey and his wife decided to try to make a little money from the fair. Their outlay was limited. Mrs. Talmey bought the ingredients for gingerbread. Gingerbread and nuts would make a traditional and popular stall.

May Day weather proved fine. As expected, plenty of people attended the fair determined to enjoy themselves and make the most of their day out. The aroma of freshly baked gingerbread tempted hungry visitors. John's stall did well.

One young man was so affected by the smell and sight of the gingerbread that he insisted on pledging his watch to John in exchange for a generous quantity of mouth-watering slices. John made a snap decision. The man could have the gingerbread plus two shillings (10p). When he received his next week's pay, the watch could be his again for three shillings (15p). The deal was made. Off went the man, with a satisfied stomach and an extra two shillings to spend. He wandered from the fair towards the High Street. [9]

John's gingerbread sold out. He was down to nuts, and not many of them. It had certainly been a successful day. Custom slackened. John could relax and watch proceedings. Quite a lot of strangers were amongst the Hurst folk. Two of them came to his stall.

John made ready to serve them but they were not after nuts, they were making enquiries about a silver watch. Had he been offered one for sale?

He was mentally prepared for it. The watch had seemed too good a thing to be true. He had acted in good faith but was in possession of a red-hot watch. He now had to decide the best course of action.

John told of the man he had obliged, a young man, a stranger. He could be described in detail. John had helped him out with money and was expecting him back the next week to redeem the watch. Here it was. Was it the one in question?

Yes, it was. It had been stolen from the brother of one of them, William Wolven across at Henfield.

John insisted he should keep the watch for the present. He directed the pair to ex staff-sergeant Richard Davey, now headborough of Hurst, whose duty it would be to search for the trickster. When the strangers reappeared with Davey, John produced the watch and retold his story.

The fair was almost over; no ne'er-do-well would be loitering now. He was probably miles away unless drinking in the High Street. Davey and the informants decided to search. The New Inn was the nearest place.

There sat the man, a look of happy contentment utterly destroyed by the informants' approach. That was the fellow, William Ede, close neighbour of William Wolven at Henfield. The brother had half-suspected Ede from the moment he realized the watch was missing the previous evening when he got home from work. William Ede protested his innocence. He hadn't stolen the watch, it had been given him by somebody.

Richard Davey reckoned that could well be the case but since the complaint was in his hands he had to ask William Ede to accompany him a few yards along the road to the black hole, there to await morning when he could explain the circumstances to a justice of the peace.

The Henfield men went home with instructions that they and the brother must be at the J.P.'s the next day if they wished the enquiry to proceed.

Next morning, they stood before the J.P. to tell their tales. William Wolven described how his watch had been hanging from its peg above the plate-shelf in the kitchen when he left for work after dinner at 1.30. On his return, it was missing. John Talmey and the brother explained their part and William Ede suggested what had really happened. It was not him at all.

Once Ede had explained his version of events, he signed the deposition with his X and awaited the quarter sessions. There, his story was ignored. William Ede would spend the next four months within the grim confines of Lewes house of correction; three on the treadwheel and the last in solitary confinement.

The harsh lines of Lewes house of correction were in stark contrast with the new building gracing Brighton's skyline. There, on a hillside overlooking the sea, stood a wonderful building of classical design with an entrance of graceful columns, Sussex County Hospital, the great charitable advance of Lords Egremont, Chichester and Abergavenny with a host of lesser benefactors. [10]

Each benefactor was entitled to recommend patients – not as an unmanageable stream but a fixed number depending on the subscription. Mr. Campion and Mr. Borrer had each given £100. They could recommend six 'in' patients and ten 'out' spread through the year. Their generous donations would help the sick of Hurst in general and their own staff in particular should the need arise.

Old John Gear was among the first to be helped. For years he had suffered from dropsy, his feet and legs so swollen that at times he could hardly walk from the house. In his days as overseer, he had dealt with Michael Harmes' eviction from Wanbarrow Farm. Now he was living in Brighton, along the London Road. Hurst paid him a weekly amount through a nearby grocer. It was as much as he or his wife could do to reach that far.

Suddenly there was hope. John was recommended as a worthy and deserving patient of the new hospital. However, before he could be admitted, one important possibility had to be allowed for; Hurst must agree to bury him in the event of his death at the hospital. [11]

The parish agreed and John became an in-patient. With hospital treatment, his condition improved and he came out considerably more cheerful and able to cope.

Dr. Weekes Tries Ballooning

D r. Weekes had a new interest to take his mind off parish patients and medical matters. He was going to try ballooning. The inspiration had been the latest amazing adventure of the redoubtable aeronaut, Mr. Green.

Mr. Green had advertised a manned balloon flight from Lewes Gas Works to take place during the town's Sheep Fair. Even more, Mr. Green would be accompanied; it was to be a passenger flight.

The Sheep Fair provided an excited crowd of spectators for the event. A band added music to the atmosphere but a blustery wind caused safety doubts. The balloon was rolling about fearfully, and with it the basket just 4 feet (1.2 metres) long and 2½ feet (0.75 metres) wide where the aeronaut and his passenger would sit on deal boards. A swinging basket could be disastrous. Delay seemed probable. [1]

Launch time passed. The band kept playing and the balloon kept bouncing at its mooring ropes. Delay was inevitable.

At last the wind eased. Mr. Green loaded his supply of restorative wine and his signal flags. He and his friend climbed aboard. Ropes were released. The balloon rose.

At first they drifted north-east gaining height until they reached a higher wind that pushed them south towards the coast. Ahead was Bexhill nudging at the sea which stretched into nowhere.

It was time to lose height and regain the favourable wind. As they did so, Bexhill began to inch towards them and then disappear west. They were over Hastings and now low enough to enjoy the view of a race meeting there.

Suddenly, Mr. Green realized the leisurely drift was becoming an increasingly rapid descent. The race meeting disappeared. Ahead were the serried poles of a hop field rushing towards them; a Quixotic regiment of lancers charging ever closer. He became a flurry of action jettisoning his deal board seat, his wine, his flags – everything to lighten the craft. A crash-landing was imminent.

The balloon swept across the field, its grapnel-anchor tattooing across the hop poles, hit ground in the neighbouring clover field and bounced to the far side before the grapnel held fast.

A group of astonished hop pickers raced over and helped the aeronauts clamber free. The flight was over, a thrilling success, but not one for the faint hearted.

Dr. Weekes would not really emulate them. His balloon was not one to navigate; just one to prepare and release. When expanded, it would be a modest five feet (1.5 metres) tall, an unmanned flight from Hurst carrying a message for whoever should find it – a probe into the unknown. At last everything was ready for the weather to be ready.

In mid November, conditions were ideal; clear sky and a light wind. The balloon was released. It rose southward at first then climbed nearly vertically until it seemed a little star drifting to the north-east. Dr. Weekes and his friends watched as long as there was a speck to watch. They went indoors well satisfied with their mission. The launch had been spectacular.

The following morning, a partially deflated balloon was found by a group of farm workers settling to a day's work a few miles from Harwich. The balloon was as tall almost as they themselves. On it was a tag stating its place of origin as Hurstperpoint in Sussex, Mr. R. Weekes the launcher.

The men took it to their master who put pen to paper relating the find. When Dr. Weekes received the letter he was over the moon. He and his friends celebrated their success. What a flight: from Hurst to Harwich – more than a hundred miles!

Just 10 miles north of Harwich was Widow Buckman. She had moved back to Woodbridge desperate to find enough work to let her children have a proper life. The only message to manage the extra ten miles to her house arrived in an unwelcome letter stating how Hurst vestry felt they had done a lot for her over many years but with her smaller family no more would be paid weekly or otherwise.

Widow Buckman pondered her best response. She ignored the letter and wrote a carefully worded one of her own to Mr. Marchant:

> *'Dec 12th Sir i have that painful task of informing you i must come home with my 2 girls i am perished for wont i have sold all my household goods one at a time till thay are all gone except my Bedstead my bed is straw But that i do not mind i am not ashamed of my Caractor you pleass to right to parish orferciers the Had oversier Mr Kemp ironmonger Market Hill woodbridge if you gentlemen misdought my word i am well known in woodbridge the 2*

pounds you sent i made youse of as i mentiend i have put my youngest boy out with it for which i am humbly oblidge to you all for your goodness i have now the orfer of a situation in a family as Cook and housekeeper ware i have no dought but i should be able to surport my 2 girls but for wont of Close i Cannot do it My Coach hire will be 1 pound which is the fare to London i wont for an answer from you sir which i hope you will not neglect for if you do not stand my friend to send Me 2 pounds i Cannot ingage with it if i Can take the plase i have a friend that will take 2 girls for 4 shillings per week the wagies is 18 gunies a year it is a situation i allways held when single and have gone out a Cooking since my husband dyed if you stand my friend i trust i shall never wont to Call on you again for it is a most exerlant family My eldest Daughter lived in the same family 5 years Dear sir plese to send as soon as possible for i must give an answer for i must take the plase the 4th January pray for god sake stand my friend for to spare my ever troubleing you again Humble servant H Buckman well street woodbridge sir plese to lay this before the Comity.' [2]

The committee instructed Mr. Ellis to write back giving the vestry's ruling.

When the postgirl knocked at Widow Buckman's door and held out the letter, a single sheet which obviously did not contain any enclosure, Widow Buckman refused to accept it. Whatever the message, there were no banknotes.

The girl took the letter back to the Woodbridge postmaster. He opened it, found who the sender was, inscribed an official 'Refused', put it in a Returned Letter sheet addressed to Mr. Ellis and sent it back to Hurst.

There, Mr. Ellis grudgingly paid the postage and pushed his letter onto the filing spike. He had done his part. The letter had reiterated that if the woman could not do without the vestry's assistance she was at liberty to return home to Hurst. She should have accepted it.

Widow Buckman knew she must keep trying. She wrote again explaining how for the whole of December her children had never eaten more than once a day and on four days there had been nothing at all for them. On top of that, the landlord had sent the bailiffs in to take her few remaining goods for the quarter's rent due Christmas Day.

She first took her letter to Mr.Kemp, the overseer. He added a footnote for her: *'I believe the above account to be correct Wm Kemp, Guardian.'*

When the reply arrived, widow Buckman was ill in bed. This time she asked the postgirl to take it to Mr. Kemp. He paid the tenpence (4p) postage and Widow Buckman had her letter. Nothing more changed hands. There was no money for her family.

Mr. Kemp decided to write on her behalf. He explained how the woman had been ill. She was up and about again but had been forced to pawn her clothes for

£2. She had nothing decent enough to wear for a place in service. He considered her entitled to their notice and awaited their reply.

The letter was effective. Hurst relented enough to send £1. Mr. Kemp handed over the full money instead of deducting the postage which he accounted for as Woodbridge parish expenses together with 2s. 6d. (12½p) he had already given Widow Buckman to enable her to buy bread.

The pound paid off the rent: her clothes stayed in pawn. It hardly seemed to matter any more. The closing date for the cook's position had passed. She would not be going to London.

She made one more plea. Only Sarah, her youngest child, was fully dependent on her. Hannah was in service with her uncle at the Saracen's Head in Ipswich. Charles had a job at a gun-maker's although he brought home only 1s. 6d. (7½p) a week. If just £5 could be sent she would be able to marry the lodger. He had offered marriage but could not finance the wedding himself. In case Hurst doubted her, they should send the money to the Woodbridge overseers who could attend the church as witnesses. If Hurst refused to help her marry she knew she would remain poverty stricken but her children could not continue to starve. She made a final effort to pen her plight: *'A workhouse is a thousand times better than living as i do.'* She would travel to Sussex with her three children – and was sorry to say there would soon be a fourth.

As soon as Mr. Ellis broke the seal, he realized the sort of letter it was and refused to pay. There was no point the postboy claiming the letter had been accepted. Mr. Ellis would not have it.

The Post Office had a procedure for such cases. On the front of the letter they scribed in bold red ink: *'Having been opened by the person to whom it was addressed I am unable to allow the postage it having a fair direction'*. It was presented to Mr. Ellis again. He had to pay the postage and accept it. The account of the widow's latest woes was pushed on the spike with his other filed papers.

The continual rejection broke Widow Buckman's spirit. She became ill again. Mr. Kemp visited her with Mr. Rose, a half pay surgeon. The living conditions shocked them. Not for years had they seen such awful poverty.

Mr. Kemp returned home and straightway wrote to Hurst informing them that his medical associate considered the woman was very ill and likely to continue in ill health being at the critical period of life when a change takes place. He described the family's condition and reached the crux of his letter:

> *'Now Sir pray do not interpret my language into anything like a threat but relief must be had immediately, as the case is made known to the magistrates. I have no choice of delaying only the necessary time for a reply before taking out orders & suspending them, however reluctant I may be or expensive the course must be if not attended to by her parish officers waiting*

for your answer regretting the occasion of troubling you being always
inclined to avoid such measures, giving me credit due to an old Officer believe
me Yours most respectfully Wm Kemp Guardian.' [3]

Woodbridge had thrown down the challenge.

Hurst responded:

'The parish officers have sent considerable sums to her & she has lately continually
been writing for more sometimes under one circumstance & then under another that they
cannot send any more relief & therefore must abide by the regular course to be pursued. I
am sir Your obt serv W.Ellis.' [4]

Widow Buckman recovered sufficiently to pen another letter. She explained
how her eldest son William had completed his apprenticeship and was remaining
in Dovercourt. He urged her to go there where she could take in washing because
linen was carried from Harwich for want of fresh water. Even if she could just
get to Ipswich she could take a small house and sell fruit. In Ipswich there was a
chance for a poor person. In Woodbridge there was none.

Mr. Ellis put the letter on his filing spike.

The Buckman troubles multiplied. Charles was
dismissed from the gun-maker's because of the
state of his clothes. The uncle at The Saracen's
Head died and young Hannah returned home.
What did not happen was the arrival of any money.
Now, with the Michaelmas rent due and nothing left
to pawn, Widow Buckman and her children were put
out on the street.

There was just one person left to give her
support, the person she had alluded to in
talk of marriage, her lodger John Mayston. They were homeless together. He had
to take the lead. He did, to his parents' house in Ipswich.

His parents knew their son was to marry as soon as his finances allowed.
When the couple arrived the real situation was instantly obvious. The woman
was pregnant.

Widow Buckman wrote to Hurst asking just enough so that marriage could
take place because the Ipswich parish officers were already threatening action
against her.

The vestry would not relent. They replied restating their position.

When the postboy called with the letter, Widow Buckman could see at once
that it was another moneyless piece of paper. She refused it. She had paid for too
many letters which did no more than tell her she could have nothing. [5]

The Post Office returned it to Hurst. Mr. Ellis grudgingly paid for yet another
of his own letters. Methodically he put it on his spike.

For Hurst, the pending marriage was a filed letter. For Widow Buckman, it remained a worrying financial problem.

Charles Buckman obtained work at an Ipswich brickyard. In the new surroundings, the state of his clothes was not so important. He soon earned notice as a very good character, a dependable boy known for industry and steady conduct.

Curtis Plumb, the overseer of St Clement's, wrote to Hurst praising Charles' attributes. It was not the main point of the letter. Unfortunately a cart-load of bricks had accidentally tipped. Charles had been behind the cart. The falling bricks had broken his leg. Surgical assistance had been obtained and the leg was set. The boy was as well as the melancholy circumstances admitted. The mother was in great distress and had approached St. Clement's for relief for her boy but, because he belonged to Hurst, orders of removal had been taken out and suspended. Would Hurst be sending relief for Charles Buckman to stay at Ipswich or was he to be taken to Hurst?

A fortnight later Hurst received a second letter. St. Clement's had not received any reply. Consequently, Removal Orders would be carried out as soon as the boy was well enough to be moved.

Mr. Kemp, the Woodbridge guardian, had also written to Hurst. His letter recounted extra payments he had personally been obliged to make to Widow Buckman on Hurst vestry's behalf during her years at Woodbridge. His accounting was being questioned by his fellow officers. He trusted Hurst would now repay him.

Mr. Kemp inadvertently addressed his letter: *'To the Overseer of Hurstpier Point near Bath.'* It went miles off course to the West Country. The Post Masters there were diligent in their quest to deliver it. Unproductive journeys were franked front and back of it; 'BATH', 'BRISTOL', 'NOT NEAR DEVIZES', *'not Lymington'*. Seven clerks added their initials and on the last available space one of them wrote: *'near Cuckfield Sussex.'* [6]

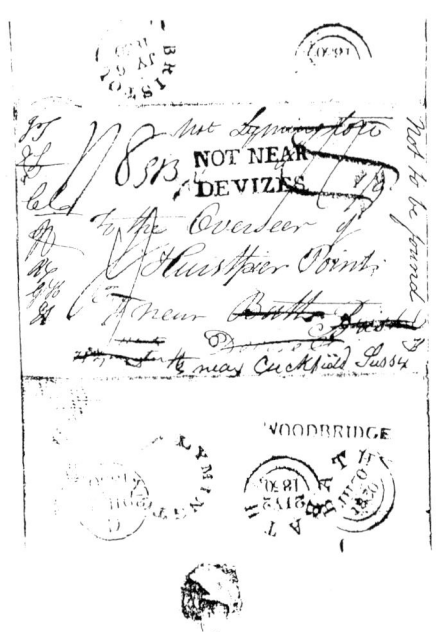

By the time the letter reached Hurst, its delivery charge had risen to 1s. 9d. (8½p) – an expensive item. Mr. Ellis paid. He presented the letter at the next vestry meeting. The response was unanimous.

Only Mr. Kemp could account for his personal actions. Hurst owed him nothing. They had enough on their hands with the injured boy.

Unknown to the vestry, Widow Buckman was dealing with Charles herself. She had worked out a way to stop him being taken to Hurst. She would claim he had been in service with his uncle. She went to the magistrates and stated her case. Her son, Charles, had previously been in service at The Saracen's Head, Ipswich, for well over a year. His proper settlement was St. Margaret's Parish, Ipswich.

The magistrates could not question the dead landlord. They accepted the woman's submission. Charles belonged to St. Margaret's.

Curtis Plumb did not mind, it would make the removal far simpler.

Widow Buckman passed the news to Hurst in December. It was St. Thomas' Day, just four days to Christmas. She had gone as far as she could. Her child by Mayston was dead and they were determined not to live together any longer without being married. She would suffer shipwreck first. She was also much spited by St. Margaret's because of the removal business and could not ask them for aid:

> 'i cannot egsist aney longer in the distress i am now in i have neither money nor food to eat nor scarcely enough close to cover me from the cold i hope you will take my miserable state into consideration and send me the sum of two pounds so as i can just go to the church though i am ever so poor.'

She was practical to the end and concluded her letter:

> 'if you do not send me some money you kneed not send me an answer for i cannot pay the postage of a letter your humbl servant hannah buckman.' [7]

Hurst were adamant the Buckmans were no longer their responsibility. They would accord with the woman's final directive: as they were not sending any money, there was no need for an answer.

1829: Henry Henty Zips the Headborough

Although Hurst had kept the Buckmans at bay, the vestry had another applicant needing help. Mrs. Henty turned up with her three children. Husband Henry had walked out on them. Governor Penfold found places for the family in the workhouse. The vestry set about finding the husband.

After a week, news came that he had been sighted some eight miles away at Lindfield.

Headborough Richard Davey was detailed to detain him. Davey's military service had been good grounding for the post of headborough. He also ran a carter's business which had quickly gained a name for reliability. In all, it made him the ideal man: disciplined, accustomed to command and with his own transport. He selected shoemaker William Randell as his assistant and away they went.

Lindfield was too small a place for a wanted man. It took a while for them to find Henry but in the evening he was sighted and quietly seized. They bundled him aboard the cart and headed back for Hurst's black hole.

It was nine p.m. and inky new-moon darkness when they arrived at the workhouse. Davey rapped on the door. Governor Penfold answered, saw who it was and went off for the key. Davey and Randell took their prisoner down the track to the black hole. It was truly black there – too black. Randell was sent to fetch a lamp.

The thought of a night in such a place appalled Henry. In desperation he thrust his hand into his pocket. His voice shrieked: 'I'll zip you up, Davey!'

Davey felt a hot sear down his cheek. Instinctively he struck out, hitting Henry a wallop that sent him crashing to the ground. Davey fell on him. There was a momentary scuffle and Henry lay clamped and powerless. Ex-sergeant Davey had spent too many years at war to be caught out by a petty criminal. Henry lay motionless until Randell and Penfold returned with the lamp.

Its glow showed a red slash down Davey's cheek and an ashen faced Henry very firmly clasped. On the ground was a knife.

Governor Penfold unlocked the black-hole. They thrust Henry inside and turned the key. The others returned to the workhouse kitchen where they inspected Davey's wound. The knife had drawn blood but the cut was not deep. His hat had taken the thrust of the blow. The crepe band was slashed, the crown dented. After this night's episode Henry would face more than an 'Idle and disorderly' charge.

He had cold, lonely hours to mull over the events. The next morning when he was taken before the J.P. and confronted with the evidence, he could only mutter: 'I did it in haste'.

He stood trial at the quarter sessions and received a year's hard labour in which to rue his haste. Henry's family had to settle at the workhouse. [1]

The Henty children were joined by two more when lame shoemaker John Henley found trade so bad he could not provide for his family. John himself had experienced the workhouse years before during his apprenticeship when his widowed mother had been forced there with her children. He did not wish the experience upon his own children but until more money was coming in they would have to endure it. He would have trouble enough finding the weekly 3s. 0d. (15p) that the vestry insisted he should contribute.

The Henty and Henley children had to attend the daily school run by Mrs. Burry who had been providing the workhouse education for many years. Threepence (1¼p) per child per week was still the going rate for the workhouse teacher. At such low pay it was as well for Mrs. Burry that the school was all-embracing with children as young as three attending. She did not have the benefit of any of her new children for many weeks before the vestry agreed to help the families leave the workhouse. [2]

Mrs. Henty was granted a few pieces of furniture from the house and a weekly eight shillings (40p) whilst her husband served his sentence. John Henley was allowed a shilling (5p) a week towards his rent. He walked his family back home. The small encouragement from the vestry was enough to reunite them.

Headborough Davey ran into more trouble at a vestry meeting when John Marchant decided to refuse an applicant. Fists up, the man threatened Mr. Marchant. Davey moved to intervene. It was like fuel on a fire. The man flared. His friend leapt to help him. They grabbed Davey and held on tight.

He could have matched them one to one. Had he been younger he would have pasted them but years were against him. They shook him till his teeth fairly rattled in his head, added a torrent of verbal abuse and went out penniless.

Mr. Marchant resumed his place. Richard Davey sat a while to recover his composure. He considered the perpetrators; Sayers and Gorringe, back from their Brixton sentence and making trouble again. They would answer through the law. There was a room full of willing witnesses. The difficulty would be in selecting the exact charges.

Kell the solicitor sorted the charges, a straightforward '---- did beat, bruise, wound and ill treat so that his life was greatly despaired of.'

George and Jesse were detained at Lewes house of correction awaiting trial at the January quarter sessions. The day before the hearing, Davey and Penfold rode over ready to appear as witnesses. They spent a comfortable evening in Lewes at parish expense: dinner, spirits, grog, ale, tobacco, a good bed and in the morning a breakfast to bolster them for the coming trial. George and Jesse had prison bread. [3]

The trial was thorough, the verdict 'Guilty' and the sentence four months hard labour with George gaining an additional month for his assault on Mr. Marchant. They were also to find recognizances of £50 each plus two sureties of £20 to keep the peace and be of good behaviour especially towards Richard Davey for one year. If they could not manage the money they would remain in prison. [4]

Nobody at Hurst felt inclined to subscribe to the release of Gorringe and Sayers, the place would be much the better for their absence. Whatever happened, George's extra month would split the pair up for a while. Perhaps it would do some good.

Another Gorringe, William, – a solid dependable man – was planning a permanent absence from the parish. William was a labourer with a wife and two young children. He had decided his options were to stagnate in farm-plodding Hurst or try the New World. He chose the New World.

William intended to establish himself in Nova Scotia leaving Mrs. Gorringe and the children in Hurst. When he had consolidated his position there, he would send for his family. Otherwise he would return. The vestry agreed.

In May, William said goodbye to his wife and children. The vestry recorded him as 'Gone abroad'. They granted Mrs. Gorringe a weekly allowance of 6s. 6d. (32½p). [5]

Hurst continued its seasonal way. At the summer haymaking, men, women and children laboured in the fields. Mrs. Gorringe turned new-mown hay in rumpled swathes of grassland green while her husband sailed far away on a salt-wet waste of blue-green waves. Each shilling she earned brought closer the day when she and her children would join him across the Atlantic.

William Gorringe landed safely in Nova Scotia. He found work, established himself and wrote telling the vestry of his success. His wife and children could follow him.

At the next vestry meeting, Mr. Ellis was instructed to write to Hurst's agent in London, Mr. Ingalls. They were about to send a woman and two young children to Halifax, Nova Scotia. Would he make enquiries about a ship to take them and the cost involved? [6]

Mr. Ingalls wasted no time. Soon his answer was in the post. Hurst were a week too late. The last ship that season had left on the 23rd September. There would not be another until mid-March. He had the London Customs Shipping List each morning which showed every vessel arriving or leaving. As soon as he saw a Halifax bound vessel he would let them know. The cost would be in the region of £16 depending on the age of the children.

Mrs. Gorringe accepted the delay. She had no wish to face the sea in winter.

In February, she was given the encouraging news that the London agent had sent word of the Blagdon, a fine vessel of some 290 tons due to leave from the new St. Katherine's Dock the 20th March. The voyage would take about four weeks. [7]

The vestry asked Mr. Ingalls to go ahead and find out all particulars of the passage for the mother, a two year old daughter and one of under a year.

The cost turned out less than anticipated at £12, but steerage passengers had to provide their own bed and bedding. Ship's provisions included beef, pork, flour, bread, rice, potatoes, peas, salt fish, barley and onions. The only drink would be water.

The vestry decided the offer was good. They agreed to pay Mrs. Gorringe's coach fare to London and allow 15s. 0d. (75p) for her to buy tea, sugar and other necessaries for the voyage.

Mr. Ingalls had the bed places built up aboard the Blagdon. Now, only the transport to London was needed. Passengers had to be aboard Monday evening before 6 p.m. or Tuesday morning. Monday was chosen as more straightforward.

Mr. Goodman, the coach proprietor, booked places on his early morning Times. It would pick the family up at the Kings Head Inn beyond the windmill and take them right to the Spread Eagle in Gracechurch Street.

The day came for Mrs. Gorringe to say 'Goodbye' to Hurst. The coach arrived. They were on their way.

Mrs. Gorringe wrapped her cloak around the children. The morning air was chill, not for them the comforts of inside travel. But it would be worth every mile of it – Nova Scotia and a new life. High on the coach, Mrs. Gorringe had views of her native Sussex that she had never seen before and would never see again.

In London, Mr. Ingalls ate an early dinner in order to meet the one o'clock Brighton coach. He hired a porter and truck for the luggage so that they could go straight to the ship.

The coach was late. By 2.30 it had still not arrived. Mr. Ingalls was obliged to return home for a business appointment. The porter remained.

Over an hour later, there was a knock on Mr. Ingalls' door. A carriage was pulling away. A young mother with two children was on his step. It had to be Mrs. Gorringe. He invited them in. His wife provided a welcome meal of cold meat and strong beer.

Mrs. Gorringe stayed there and took tea with Mrs. Ingalls. At 6 o'clock she was escorted to St. Katherine's Dock. Mr. Ingalls saw her aboard to her bed space. Three other ladies were travelling steerage, one with twins at her breast. Mrs. Gorringe and her girls were in safe hands. Mr. Ingalls took his leave and returned home.

There was still cargo to be put aboard; foodstuffs, cloth, millinery and haberdashery for the colonists. The Blagdon did not sail until the Friday's evening tide.

Illustrated London News 17-8-1850 Copyright The British Library Board. All Rights Reserved

The captain proved worthy of his reputation. Although the voyage had its uncomfortable moments, it had a successful ending. At Halifax, William Gorringe was reunited with his family. Their new life could begin. [8]

Mrs. Harmes Bids at the Auction

For Henry Muzzell in Hurst, life was nothing but sadness. His wife had died. They had enjoyed 21 years together with the only regret being the lack of a child to bless their marriage. He had persevered through years of financial hardship: now he had the added trauma of bereavement. Henry sought solace in work.

His industry and dutiful attention to the niceties appreciated by the gentry were helping him become a man of consequence in the village. Whatever the task, he was always efficient. He was now called for jury-service, a duty that brought him level with the small-business shopkeepers. People requested him as executor of their will. He was agent to Dr. Dodson whose time in London was mostly spent on affairs of the church. Mr. Campion appointed him reeve of Hurst Manor, an acknowledgement of his ability and proven integrity.

Being reeve included the position of beadle at Hurst Manor's Court Baron. At Henry's first court, there was the inheritance transfer of 10 acres (4 hectares) of land to two sisters who had to pay an entry fine of 2d. (1p). Because the sisters had not attended court, Henry was instructed to obtain the money. It would be a gentle introduction to his duties. There were bound to be trickier situations. [1]

It was to Henry as Dr. Dodson's agent that the vestry paid the twice yearly rent for Michael Harmes who occupied one of the doctor's houses. Michael did not mind who handled the rent as long as he was not doing the paying.

At the annual parish meeting, he had a shock: his name was struck off the list of parish-paid rents.

Michael grimaced. The parish had tried to play him false many a time. Experience had taught him the best thing to do – just carry on.

When the next rent day arrived, Henry Muzzell turned up at Michael's door for his money. Michael was ready for him. The money was not available at that moment because Dr. Dodson kept delaying the work Michael was to do in cutting Mrs. Marchant's name on her tombstone. Henry explained that Dr. Dodson had not yet come to a decision about the tombstone. He had, however, expressed surprise that Michael had not paid his rent. Michael said he would see Henry about it in a few days.

When Henry called again, Michael had good news. If Dr. Dodson would graciously wait a month the rent would be settled because a friend had promised to pay the full £4.

Henry could have told Michael to pull the other leg, so little was his word worth. At the end of the month it was all as Henry had anticipated; no rent and no sign of it coming. It was time to call in Mr. Kensett, the auctioneer, to levy distraint upon Michael's furniture. Doubtless it was of poor quality but its auction should raise enough to cover the rent.

Mr. Kensett chose early morning for his visit. He and his man approached Michael's house. It was a bit like the wolf and the third little pig. Michael saw Kensett approaching. A visit from him on such a morning could mean only one thing; trouble. Michael locked and barred the door.

Kensett knocked, waited and knocked again. Michael's family took no notice. A battle of endurance followed. Kensett knocked and Michael ignored until Kensett finally accepted that Michael was too determined for him.

The auctioneer retired and consulted with Henry Muzzell. A strategy was evolved. Michael Harmes would have to leave the house sooner or later. A watch would be kept. As soon as the opportunity came, they would strike and serve the warrant.

Michael more or less read their thoughts. He detailed his sons to ensure one remained at home with the door locked at all times. He did not intend being thrown out of his house by anyone, be it absentee landlord or upstart agent. His simple strategy worked.

Through October into November the impasse continued, more damaging to Henry Muzzell than to Michael. As far as possible, Michael continued a normal life. He was as affable as ever to his fellow men provided they offered no threat to him.

If Michael had learnt one lesson in life it was 'Never be hard-hearted'. Since his time years ago as an efficient, unfeeling overseer he had taken so many knocks himself he was now more willing to help others if he could.

Such a chance came one day when a labourer asked a light for his pipe. For him, the door could and would be unlocked; a small ember from the hearth, the pipe alight and a contented labourer puffing happily on his way.

Michael unbarred the door. The labourer stepped inside and produced a distress warrant. Michael flared in fury and the bailiff placidly stood his ground. Michael could rant and rave, he could expend his energy in temper but the warrant was there. Henry Muzzell had duped him as only an efficient, unfeeling agent could. [2]

Michael went to the vestry. He was being distrained for rent arrears plus unjustifiable legal costs of over £8. Misfortune had brought him level with the village pauper and he was about to be put out on the street. They had helped others in a similar position. Now they should help him. [3]

The vestry considered Michael's request. They did not mention the disputed 40 shilling note of hand with the counterfeit Mr. Ellis signature or any of Michael's other dealings. They simply did not think it proper to pay.

Nearly all the furniture was auctioned for the debt but Michael vowed not to quit the house until Christmas. He would just carry on.

Although Michael had no regular income, he did have intermittent work as barber to the workhouse. He made out his monthly account with his customary neatness and presented it for payment. His receipted bills went to Mr. Ellis for the parish file.

Mrs. Harmes concentrated on replacing her furniture. There would be plenty of opportunities at the local sales of household effects. She would rebuild her home even though she could never regain the far off days of Wanbarrow Farm when she was the lady of the house with servants about her. How times had changed. Now, even servant girls had more money than her. [4]

The sale of West Town furniture was like a thumb-screw as she recalled what might have been; four-post and tent bedsteads, Marseilles quilts, Brussels carpets, Pembroke tables, ---- the list went on. She could wring her hands for the mangle and ironing stove – and would wring them more next wash day and for ever. The dairy utensils, the watering machine, the melon and cucumber frames were all a dream – once, once upon a time a possibility but now a mocking voice calling bids beyond what she saw in a year.

Mrs. Harmes was determined. When Mrs. Scrase died there was another home to be auctioned. The house was not grand. Mrs. Harmes had more hope.

Among the people at the sale was a person unfamiliar to her, Mr. Fisher, the newly appointed assistant overseer replacing Mr. Penfold who had been sacked for impropriety towards a woman in the workhouse. Henry Muzzell was also there, no doubt still self congratulatory about the bailiff's 'Light for my pipe, please,' trick. The majority were people like herself, intent on improving their homes.

There were 69 lots, from beds down to a box of sundry knives and forks. The most valuable item was a clock. Mrs. Harmes would not be bidding for it.

Mr. Fisher was not at the sale for long. The eighth lot was the box of cutlery. Mr. Fisher bid 1s. 6d. (7½p) and carried it off to the workhouse. He must have been there on parish business.

Henry Muzzell seemed set on staying to the end. He bought Mrs. Scrase's books for 2s. 0d. (10p), a deal chest for 16s. 6d. (82½p) and still had money to hand. Yet times were when he had been happy to accept beef from the Dog Smith charity.

Lot 21 was offered: three flat irons. Mrs. Harmes bid and had the joy of success. They were hers for 1s. 6d. (7½p) to help keep her family looking respectable. She was successful again with a frying pan for a shilling (5p).

Mrs. Harmes waited and watched as Henry Muzzell kept spending: 4s. 0d. (20p) for a table and 3s. 0d. (15p) for a night commode, an item most families did without well enough. She knew she could not bid for luxuries. Her money was for a bed and blankets, even the thin ones would do.

Henry Muzzell's bids bought two more boxes before the stump bed came up. This was what Mrs. Harmes needed, a space saver that could be stored beneath her own bed. Other people showed little interest. They were waiting for the full beds with bolsters and pillows. Mrs. Harmes bid. At 9d. (3½p) it was hers.

The blankets proved out of reach, even the thin ones, but Mrs. Harmes was satisfied. For an outlay of 3s. 3d. (16p) she had another bed, a good frying pan and three irons. There would be more sales. She would have a home for her family again. [5]

Henry Muzzell, too, was concerned with new homes as executor for Sarah Wickham, the widowed owner of two small farms, High Fields and Goldbridge. In her will, High Fields was to go to her oldest sons, Henry and Jesse. Goldbridge, on the other side of the parish, was for William and young Luke.

Sarah Wickham was not in good health but, with the welfare of her sons ensured, she should have been able to live her days peacefully. Instead she had to endure a cowardly robbery. Thieves broke in and took anything portable that seemed of value. Her sons comforted their mother and went straight to the constable.

It was common knowledge that one of Hurst's laggards was fresh out of gaol. He became prime suspect – Jesse Gorringe, once more running free after his sentence for assaulting Richard Davey. He was questioned. He could not give a good account of himself. Nor could he explain being in possession of some of Sarah Wickham's property.

He was tried at the county assizes together with his new accomplice George Marchant. Both were found guilty and sentenced to death. They had one lone hope of avoiding the rope. The judge would almost certainly commute some death sentences to transportation. They clung to that desperate hope.

Gorringe and Marchant had the joy of hearing they were reprieved. They went to the hulks ready for Australia. The George and Jesse partnership was irrevocably broken.

At the end of the year, Sarah Wickham died. Henry Muzzell carried out his duties as executor. He completed the legal formalities and the four sons inherited their farms.

Luke's wife had just given birth to their fifth child, a little girl christened Sarah after her mother and grandmother. Mrs. Wickham was a capable wife and mother. Their old home at Poplar Cottage, rented from solicitor George Faithfull, had been handy for High Fields but to move across the village to their own farm was a dream come true.

T WELLS.

Goldbridge would be tough going with the children so young but they were a strong family unit in good health and Luke was content to work the long hours needed.

1830: Miss Campion Enjoys Her Archery

Grocer John Lempriere, Clement's successor, was providing the opportunity for a family to set up business on part of the old Royal Oak complex. He placed a front page advert in the Sussex Advertiser:

'TO BE LETT. A CONVENIENT DWELLING HOUSE, CONSISTING OF A FRONT SHOP, LARGE BACKROOM ETC. FOUR LARGE BEDROOMS, ETC. ETC. IN GOOD REPAIR, SITUATED IN THE CENTRE OF THE WELL-KNOWN PLEASANT VILLAGE OF HURSTPERPOINT, WELL ADAPTED FOR CARRYING ON ANY RESPECTABLE TRADE, OPPOSITE THE NEW INN.' [1]

He was pleased to announce that his own shop now stocked Morison's Universal Vegetable Medicine, the most effectual yet on offer for the cure and prevention of all diseases. He could also provide a complete manual on health, Morison's 470 page volume at 16s. 0d. (80p). Furthermore, he was now agent for Messrs. Beaufoy and Co.'s concentrated Disinfecting Solutions of Soda and Lime with their wonderful qualities in preserving meat, bleaching linen, preventing contagious diseases in cattle, rendering unwholesome and fetid processes innocuous and instantaneously purifying putrid water and holds of drains, water-closets and night-chairs. Chloride of Soda 3s. 6d. (17½p), Chloride of Lime 2s. 6d. (12½p), quart bottles included and ample directions for use.

John Lempriere let his shop to Thomas Wyborn who set up as a dispensing chemist and patent medicine vendor. Perhaps 'Morison's Universal Vegetable Medicine' would find some rivals.

Danny House did not rely on village shops for its needs. Many groceries came from Brighton. A servant could be dispatched there and return with the item within hours whereas the village shop would probably not stock it at all. 14 year old Charles South did the shopping on one occasion; a pound of preserved apricots, a pound of preserved plums and two pounds of ginger-nuts. It put another 18s. 0d. (90p) onto Mr. Campion's account which at times was almost £100.

It was business on trust by them all; by the company trusting Mr. Campion to pay, by the assistants trusting the honesty of the Danny servants, and by Charles South trusting nobody would realize he was nothing at all to do with Danny. His was a misplaced trust. He had to undergo the trauma of a quarter sessions trial. Somehow he was acquitted. He did not go shopping for Mr. Campion again. [2]

The old Danny men blessed Mr. Campion for keeping them from the workhouse. Every month they received a pension payment from him. If any of them were in extra need, he did his best to provide for them.

Passing vagrants too were pleased to thank him when Danny House gave food from the beggar basket or, better still, put a shilling (5p) coin in their hand – half a day's wage of the estate labourer working in the field.

The village poor also received gifts. Each St. Thomas' Day, Mr. Campion had bullock killed to provide Christmas beef. With the beef, came flour and cash. In the depths of winter, coats and blankets were given to the most needy, and there were generous contributions to the soup, bread and coal funds. Surplus spectacles went to people with failing sight.

Mr. Campion's charity spread wider. He ensured that little Elizabeth Peachy, who never heard the church bells ring although her home was beside the churchyard, could have a place at London's deaf and dumb institute. Each year he gave towards the welfare of the debtors in Horsham gaol.

An annual 10 guineas went to the National School. Mr. Campion paid for the boys to have special singing lessons and he supported the school money-raising bazaars in a practical way always finding something or other to buy. Children knew that when May Day came they could take their garlands to Danny House and come away with pence to reward their efforts.

Curate Rev. Tufnell was always sure of support for his ventures; the book club, the poor person's penny club and the mothers' lying-in charity.

There were annual subscriptions to both the old Hurst Friendly Society and the new Union Friendly Society where William Bartley handled the money and proved the Bartley name worthy of people's confidence. [3]

Mr. Campion's private life at Danny was strictly his own as any person's was. He mourned the death of his child as his employees did of their children. He rejoiced at the marriage of his child as they did theirs. Such times were family times.

On some occasions people saw arrivals and departures. Newspapers carried reports of local events.

Mr. Campion was a member of the East Sussex Hunt paying £26 for the year's sport. When the hunt assembled at Danny it was still private, but the chase across the surrounding land was public spectacle. The Brighton papers reported its success or failure.

One of the best days was a meet when 130 huntsmen gathered. Although dawn had been frosty, the sun's warmth thawed the ground leaving it heavy and wet; tough going for the horses. The first fox gave little sport. A second broke at the foot of Clayton Hill. It took the hunt through clay-clogged fields to the Friars Oak and wheeled round again to head across towards Hurst.

Fired by the thrill of the chase, huntsmen urged their horses on across Danny, round Wolstonbury Hill and on into Pyecombe parish. There the dogs seized the fox and the hunt was at an end. An exhilarating morning; free running without check – Downland sport at its best.

Game birds were also important on Danny grounds. Michael Marchant was an efficient gamekeeper who rightly enjoyed Mr. Campion's full confidence. The vast Danny oaks, some of them many hundreds of years old, dropped myriads of acorns each autumn. It was Michael's task to ensure sufficient were collected to fatten the pheasants. Poachers occasionally shared some of the Danny fare but Michael and deputy John Jupp, encouraged by Mr. Campion's £5 bounty for each successful conviction, ensured as little as possible went astray.

During summer, the South Saxons and the Foresters Archery Societies were supported. Archery was not a male domain. The Miss Campions enjoyed the sport and practised regularly. Archery at Danny was a social occasion on the east lawns with afternoon tea in the shade of a marquee. Fashionable ladies participated, and some were acknowledged experts.

Archery at Danny House

The Miss Campions themselves were invited to take their bows 15 miles to Firle Place beyond Lewes for Lord and Lady Gage's grand archery display. Most of the neighbouring gentry were present. A hundred guests sat to a sumptuous three o'clock dinner in the Great Hall. They spent the next two hours dining and imbibing before assembling on the lawns for their archery.

They loosed their arrows and exchanged social pleasantries between times. At the end of the contest, the judges set about determining who had shot the truest. The winning arrow was selected and the champion announced: Miss Campion of Danny shooting at 60 paces. More pleasantries were heaped upon her and then the company retired to prepare themselves for the evening's grand ball. With dance and conversation, the hours slipped by to midnight when the guests bid each other: 'Goodnight,' and dispersed to their rooms. It was a happy group that set off next day for Danny House with a trophy for Miss Campion and enough news for several weeks' discussion over afternoon tea. [4]

Mr. Campion himself preferred the race meetings. Brighton and Lewes were enjoyable days but in no way did they compare with Goodwood. There, the races, the company and the setting could never be surpassed.

The family enjoyed music festivals at Brighton and at London where they experienced the thrill of one of Paganini's concerts. The magic of his violin and his rapturous enthusiasm could never be forgotten. The opera, Drury Lane theatre and Vauxhall Gardens all attracted the Danny patronage. [5]

A Broadwood grand-piano had been delivered to the house, an event that could not pass unnoticed. Young Mrs. Campion was an accomplished musician with piano or harp and she had a lovely singing voice. At her father Thomas Kemp's luxurious house in Brighton she had entertained foreign dignitaries at extravagant dinners. At Danny her musical talents were equally appreciated. As the winter evenings lengthened, the family enjoyed music and dancing along with the diversions of cards and backgammon – while the estate families patiently awaited the St. Thomas Day beef, the flour and the cash of Danny House benevolence. [6]

William Sharp Has a Bad Night

T here was discontent among the workers, a growing awareness that too close an adherence to the 10th commandment would keep them forever poor. New machinery on the farms was threatening the day labourers' livelihood. Accounts of insurrection on the farms of Kent and Sussex appeared. Rick-firing was engulfing the region like a dread new disease, 'Arsonic Plague'. Land owners and farmers were alarmed. Somebody had to find a cure.

The prospectus of the proposed London to Brighton Railway reported in The Sussex Advertiser offered a little hope. Disgruntled farm labourers could perhaps find better employment as navvies on the railway. The security of the rail-road between Liverpool and Manchester had been proved with speeds up to 25 M.P.H. At such speed, Brighton would be within 2½ hours of London. 500 passengers daily took more than twice that time by coach. [1]

The advantages of the rail-road were so obvious that route plans and financial details were prepared ready for a petition for an Act of Parliament. Messrs G. and J. Rennie were surveying a 47 mile line from Kennington Common to the entrance of Brighton.

When the actual route became known there was rejoicing and wailing. The rail-road would go straight as a die through Hurst to pass between the church cottages and the White Horse Inn, cross the grounds of Danny Estate and exit via a tunnel under the Downs. London, Hurst and Brighton linked by direct train: happiness for farmers wanting good markets; joy for travellers wanting a swift service to London; alarm for the wary who distrusted change and feared easy access to their property by criminals. [2]

The rail-road was a ray of hope but it would not help anyone that winter. In November, Hurst vestry met to decide the pay and conditions of winter work for the unemployed. It was an annual event normally attended by the curate, churchwardens and overseers who passed the pre-arranged resolutions and sent the assistant overseer round the parish with the minutes book to obtain the farmers' signatures. [3]

With problems of agricultural unrest uppermost in people's minds, more landowners and farmers attended the meeting. The Rev. J.C.F. Tufnell was joined by Mr. Campion, Mr. Borrer, Mr. Marchant and Mr. Jenner covering most of the richer southern lands. Smaller farmers from the north rode in and so did William Sharp from his lands straddling Hurst and Twineham. For him, Hurst was only half the issue. He would also have to attend Twineham's meeting.

Although the Hurst agreement did not concern the wages of the regular contract labourers, it had an important bearing. If the unemployed were seen to be receiving better money for their parish work, the contracted farm labourers would be more ready to keep faith with their employers because it was accepted by everyone that those on parish work were paid less than the regular men.

The vestry resolved that parish rates for married men should be two shillings (10p) per day and that single men aged 18 upwards should have 1s. 8d. (9p). Work would be guaranteed until the first of April and men would continue to receive their pay even during wet weather. The meeting carried the resolution and felt it a very fair deal.

The next week at the Castle Inn by the Hickstead toll-gate, Twineham held its parish meeting. This time William Sharp attended in his capacity as overseer, a sensitive position as he was none too popular with the Twineham labourers. Rector Goring and his churchwardens were there together with the parish farmers to set the new wage levels for the contract day-labourers. Reporters from several Sussex papers were also there as it was rumoured the labourers were planning their own corporate action. [4]

True enough, the Twineham labourers had been out drumming up support for higher wages. Anyone willing to join them was welcome, even men from Hurst, Bolney and Albourne. Any doubting Twineham man was soon persuaded the benefit of a united front and what might otherwise happen to him.

There had been determined talk amongst the men and they had decided their claim, 2s. 6d. (12½p) a day. They wrote their demands formally on paper bearing the two-penny (¾p) stamp impress of officialdom. It was a just claim legally presented.

As the farmers talked inside the Castle, the men gathered outside. They presented their legal document claiming the half-crown day. The farmers rejected it. They would be paying 2s. 0d. (10p) a day and were not prepared to discuss it further.

The labourers disagreed and took steps to ensure they did discuss the matter. They pushed their way inside. The farmers felt themselves driven into a very tight corner. If it was not mob rule it was a fair imitation of it.

More men crowded in; familiar faces, strange faces; some threatening, some blank, a few embarrassed but the vast majority determined to improve their wage. The farmers were equally determined to hold wages down. They stated their case and challenged some of the men: they were foreigners. If they were not Twineham men they must go. Nobody left.

Discussion began. Neither side would compromise. Soon it was deadlock. The rector felt he could achieve nothing and made to leave. Men made room for him but declared no one else would go. When someone else made a move towards the door, the men's determination was at once clear. They became more outspoken and accused the farmers of starving the poor by making them work for only tenpence (4p) a day. The farmers explained how hard pressed they were by the landlords' rents and the rector's tithes.

The men responded to the tithes tactic and sent a group off to fetch the rector back. He had the uncomfortable experience of being preached to, after which he pledged himself to lower his tithes and take care of the poor. Having done so, he was allowed to leave again. The rest remained prisoners at the bar with the landlord anxiously watching developments.

The farmers felt their only hope was a quiet but continued rebuttal of the men's claim. More accusations were hurled, the half-crown claim became louder. By 6.30 p.m. the claim was a clamour but still no farmer budged.

At that point, the press reporters were drawn into the discussion. A farmer observed that they must have been to similar meetings and perhaps one of them could say what transpired at them. At last there was agreement to listen to somebody. The Brighton Herald man explained that parishes varied with some paying according to the season while others gave a flat rate. The wage, allowing for seasonal adjustment, was generally between 2s. 3d. (11p) and 2s. 6d. (12½p) for married men.

Mr. Wood proposed this to his fellow farmers. They rejected it but Mr. Wood prevailed upon them to accept 2s. 3d. (11p) from Michaelmas to Lady Day and 2s. 6d. (12½p) during the months of more daylight when the men would work longer hours. The majority decided they would go along with it as long as the single men were held at 1s. 8d. (9p).

At last an agreement could be made. It was drawn up and read to the men. The farmers signed approval. Everybody could relax. Common sense negotiation had calmed an eruptive day to enable an amicable settlement to be made. The farmers showed their practical sense in a goodwill whip-round to buy beer for the men. The landlord immediately perked up and provided the drinks. The Castle was suddenly a happy house.

It was 9 p.m. before the men dispersed. Back at his farm, Mr. Wood could feel private satisfaction that he had finally brought a difficult meeting to such a conclusion. Mr. Sharp, at his house across the boundary in Hurst, could again relax now that the wages question was settled for both parishes. For them all, it would be a well earned night's rest.

Not everybody slept.

Sometime after midnight, Mr. Sharp was awakened by a shout: 'Fire! Fire!'

A glare lit the sky. As fast as possible he made towards it. One of his own barns was alight. The seat of the fire was in a bay stacked with oats ready for threshing. There the flames were out of control but in an adjoining shed several men were hard at work pulling ploughs to safety and throwing out boards.

The salvage efforts were interrupted by a late arrival who took one look at the men and rushed towards them shouting: 'You damned fools, what are you doing there?'

He seized a board and hurled it back into the flames.

'Burn one, burn all!' he yelled and pushed the door shut.

Another labourer immediately struck him to the ground and reopened the door. The man leapt to his feet again, dashed forward and swung the door to in the face of William Cook trying to escape from the beam where he had been loosening boards.

Cook threw himself at the door. It gave. He was safe outside. Hard on his heels came Nicholas Wood. Their assailant stood eyeing the blaze. Cook stepped forward and punched. All his anger was there and he had the satisfaction of seeing the man reel back, blood pouring from his head, then turn and run into the night.

Loyal men saved what they could but the heat was too intense. Deal boards and oats roared fierce yellow-red flames and became glowing ash. Sparks danced upwards to the sky in a towering funnel of heat. Mr. Sharp had to watch his barn burn before his eyes. No amount of loyalty could save it. The men dispersed to their homes.

Back at his cottage in Hurst, Richard Reeves rested as his wife dressed a nasty head wound. Next door, old Dame Turner sat listening as ever to the conversation through the flimsy wall. Reeves was in pain. He talked to his wife.

'There will be two more fires before morning,' he declared.

There were no more fires but there was a thorough investigation. People were questioned, statements were taken. Richard Reeves agreed he had been at the Hickstead meeting but he had been forced there by foreigners from other parishes and the mob turned on him because he didn't stand up for his rights enough. Henry Payne said that he too had been forced from his work as gardener and was compelled to join the mob.

Mrs. Gander lived two doors from the Reeves. She said Mrs. Reeves had come to her in the wash-house and declared if her husband was taken she would tell all she knew about who fired the barn.

James Gander swore it was Reeves shouting an alarm that awoke him. He had asked where and was told at Sharp's. When he had suggested it couldn't be right, Reeves yelled that he'd be damned if it wasn't and there'd be two more before morning. Reeves's wife had told his wife that Sharp's barn was not meant to be burnt but Botting's stacks were. When his wife asked how it was to be done, Mrs. Reeves had said touch-paper. Now his wife was so frightened she didn't know what she was saying.

Those who had been at the fire named Reeves as the trouble-maker. With so much evidence against him he could hardly have expected less than to be arrested. His house was searched. In his bedroom was some paper which on test proved to be touch-paper. His future was black. Death and transportation were being meted out to the agricultural arsonists.

He stood trial at the winter assizes. The grand jury set aside the bill against him for arson. At that news Reeves could afford a sigh of relief.

For his assaults at the fire, he was imprisoned for three years, the maximum permissible sentence. The judge observed that it was imperative to make a severe example of him. Richard Reeves may have reflected on his luck. If he had stolen a bag of the oats instead of burning the lot he could well have been on his way to Australia.

1831: Nathan Marchant Starts a Sparrows Club

In May 1831, the fourth national census was made; a census enquiring more closely into the make up of communities. 1484 people now inhabited Hurst in 267 families with more than 40 of them sharing houses. Agriculture employed most men. About a fifth were craftsmen or traders. The final statistic recorded the 90 female servants: women still at the tail end. [1]

Everybody soon had an event to celebrate: William IV's coronation. The village greeted their monarch's day with enthusiasm. Dr. Weekes set the scene at Mansion House with a roaring royal salute from his seven-pounder canon. The echo mingled with the church bells' pealing acclamation that was to ring and re-ring through the day. [2]

At Danny and Pakyns, the workers' families enjoyed celebratory roast beef, plum pudding and beer. The curate entertained a hundred of his poorer families with bread and cheese washed down with beer. For the National School children, there were buns and beer from Mr. Campion. All was bon appetit and happiness.

In the evening, the band paraded the High Street shadowed by dance-stepping villagers. At intervals there were firework festivities to enjoy and then, as September dusk settled deeper, householders drew back their curtains and lit carefully sculptured secrets – their royal illuminations to dazzle the eyes of the revellers.

The band played on, transparencies twinkled with greater brilliance, impromptu halts were made and rousing cheers given to reward every ingenious illuminator. The cheers rang loudest for curate Tufnell, Dr. Weekes, Mr. Ellis, and Mr. Edwards, landlord at the New Inn. And Mr. Edwards cheered too as his customers drank their king's health amid banter and good humour to a late hour.

With autumn setting in, a group of farmers decided to get to grips with a perennial problem, sparrows. Sparrows and their ilk were more than a peck of trouble plundering grain in the fields and in the quiet shelter of the barns. Sparrows could never be eliminated but their control could be a competitive sport with an awards system and a social gathering into the bargain. The instigator was Nathan Marchant, the heir to Little Park, borrowing an idea from Twineham.

There they had formed a Sparrows Club. Each member pledged to produce a dozen sparrow heads per month. It did not matter how or where he got them but failure incurred a fixed penalty. Nathan had been an enthusiastic member with a bag of sixteen hundred heads in just seven months. [3]

Now he promulgated the idea in Hurst. The premium would be two dozen heads per month from September to April or pay the forfeit. In April they would wine and dine at the New Inn, present the prizes and enjoy more drink. Sufficient farmers liked the idea and Hurst Sparrows Club, 12 guns strong, was in being.

At Little Park Farm, they had to deal with a different threat to the harvest. It was early morning. Mr. Marchant was standing between the barns in his stack-yard with William Bartley, son of Thomas from the Royal Oak. William was contemplating the prospect of tending the garden at Little Park, a job with a reasonable wage that would please his wife and perhaps enable them to live without having to grovel to the vestry for aid.

As they stood, Mr. Marchant caught the scent of tobacco smoke. Neither of them was smoking, a golden rule when near the corn-ricks. Mr. Marchant motioned William to follow and quietly went round to his stacks. There crouched Jasper

Burt, clear as a bell, loosening straw at the foot of the stack. In his mouth was a pipe, well drawn with tobacco glowing in the bowl.

There was little love lost between Mr. Marchant and Jasper Burt. Mr. Marchant could not move quickly. William could. Rushing forward he grabbed the man and held him fast. Jasper blustered. Fire the stack? Not he. Not that he cared if Mr. Marchant had to watch the whole lot blaze one after the other, stack to barns to house. Mr. Marchant knew he had an arsonist.

Jasper was taken before the magistrate. A search revealed three matches, tools enough for a fire raiser. He was committed to await the next assizes. There the grand jury found a true bill. Jasper stood trial. [4]

The facts were clear and Mr. Marchant's evidence concise: the man had a lighted pipe by straw which he was about to ignite. He had three matches and the straw had been loosened.

When cross-examined, Mr. Marchant had to agree he had not actually seen Jasper Burt in the act of lighting anything. William's evidence was similar.

Jasper explained that he was a labourer smoking his pipe. He did not deny being where he was but it was nothing more. He had no intention of lighting anything, only his pipe.

The jury considered their verdict. They decided it was 'Not guilty'. Jasper could smoke his pipe in peace – but not in a stack-yard.

Mr. Marchant's fear of fire raisers, worry enough in itself, was dwarfed by the national alarm over the cholera-morbis. The dread disease had been plotted across Persia and Russia into Europe. In October it had appeared in Sunderland and was now moving relentlessly down the country. Diarrhoea, stomach cramps and a 50-50 chance of death. People sweated at the thought.

In Hurst, a special vestry meeting was called. The notice at church was kept to a minimal three days: 'A meeting at the Workhouse in order to consider and provide the most efficient means to check the progress of the cholera-morbis should we be visited with such a dreadful calamity, the disease having already shown itself in a distant part of the kingdom.' Rev. J.C.F. Tufnell took the chair. The meeting set to business. [5]

Every possible precaution had to be taken; nothing was to be considered too difficult or too expensive to embark upon. Not until they had thoroughly considered every safeguard did they draw up their resolutions. The wording was precise:

'Resolved – that the Householders be earnestly recommended to remove all accumulations of filth from their premises and to keep their premises in as airy state as possible.

Secondly – That such arrangements be made so as the upper dormitory of the Poorhouse may be appropriated at once for the purpose of a Hospital should occasion require.'

A subscription raised £10 to be banked ready to spend on remedies. [6]

The defence strategy was complete. It remained to carry it through and then wait. Apart from those precautions, they were in the lap of the gods.

In early December, the vestry received a letter reminding them of another calamity:

> 'Cox Lane
> Ipswich
> 2 Dec 1831
> Genln, I beg to acquaint you that Hannah Buckman the widow
> of Wm Buckman is in the greatest distress imaginable – She has
> no gown to put on & has been obliged within a week to part with
> a table for 9d – she is starving – I am authorized to distrain her for
> nearly £2 – but poor creature, her whole store wod not fetch a
> quarter of that sum – she belongs I understand to your Parish –
> Pray assist her in some way – I think if she was relieved with a
> trifle & a small weekly allowance thereafter, she wod do & save
> expence to you – she now resides on the Dunghills in Ipswich
> Yr early answer is requested – I remn Yrs &c Christ I Wright'. [7]

Christmas passed, New Year passed and most of January. Then there was news from an Ipswich landlord, Mr. Kerridge, explaining how a tenant of his, Widow Buckman, with her little daughter was in the greatest distress. Unless relief was immediately given he would be forced to take legal means to recover over £2 that she owed him. He allowed her to use the back of the letter to write her own plea:

> 'now sir as Mr Kerridge gave me
> leav to put a word in i hope your
> godness will feal for me and lay
> this before the Comity as no one
> but god and my self knows what
> i have sufferd i have been neerly
> perished with hunger it is a hard case
> for me more so for my little
> girl i hope the gentlemen will have
> mersey on me and send me some
> acknowledgement what ever they may
> think proper if i can but git out
> once more i shall git work i do not
> the least fear i have been confind
> to my room 13 weeks this day and
> have never been even to the gate

which is not more than a stones throw
from the street Dear sir have for me
a feeling and state my case
plese to direct this
H Buckman widow near the
pound corner St Clements
to be left at the Cow and pail.' [8]

The vestry debated the matter and agreed their response. Mr. Ellis wrote his instructions on the letter: 'not to be replied to'. If the woman was incapable of supporting herself, the Ipswich magistrates would issue Removal Orders. The vestry felt certain she would get by without their interference. They would wait for proof of her condition by her arrival in Hurst.

The vestry had gauged the situation correctly. Not until the following November did they hear of her again. The letter came from Curtis Plumb, overseer of St. Clement, Ipswich: Widow Buckman was very ill and in great distress. She had called on St. Clement's for help. She needed at least 7s. 0d. (35p) a week during her illness. Curtis Plumb begged Hurst's immediate answer or orders of removal would be taken out and suspended until the widow regained health enough to be moved. [9]

Hurst held on. Widow Buckman failed to arrive.

Henry French Makes New York

Hurst was considered a pleasant location for country summer cottages. Several had been built by a Brighton man, Mr. Cheeseman. He was about to build more.

He invited guests from Brighton to the ceremony of laying the first stone and made the occasion a treat for the village children. It was the usual treat, roast beef and plum pudding. That day it was as popular as ever. About 300 children turned up. All went home satisfied.

Mr. Cheeseman's elect company of guests confined themselves to the comforts of the New Inn for dinner where they politely praised the facilities of the country village, a quiet retreat from the noise and bustle of town life.

Next door at the workhouse, Mr. Fisher was used to receiving people from Brighton. Sometimes it was a lone traveller, sometimes a group or a family. Invariably, they handed him a pass entitling them to relief. The intention of them all had been to stay in Brighton but the town authorities had become somewhat fastidious: not everyone was welcome there.

The Brighton Gazette listed eminent visitors who rented a house or took their entire household to one of the grander hotels. They were valued guests bringing prosperity to the town. Impecunious visitors were a liability. Amongst them were the vagrants, a veritable blight on the town: idlers, tricksters, hawkers thrusting their wares at any lady whose carriage came to a slow pace and beggars exploiting the kindness of vulnerable guests.

For too many years the problem had not been dealt with properly. At last, more effective measures were being adopted. The Brighton Provident and District Society's main task of providing support for the town's poorest labourers was enlarged to include the distribution of 'mendicity tickets' to anyone who seemed in need, particularly newly arrived visitors. Many accepted tickets, few made use of them – the lodging house proprietors warned what the consequences could be.

People who did take their ticket to the society's agent were closely questioned by him about their occupation, their reason for being in Brighton and anything else he considered necessary. The agent's brief was to prevent the idle and dissolute from gaining lodgings. [2]

The authorities were convinced that once the vagrants were in lodging-houses the more decadent of the owners provided them with matches, song sheets and laces to be hawked around areas where useful information could be gathered for future robberies.

To combat the evil, town constables were detailed to apprehend any visitors failing to give a good account of themselves. This was no longer to mean just the traditional admonishment, overnight detention and being put out of town. Under the new instructions, vagrants apprehended in the street were taken before the magistrates charged with being idle and disorderly by wandering abroad and begging in a public place. Most were sentenced to hard labour for a fortnight or a month in Lewes house of correction.

As soon as they entered the prison, they were thoroughly washed and cleansed. All clothing was taken away, baked to destroy infection and stored until the prisoners' release. It was all part of the fight against cholera. Fear of an epidemic was as rife in Lewes house of correction as it was anywhere. Squalor was pinpointed as conveyor of the disease.

The prison surgeon and visiting justices had laid out strict procedures. Portable vapour baths were put in the infirmaries, the cold bath was adjusted to tepid and braziers were lit in the passages to alleviate dampness. The keepers were ordered to give their utmost attention to ventilating every part of the prison and cleansing the privies, drains and sewers. Cleanliness was the order of the day. [3]

Hard labour for men still meant the treadwheel although the Lewes wheel no longer linked with the miller's grindstone to produce wheat. Nor did it have any tangible end product. It was a new design geared with a flywheel as a copy of Petworth gaol's wheel. There, they had developed an ingenious system, a clever invention to measure the amount of work each prisoner performed. Intricate calculations determined the time spent on the wheel, the height of the step and the setting of the gear ratio to ensure labour really was hard. The men now exerted optimum energy to produce prison punishment sweat. The system had been perfected.

Lewes prisoners did not like the change and they objected, just as the first men on the original wheel had done. This time, the authorities dealt with it better. Some objectors were placed in solitary confinement and two were whipped. It had due effect. Prisoners returned to their work and conducted themselves quietly. The wheel was soon judged to be extremely beneficial.

When not at the wheel, the men returned to their day room, 15 feet by 14 (4.5 metres by 4.2) shared with 20 or 30 fellow prisoners, awaiting the lock-up transfer to their cell with its tier of three narrow beds: a soulless routine until the day came to reclaim their baked clothing.

On release, vagrants were issued with a prison pass ordering them back to their settlement parish and authorizing payments of 1½d (½p) a mile to be given them at designated places on the direct route home. Armed with their pass, Brighton's rejects began their journey home. It was those whose road took them via Hurst who found their way to Mr. Fisher at the workhouse.

When Thomas Jones and John Bingham arrived they were each given 1s. 2d. (6p). John Bingham was heading for Manchester. Thomas Jones would continue to Liverpool. They had been stopped in Brighton on the 1st of August and sentenced to a fortnight's hard labour. They walked the Lewes treadwheel and on the 13th were discharged with a prison pass. Hurst workhouse was their first call. [4]

On the 26th September, the Brighton constables found Mrs. Cain begging with her six children. They were sentenced to seven days at Lewes. She and the three oldest children, Catherine, Mary and Rosannah were put to making mop heads.

They completed their sentence and on the 8th October arrived at Mr. Fisher's door. He honoured the family prison pass with 4s. 1d. (20p). For the Cains, home was 300 miles away at Cockermouth beyond the mountains and lakes where Wordsworth's golden daffodils danced and fluttered in the breeze. Mrs. Cain would have many more workhouse calls to make.

Mr. Fisher carefully recorded the payments in his book ready to reclaim his money from Lewes; D. Mahoney to Liverpool, 2s. 6d. (12½p), William Jackson to Lancaster, 1s. 2d. (6p), John Parsons, Sheffield, 7d. (3p), William Griffiths, wife and children, St. Bees, 2s. 4d. (12p). The visitors seemed endless with people heading for Penrith, Preston, Chester, Carlisle, Birmingham, Gloucester, Stockport and Salford. In all, Mr. Fisher had 80 callers bound for 18 different destinations, particularly Liverpool, as Brighton cleansed its streets of unwelcome intruders. [5]

Henry French, whose motherless childhood days had been spent in Hurst workhouse, had a far longer journey in mind. The workhouse had apprenticed him to farm servitude – put to scare birds, pull turnips, turn hay, be plough boy, help at harvest or do whatever the task demanded.

That life was now distant memory. He had walked the Downs from Hurst to Lewes and proved worthy enough to hold a place on a farm. He was married, had five children about him and his wife again expecting. He had found the joys of independence but he had just had to move house again: not from choice but to make way for the farm shepherd, the second time he had been pushed aside for others – his childhood stigma still hooking him to a line linked inextricably to the workhouse, threatening to reel him back in. It was not the life for his children.

Henry had a dream: New York. In America men were free to make their way in life. There they did not bare their heads to a vestry committee. It was a dream worth pursuing. He applied to Hurst for help with the passage money. They would not be able to suggest that his settlement was elsewhere.

The vestry decided Henry's emigration was in the best interests of the parish. They would support his passage out but there would be no 'return' clause, it was to be a one-way ticket west for himself, his wife and six children. Just oldest son, Henry junior, would remain. He preferred England. [6]

Hurst first had the task of finding people to back the venture. There were willing subscribers: Mr. Campion, Dr. Weekes and Mr. Goodman all happy to provide at 4% per annum over three years. The money, £50, was there.

Steerage places were booked on the 453 ton Joseph and Henry Cumming recently in from New York with logwood, barrels of turpentine, hides and wool. The family's passage across the Atlantic would cost £27 10s. 0d. (£27.50) plus £1 16s. 0d. (£1.80) hospital money. [7]

Mr. Fisher settled the final rent and paid Henry £3 to buy clothing for his family. They spent their last few days in Hurst at the White Horse and left for London in style aboard a private coach of Mr. Goodman's fleet.

In London, Henry was given a final £10 for provisions during the voyage.

On the 17th August, the Joseph and Henry Cumming received clearance to sail. The dream was coming true.

The Lloyd's List charted the ship's progress. On the 18th, they cleared Gravesend. 13 days later they were at the far end of the Channel, clearing Plymouth.

In early October, a vessel docked in London and reported that on the 14th September it had passed and spoken with the Joseph and Henry Cumming amongst the mid-Atlantic waves at latitude 46, longitude 28.

Finally news came that on the 9th October the ship had docked in New York. Henry French had achieved his dream. [8]

1833: George Faithfull Becomes M.P. for Brighton

Brighton retained its magnetism for some of Hurst's own paupers. Henry Manners was still there seeking a medical career. His great achievement had been to court Elizabeth Glazebrook and win her as his wife. Now, his old difficulties – lack of a suitable situation and money – beset him yet again. He felt forced to request more parish aid from Hurst vestry. They obliged with a week's relief but when he still failed to find employment they ordered him to dig flints on Wolstonbury Hill.

Henry was quick to remind them of his poor health and his doctor's training. To his delight, they sent him £2 towards purchasing the necessary equipment to carry on trade as a barber. The proviso was that he did not apply for help again. Henry happily agreed. As a barber, his life in Brighton was assured; Mr. and Mrs. Henry Verral Manners of the medical fraternity.

Michael Harmes had taken his family back to Brighton helped on his way by a parting gift from the vestry, a bed. He felt at ease in the town's hustle and bustle where strangers could mix harmoniously without having to discuss past difficulties. When circumstances forced him to seek relief, he too asked Hurst for aid. They allowed a weekly 5s. 0d. (25p) on a short term basis. He saw it as permanent income.

With the allowance, life went along steadily for several months. Then Mrs. Harmes fell ill. Michael applied for more aid. The vestry obliged until she regained her health. The next time he asked, they turned on him. If he could not live without appealing for parish aid he must join the Wolstonbury flint diggers.

Wolstonbury would mean an eight mile walk morning and night. Michael had no intention of doing such a thing. He managed another month until the landlord called for his rent.

Michael kept him at bay as long as possible but it came to an abrupt end when the bailiffs arrived and seized his goods for auction. Mrs. Harmes' efforts to rebuild her home were as nothing. This time the vestry ordered the family home. Michael was pondering such a move in any case.

When Michael arrived in Hurst, he politely asked assistance in procuring more furniture. The reply was an ultimatum. If he could not maintain his family they must go into the workhouse. It was the nadir of his career. [1]

The threat spurred Michael to greater effort. He held on, procured a variety of work and proved his adaptability by becoming a proficient member of the bell ringers' team. They were all men of the village. Such was their enthusiasm and pride that one of them wrote a poem incorporating them all by name. He inscribed his verse on a wooden plaque:

> *'The ringers names at that time*
> *I thought no harm to book*
> *The first that I shall mention*
> *His name is Thomas Rooke*
> *Henry and Stephen Pierce*
> *Two Williams and John Wicks*
> *Edward and Michael Harmes*
> *And George and Thomas Cripps*
> *Richard Davey the Parish Clerk*
> *Makes up in number eleven*
> *I hope when they do ring their last*
> *They all may go to Heaven.'* [2]

For Michael Harmes, recognition on the belfry wall was important. He had been to social depths unimaginable for a respectable ex-farmer like himself. The plaque was firm evidence that he was part of society again. He had regular work doing painting and repairs for the vestry. His contribution to worship was being recognized. He may still be poor but he was a person.

Michael's bell-ringing parish-clerk was ex-sergeant, ex-headborough Davey. Steadfast in faith and strong in arm, he doubled as both clerk and sexton. He ensured everything was in place for Divine Service, he sang the measured responses to curate Tufnell, he dug the graves and he kept the church surrounds in good order. As parish-clerk, he felt confident enough to join the Rev. Tufnell in registering to vote at the forthcoming general election. His application was rejected but he still aspired to 'The Vote'.

It was the first election under Parliament's new Reform Bill designed to eliminate old malpractices and widen the franchise. The previous year had seen the end of the old rotten and pocket boroughs, including Bramber and Steyning. Sussex was now split into West and East, each returning two M.P.s. Hurst was included in East Sussex constituency but Brighton was now to have its own two members.

In Brighton, election fever had been building ever since the Reform Bill became law. The town's newspapers published the latest campaign reports. The Guardian backed the ideals of the new radicals. The Gazette exposed their faults and warned of the consequences.

A Political Union was already in place promoting reformist ideals. Now it needed suitable middle-class advocates as candidates for Westminster. Two suggestions were Mr. Isaac Wigney, son of the Brighton banker, and George Faithfull, the solicitor from Hurstperpoint. Each needed to prove he had sufficient backing to merit the Union's support.

Opinion at first doubted the choice of Mr. Faithfull whose indifferent health made him unlikely to stay the course. His supporters advertised a meeting at Brighton in the largest room of the Royal Sovereign to further his cause and propose him as the main candidate. Handbills were distributed about the town, particularly at the beer-shops and pubs where the workers gathered. The workers, whilst understandably not worthy of the vote, could nevertheless be useful voices.

The meeting proved popular despite strong rumours that Mr. Faithfull himself would be unable to attend. Supporters crammed the room and overflowed down the stairs into the street. [3]

Upstairs a chairman was elected. He called the meeting to order and made a glowing speech praising the attributes of their candidate who so sadly was not amongst them that night. Such a man as he, an eminent solicitor, would make Parliament itself sit up and know that the new men of Brighton had a voice.

At that point, an inner door opened. There stood George Faithfull himself with brother Hugh at his side. It was the perfect entry. The room roared its delight. This was the man to promote their cause. Here was their champion. Way was made for him to enter.

When calm was restored, George Faithfull expounded his ideals. They were a duplicate of the Political Union's precepts except that he first stressed the sanctity of private property; his land at Hurstperpoint would not be part of the bargain. Parliament, however, should dispose of all public property – the Church lands, crown land and military academies. Out should go that threat to civil liberty, Peel's new police in their blue frock-coats and fine buttons. Elections should be every three years and an extension of the franchise should be made to those capable of forming an educated opinion.

Mr. Faithfull sat down to tumultuous applause. Brother Hugh rose to address the meeting. He explained how he had not wanted his brother to stand for Parliament. A man of recent ill health, a family man with eight children dependent on him, should not sacrifice his health for his country. But all cautioning was in vain, for brother George was determined to go on, to present the interests of the townsmen of Brighton in Parliament.

The crowd again roared their approval. 'Faithfull and liberty,' was the cry. They knew what their vote would be.

So Isaac Wigney and George Faithfull stood together for the new borough seats. They derided their opponents – long-standing Tory Sir Adolphus Dalrymple, conservative Mr. Crawford and Captain Pechell R.N., an equerry to the queen dowager coming straight from duty as if on a royal errand. The forthcoming election would put them in their place.

The day came for the official proclamation. To ensure Brighton was fully informed, the proclamation was being made at the Town Hall and at nine other locations throughout the borough. [4]

First were the trumpeters heralding a dignified procession: the town crier, the headborough, the returning officers, a guard of uniformed police, and the Brighton Band. They took station at the Town Hall.

'Oh Yes! Oh Yes! Oh Yes!' hailed the crier and all were silent for the High Sheriff's announcement: two burgesses were to be elected to represent Brighton in Parliament.

Mr. Ridley, the returning officer, announced the day and time for the election. That done, the town banners were raised and the procession moved off to its next station closely followed by a bevy of Wigney supporters sporting flag and banner favours. The band faded and daily life continued.

Five days later, scheduled for 10.00 a.m. precisely, was the election itself at the hustings beside the Town Hall. At a quarter to ten music was heard. An approaching band was bringing the first candidate. It was Isaac Wigney. Following him came Sir Adolphus Dalrymple in a barouche bedecked with yellow and purple flags. He too had a band to play him in. Next were George Faithfull, surrounded by blue banners proclaiming his ideals, and Mr. Crawford who arrived quietly without any ceremony. When Captain Pechell's flag-flapping cavalcade had joined the throng some 4000 people were crammed in the square.

Mr. Ridley was sworn in as returning officer, and the formality of proposing the candidates began. That done, the candidates made their speeches. First was Mr. Wigney. The crowd acclaimed him and cheered.

Next was Captain Pechell. He stepped forward. A flood of jeering cat calls greeted him and drowned his words until at last the returning officer held aloft the proclamation of adjournment. He would allow only five minutes for calm to return or the election would cease.

The trouble makers were persuaded to heed the warning. Captain Pechell delivered his speech. The crowd remained silent. They accepted Crawford and Dalrymple with hardly a murmur and cheered Faithfull to the echo.

Once the speeches were over, questions could be put. Mr. Hugh Faithfull had a question for Sir Adolphus Dalrymple. Had Sir Adolphus ever directly or indirectly offered bribes?

Sir Adolphus assured him he had not.

Up spoke a fruiterer claiming a bribe had been offered him – a good dinner and two or three sovereigns as well if he voted for Sir Adolphus Dalrymple. A coach builder told how he had met Griffiths the painter who told him of the offer. He had been given cards and bills to distribute but had not used them.

More accusations followed and Henry Faithfull declared it a shame and disgrace to tempt poor men.

The election had become a slanging match. Dalrymple's men denied any wrong doing. Henry Faithfull launched into a long defamatory speech. Sir Adolphus listened calmly, rejected the charges and gave ironic credit for an excellent example of pure, faithful rhetoric.

Recriminations were ended by Mr. Ridley declaring it was time for a show of hands to determine the successful candidates.

Hands were raised, the count made and the result announced: Messrs Wigney and Faithfull were elected. Captain Pechell's proposer immediately demanded a poll. Mr. Ridley announced an adjournment to allow two days of recorded votes.

The first day saw several intimidating incidents by voteless supporters of Wigney and Faithfull. A small but noisy mob harangued Captain Pechell's men and broke windows of any shopkeeper sympathetic to the wrong cause. The constabulary were summoned, Wigney pleaded for seemly behaviour and peace returned.

At the end of the day Wigney headed the poll but Faithfull was behind Captain Pechell. The news was sobering.

The second day saw Faithfull recover his ground. At the close he was safely returned with Wigney. Much to the amusement of the crowd, Sir Adolphus Dalrymple gained only 32 votes.

The successful men thanked their supporters and shook hands with the losing candidates. George Faithfull Esq, M.P. elect for Brighton, rode home to Hurst a tired but happy man.

Luke Wickham Goes to the Asylum

At Goldbridge Farm, Luke Wickham was enjoying the first fruits of his inheritance. He worked long hours to make the land more productive. Mrs. Wickham, heavily pregnant with her seventh child, was unable to do as much as usual but her older boys were now employed on the farm and they proved good workers.

Suddenly everything went wrong. Luke was struck down by a summer fever. It proved severe. For weeks his life lay in the balance.

When the fever finally abated, Luke seemed unable to comprehend what was going on around him. He was incapable of doing anything. Mrs. Wickham did her best but in the end she had to call on the vestry for help. Her husband's handicap was too much.

The vestry decided Luke must be nursed at the Pest House. There, further weeks passed with no improvement. It was obvious he was not going to recover his faculties. The only recourse was to place him in an asylum.

Richard Davey escorted Mrs. Wickham to Lewes to have her husband certified. That done, Luke was moved to Hoxton Asylum.

Mrs. Wickham determined to keep the farm running despite the loss of her husband. The parish showed a positive approach by purchasing potatoes from her. She would start with their support but where she would end was not so certain. [1]

Soon the vestry had to face a situation affecting the whole parish. The latest Parliamentary Act for employing the poor set out specific targets to be achieved within parishes but left vestries to provide the necessary money.

The timing exacerbated the problem. The November poor-rate had been assessed to last three months. That money would not cover the additional expense necessary to implement the new Act. The vestry were in a quandary.

They decided that the Act now allowed them to levy an additional rate, a labour-rate. By it, everyone liable to pay poor-rates would also have to employ a proportionate number of labourers. Anyone not using their full quota would pay for the remaining part in cash to the overseer.

The necessary vestry meeting was announced. It was open to all rate-payers. Mr. Marchant and Mr. Goodman were there as churchwardens and Jesse Wicham as overseer. Only 12 parishioners attended but the importance of the meeting was demonstrated by the presence of Mr. Campion, Mr. Borrer and Dr. Richard Weekes. Henry Muzzell was there too as agent for Dr. Dodson ensuring his interests were served. [2]

The Rev. J.C.F. Tufnell took the chair. He explained that a calculation of the cost of all the labourers in the parish, men and boys, required a labour-rate at 5s. 0d. (25p) in the £ for the next six weeks. A resolution was proposed and seconded. The vote was taken: unanimous agreement. The labour-rate was entered in the minutes book and all present signed their agreement.

Mr. Fisher took the book to the Lewes magistrates for their approval. Five legal signatures were appended. It now remained for him to visit the farmers and ensure everything was in order. He was not well received.

At the end of the six weeks, a second labour-rate had to be made. There were grumbles of discontent around the parish. What if a third rate was demanded? They could not go on and on producing money.

A third rate did indeed follow. It coincided with the new poor-rate. Both were proposed at the vestry's February meeting: a 5s. 0d. poor-rate for twelve weeks and a 5s. 0d. labour-rate for six weeks. When Mr. Fisher rode round the parish with the latest demand he was confronted by determined opposition. Farmers, traders and householders refused to pay.

The labour-rate became the paramount topic of discussion: a kaleidoscope of views highlighting the strains and stresses of parish life. Arable farmer clashed with grazier, shopkeeper with the independent gentleman, smallholder with larger landholder, and dissenter with Churchman. The discord was vociferous enough to persuade the vestry to seek further legal advice. They consulted solicitors Kell and Co. who referred the matter to the learned Fred Thesiger (Temple). The labour-rate was suspended pending Mr. Thesiger's reply.

At the same time, His Majesty's Commissioners opened an enquiry into the Practical Operation of the Poor Law. People could forward facts about their area by writing to the commissioners. Hurst residents provided information about the labour-rate. [3]

Doctor Hampton Weekes described how previous winters had seen up to 30 of Hurst's unemployed put to digging flints on the South Downs and using the time to plot poaching, pilfering and even sheep stealing – plans which were perfected in the evenings at the beer-shops. The labour rate worked well in the parish and had put an end to the flint digging.

John Marchant was convinced that the flint diggers became changed men when they worked for him at Little Park. William Jenner complained that his farm, being mainly meadowland, was rated higher than arable farms although it did not need so many labourers. It meant he had to take on five more men than he needed. James Vallance claimed it was the farmers with arable land who were disadvantaged. He had found work for his full quota of extra labourers but the quality of the 'parish men' sent to him was shameful. They were the most idle and dissolute individuals, with the least skills, yet they received a wage little short of the best and steadiest workers. In his view they should only have task-work; that way they would be paid only for what they did.

Thomas Mercer was determined to make his feelings known. A pen was no use in his hand so a friend wrote for him. There he was, a labouring man out of employment with nothing else to look to for support. Yet he was still charged both poor-rate and labour-rate. To avoid paying cash for nothing, he had hired a man to work for him even though he had no work himself. The rate pressed people like him very hard. Thomas signed his 'X' confident his views were being expressed accurately.

Curate Tufnell was adamant the scheme would be good for every agricultural parish provided it was properly assessed. He highlighted the action of Hurst's few dissenters who were contriving to make the vestry's labour-rate null and void.

Strident among the dissenters was John Lempriere of the old Royal Oak complex, now with a chapel beside his shop. He lambasted the rate and the Established Church alongside it. The rate was a landed interest measure from first to last designed to ease the pockets of the rich who had little care for the poor. If the tithes had remained in their original form as a provision for the needy, the poor-laws would not be needed. The clergy should stop putting the tithes into their own pockets. Landowners should lower rents so that farmers could employ more hands instead of the land being neglected, the poor becoming worse off and the middle class being called upon to support them in a country flowing with milk and honey. Englishmen would not then be obliged to go tottering in their rags for parish relief.

Peter Wells went straight for the cheats who defrauded the system by avoiding payments. He had employed a man for the full six weeks when the labour-rate was introduced. He then discovered abuse of the system with people claiming ordinary employees as paupers working under the terms of the rate. Gentlemen claimed for footmen and stable boys; farmers for their yearly servants. An Act of Parliament should be passed to employ the poor man decently and raise his comforts above that of the labouring beast.

Doctor Richard Weekes' assessment was radically different. All attempts to lessen pauperism would be in vain unless the poor-laws were remodelled to accord with the original plan of Queen Elizabeth's time. That would produce an industrious, economical and sober set of poor whereas the present law was a bonus to every drunken, idle and debauched vagabond. The solution was to consolidate every 10 or 20 parishes around a central house of industry with Government controlling all money for the poor.

Off went the letters. Whether they would have any influence nobody knew, but His Majesty's Commissioners were pleased to include them in their report ready to be printed and published by order of The House of Commons.

Whilst the Hurst letters were being penned, an exciting new phase of life was beginning for George Faithfull M.P. in the House of Commons. There he quickly found his feet during the debate on the re-election of the Speaker who during the previous Parliament had been voted a pension of

£4000. Most M.P.s supported the Speaker. A pocket of reformers ardently opposed him, among them Cobbett, champion of the English underdog, and O'Connell, champion of the Irish. George Faithfull seized the chance to make his mark with Cobbett and O'Connell. He proposed the withdrawal of the pension or he too could not give his support for the Speaker. [4]

Sir Francis Burdett rose to put down the upstart radical. The Hon Member's proposal was very extraordinary. Those who considered the Speaker was overpaid should try the experiment of filling the chair. The House laughed and George Faithfull was silent: there were bigger men than him around.

Large among them was Lord Althorp, Chancellor of the Exchequer and Leader of the House, who had guided the Reform Bill through the Commons. It was Lord Althorp who announced the continuation of duty on West Indies sugar declaring that although it was undoubtedly desirable for the poorer classes to have lower taxes, the sugar duty was not the one to reduce first. He did not mention the immense sum raised by the tax.

George Faithfull's zeal was roused. He rose to speak. He regretted hearing from his Noble Lord that the country must not expect the Government to propose much, if any, reduction of taxation. The people had looked to the Reformed Parliament for relief from their burdens. If they should be disappointed, he feared they would be driven to a state of desperation which would produce some convulsive movement.

M.P.s were not comfortable with the new member. Already he had given moral support to insurrection in Ireland by backing O'Connell and voting against the Irish Disturbance Bill, designed to ensure maintenance of law in the rebellious region. Was he now hinting at more trouble on the streets? The Brighton M.P. had to withdraw again.

Snubbed but not destroyed, he continued his crusade. His finest hour came when he rose to present a motion to the House – a sensitive motion on an issue of religion. First he quietly reviewed his credentials and convictions: he, a dissenter as Honourable Members knew full well, was not against the church. Let it remain, bishops and all. Christianity was a religion of goodwill and charity. The church he revered, the Establishment he hated.

Having set his position he was ready to fire his broadside: 'What does the Protestant Church Establishment do? It makes men uncharitable, it breeds quarrels and in no case more so than in unhappy Ireland. The opposition to the Establishment is spreading to this country; and if tithes are not abolished, and taxes reduced, the people will take the work into their own hands. The tithes were originally Catholic property for the relief of the poor and the repair of churches. How are they now in the hands of Protestants? Why, by Acts of Parliament. If my Noble Lords wish to give the people the benefit of the Reform Bill and relieve them of the burden by which they are ground down to the dust, let them use some of the property of the Church Establishment. The greater part, if not the whole, of the revenues of the Church of England should be for the use of the nation.'

Mr. Faithfull sat down. His mentor William Cobbett rose to second the motion. The Hon Member for Brighton was a man after his own heart.

Lord Althorp remarked it was hardly necessary to answer the M.P. for Brighton. The question was not fit for discussion. 'Here, here,' echoed the Hon Members.

Another member rose to say that he as a Roman Catholic would move that the money should go to the Church that it was originally meant for.

'Withdraw, withdraw,' demanded the incensed House. The dissenter was bad enough. The Roman member was adding stinging insult to grave injury.

When the motion was put to the House not one 'Aye,' was heard. The 'Noes,' were everywhere. There was no division and the House moved swiftly on to the question of bribery at elections. George Faithfull, Hon Member for Brighton, was not going to upset the Established Church of England. [5]

Sir John Dodson Eyes Little Park

Whicle George Faithfull thundered forth at Westminster, his fellow Hurst landowner, Sir John Dodson, was influencing church affairs in Doctors' Commons a little further along the Thames by St. Paul's Cathedral. Sir John had progressed far beyond the status attained by his parish rector ancestors. His career had included a term as M.P. for Rye, a time not marred by unseemly speeches. Now, his energies were almost fully concentrated on affairs of the ecclesiastical court ensuring continuity in the law and traditions of the church.

Sir John had certainly not cut himself off from his parish home. He maintained a great interest in the farming community there, particularly where it offered an opportunity to increase his land holdings. The better Hurst properties were advertised in town at Garraway's Coffee House but they tended to fetch more than he considered appropriate. He had, however, been able to step in as saviour for several small farmers needing to leave unprofitable holdings.

The present information from Hurst was that Little Park might be worth his attention. Sir John liked the idea of Little Park – at the right price. He briefed his Lewes land agent to investigate the state of all Mr. Marchant's freehold and copyhold land.

The agent rode over to Hurst and made his inspection. He reported Little Park as old and run down with Edgerly buildings out of repair. Although the estate was a compact desirable property, the land was badly managed and needed a lot of improvement. An offer could be made at £8000 including £50 for the ½ acre (0.2 hectare) Bowling Alley. Sir John considered it a sound investment and instructed his agent to initiate negotiations.

Sir John had been misled: his plans would have to be put on hold. Little Park was the Marchant family estate. There was no way it was going on the market. [1]

Privately, John Marchant was finding the mortgage debt to Mr. Borrer a greater encumbrance than expected. Repayment of the complete loan was proving difficult but he was confident he could find most of the money by releasing small parcels of land to the building investor. The remainder could then soon be found.

An advertisement was placed in the Brighton Gazette:

'To be sold by private contract, several plots of freehold building ground, in the preferable part of the beautiful village of Hurstperpoint, eight miles from Brighton. Terms and particulars may be ascertained of Mr. Marchant, Little Park, Hurst, and of Mr. Ridley auctioneer, Brighton.'

Mr. Marchant's land bordered the road from opposite the church right through the village. It would provide prime building sites. A good price was guaranteed.

Dr. Richard Weekes did not hesitate. He was well known as a shrewd investor in the property market particularly in houses for the less well off. His houses would not be ostentatious.

George Cheeseman, the Brighton builder, was also quick off the mark. His houses for letting out to summer visitors had been a great success. Now he purchased land for ten more which would be sold on the open market. His most ambitious venture was an impressive mansion with a sweeping drive in front and enough land for a large orchard behind. He named it, St. George's, coating it with patriotism.

English Corney, the new wheelwright back in the village from Brighton, bought a plot. He had two workshops behind his house, one for himself and the other a smith's. It was ideal: his wife and children one side and a blacksmith the other.

Hurst was certainly expanding at an alarming rate. John Marchant had no more wish for the ribbon development than the majority of inhabitants but it would help him pay off his debts and be master of his own lands again.

The vestry had a problem of their own. A legal opinion had just been received in reply to the controversial question about the labour-rate. It came from the learned

Fred Thesiger (Temple). He found the nature of the powers given to the vestry under the Act of Parliament difficult to establish, but in his opinion the legislation was not allowing any additional labour-rate to be made: it was simply enabling the old poor-rate to be used for wider purposes. Such a labour-rate could not be enforced, and certainly it could not be raised unless three-quarters of the parish ratepayers consented, not merely those assembled in vestry. [2]

Bang went the labour-rate. With such a legal opinion, there seemed a distinct trace of democracy in the air. Were Messrs Campion, Borrer and their entourage no longer to call the tune? Altogether it was a considerable rebuff for the gentlemen of Hurst; a check on their influence and power.

The abortive labour-rate was Mr. Fisher's last assignment before he became ill and died. He had been a reasonably efficient assistant overseer. Once or twice he had not organized the finances too well and had asked for money in advance but the vestry had never doubted his honesty. He left his worldly wealth to his wife and daughter: except six guineas set aside for the trouble taken by his executor, Henry Muzzell. [3]

Henry also took over Mr. Fisher's duties whilst the vestry advertised for a new man. He was certainly having more parish business thrust upon his shoulders. He was ready and keen for it. There was an added dimension. Henry had a new wife. No longer was he ploughing a lone furrow.

Henry's manorial duties as Mr. Campion's reeve entailed close liaison with solicitor George Hoper at Lewes who dealt with legal matters. He also had the task of collecting quit-rent arrears. He managed all except those from Dr. Weekes. The doctor was adamant he would not pay a penny until the next manorial court in accord with what he claimed to be his copyhold agreement. If Henry had not realized before, he would now know that Dr. Weekes was not a man to be pushed.

Dr. Weekes caused further disturbance by digging out sand close to the Hurst Turnpike Road. It was Danny ground.

Sand had a commercial value, as did everything else at Danny. 4s. 0d. per load was the price for sand taken from the estate but it was not so much the loss of revenue that concerned Mr. Campion as the audacity of the doctor presuming to take matters into his own hands.

Mr. Campion sent Henry Muzzell over to Lewes with a letter for Mr. Hoper outlining the matter. Henry was instructed to explain all the local particulars.

It was the start of a long exchange between Mr. Hoper and Dr. Weekes until the exasperated doctor saw red and put his thoughts to paper:

> 'Dear Sir,
>
> Really the subjects of your letters are as frivolous as scarcely to be worth the ink and paper required to answer them. The Road from which I take

this sand belongs to the Trustees and never did belong to Mr. Campion and many people have for years past taken sand from the same place without any consent, therefore I, having taken it by permission of the Hurst Road Surveyor, thought I was improving the said Road by so doing. Mr. Borrer and Mr. Tufnell have taken and dug sand from the same place therefore why spit your venom at me alone. If any damage has been done I am very willing to pay for it as settled by any jury of Hurst people – I deny its being waste land but entirely belonging to the Hurst Road which just below is flinted as wide as the Road is, where the said sand has been taken away – Was you to see it you would be able to inform Mr. C of his error in judgement. Even allowing it to be waste I claim a right to dig sand being a Tenant of the Manor a similar right which I exercise in the Manor of Stretham, in common with many other Tenants – At this time of day Mr. Hoper, you and Mr. Campion should be better employed than in acting up to the vile Tyranical system of the barbarous feudal times I remain your most obt R.Weekes.'

Mr. Campion felt able to consider the contents coolly. In his opinion it was just what might be expected of Weekes, inaccurate in its claims, bleating in its protestations. The truth of the matter was that Mr. Borrer had dug sand from the opposite side of the road where his own lands were. Mr. Tufnell had dug sand only since Weekes' example and now had no intention of removing it. The road itself was only 24 feet (8 metres) wide and the waste each side was not the property of the trustees. It was never a sand-pit and the only occasions sand had ever been taken were when poor people living nearby sent their children for a bagful to use on the cottage floors.

Mr. Campion was happy to condone quiet use by the cottagers but wholesale removal by the likes of Weekes was beyond the pale. Flagrant flouting of manorial law would not be tolerated.

Henry Muzzell set out to track down the missing sand. Within days, he was able to report to Mr. Campion. Nine cartloads of sand had been carried away and laid down in the back-yard of Mansion House. A further three or four had been laid down at the side of the road on land that Mr. Weekes had purchased from Mr. Marchant. The case against the doctor was proved beyond doubt.

Soon after the conclusion of the disappearing sand episode, Henry handed over the reins of the workhouse governorship to Mr. Billy Heaver from Slaugham whose wife, Elizabeth, would be matron. Their combined salary was agreed at £40.

Henry Muzzell was able to introduce Billy Heaver to his new home and to ensure he understood essential procedures. That done, Henry reverted to being Sir John Dodson's agent and sent in a bill for rents owed by William Bartley and Henry Henty.

William had one of the small cottages above the Old Hollow by the church. He was known as an upright man who always did his best for his family. Henry Henty had been of good behaviour since his year's gaol for 'zipping' headborough Davey but it had not helped him pay his rent. Billy Heaver paid both from the parish purse.

Mrs. Heaver found one cause of concern at the workhouse. The kitchen oven was in such a state it could not be used. The vestry authorized repairs. 50 new paving tiles were fitted. Blacksmith Chandler made a decent hoe for raking out the hot embers. Billy Heaver purchased a stock of 36 'three-farthing' ($\frac{1}{3}$p) brooms to sweep out the last of the ash. Workhouse baking was about to improve.

In one respect the place had been modernized. A few months before Mr. Fisher's death, the vestry had decided that having only one privy for both males and females was unsatisfactory. It had been agreed to make another for the females. It was now ready. [5]

The only problem the Heavers encountered among the residents was old Stephen Jupp who periodically disregarded workhouse rules by wandering away to enjoy a few days of precarious independence begging around the parish. Nobody wished him harm and he wandered back as regularly as he went. Old Stephen had been a good man in his time so his absences had always been overlooked. Billy Heaver accepted the situation.

He did have to deal with Edward Heaseman who was far from his proper home. Heaseman had been accepted in Hurst all the years he was self sufficient but as soon as he was forced to apply for parish relief he was taken to Lewes magistrates. They determined his home parish as Southampton. [6]

Once the removal papers were processed, Billy Heaver was instructed to take Heaseman the 70 miles to Southampton and deliver him to the overseers there. That done, he was to continue to Ringwood and check on the Davieses, a Hurst family receiving regular relief from the vestry. Their landlord had written explaining that Mrs. Davies had been obliged to borrow £1 4s. 0d. (£1.20) from him to buy food because one of her children had been very ill and the money allowed by Hurst was inadequate. Heaseman's removal provided an opportunity to check on the true position at Ringwood. [7]

The two men travelled by cart to Brighton. At Stonepound, Billy Heaver paid the 4d. (2p) toll and called in at the beer house where Edward Heaseman enjoyed a gin and beer at Hurst parish expense. From Brighton they travelled by the Red Rover coach. More refreshments were had on the road to Chichester where they stopped for dinner. Further stops were made before Southampton was reached. In all, Edward Heaseman enjoyed a reasonable journey home. Finally, Billy Heaver handed him across to the Southampton overseers. He was off Hurst's hands. [8]

Billy Heaver carried on a further 20 miles to Ringwood. All proved in order at the Davies house. Their poverty was acute. They obviously depended on Hurst money and needed more.

He returned to Southampton. The next day he started for home on the Brighton coach. When he got back to Hurst, he presented his expenses bill, £4 12s. 6d. (£4.62).

At Southampton, Heaseman explained the temporary set-back which had caused his removal. He wanted to live in Hurst. With a little help he was sure he could manage it.

The Southampton vestry listened to his case and decided to support him. A letter was written authorizing Hurst to pay Edward Heaseman 2s. 0d. (10p) a week which would be repaid whenever requested. [9]

Armed with the letter, Heaseman set out for Hurst. For this trip he did not have the comfort of a coach, but arrive he did, to cause a few raised eyebrows until he produced his letter. It made all the difference. Edward Heaseman was no longer a liability, he could stay. Work was soon found for him, cleaning the church clock.

Billy Heaver had arrived back just in time for the May Day Fair. There were 39 paupers in the workhouse. He distributed parish-pence to them all and they set off to make the most of their afternoon's freedom. Old Stephen Jupp decided to extend his time out and set off on another walk-about. Mary Sayers, one of the young girls, returned far from well. She was at fever heat and a nurse sat several nights with her. To everyone's relief she recovered but the illness left a very limp little girl. Oranges were purchased for her, a rare fruit for the workhouse. With careful nursing she slowly regained her health. [10]

There was trouble of another sort at the Sparrows Club Annual Dinner. After the members had enjoyed their usual satisfying meal, chairman Nathan Marchant proposed the toasts. Liquor flowed free as healths were drunk, 'three times three' from first to last.

Next, Samuel Goodman announced the year's most successful guns. The greatest score of sparrow heads during the winter had been achieved by first Mr. Bull, second Mr. Marchant and third Mr. Hider. In the four years of the club's existence 19,777 heads had been produced. Great praise was due to all members for decimating those enemies of agriculture. The benefits had been noted far and wide. Sparrows Clubs had sprung up not only in Sussex but also through Kent, Surrey and Hampshire.

On such a note, the members began their session of merriment. Good beer and song intermingled until a boisterous chorus tweaked the sensibilities of a member whose land had been invaded by the hunt. Up he stood. Face glowing, broad arms waving, he proclaimed his candid opinion of huntsmen who damaged his land.

Colleagues were alarmed. They knew the huntsman involved and they feared their member's propensity for stupid talk. Nobody was going to target the parish elite. They quickly calmed their man and the evening continued in song. The Sparrow Club's shot was strictly for the birds.

1834: Mr. Marchant Promotes Cricket

John Marchant enjoyed cricket. He was the power behind the new Hurst Cricket Club. His grandfather, William, had enjoyed playing when he had been in charge at Little Park. In those far off days the games against neighbouring parishes had been played at the Danny Sand Field. Now John Marchant provided the ground, his Home Field.

The Home Field slope was pronounced – some would say a hill – but it was perfectly playable and visitors used to level ground would just have to adjust. First visitors were the Brighton Clarence Club. Hurst gained the victory by 56 runs, a grand start for them.

One of the keenest players was wheelwright, English Corney. He shared the excitement of the club's six run victory on the Home Field slopes against Chailey and the humiliation of a thumping defeat by the Brighton Hereford Club at their ground high on the Downs near the race course. [1]

Cricket also featured when Mr. Campion invited the children of the National Schools to Danny as part of his birthday celebrations. It was to be a benevolent occasion for the working class children. Parents of children attending the other schools would prefer it kept that way: they had no wish for their offspring to mix.

The chosen day still entailed a morning of school – with an uncommonly high attendance. Lessons over, the master led the 140 children soberly along the estate paths to their afternoon of festivities.

Full in the face of Danny House, the children enjoyed cricket and other seemly school-games watched by the guests gathered for the house celebrations.

The games were within striking distance of the dinner tables prepared in the shade of the ancient Danny oaks. At two o'clock the children settled for the birthday dinner. The ladies served them roast beef and followed it with plum pudding. The gentlemen served strong beer, and smiled at the children's pleasure.

At the conclusion of the meal the children were invited to drink the king's health. They did so with gusto 'three times three' in the best tradition showing wonderful loyalty to the crown. Next they drank to Mr. Campion with even greater goodwill for their generous host. At the third health, 'Mrs. Campion and her family', the children responded with such fervent enthusiasm that an astute observer suggested the source of their energy – strong beer proving its strength. It was time to depart if propriety was to be maintained.

The master mustered his boys, the mistress her girls. Humble thanks were cheerfully given. The master spoke. School discipline ruled. A line of happy children wound back along the estate paths out of the Danny grounds and safely home round meat, plum-pudding and good strong beer.

Mr. Campion also gave some of his Danny workers time off for cricket against Mr. Marchant's men. The match took place on the slopes of Little Park. Stumps were positioned and battle began.

The bat did not swing easily for the Danny players and they hit out with more enthusiasm than skill. It was still a great game. At the end of the day Mr. Marchant's men had triumphed by 195 runs. Cricket over, the players returned home ready for harvest where hand and wrist would show far greater skill with the sickle.

First came the Horticultural Society's July show on the Town Field. This was the society's big show. The Town Field was the ideal location with its two lines of fine elm trees and the wonderful view to the Downs.

Dignified gentlemen with their ladies strolled in the shade of the elms and admired the grand arch at the entrance of the marquee. There, against a background of evergreen foliage, an array of bold and colourful dahlias stood out in letters two feet (0.6 metres) high proclaiming: 'Hurst Horticultural Society'. Beneath it, visitors entered the spacious display area to inspect the exhibits and praise the prize winning entries.

Dominating everything were the wonderful plants sent in from the gardens of the gentry to enhance the day. Mr. Campion had contributed a wonderful Fuchsia Fulgens, Mr. Borrer a Magnolia Grandiflora, and Mrs. Marchant an amazing clump of Paradise Grass.

The fruit, flowers and vegetables of society members were acclaimed as of outstanding quality and there was high praise for the cottagers' produce. The bouquets of wild flowers gathered from the hedgerows by labouring class families also brought comment: how uplifting for the owner of the winning bouquet to be named alongside show members who cultivated their entries.

At prize-giving time the curate presented the cottagers' awards and remarked on the greatly improved standard of their produce. He heaped further praise as he recounted how impressed he had been prior to the show when looking over the cottages and gardens. It gave him great satisfaction to be able to report so favourably on the cleanliness everywhere and the obvious industry of the occupants.

The curate himself was a proud winner with his gardener taking prizes for best onions and best blackcurrants.

Henry Muzzell was also rewarded. His flower garden was an engrossing hobby to take his mind off work. His bright displays of stocks and Busy Lizzies both gained first prizes in the Amateurs Class.

Henry had a bonus. Once the final prize had been awarded, the cottagers were all bid farewell and sent off home. The amateurs joined Mr. Campion, Mr. Borrer and the other parish gentry for the celebratory dinner at the New Inn, after which they returned to the seats set among the Town Field elms for a dessert of the prize winning fruits of the show and for dancing through the evening until ten o'clock.

The Brighton Gazette failed to notice the excellent standard of display described in the Sussex Advertiser but they were pleased to record the encouragement given to the poor and explain how prizes for wild flowers would teach the labouring classes to appreciate the beauties of nature and bring to their notice many useful vegetables that could be found along the hedgerows.

That August, a group of farm labourers on their way to harvest made a startling hedgerow discovery. In the undergrowth lay a corpse, soft and decomposing, peacefully reposed with folded arms. The features were no longer of anyone, but the workhouse round-frock hallmarked old Stephen Jupp. His May Day excursion was over.

The coroner decided the death was natural. Stephen Jupp was allowed the dignity of a pauper funeral in an unmarked grave. [2]

The whole question of pauperism and workhouses was in Parliament's melting-pot. The statutory parish returns to the Poor Law Commissioners were more voluminous than ever with questions that had ominous overtones. Mr. Marchant had to find the answers. The first provided a clinical analysis of Hurstperpoint.

The parish needed 200 men and boys for year round cultivation of the land. It had 240 labourers. In summer, there was work for everyone. In winter, about 40 had to be given parish work, mainly digging flints. Men on parish work were paid 10s. 0d. (50p) a week. Wages otherwise were uniform throughout the year at 12s. 0d. (60p) a week plus beer. Piece-work was general so the industrious labourer could boost his annual earnings by as much as £5. At haying and harvest, women and children could earn 9s. 0d. (45p) a week, and in winter 3s. 0d. (15p).

Very few labourers owned their cottage; most were rented from the farmers at around £3 per year. Families had enough to live on with bread, meat, and vegetables, particularly where the garden was properly cultivated. They did not have enough money for savings. Relief for men in employment was given if they had more than three children aged between 3 and 10. If parents could not provide for children over 10, the vestry found work for the child or placed it in the workhouse.

Next came searching questions. Should magistrates be prevented from ordering relief for persons refusing to enter the workhouse? What would be the effect of a Union of parishes? Could he tell anything about the causes and consequences of the Agricultural Riots of 1831?

Mr. Marchant gave answers as best he could but how would the Government choose to interpret them? The thought gave him little pleasure. Everybody knew that plans were afoot for parishes to lose their independence through a series of Poor Law amendments being guided through Parliament by Lord Althorp.

In the House of Commons, the Hon. George Faithfull, Brighton, kept true to his ideals and opposed the new bill that threatened to exacerbate the plight of the labouring family. But Mr. Faithfull had no influence in Parliament, he was still a vote in the losing lobby. The bill became law and the Poor Law Amendment Act was on the Statute Book.

Unions of parishes were to be formed to administer relief. Able bodied paupers would do task-work and be paid considerably less than an independent labourer. If no work was available the relief would be mainly food or other necessaries of life. The system of payments to paupers outside the parish was to be carefully revised.

The final directive was the most ominous. Any able-bodied pauper asking relief could be offered a place in the workhouse with food and a bed for which a set amount of work would be done. A refusal to enter the workhouse constituted a rejection of aid. No alternative would be offered.[3]

Parish payment of paupers' rents was also to stop. At the vestry's June meeting it was agreed that notices ending rent-relief should go to the fourteen landlords still having agreements with the parish. Printed forms were distributed. No longer would landlords be assured their rents.

The new ruling affected Dr. Weekes more than most. Never before had there been doubt over the income from his houses. Whenever his tenants were unable to pay their rent, the parish had footed the bill since time out of mind. He paid the poor-rates, the vestry paid him the rents Lady Day and Michaelmas. How now was he to be sure of his money from such old timers as Hazelgrove, Lewry and Tugwell, parish paupers since the start of time?

The doctor was able to find more peace of mind over his new venture, a north-south toll road through Hurst. The southern part from the church down to the Brighton Road had just been completed. Now he had to ensure finance for the Cuckfield section. He wrote to Sir John Dodson in London pleading with him to pay his share and lead the way for others.

Sir John responded. Others followed and the finance was there. The new road would provide such an improved route for London/Brighton coaches by avoiding the notorious Clayton Hill that proprietors would inaugurate a service through Hurst. Direct stage-coaches to London and Brighton! It was what the parish had been waiting for. [4]

Not everyone agreed. Opponents feared the increased attraction for housing development. They had only to cite the old toll road as example. Five Hurst properties were up for auction. The main lot was claimed as of interest to capitalists whilst another with smithy and stabling was said to be well worth the attention of coach masters. Most controversial was the barn advertised as a property which 'for a trifling expense might be converted into a Dwelling House'. Anyone wanting to turn a barn into a house could call on land surveyor Henry Muzzell for details. [5]

In the High Street, a piece of property development was causing unusual hostility. The argument concerned the boundary between butcher Luke Humphrey and grocer John Lempriere. Luke Humphrey was building a shop by his slaughter house. John Lempriere said it was extending onto his Royal Oak complex. The men were at loggerheads.

The shop was completed but Lempriere would not withdraw. The dispute had to be settled in court. There, after six hours of legal wrangling, Luke Humphrey was found guilty. He had encroached 16 inches (40cm) on his neighbour's land: fine £2 10s. (£2.50).

That autumn, old Thomas Bartley died. He had known the Royal Oak better than anyone; it was his family home. Its loss back in 1813 had been a body blow to him but he had slowly rebuilt his life. He had risen from occupying parish-paid accommodation to having his own place again. He had made bell ropes for the church. He had supplied the workhouse with potatoes from his own ground – the independent man helping the poor of the parish. He had earned enough money to pay the poor-rate. He had regained respect. [6]

His family gave him a good funeral and placed a large headstone in his memory.

Mr. Faithfull Campaigns Again

The autumn of 1834 brought a national disaster: fire at the Houses of Parliament. The Brighton Herald reported it as truly awful, flames bursting from the roofs and molten lead pouring down upon the street like water; the House of Lords and the House of Commons completely destroyed. [1]

King William immediately made the newly erected palace in St. James' Park available to his ministers. At the end of the year, Parliament was dissolved and a general election called.

In Brighton, the radicals were once more pitched against the establishment. Sir Adolphus Dalrymple and Captain Pechell again provided the opposition. The radicals were no longer a united front. George Faithfull's reform zeal at Westminster had left him with a tarnished image to the extent of being labelled among the worst of some very bad characters in Parliament.

On election day, the candidates made their way to the Town Hall. Wigney was first, arriving quietly in accordance with the candidates' agreement not to use bands or make intrusive noise. Pechell and Dalrymple followed with cavalcades of flags and banners. Then the music of a band was heard and George Faithfull arrived with a procession of flag waving supporters. [2]

It was time for the election addresses. George Faithfull moved to the front of the hustings. The crowd acclaimed him. Eloquent as ever, he took time to dismiss the opposing candidates, review his achievements and finally launch his battle cry: 'The rich are never satisfied; they have gone on grasping and grinding the poor until they can do so no longer. I oppose the ways of the rich. I stand for the repeal of the Corn Laws so that the poor can have cheap bread, for repeal of the malt tax so that everyone can afford good beer. I want to see the man, who from the rising to the setting of the sun toils to the utmost of his power – the man who returns home to his family with an exhausted frame – I want to see that man able to sit down by a good bright fire, to have a good piece of wholesome bacon or pork, a good bed to stretch his limbs on, and good clothes to his back.'

Mr. Faithfull sat down to the ringing acclaim of his supporters.

When the last of the candidates had finished, the Returning Officer called for a show of hands to determine the winners. Up went the hands. The victors were announced, Mr. Faithfull and Captain Pechell.

Wigney's men would not accept the result. The next two days were assigned for the recorded poll.

The first day ended with Pechell and Dalrymple ahead. The pundits were taken aback.

When the poll closed next day at four o'clock the result was decisive; Pechell 960, Wigney 524, Sir Adolphus Dalrymple 479 and last of all George Faithfull on 469. Ordinary Brighton man might want George Faithfull but the enfranchised voter wanted an M.P. of respectability, not a radical firebrand.

Mr. Faithfull could not entirely conceal his disappointment. In his post election address he poured scorn on the victors and assured the people of Brighton he would be ready to represent them at the next election when the present pair had proved themselves unworthy of their office.

He then had no option but to accept the result, go home to Hurstperpoint and satisfy himself with local politics. But his achievements could not be taken from him. He had called for reductions in taxes on sugar and malt so important to the working man; he had supported Lord Ashley's endeavours to improve conditions for factory children; he had spoken for public gardens in towns. That August he had voted for the freedom of all colonial slaves, he had supported the unsuccessful motion for them to be paid during the obligatory apprenticeship period following their freedom and he had voted for the plantation owners' compensation to be reduced. Mr. Faithfull had no doubt he had played his part for the common good.

He soon had another part to play. The Hurst toll roads were losing revenue because farmers made use of side roads and the Danny Lane as a free way towards Brighton.

Dr. Weekes had suggested a remedy. The White Horse Gate should be moved east to Danny Lane where a side gate would be erected. Travellers could choose. Pay at Danny Lane or along the new road by the church. It just remained to canvas support amongst the trustees and include the proposal on the agenda for the next meeting. [3]

The proponents had overlooked one vital factor, Mr. Faithfull. In Mr. Faithfull's eyes the toll road trustees were meeting to further their own ends instead of the community's. He would do something about it.

First he visited Mr. Campion and discussed the issue with him. Mr. Campion was equally oppposed to a gate at the end of his lane. He pledged his full support as an objector and promised to canvas the trustees himself. Mr. Faithfull left. Now he could confidently orchestrate a public protest.

His close friend and fellow solicitor, Charles Sharood, had the ideal venue at the New Inn. Mr. Sharood had married the inn keeper's daughter. In due course, he had inherited the inn, to the knowing nods of cynical sceptics who had never accepted that the marriage to the crippled heiress was for love alone.

The protesters gathered in the New Inn. It was Charles Sharood himself who took the chair. He proposed a carefully worded resolution opposing the re-siting of the toll-gate. Everyone agreed.

Mr. Campion took the papers with him to the trustees' next meeting. There he quietly expressed his views. The majority understood what it entailed and voted accordingly. By 15 votes to 5 the gate would remain at the White Horse. Mr. Faithfull was victorious. Dr. Weekes and the thwarted trustees nursed their wounds. They determined to try again another day.

Mr. Faithfull's victory over the parish toll-gate just missed the launch of a new Brighton paper, The Patriot. The editor explained the paper's policy by printing an extract from a speech delivered at The Globe by none other than G. Faithfull: 'The reformers of Brighton and Sussex will now abandon the apostate Guardian to its fate. A press must be either the greatest national blessing or the greatest national curse because it is the only medium of communication for the public. What is it we want in Brighton? An independent and fearless press.'

The Patriot declared itself determined to fight for the good of the people, to promote the cause of civil and religious freedom and never become engrossed in parochial affairs. It was the friend of the working family man. [4]

About the same time, Hurst vestry received a communication from a gentleman who was entirely engrossed in parochial affairs. He declared himself as their very obedient servant W.H.T. Hawley, Assistant Poor Law Commissioner. His letter requested the vestry to meet with him at the inn in Hurst the following Friday with all parish books for the previous three years and with answers to 13 questions plus abstracts of 10 accounts. The vestry had just three days to comply. [5]

Mr. Hawley proved a true devotee of the New Poor Law with all its ramifications. His visit was to assess the position in Hurstperpoint. The vestry produced their books and answered his questions. He was thorough in everything. When he left, the vestry fully understood who were the servants.

Mr. Hawley's report lamented the state of affairs in Hurst. The curate there worked hard for the improvement of his parish and his fellow men. He had an able and intelligent staff of parochial officers. Yet mismanagement was so prevalent it proved the necessity of a more authoritarian power. [6]

Of the 1500 inhabitants, 630 were found to be in a state of pauperism. Although the parish had an excellent workhouse perfect for classifying inmates and providing them with employment, it failed through a lack of proper discipline. At Hurst a pernicious system prevailed with the out-relief given as articles through a system of tickets issued to paupers who changed them for goods at local shops. It was a system geared to the benefit of millers and shopkeepers including the vestry clerk himself.

Equally reprehensible was the practice of putting-out boys as farm hands and girls as servants. The parish paid a shilling a week for each of them and provided clothing. This had an invidious effect on families upright enough to keep independent of parish assistance whose own children were denied the positions occupied by 'parish-children'. Commissioner Hawley was not enamoured of the state of affairs in Hurstperpoint.

The vestry were informed that on 26th March 1835 the Cuckfield Union would come into existence being formed from 15 surrounding parishes. As a member parish, Hurst was to provide two elected guardians. [7]

Cuckfield was designated for the able-bodied adults, Hurstperpoint (five miles south) for the old people plus the girls, and Lindfield (three miles east) for the boys.

In the summer, the big move round took place. It was completed efficiently. Nothing had been left to chance. For the paupers involved it was a dramatic day, traumatic for some, but pauper reaction came into the reckoning only as a factor that required discipline. Cuckfield, with an influx of 53 able-bodied to swell the 36 already there, could have seen discord. The careful planning and effective use of authority ensured an orderly day.

The 35 boys accommodated at Lindfield included nine Hurst lads able to boost each other's spirits in the new surroundings. The lone boys from Slaugham and Horsted Keynes needed to make friends quickly.

Hurst had fewest new arrivals, 32 to join the remaining 25. Mrs. Heaver would add to her duties by being schoolmistress for the girls. [8]

Opponents of the new Union were vociferous in their attacks. They inveighed against legislated cruelty that forced any man laid off from work to lose both his home and his family because of the iniquitous classification system which separated husband from wife in one building and pushed their children miles away, boys in one direction, girls in another. How barbaric was the nation? [9]

When a vestry meeting was announced to formalize the sale of the workhouse and its furniture to the Cuckfield Union, Mr. Faithfull determined to oppose it. He led a team of six supportive dissenters to the meeting.

John Marchant, as Hurst's representative on the Union Board, explained that they had assembled to appoint valuers because the Poor Law Commissioners were now having the workhouse.

Mr. Faithfull was astounded. The building was the Poorhouse, the property of the poor of Hurst who through no fault of their own had to use it. Only they, the poor, could authorize its sale.

Dr. Weekes retorted that the parish had better make the most money it could from the house.

George Faithfull was inflamed by the suggestion He rounded on the doctor. They transformed the meeting to a verbal duel each attempting to out phrase the other.

When they paused for breath, solicitor Charles Sharood took up the cause and moved that the present proposal would sanction an unjust and injurious system of treating the poor. Mr. Faithfull seconded the motion, his supporters voted in favour and the workhouse was saved. Legislation may dictate that the house would accommodate the young girls and old people from 15 parishes, but the building was still the property of the parish. The Union would pay £40 per year for its use.

1835: Mr. Marchant Hits Out

A more cheerful side to village life was the June cricket match between the old Hurst Friendly Society and the Union Society. There was a festive air about the place. At noon, a band began playing outside the New Inn. The two sides assembled, each sporting their Friendly Society colours, and marched up the road to Mr. Marchant's Home Field. [1]

At the side of the field was a specially erected stage decorated with evergreens ready for the band. Ready too were the stumps marking a pitch carefully set to minimize the slope. Three to four hundred spectators arranged themselves around the field. The game was ready to begin.

The Old Society batted first. Top score was the 22 by John Marchant of Little Park, 67 years old and still a keen hitter of the ball. The team made 70 and everyone rested while the band struck up an interlude of music.

Sadly, the Union batsmen were not so effective. Three of them were run out and the score closed at 30. There was more music from the band.

The Union bowlers did better when the Old Society batted again. At 43 the last man was out. The musicians played for the final interlude.

As the Union Society began their fight back, the glorious afternoon was becoming evening. One of the Harmes boys, Henry, led the way with a fine 21 before John Marchant caught him. Hopes of a Union victory disappeared as George Marchant bowled the last three men in swift succession. At 61, the innings and game were over; a victory to the old Society by some 20 runs.

The next month the cricket club went down to Brighton to play the Blue Club. Mr. Marchant opened the innings. He was in fine form again. In no time, he had 16 to his name. Then came a ball so bad it just had to be hit out of the field. Somehow he missed. The ball finished up lodged in his jacket. Unabashed, he recovered the ball and handed it to the wicket keeper. The wicket keeper appealed. The umpire gave Mr. Marchant out: 'Held the ball!' A surprised Mr. Marchant left the field to be replaced by an equally surprised Henry Harmes. [2]

The remaining batsmen brought the side to 115 and the bowlers saw the Blue

Club out for 81. It was time for Mr. Marchant to bat again.

They got him in the end, caught for 78, a truly magnificent innings which quite knocked the heart out of the Blue Club bowlers. Hurst batted on to 207 which left no time for an answer. It was not really necessary, the victors were already known. Mr. Marchant took his team home in happy mood.

Mr. Marchant now had to turn his mind to more serious matters. The Poor Law authorities had refused to be beaten over the workhouse. The question of valuers for its sale to the Cuckfield Union was to come up for another reading in a week's time. [3]

It became a week of activity and confrontation with 'Pro' and 'Anti' advocates out drumming up support. Mr. Campion intimated that he would be in attendance. He asked his rate-paying tenants if they could manage to be there as well and he stressed the importance of punctuality. He also made clear his views on the question.

Thomas Wadey the bricklayer and English Corney the wheelwright understood the drift of things. They considered a vote for the sale a good insurance for continued patronage at Danny House. Henry Muzzell knew which side his bread was buttered and he was out for jam. They got themselves to the workhouse on time.

The radical opponents too had been rallying support although they lacked the economic angle of the pro-sale lobby to persuade disinterested voters.

Over 40 rate-payers crowded the workhouse vestry room for the meeting. At 6.00 p.m. Rev. Tufnell took the chair. He reminded everyone they were there in response to an official notice to appoint a valuer for the sale of the workhouse to the Cuckfield Board.

Mr. Faithfull rose to make a legal point: because the vestry notice had been signed by only one parish officer, the whole meeting was out of order. Dr. Weekes retorted that they had come to carry the question and would do so.

For a few moments their feud flared until Rev. Tufnell called them to order and declared he was using the authority of the chair to put the motion to the vote. Mr. Campion gave his backing.

The radicals claimed it could not be done because a previous meeting had already rejected the motion. Rev. Tufnell was determined. He called upon all those in favour of appointing a valuer to raise their hand. The count was made, 24, – all Mr. Campion's men, all Dr. Weekes' entourage, the parish-clerk and the Rev. Tufnell himself. He called for votes against.

The 18 radicals were in a corner. They were being asked to vote on a motion that had already been decided. It was totally out of order. They kept their hands down.

'Carried unanimously,' declared the curate and signed the minute amidst the rejoicings of the pro-lobby. The radicals considered their position. They placed a protest motion on the grounds of the procedures being illegal. It achieved nothing. The sale would go ahead. This time the establishment had triumphed.

The next clash was the annual meeting to set the church-rate charged on all but the poorest parishioners. The previous year's rate of threepence (1¼p) in the pound, had raised over £50: important income for the parish church. [4]

Hurst now had a Wesleyan Methodist Chapel as well as the chapel on the old Royal Oak complex. Families had choice in their place of worship. Those who preferred the chapels objected to paying a rate to the Church of England. They signed a petition seeking redress. The radicals decided to champion the dissenters.

The new church-rate would be set at the evening vestry announced for the end of July at the workhouse before the farmers' corn harvest began. The news spread.

An unusual number of people turned up for the meeting. Mr. Borrer, Mr. Jenner and Dr. Weekes sat together a little apart from sexton Richard Davey and other stalwarts of the church. Their conversation deepened as numbers swelled – George Faithfull and Charles Sharood with Messrs. Lempriere and Rowland who prayed each Sunday at the General Baptist Chapel in Ditchling. Others never before noted at a vestry were there.

When Mr. Campion arrived the curate commenced the meeting and announced the business, the expediency of a church-rate. Everybody knew they had to act as conscience dictated. Opinions had to be explained lucidly. They were. Each man knew he was as right as his opponent was wrong.

When the exchanges ended, churchwarden Mr. Packham proposed a threepenny (1¼p) rate for the coming year, Rev Tufnell asked for a show of hands. 13 were in favour. The opponents felt quiet satisfaction, there were 14 of them: victory for the dissenters. [5]

It was a church disaster. For both the rector away in Kent and the curate in the thick of things, the loss of local income was an impossible situation that could not endure.

The radicals were not finished. The Brighton Patriot engaged itself in parish affairs and accused the curate of entering labourers' cottages and literally poking his nose up the chimney to see what was hanging there. If there was bacon, he tried to persuade the housewife to sell it and buy cheaper food. If he found a meat pudding in the pot, he lectured the wife for extravagant and luxurious living. [6]

The curate was determined to help and guide the labouring family all he could. To this end he devised a Society for the Encouragement of Industry and Prudence: a savings club with a difference, open only to men in trade or agricultural labour. It had the financial backing of parish landowners Campion, Borrer, Dodson, Weekes and Marchant.

Members paid a weekly subscription; a shilling (5p) for 20 year olds, 6d. (2½p) for 14 year olds or 3d. (1¼d) from parents paying for younger boys. Each three years they would be credited with a premium from the backers until they reached the age of 27 when they withdrew their savings plus interest and received a silver watch engraved on the back: 'Industry and Prudence'.

There was just one penalty clause. If you married, you lost your savings which were distributed among the other members. For the labourer with resolve the society had potential, for those smitten by love there could be problems.

The Patriot vented its ire. It was an immoral and un-Christian like scheme. Never would the independent farmer of 70 years back have condescended to pay his men from the poor-rates. In those days the labourer had his comfortable house, his garden, his pig and his beer barrel. It was the heavy taxes imposed for wars that stripped the labourers of domestic comfort. Now they were reduced to living in hovels: their young men penalised if they desired to marry. The tiller-of-the-soil had passions, strong and uncontrollable, driving him to seek unlawful consort where only he could find it – in the society of the depraved and vicious. And the young women huddled off to servitude in the towns became the victims of its crimes and finally sought a refuge in the stews. Thus was the reverend curate responsible for the downfall of his young parishioners. [7]

Samuel Goodman Meets
The Marquis of Worcester

Samuel Goodman had a newsworthy encounter in London one evening with one of his passengers on the Times Coach. The passenger was the Marquis of Worcester who commuted regularly between Brighton and London on Parliamentary business. He was well known as an accomplished coachman accustomed to driving whichever coach he used.

As the marquis boarded the coach for the journey home, he asked to take the reins. Mr. Goodman refused him. The marquis explained his credentials and Samuel Goodman explained his own position. The Times was his coach. He was responsible for passenger safety. He would drive.

The marquis had to acquiesce. It angered him. His anger lasted. He resolved that Goodman should be taught a lesson.

Negotiations were begun with a London coach contractor. Soon a smart yellow coach, the Quicksilver, was advertised to leave Brighton the self-same hour as the red Times. Both would complete the journey within five hours – speed was of the essence.

A bigger than usual crowd gathered in Castle Square for the Quicksilver's inaugural run to London. There were officers of the Dragoon Guards and fashionable visitors eager to watch the new coach. And in the coachman's seat was the Marquis of Worcester himself. The lesson was about to begin.

The contest was fierce. Both the Quicksilver and the Times had crack teams. For a fortnight neither could claim the mastery but the new coach was enjoying heavy bookings.

The decisive journey was by the early morning Quicksilver from Brighton. As usual, it was a heavy booking; four inside passengers and nine outside. There was a last minute change of driver with the regular man being replaced by Mr. John Snow, the son of a Brighton coach proprietor.

The horses set off at a smart rate out of Castle Square and along the new road behind the Royal Palace. As the coach entered Marlborough Place, the pace accelerated. People turned to watch. The Quicksilver was certainly outshining its rival in a breathtaking display of horsemanship by coachman Snow.

As he guided the horses into narrower Gloucester Place, a large wagon loomed into view pulling out ahead of them. The Quicksilver's horses swerved. The offside wheels hit deep rainwater, the coach tilted, balanced briefly on two wheels and capsized. Outside passengers were hurled through the air to crash against roadside railings. Inside passengers were dragged helpless in the upturned coach until the horses could be stopped.

Onlookers rushed to help. The injured were taken to the King and Queen Inn where the landlord called upon his staff to give every help and comfort they could.

Help was certainly needed. Five people had fractures. Doctors cleansed wounds, set bones, tied up a man's broken jaw and amputated the crushed finger of a ten year old girl. John Snow, a mass of bruises from head to toe, would answer for his actions.

The Gazette saw the accident as the inevitable outcome of the dangerous mania for fast driving and hoped it would put an end to amateur stage-coach driving whether it was done by the Marquis of Worcester or by a commoner. Samuel Goodman agreed whole-heartedly. [1]

Good road manners and gentle speed were observed when over 500 Brighton radicals set out for Hurst. They had all supported Mr. Faithfull's election campaigns and were now invited for a day out at his house, Jackets. Vehicles were on the road by 6 a.m. [2]

The weather proved glorious. At Jackets there was something for everyone. The energetic could play cricket, trap-ball or quoits. A band played and there were large grounds to wander through with a wonderful view across the Sussex Weald. Mr. Faithfull moved around his guests ensuring his hospitality was being enjoyed by them all.

At three o'clock, the band led the guests to a field nearer the village where huge marquees had been erected. From the corners hung welcoming banners of blue silk lettered in gold. Inside were festoons of flowers and evergreens. White clothed tables were laden with food.

The guests took their places and commenced the feast. At its close they were invited to line up and walk through the village street. It was an impressive sight, 500 visitors preceded by the band. As they passed the curate's house they sang 'Rule Britannia', perhaps not realizing they were singing to make him fully aware of the immense support the radicals could call upon.

The song sung, they marched back to the dinner marquees for sherry and Mr. Faithfull's address. By the time he finished speaking, the bottles were virtually empty with just enough left to toast success to the Brighton Patriot.

The evening finished with games and dancing watched by a growing crowd of villagers. As night closed, the guests departed for Brighton.

The next evening was an open invitation for all the Hurstperpoint poor to attend and enjoy themselves. The evergreens and flowers remained, the white cloths were on the table and almost 400 villagers sat down for a meal of beef and strong beer to the background music of the Hurst band.

Afterwards, old men enjoyed their pipes, the women enjoyed a leisured chat and the younger ones enjoyed dance and flirtation. The evening finally over, everyone gave three cheers for Mr. Faithfull and returned home happily appreciative of his generous hospitality.

In the morning there was further proof of his benevolence as he went about the village distributing gifts of cotton and flannel cloth to the poor.

At the Horticultural Society's August show it was the curate who was able to offer practical support. When the last of the cottagers' prizes had been presented the curate congratulated everyone, made a short exhortation for them to renew their efforts, and then made his great announcement. Through the generosity and kindness of Mr. Borrer, a field was being set aside to provide allotment gardens for labourers.

Members were delighted. The labourers would quit the infamy and vice of the beer shops in order to cultivate their allotments to provide food for the family and satisfaction for themselves. Rev. Tufnell and Mr. Borrer should be congratulated.

The only dissenting voice came from the Brighton Patriot which calculated Mr. Borrer as reaping an annual £20 in rent, far more than the field's real value. It was the poor providing for the wealthy.

Mr. Borrer had agreed to five acres being used at an annual rental of £1 per quarter-acre. Provided the men manured their plots, kept the paths free of weeds and did not smoke their pipes, they could cultivate the land in whatever way they felt best. There would be an overseer of allotments to ensure good husbandry, Mr. Henry Muzzell.

Word of the allotments spread. Requests for places were made to Henry Muzzell. The curate arranged an official hand-over where the applicants could stand by their selected plot and thoroughly satisfy themselves it was what they wanted. This was going well when rain began.

The rain threatened to soak the lot of them. The curate suggested they retire to the rectory to shelter from the elements and drink to the venture with a glass of hot elder wine. They cheerfully complied and one happy applicant quipped they were bound for success because what better omen could they have than a good shower of rain?

Henry Muzzell was again to the fore at the vestry's September meeting, held in church because the workhouse had been made over to the Union. A new vestry clerk was to be appointed. For 40 years the post had been held by an Ellis, first Charles and then his son William. Both had been exemplary. The vestry trusted that the new clerk would continue in like manner. They had one candidate in mind, the man who had shown ever increasing integrity and understanding of parish matters, Henry Muzzell. His appointment was a unanimous decision.

Within a month, the assistant overseer's post was also vacant because Billy Heaver became responsible to the Cuckfield Union as relieving officer for the Hurstperpoint District under the new Poor Law Amendment Act. Henry Muzzell willingly accepted the position. He would now have to find work for the unemployed, keep account of flint production and sales, undertake all necessary parish journeys and, above all, keep the parish accounts in order. For this he would receive £40 per annum plus expenses and allowances for journeys. Henry's years of unstinting service were having their reward.

Dr. Richard Weekes, who had once written so forcibly to the Poor Law Commissioners advocating central workhouses, found himself caught by the side effects of the Amendment Act in his role as landlord. Because vestries could no longer give rent relief, he had to take his own action against two non-payers, James Hazelgrove and William Lewry.

Both were way behind with their rent. Each had received a letter from Dr. Weekes' lawyer warning that bailiffs would be sent in to seize household belongings if payment was not made. No money had been paid.

Two bailiffs were sent from Brighton to take the necessary action. The men at first had difficulty locating Hazelgrove's High Street address. They were directed to a narrow alley opposite Dr. Weekes' Mansion House. It led to a yard behind a shop. There they found his home, a small tenement comprising a cellar, ground floor room and first floor bedroom. The floors were bare and there was no ceiling. A small latticed window was the only source of light. [3]

When the men announced their business, Mrs. Hazelgrove was distraught. Her husband was a good hay trusser but there was little work for him. She had six children to feed with hardly any money coming in. What with her being in child again, she had struggle enough to cope and the extra worry was more than she could take.

The bailiffs were appalled at the poverty around them. On the floor upstairs were two chaff mattresses, two chaff pillows, three old blankets and a rug coverlet. There was not one item of furniture in the room.

They returned downstairs. The complete ground floor furniture would have to go. Even then it would raise hardly £1: the debt was £1 12s. 0d. (£1.60).

Mrs. Hazelgrove complained bitterly. Her husband had offered 6s. 0d. (30p) the previous week, only for Dr. Weekes to insist the whole debt should be cleared.

The men were lost for words. If they took everything, they would be responsible if the woman became ill. If they did nothing, they were answerable to Dr. Weekes.

Mrs. Hazelgrove hinted at a solution by explaining that she had sent the lawyer's letter to Mr. Faithfull. He had told her he would never stand by and see her thrown out of her home.

Mr. Faithfull was consulted. He suggested a petition be taken to the main houses. Apart from Dr. Weekes' own Mansion House, the nearest place was the rectory. The Rev. Tufnell contributed a shilling (5p). Another 31 were needed. The bailiffs gained one more. They returned to Mr. Faithfull and explained the position. He paid off the debt and instructed the men to replace Mrs. Hazelgrove's property.

It was now the turn of William Lewry to receive a visit. His was a better home. In past days the furniture had been quite respectable. Even now, a selection of it would easily raise the £2 4s. 0d. (£2.20) owing in rent.

William declared it a harsh judgement. He was a day labourer earning barely enough to keep body and soul together. He never visited the beer shops and the only time he had enjoyed a real meal recently was when he had taken his family to Mr. Faithfull's feast. And for that one occasion the curate had warned him he would no longer qualify for the rector's bread distribution at Christmas.

Mr. Faithfull's name again. The bailiffs sensed something of a plot. Were they on a fool's errand? Was Mr. Faithfull going to step in as benefactor again?

Mr. Faithfull had a second visit. Again he provided the necessary money. Dr. Weekes received his rent. The bailiffs went home to Brighton.

The Brighton Patriot reported the incident. Richard Weekes had been highlighted as a heartless landlord exploiting the defenceless; a 'Builder of hovels for the parish poor' putting as many as four families into one house. Into the hands of such men were the paupers delivered now that the vestry could no longer give rent relief. [4]

Mr. Faithfull was about to have his own integrity tested. The toll-road trustees were making a second attempt to change the toll-gates. The revised plan would keep the toll-gate by the White Horse and place a new one between the village and Danny Lane some quarter of a mile nearer than the previous suggested site. Tolls would be unavoidable whether travellers headed north, south, east or west.

People knew Mr. Faithfull had been instrumental in preventing the previous scheme and his opposition was expected again. To the surprise of many, he made no protest and the gate was moved. [5]

The Brighton Guardian seized the chance to attack Faithfull. Hurst people could scarcely put their noses out of the village without paying a toll while Mr. Faithfull, mighty Mr. Faithfull, paid nothing because the new position of the gate between his home and the village meant he would incur no extra cost whatever for the journey to his office in Brighton. Where was the champion of the village now? Mr. Faithfull was shining in his true light.

Before the dust could settle on the toll-gate issue, another one was raised. The church was still having to function without church-rate income. Rev. Tufnell knew it could not continue. He determined to rectify the matter.

At the Sunday Divine Service, notice was read of a meeting to be held in church at 10 a.m. Thursday morning to rescind the previous order against making a church-rate and to set a new one. The congregation noted the time. Non-attending dissenters were at an acute disadvantage. [6]

There was determined lobbying on behalf of the church. All who could possibly manage were urged to attend. English Corney the anxious wheelwright, Adam Adams the new landlord of the White Horse, Henry Pierce a devout carpenter, and the inevitable Henry Muzzell all gave their word.

Thursday was wet, a dreary day heavy with the threat of thunder. The dutiful churchmen walked through the rain to cast their vote. Of the opposing force, there was but one representative. Undismayed, he spoke for his beliefs and moved that a church-rate for the established church should not be made compulsory upon men of a different persuasion. Nobody moved to second his motion.

Churchwarden Mr. Packham proposed a rate of threepence (1¼p) in the pound. Mr. Jenner seconded it and the inhabitants raised dutiful hands in support. The church income was secure.

The dissenters were taken to task for not having attended the meeting but they were adamant it was not the end. The setting of a rate did not mean the money would be forthcoming. Dissenters would never pay; it was a matter of conscience. [7]

The curate also had a matter of conscience for Hurst parishioners to consider. He asked them to contribute to a special subscription being made throughout the kingdom to help ease the great suffering being experienced by a section of the community in Ireland. Everyone should be as generous as possible. Lord Sheffield had subscribed £100.

Hurst's lords of the manor did their part with both Mr. Campion and Mr. Borrer giving £10. Rev. Tufnell himself gave £5 and others were equally supportive. The money was needed to help relieve the terrible hardships being suffered by clergymen of the Established Church in Ireland where Irishmen were refusing to pay their tithes.

The dissenters of Hurst, sensitive as they were to the needs of others, did not feel their conscience pricked.

Edward Oram Enjoys an Evening Drink

Edward Oram did experience an unfamiliar sensation akin to conscience. It happened during a rare evening he was able to spend in Adam Adams' White Horse Inn. It was not that he started with any intention of being public spirited. He was just there at the crucial time.

Edward was making the most of his opportunity. He doubted he would be drinking there the next night, the root cause being that he did not have work often enough – and being an illiterate parish-child he was not likely to. He still had brushes with the authorities, just as he had done many years before when the beadle enticed him out of the workhouse to celebrate Guy Fawkes. Even now, his periodic lack of earnings drove him back to the Union Workhouse, much as he loathed the place. But that night he was in funds so he sat enjoying his drink.

Across the room, two men sat playing cards, keeping themselves to themselves and conversing in undertones. Edward was certain they were strangers – and that meant they were suspicious characters probably up to no good. He made a mental note of them, just in case.

At nine o'clock, the card players left. They headed north to William Hallett's farm close by Little Park. They had visited there the previous afternoon, one calling at the farmhouse and the other crossing the field by the hen-run to meet together at the far side and disappear east towards Wickham lands. A farm worker had watched them closely.

Now the pair had the darkness to themselves. They crossed the field to the hen-house, loosened a board below the window, reached inside and withdrew the bolt. Seven hens and three cockerels were lifted from the perch. From there, the men visited Wickham Farm and collected another 11 birds. It was time to go: a heavy load and a long walk back to Brighton.

In the morning there were two angry farmers. William Hallett's man recounted seeing the strangers. He had watched them well and gave good descriptions; clothing, height and appearance.

Mr. Hallett wasted no time. He knew as well as anyone that the rogues' probable destination was Brighton and that they would waste no time disposing of the birds. He rode to Brighton himself and reported the theft. Two constables were detailed to search for the men.

The likely places for chicken sales in the centre of town proved fruitless. The constables widened the search. By early afternoon they had almost reached the end of their area, the boundary with Hove Parish. There, walking down Western Street towards the sea, were two likely suspects. From the descriptions, they just had to be the men. The constables decided to intercept them by going down the next road to the sea-front and back up Western Street. They were in luck.

One of the men stood inoffensively at the roadside. Nearby was a beer-shop. The constables went in.

A customer was holding a basket. In it were dead hens. The man was quietly arrested.

The other suspect had guessed what was happening and was walking from the scene. He was not quick enough.

The pair were taken to the Town Hall where they were charged with felony; Thomas Brooker and William Todman. They explained that they had bought the hens for 1s. 9d. (9p) from a man near the King and Queen Inn. They were unable to name him but they would recognize the dirty green frock he wore. The constables preferred to inspect the men's lodgings.

The lodgings were in Pimlico, an alley off the North Lane with no exit at the far end. Pimlico was home for those who had lost hope of finding anywhere better. There was no sanitation. Houses were little more than huts. Most held fishermen's families, fishermen who had fallen on bad times. Young children roamed the alley playing in a litter of fish offal. The ground was fish, the air was fish. With one way in and the same way out, there was no privacy in Pimlico. Somebody or other saw everything. [1]

Brooker lodged at 22. He had been with his friend Todman. They had left the alley together midday Monday and returned about daybreak Tuesday. Eliza May was certain of that because she too lodged at 22.

Number 22 proved an Alladin's cave. More plucked birds were in the room, and any amount of feathers in the coal-hole – duck, chicken, goose and turkey. The constables knew they had done a good day's work. These were no petty purloiners of poultry.

It just remained to identify the birds. Farmer Hallett had no hesitation. The birds might be featherless but he still knew one from its crooked comb. Two he could swear to from markings on the head and another by its five claws. It was all quite elementary.

By the time a man from Wickham had identified some of his master's birds, and Oram had identified the men as the ones in the White Horse, the pair had nothing to say.

They were held in custody until the Easter quarter sessions at Lewes. There, they stood trial on two counts of chicken theft. The verdict for both was 'Guilty'. Sentence for the first offence was 14 days solitary confinement. For the other it was another 14 days with an extra punishment for it being a second offence – seven years transportation south beyond the seas. Todman and Brooker went to the Leviathan hulk in Portsmouth to await a convict ship to Van Diemen's Land. [2]

Illustrated London News 21-2-1846 Copyright The British Library Board. All Rights Reserved

The parish poor felt themselves being transported when they went to the Union Workhouse. What they hated most was its destruction of family life. Lindfield workhouse had closed in March. Accommodation had been prepared for the boys at Hurst which still left five miles and two pairs of locked gates between parents and children. The 'Cuckfield Union' mark on the official clothing was the one unifying factor. [3]

The only acceptable thing was the Union bed. A regulation iron bedstead with flock mattress, linen sheets (changed at least once a month) and blankets was far preferable to the home conditions of families like the Hazelgroves with their bedless sleeping room.

Union clothing was better than rags but it was coarse and plainly fashioned for institutional recognition – functional and ugly. Women wore flannel petticoats and grogram gowns over black worsted stockings. Men had striped calico shirts, drugget trousers and Scotch sheeting round-frocks. To keep out inclement weather, there were rough wool 'fearnought' jackets. [4]

Food quantity and variety were carefully assessed. Breakfast was bread and gruel. Dinner was 1½ pints (¾ litre) of soup or 12 ounces (360 grams) of potato with 14 ounces (420 grams) of meat pudding – except on Friday, meatless Friday, when it was plain suet pudding. Supper was bread and 1½ ounces (45 grams) of cheese. [5]

Word got out that actual workhouse dinners consisted of pork and cabbage without either suet pudding or potato. The Cuckfield governor, William Kerby, – an ex-turnkey from Lewes prison – was so taken aback by the food that he drew the attention of the guardians to it. The guardians reminded him to attend to his duties: the medical officer knew the correct food for the workhouse. [6]

There was no deviation from the work schedule. Wheat was purchased 'in the straw' and the men threshed it. A gang walked the treadwheel powering the workhouse corn-mill. They began at 7.30 a.m. walking an hour and resting for 15 minutes until 6.00 p.m. except for their dinner break. The younger women worked the bolting-mill to sift the meal. Other men had to break a cubic yard of hard stone specially purchased for the task or to pick 3 lbs. (1½kg) of old rope, separating the strands as oakum for caulking ships. Women had to pick 1¼ lbs. (½ kg).

Most paupers were compliant but a handful refused to toe the line. Mary Tugwell was a rebel. Her first workhouse experience had been at Hurst as a seven year old with her two sisters, Frances and Ann, when their father was sentenced to a month's hard labour for neglecting his family and refusing to work. His girls had spent the month in the workhouse. It was their father's fourth sentence. Since then the girls had not known a proper home. Life had meant stretches of service as menial under-servants with intervening time in Hurst workhouse. Either way, the order of the day was submissive obedience – anything else was misconduct.

The Tugwell girls were not submissive enough. As soon as each sister neared her 15th birthday she was transferred to the Cuckfield house. There they encountered the daily dirge of oakum picking and the depression of hopeless adults. There were no allowances for teenage years. The young would learn to linger or rebel. [7]

Mary somehow teamed up with 17 year old Henry Richardson for an exciting Guy Fawkes Night escapade. They managed to let off a firework. For the authorities it was an unacceptable breakdown in discipline. It led straight to the quarter sessions and punishment in Lewes house of correction. [8]

Mary returned from her imprisonment determined and resentful, liable to angry outbursts at the slightest provocation. One day as William Kerby read family prayers to the females, a shrill voice inveighed against him, loud and abusive. Others quickly joined in. Prayers ended abruptly. Mr. Kerby dealt with the troublemakers; Mary Tugwell, sister Fanny and two friends. They were taken into custody and committed to Lewes house of correction. [9]

The second imprisonment reinforced Mary's resolve. Within weeks of returning, she seemed to explode, throwing herself at Kerby and threatening to tear his heart out. He fended her off and sent for the constable.

As the constable removed Mary from the workhouse, three of her friends tried to free her. They were taken as well for using indecent language and trying to release a prisoner in his custody.

They all appeared at the quarter sessions. Mary's friends were sentenced to 21 days hard labour. Mary was fined £5 and had to find two sureties of £5 to keep the peace. She was penniless, and friendless too when it came to sureties. Mary remained in prison.

The Brighton Patriot took up the case of the female paupers. It felt the workhouse governor had been a little hasty in his manner to them. Paupers they may be, but they were not bereft of feeling. An end needed to be put to the continual uproar, obscenity and annoyance that was said to prevail. To that end the wishes of the ratepayers should be met by setting up a committee of enquiry.

The Brighton Gazette leapt to defend Mr. Kerby. The cause of the disturbances had been four young girls whose conduct was of the most disorderly nature singing indecent songs, inciting the inmates to open rebellion and threatening the life of the governor. [10]

Secure within Lewes house of correction, Mary knew nothing of newspaper reports. She spent many weeks inside awaiting sureties who would never appear. At last the court decided to accept her promise to be of good behaviour. They returned her to the workhouse.

Although Mary may have made the promise in good faith, she soon slipped into her old ways, speaking her mind and refusing to work regardless of the governor's attempts to control her. The Board of Guardians wrote to the Commissioners for help explaining that Mary Tugwell's behaviour was beyond correction either by the workhouse master or by the infliction of heavier punishment at the magistrates' court. She constantly gave way to violent and ungovernable passion, used outrageous and abominable language, refused to work and seriously alarmed the other inmates. All attempts to bring her to her senses had failed. The guardians felt their only recourse was to exclude her from the workhouse. Could they do so?

Back came the answer. The board could not refuse relief to a destitute person on grounds of misconduct. At the first indication of disruptive behaviour, the governor should restrain the woman and reduce her food allowance in accordance with the rules laid down for such occasions. Mary Tugwell must remain in the workhouse.

Despite the handful of troublesome inmates, the Union Board felt they had achieved an efficient house. There was suitable accommodation for those who needed it, an equitable work schedule and clearly defined rules to ensure cleanliness and good order.

Yet, such was the class of people they were dealing with, the measures failed to ensure good health. Fever broke out in the Cuckfield House. The guardians took the extreme measure of sanctioning the expense of medicinal fumigants for all male inmates – a pipe of tobacco morning and night. For once there was full co-operation. The medical officer also advised that the admission of any pregnant woman would put her life at risk. A room at Hurstperpoint was quickly adapted as a lying-in room. [11]

Hurst with its mix of younger children and aged inmates was spared the disruptions of Cuckfield.

Provisions were still put out to competitive tender. A Brighton butcher beat the local shops to the meat contract by providing beef 'clods and stickings' with suet at 4d. per pound (1¾p per ½kg) and 'neck and breast' of mutton at 6d (2½p). Dissenter Henry Rowland at his shop on the old Royal Oak site pared his prices and won the groceries contract with 3rd quality butter at 9½d per pound (4p per ½kg), flat Dutch cheeses and yellow soap equally priced at 5½d (2¼p), best bacon and bastard sugar at 6d (2½p) – or raw sugar ¾d dearer – and Chinese congou tea at 4s. 7d. (23p). For workhouse lighting, he provided best dipped-candles at 6s. 2d. (31p) per dozen. Hurst inmates would not dine on pork and cabbage.

Billy Heaver could leave much of the discipline to the schoolteachers Mr. and Mrs. Bubb who had been appointed when the Lindfield workhouse closed. The Bubbs had proved eminently suited to obtaining the best from the children. So efficient was their teaching that Rev. Tufnell in his position as chaplain to the workhouse felt able to arrange an open day to demonstrate the school's achievements. Guests from the Union's 15 parishes were invited to an examination of the scholars.

Mr. and Mrs. Bubb had been preparing their 53 pupils for the big day. Also on view, was the new Work Shed that had been provided for the boys. Built of fir poles and well slated, it was excellent value costing no more than £4 to erect. [12]

The Work Shed impressed everybody, efficiency in both finance and construction; poor-law administration at its best. Would the education prove as efficient?

The weather was fine enough for the examination to take place in the fresh air of the boys' play area. First, 10 boys and 10 girls stood up to read from the New Testament. The chaplain asked his guests to choose the reading they would like from four chapters of St. John by the boys and from two chapters of St. Luke by the girls. The choice made, the company settled to the lengthy readings. They were impressed. The children – offspring of paupers, every one of them – spoke accurately and distinctly, their voices showing just the right amount of expression, sensibility and feeling; a remarkable achievement on the part of schoolmaster Bubb.

The Rev. Tufnell then invited the guests to inspect the reading books. The variety bewildered them. How had the children done it? The Rev. Tufnell explained. The readers had learnt it all by heart. It was the vogue! An excited buzz went round the guests.

Next was arithmetic – again a modern approach, and on very practical lines affording much amusement to both children and guests.

Fifteen children then underwent a rapid-fire questioning on the collects for the whole Christian year. The answers came without any hesitation or confusion. Not a mistake was made even of a petty kind.

To the polite applause of the guests, each of the 24 children who had participated was given a copy of the New Testament and Marsh's Catechism of the Collects subscribed by the S.P.C.K.

As a more gastronomic reward, every child in the school was given a plum cake for immediate consumption. The expressions of delight on those pauper children's faces were a picture to behold. How the guests themselves delighted in it.

When the last crumbs had been demolished, the guests took their leave expounding on the achievements of the dedicated Mr. and Mrs. Bubb.

The Bubbs had their own reward when shortly afterwards they tendered their resignation. The Committee resolved that in consideration of the uniformly good conduct and efficiency of the workhouse schoolteachers they should be excused payment of all money still owing to the Union for their child's board at the workhouse. [13]

1836: Samuel Goodman Braves the Christmas Snow

The Hurst allotment holders had been working their plots for a year. They now had the chance to prove themselves at the first Allotment Gardens Show.

In the morning, the allotments were open for the general public to inspect. At noon, the curate and his team began judging the exhibits. There were nearly 40 prizes to award. Not until 2 p.m. were the winners announced. [1]

John Talmey found his crop of carrots almost as rewarding as his fairground gingerbread had been. Thomas Rooke, of the bell ringers verse, took firsts for his cabbages and lettuce. Most successful of all was William Bartley; best parsnips, best French beans, second finest cabbages and best tray of vegetables. Mr. Borrer presented him a special award for his indefatigable industry in achieving such a high standard throughout the allotment and keeping an exact account of expenses and receipts. William Bartley could justifiably feel proud.

Next, the vegetables were put up for sale at the bazaar where any of the parish cottagers could sell their produce.

There was fun afterwards for all who wanted it in sports, strictly without tobacco or drink, held on Mr. Marchant's Home Field. After the sports, came dinner. This was an event with no losers; mouth watering portions of beef and veal with large helpings of hard-pudding followed by plum pudding – and then hot elderberry wine to toast the day's benefactors one by one. At 7 p.m. proceedings came to an end. Rev. Tufnell felt content that his efforts for the poor were bearing fruit.

John Marchant was having less success with Little Park Farm. His efforts were continually thwarted by the temporary loan he had accepted from William Borrer. It had dogged him for years. William Borrer had passed away peacefully but not the loan. Now £7000 was due to heir Nathaniel Borrer and there was no escape. [2]

Mr. Marchant sought the advice of solicitor Edward Duke in Brighton. The unpalatable conclusion was that more land had to go on the market. Mr. Marchant advertised 30 acres (12 hectares) opposite the church. The speculators swooped. [3]

The sale still left a deficit of over £4000. Mr. Duke helped negotiate a new loan. East and West Edgerly were now in pawn to Mr. John Duke! Little Park Farm needed a run of good years.

That year's corn harvest did nothing to help. Poor growth in the straw boded ill and the August weather was grim. The yield was not as low as feared but there was certainly not going to be any surplus. The farmers' only consolation was that the price of wheat would rise.

The poor weather continued into the autumn. An evening of wind and rain at the end of November increased through the night. The wind boomed along the streets and around houses. Loose fittings rattled and banged. Animals huddled together in the fields. Twigs and small branches showered the ground. [4]

By daybreak, everybody knew they were experiencing the worst hurricane they could remember. Tiles slid from roofs to smash shrapnel shards across the roadways. Chimneys crashed. Earth round trees heaved and buckled as oak, ash and elm fell, wrenched from the ground with chunks of clinging soil scouring deep pocks where the roots had been.

When the storm subsided, there was a clear sky – and widespread damage everywhere.

The Brighton papers reported disaster across the county from Chichester to Hastings. Dr. Dodson's Lewes agent informed him that one of his Hurst lodges had been blown down. The other damage to his property was not serious. [5]

The general state of the land left the poor in a worse position than ever. Fields could not be ploughed. Grubbing, ditching and hedging were suspended. There was little wheat or clover to keep the threshers employed.

James Hazelgrove, the hay trusser, found it particularly hard. Every lost day reflected in less food for his family. With seven children to feed, even a full week's wage of 11 or 12 shillings (55 or 60p) was inadequate. The previous year, George Faithfull had plucked him from the bailiffs. Now, with virtually no work, and the Union unable to allow out-relief, his family seemed doomed to Poor Law classification. [6]

By December Hazelgrove's position was so serious that the Union Board wrote to the Poor Law Commissioners requesting permission to give out-relief. The letter was passed to Assistant Commissioner Hawley.

Assistant Commissioner Hawley examined the case thoroughly. By dint of careful research, he came to the conclusion that the ordinary hay trusser would tie two tons a day at 2s. 6d. (12½p) per ton giving a weekly wage as high as 30s. 0d. (£1.50). The case did not require the least relaxation of the rule. The only proper course was to offer to take Hazelgrove and as many of his family as were dependent on him into the workhouse.

The Union took note and dispersed the family in accordance with Poor Law rules. The five children not needing their mother's nursing were put in Hurstperpoint workhouse. The parents and the two youngest children were taken to Cuckfield where James was assigned to the men's quarters.

It meant Christmas in the workhouse – each part of the family in their own section – although it would include a better meal than at home if the gentlemen of the district remembered to subscribe a little for the inmates to celebrate with beef and plum pudding.

That Christmas proved memorable for everyone. It began with quiet snowfall. Households awoke to a white Christmas freshly laid for their celebrations. [7]

People still needed to travel. At the Red Office in Brighton's Castle Square the Times made ready for departure to London. A chill wind blew snow flurries around the coach but passengers, driver and guard were well protected. They set off. The horses were keen to go, stages were reached on time and teams changed.

The afternoon dusk came early with gathering clouds. The strengthening wind became a gale blowing fierce and cold from the north-east. The horses were head on to driving snow.

At the outskirts of London, they passed the Brighton-bound coach whipped on by the wind in its tail but still with many uncomfortable miles ahead.

For passengers on the inward Times, the journey was nearly done. They arrived cold and cramped, thankful for the coachman's safe handling, glad to find indoor warmth.

Outside, the storm ran on. Snow gathered against houses, along streets and in the city squares. Southwards, it lay deep against the hedgerows, blotting out roads and forming ever rising drifts. The Brighton coach moved slower and slower until on the Downs the drifts had become too deep. By Pyecombe the driver gave the reins to a passenger and rode postilion on one of the horses.

They continued in the strange snow-darkness to reach a silent Castle Square just before midnight. All hopes of seeing them had been abandoned but the guard's blast on his horn brought a quick response and everyone was found shelter.

The mail coach through Cuckfield found the going even worse. All other coaches were safely in and people had been asleep for hours. The coach at last passed the Stone Pound gate and began the ascent of Clayton Hill. And there it remained, caught in drifted snow stacked almost as high as the horses. It was 4.00 a.m. The coachman and his solitary passenger bedded down as best they could. The guard determined to get the mails through and set off on one of the horses.

When day broke, the coachman and his passenger managed to turn the coach and make their way back to the Friars Oak Inn. There they were happy to stay.

The guard was still struggling towards Brighton. Not until 1.00 p.m. did he arrive. He was in a state of utter exhaustion. They bathed him and put him to bed.

He had got his mails through but it had come near to costing him his life.

Boxing-day proved a 'No Go' day for any stoic stubborn enough to try. Mail-men set out from Brighton and had to give up five hours later at Pyecombe – at less than two miles per hour they were never going to reach London.

The next morning, Samuel Goodman determined to venture from home and try the eight miles into Brighton. Travel by carriage was out of the question, it had to be horse-back. It was a long ride that gave no pleasure apart from the satisfaction of arriving.

He at once saw to it that the main road clearance was speeded up. Men were put to work with shovels. Within days, a sufficient clearway was made. A team of six horses was hitched to the Times and the morning coach to London set off. The snow was negotiable.

When Carey Borrer went down from Hurst on New Year's Day, there were still long runs of snow banked as high as the carriage on each side.

Whilst men had cleared snow from the roads, the snow had cleared men from the fields. Farm labourers were forced to seek help from the Cuckfield Union. On the worst Friday, there were 60 able-bodied men wanting out-relief. Out-relief was refused but each went home assured he could bring his family into the house the very next day. They knew what that meant.

Only five families took up the offer. The men were detailed to the corn-mill – at which news three returned home.

Mr. Hawley was delighted with the outcome. He reported back to the Commissioners explaining how, of 60 applications, only two proved genuine requests. The severity of the weather had afforded the finest opportunity for listing the excellence of the workhouse system. A more satisfactory proof could not have been offered the guardians. It was a well won battle against pauperism.

Those sentiments were not shared by the parishes. The weather dictated life. Clear calm days ended in rich sunsets that foretold mornings of numbing cold. When winds blew, they blasted more frozen air from the east. In town and village alike everyone shivered but the poor shivered more than most and the gentry of the area dug in their pockets to provide succour for the suffering.

Danny House gave food, bedding and clothes. Public subscription raised money for bread, soup and fuel. The bread was given out from Henry Muzzell's house several times a week: 110 loaves needed each time. [8]

Carey Borrer spent a complete morning at the rectory ensuring the 80 families collecting coals had their proper quota. He was down from Oxford, freshly qualified to minister in the Church. He had studied at Oriel College under the influence of Newman's controversial preaching and Pusey's crusade for the Holy Eucharist to be celebrated every Sunday. Carey hoped to have his own parish before long where he could introduce the style of worship that he found so stimulating at Oxford. For the moment he was determined to play his part in Hurst giving help wherever he could.

He led pre-breakfast prayers at the workhouse, except the morning another inch (2½cm) of snow fell, read to the old men and inspected the boys in their schoolroom. He visited the National School for an hour at a time ensuring himself all was in good order. When the chance came, he gave advice to the cottagers. If school-aged children were at home he urged the mother to enter the girls in the penny club and to send the boys to school. He handed out soup tickets to those in need, read to the elderly and visited the sick.

Influenza was rife: children and adults miserable in bed with pains in the head, pains in the bones and pains in the bowels. Carey took them nourishing rice pudding and offered kindly words of comfort. Two of the women were so ill they were taken to the Royal Sussex Hospital. Carey visited them there and to his extreme pleasure found everything as comfortable as possible. [9]

Rev. Tufnell used funds set aside for the sick from the collections made at the monthly celebration of Holy Eucharist. The money provided greatcoats for 15 of the oldest men – prevention was far better than cure. A special presentation was arranged.

The men gathered in the rectory hall and the curate distributed the coats. Each man put his on, thick, warm and comforting with a cape down to the elbows. The curate felt a comfortable glow too; such a worthy group of aged labourers, all enveloped in dark coats with high stand-up collars to their very ears so that nothing of the men appeared but their venerable heads. What a pleasing sketch it would make.

The curate satisfied himself by inviting the men into the parlour. When they were all seated at the table, elder wine and cakes were handed round. He led a discussion about the sacrament and then they got on to personal anecdotes and memories of days gone by.

Grandfather White proudly declared how in all his years he had never once slept outside Hurst. His tale was countered by the man whose early days had been in the employment of a lady fond of travelling. In her employ he reckoned he must have slept in every county in England and pretty well every large town.

Grandfather White was not put out. His mate alongside him had been ploughing on the same farm as him 50 years before, nimble as could be, yet here he was now having to reach out for his crutch to help him along. Who would have thought it?

When the tales had run their time, the curate suggested the men should make sure nothing had accidentally slipped into their pockets before setting off home. They were a little taken aback at first until one reckoned there was something 'wruxelling' in his pocket and another reckoned he felt 'soment' in his whereupon they each discovered a package of tea tucked deep down to take home. What a man their curate was!

The next Tuesday, another 132 of the curate's poor had gifts; blanket, sheet or length of flannel, whichever was requested.

The bad weather meant workless weeks for the farm labourers. Unemployment remained rife and the excellence of the workhouse system was suddenly in doubt. The Cuckfield Union Board were so overwhelmed by the numbers going to them that they resorted to giving cash and flour as out-relief.

The Poor Law Commissioners wanted a more positive strategy offering a permanent solution for the labourer and easing the unemployment problem. They instructed the Union Board to promote the opportunities on offer for people to move north to the industrial towns of Lancashire. Interested families would be found work there and know the terms of employment before they went. The only restriction was that applicants should have large families because the main openings were for younger employees.

Boys and girls aged 9 could start in the wool, cotton and flax factories at 1s. 3d. (6p) a week. The 9 to 13 year olds worked only eight hours a day. They quickly learnt what they had to do and most liked it. After work they had two hours at school. The weekly wage rose annually to 8s. 0d. (40p) for 18 year old boys and 7s. 0d. (35p) for girls. The father would normally not have work in the factory. He would be hired as a labourer, carter or porter depending on his capabilities. His pay would be from 10 to 13 shillings (50p to 65p). [10]

The northern houses were much better built, of brick or stone. Generally, they had a sitting room, a back-kitchen fitted with an oven and boiler, and two or more sleeping rooms. Rents tended to be higher but coal, clothing and food were all cheaper.

A family had only to let their parish know they wished to go and everything would be arranged for them.

There might have been a better response if the local papers had not carried details of a Parliamentary Report on conditions in the north. It told of men being refused relief because they did not send their young children to the mill, of children too tired for evening school and of others in the mills 16 hours a day, beaten to keep to their work and growing deformed by the tasks they had to do. Nothing about factory life seemed good and the house description was tainted by tales of overcrowding in shared rooms.

None of the Cuckfield Union men risked the move north. Sussex farm life was what they knew and they preferred to stick where they were and hold on for better days.

The severe weather continued through March causing crises in agriculture and trade. In Parliament ministers were reported on the verge of resigning: Sir Robert Peel standing by to form a new Government. [11]

It was mid April before warmer winds saw the end of the snow. The White Christmas was at last over.

9: 1830: From her vantage point on the coach, Mrs. Gorringe had views of her native Sussex
that she had never seen before and would never see again.

10: 1831: Mr. Campion was a member of the East Sussex Hunt.
When the hunt assembled it was a private affair. The chase was public spectacle.

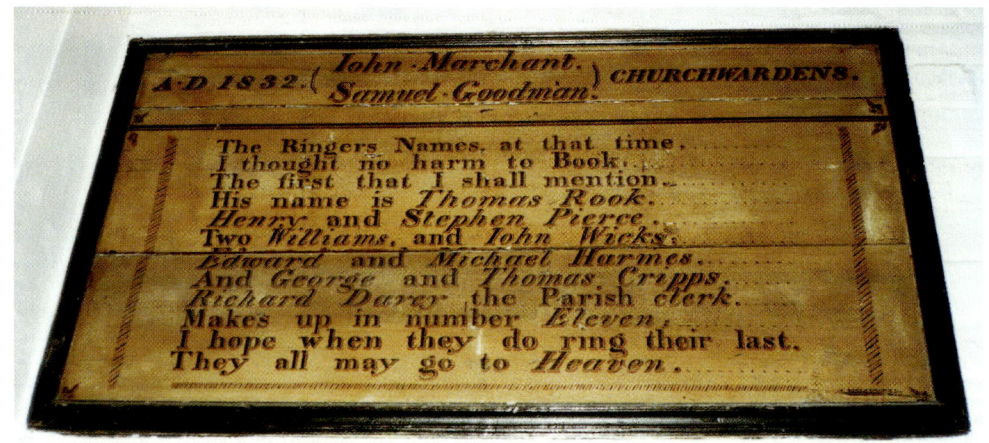

11: 1833: The bell-ringers verse named eleven men; fellmonger, carpenter, flint digger, workhouse barber, day labourers and parish clerk.

12: 1833: Richard Davey was sexton at St. Lawrence Church.
He sang the service responses to Rev. Tufnell and kept the churchyard in spotless order.

13: 1835: Stage-coach proprietors stressed the comfort and elegance of their London/Brighton vehicles: good springs, fine lines and padded seating.

14: 1835: The yellow Quicksilver coach was introduced as a direct challenge to Samuel Goodman's red Times. Both did the London run within five hours.

15: 1835: Edward Oram sat drinking at the White Horse.
Across the room, two men sat playing cards and conversing in undertones – suspicious characters.

16: 1836: Boxing Day snow made conditions impossible. Mail-men set out from Brighton only to give up
five hours later at Pyecombe – at that speed they would never reach London.

1837: Dr. Weekes Builds
a Grand Hotel

Rev. Tufnell was again doing his best for the Hurst working man at the annual meeting of the East Sussex Agricultural Association. He was under pressure to justify being allowed £5 for prizes whereas other parishes had only £3.

He explained how in Hurst there were 20 allotments. They were well cultivated and one man, William Bartley, deserved particular mention. He had a large family and rented a quarter acre. On it he kept two pigs, cropped 40 bushels (1.5 kilolitres) of potatoes, supplied his family with vegetables and grew enough beans and peas to pay his rent. It was a delight to see crops flourishing on that man's small plot. This was the reason for Hurst's extra money: it was needed for awards at the annual Allotment Show.

The noble chairman declared that other parishes wishing to do likewise should send in rules before the end of May. He moved business on.

In June, the Association held their shearing competition at Firle Park. The sheep were from one of the renowned Southdown flocks bred by Mr. Ellman. 34 men were competing including William and John Walder who had walked over from Hurst. Each had to shear five sheep efficiently and within a good time.

Spectators and judges alike were impressed by the skill shown; men shearing a sheep in less than 30 minutes with hardly a blemish throughout the pens. By three o'clock most had finished. Neither of the Walders gained a prize but both were content with the half-crown (12½p) awarded to non-winners. [1]

In December, members gathered at the Star Inn in Lewes for the distribution of the year's prizes. Rev. Tufnell was given the opportunity to speak. He advised the prize winners to put what they could into the savings bank. He told them of the one in Hurst used by 25 young men. There the children too were saving, girls as well as boys. Perhaps it was as little as a penny (½p) a month but it all added up and for the boys it would hopefully go towards a future apprenticeship for them. Not only did they save, they used their time profitably. [2]

To prove his point, the curate exhibited a piece of well finished straw plait made in Hurstperpoint from British grass. There, labourers' boys at the National School went to the workhouse each afternoon from 1.00 p.m. to 5.00 p.m. to be profitably employed learning the art of plaiting. Another poor girl, crippled by fever, had in three years made plait to the value of £16. The curate gave each of the labourers printed directions for making it. He sat down. Prize giving could begin.

The Earl of Chichester rose to present the prizes. With each was a certificate signed by himself and mounted in a varnished oak frame, perfect for display in the cottage.

First, the earl impressed upon the winners how the award gave them greater influence among persons of their rank in life. By being placed higher, they were in the sight of God responsible for their good conduct and should be an example to their neighbour. His homily complete, he called the first man forward.

The curate's nominees were among the prize winners. James White gained one for long service and another for placing three of his girls into respectable service at an early age. Two girls gained theirs for being farm house servants more than five years, and three of the 'Under-16' boys for being permanently employed in agriculture more than three years. Rev. Tufnell was a happy man.

Pleased as he was to provide encouragement for his Hurst labourers, he felt unable to help some of the needy families. Wheelwright English Corney was a case in point. He was an independent craftsman, determined to find his own solutions to life's problems but the family was obviously going through a difficult time.

English's business had started well enough and he had enjoyed added success with the cricket club. Trade had later fallen away. Income had been so little for so long that he finally felt forced to put his house up for sale. He placed an advertisement in The Sussex Agricultural Express. The property was an attractive investment: a new eight roomed house with dry cellarage and detached wash-houses with fine spring water obtained by an engine pump. The walled garden was well stocked with young fruit trees. In the yard there were two workshops, a wheelwright's and a smith's. [3]

The advertisement caught the eye of Nathaniel Borrer. He made English an offer and was pleased to add the place to his holdings.

English felt the sale a hard return for all his endeavours; the craftsman working himself to the bone for scant reward. For the moment, he was back on a level with the day-labourer striving to maintain dignity without recourse to vestry relief. He would do anything necessary to see the bad times through and keep free of the Union workhouse.

Dr. Richard Weekes also had some property for sale. He had invested capital in building a family hotel and posting house at the top of the new road to Cuckfield. He was convinced it would provide an excellent opportunity for returns on investment once coaches began using the London to Brighton route through Hurst.

The doctor advertised in the Brighton papers that the complete holding was to be sold by auction: a hotel with excellent stabling, two double coach houses, a detached tap room and a large garden overlooking richly wooded country. The location was in a favoured resort for visitors and others on account of the beauty and variety of the rural rides and the celebrated benefits of the air which was strongly recommended for invalids. [4]

Investors did not seem at all impressed by the potential of Dr. Weekes' property. Only a handful of buyers appeared at the auction. The hotel remained unsold. The tap room eventually opened as a beer house with Edward Harmes as landlord. No more would he rely for his income on the daily walk up Wolstonbury Hill to supervise the flint diggers.

The coach route through Hickstead satisfied Carey Borrer. His great triumph was the journey to and from London in a single day. It proved the speed and reliability of Samuel Goodman's Red Coaches: which was more than could be said of the patent steam carriage that had powered its way from London to Brighton amid a fanfare of publicity only to breakdown into a mass of immovable metal. [5]

Carey's favourite travel destination was Ireland, the land of lovely Elizabeth Orr, the lady of his dreams. When Elizabeth accepted Carey's proposal of marriage, there was great rejoicing. He would have to travel to Belfast for the wedding: what a wonderful day it would be.

On his last full day of bachelor life in Hurst, Carey rode with his father to Lewes and indulged in their hobby at the South Saxons' archery meeting. It was a good farewell. His own arrows were accurate enough for second prize, though well behind the winner. His father took a prize for the best 'gold'.

They were prizes quickly forgotten as Carey set off next morning soon after eight on the leisurely cross-country journey to Ireland. Twelve hours later he was arriving a comfortable sixty miles from Hurst at Winchester. The satisfaction of travelling at an easy pace was the lack of fatigue when the destination was at last reached. Carey appreciated it. There was no rush. [6]

He finally landed in Ireland to arrive at Belfast in good health and with time to spare. Had he been going further west to Galway, he would have stared in horror at poverty which made Hurst's workhouse seem rich. In Galway, Irishmen were labouring against famine. Potato and oatmeal were so priced out of pocket that the weakest perished, starved to death. But Galway was a world beyond Belfast. Carey knew nothing of it: for him, all was peace and tranquillity.

At last the wedding day dawned. The ceremony was a service of bliss. Carey and Elizabeth were man and wife.

After four quiet days together, they travelled back to Hurst. Not so leisurely this time; coach to Dublin and a boat across to Liverpool where they entrusted themselves to the new experience – the speed, rattle and smoke of railway travel in a whirl-away journey to Birmingham. Then it was the easier sway of a horse-carriage to Oxford where Carey took his wife to listen to one of Newman's excellent sermons. And so they came down into Sussex; a final night in Horsham and then the quiet retreat of Pakyns. [7]

This time Pakyns was just a temporary haven. In a few days, Carey and Elizabeth were off again in their phaeton to London, the start of a six week continental honeymoon. At London's Tower Stairs, they boarded the Steam Navigation Company's ship Soho bound for Antwerp. [8]

The weather was fine. Carey relaxed to watch the Thames traffic as the ship threaded through a maze of masts among busy steamers plying between London and Greenwich.

Just offshore from Greenwich, lay one of the old Nelson ships, the Dreadnought. Inscribed on her was the message: 'Hospital for seamen of all Nations', whilst on the river bank stood the beautiful hospital itself which for Carey summed up British feeling towards her brave sailors. Carey had 23 hours to rejoice the exploits of Britain's sailors before Antwerp was reached, a long yet enjoyable crossing.

The next stage was far different with extremely hot weather and a packed train to Brussels. It was 24 miles of discomfort but took less than 1½ hours; they could hardly complain.

Now came the most patriotic part of their honeymoon: a trip to the battlefield of Waterloo. They visited the church where regimental tablets recalled the officers who had died there. At Mont St. Jean they left their carriage and continued by foot climbing 200 steps to the top of the specially erected memorial mound overlooking the ridge where Wellington's heroic infantry had repulsed the furious charges of Napoleon's cavalry. Thunder rolled in the distance and storm clouds gathered.

Undeterred, Carey continued to the shattered chateau of Hougoumont, its battered walls unaltered the 20 years since glorious victory. There inside the chapel was the crucifix which had caught fire during the conflict yet burnt no higher than the feet of Christ. And there Carey sheltered Elizabeth a full hour caught by the storm: a darkened sky, fierce lightning flashes, thunder claps bursting above and around them – a private 'Son et lumiere' Battle of Waterloo while the rain fell in torrents. At the end, the coachman sought them out and took them clear of the mud back to their hotel.

Although the honeymoon had much more, there was nothing to evoke comment like Waterloo. There was the frustration of a heavy cold making Carey housebound three days; the joy of a letter from Hurst and the discomfort of continental travel. Carey liked the vehicles well enough but the roads were anathema to him. They ran straight and level for miles on end and were paved – so different from the meanders of his flinted Sussex roads.

The time came to sail again for London. It was another long voyage lengthened by fog that caused them to wait offshore three hours. They eventually landed and then had the unforgettable experience of zealous customs officials: a five hour wait to have their luggage checked. They were back in England.

Their first night was spent at the famous Spread Eagle Inn. When they arose they knew they were really home: a frost-cold morning with everywhere deep in snow.

The final part of the journey was by the Sovereign coach to Hurst where at last they were able to thaw out and enjoy a Pakyns family dinner.

1838: Peter Pratt Breaks His Leg

The great event of 1838 was the coronation of Queen Victoria. Towns and villages everywhere were staging events to mark their loyalty. Hurst gentry and traders had raised a subscription to ensure the celebrations for their inhabitants were memorable. Rev. Tufnell distributed 4d. (1½p) to every poor child. [1]

The day began with the church bells pealing out. It was a peal to be repeated throughout the day. At 10.00 a.m. there was cricket on Mr. Marchant's Home Field. With such a well supported club in the village, enthusiastic participation was guaranteed.

In the afternoon, the inmates of the workhouse and the children of the National Schools were treated with buns and strong beer. The children then took their place in the parade forming up in the High Street. At the head was the standard bearer who wore a large crown of cut flowers. Next came the 12 stewards with their blue rosette badges of office, and a quartet of members from the parish benefit societies carrying their society banners. In the centre was the Hurst band. Behind it stood the children, 300 of them, each with a nosegay of flowers and a small flag.

The band began playing. The long crocodile swayed into motion. Parents joined the ever lengthening tail to march up the road as far as the absent rector's house where they wheeled right beside his garden and into the Home Field ready for the excitement of family sports.

There were races for all and wonderful prizes for some: work boxes and needle cases for the girls; shirts, caps and stockings for the boys. Women ran for lengths of calico. The men ran for money, had sack races for shoulders of mutton, blindfold races wheeling a barrow for round-frocks and jingling races climbing the pole for legs of mutton. They were prizes worth winning.

The sports were followed by music and dancing for all who still had celebratory energy to expend; a string of quadrilles and country dances to enjoy into the evening.

At last, as the shadows lengthened and a cool mist rose, children gathered with their parents for the final spectacular event, the flight of a fire balloon.

The balloon teased at its moorings. There came the moment of release and it rose gracefully into the sky – flight, a magic escape from earth, a new monarch's reign. The glee singers sang 'God save the Queen,' three hearty cheers from the crowd wished her a long and glorious reign and people slowly returned home to the realities of everyday life.

Just two days after the coronation, as if planned to welcome Queen Victoria's reign, the vestry had a barrel organ installed in the singers' gallery of the church. Rev. Carey Borrer listened to it the following Wednesday evening and liked what he heard. For him though, it was not enough. On the Saturday, he decided on a second set of tunes. Carey Borrer was a man of action. [2]

The next Home Field excitement was cricket with the Priory team from Lewes. The weather was wonderful, sun and such perfect stillness that people claimed they could hear the firing of guns at the Grand Review in Hyde Park almost 50 miles away. [3]

Hurst were out cheaply in their first innings but fast bowler Hudson kept the Lewes score almost as low. In the second innings, Hudson proved himself a free scoring batsman as well. Then he hit the ball high. A fielder went for the catch, the batsmen went for the run and there was a collision. Batsman, fielder and ball were in a heap on the ground. Lewes appealed for the wicket; the batsman had plainly impeded the fielder.

'Not out,' was the decision. It was the Hurst umpire.

Play continued. Hurst made 156. By now, the sun was setting. The game came to an inconclusive end.

It was afterwards that the collision and Hurst cricket in general were discussed among the Lewes men. The batsman should have got out of the way; the umpire was wrong. The Hurst ground's slope made runs easier to score there than anywhere else. A couple of hitters could soon have knocked off the runs. Hurst Club took players from miles away. Hudson was really a Brighton man.

Thoroughly disgruntled, the visitors set off home. Cricket had its darker side.

At Pakyns, they kept an even pattern of life in pace with the seasons. When summer's harvest was safely gathered in, Mr. Borrer and his men joined together for their Harvest Home celebration where cricket would be a unifying game with no undercurrent of bickering.

The New Inn marquee was erected in the estate grounds and at two o'clock the Pakyns labourers and the invited traders from the village sat down to the harvest feast. Nathaniel Borrer was hospitality itself at the head of the table, his workers and their families ranged before him and Mr. Bull, the steward, in supportive roll at the far end. The tables held beef, puddings, bread and beer. The families provided friendly banter and copious good cheer. People ate their full, quaffed their beer and were soon in festive mood for cricket.

Cricket provided its usual abundance of incident and amusement as unaccustomed batsmen thrilled when a wholesome whack of the ball sent fielders scurrying. At the end of cricket, they repaired to the marquee again for a session of song and loyal toasts to their master and mistress and steward and all. Steward Mr. Bull thanked the men for their sentiment and expressed his conviction that there were no better workmen than them, the honest, sober and industrious men of Pakyns. At 10 p.m. they all rose and sang 'God save the Queen' to conclude their harvest home of laughter, happiness and unity. [4]

Mr. Borrer was among the group of gentry and villagers who showed kindness when Peter Pratt had a ghastly accident whilst helping hoist timber on a wagon out at Sayers Common. When the load unexpectedly shifted, a trunk rolled onto his legs breaking both of them. He lay in agony. His workmates levered the tree away and sent for the doctor. [5]

As soon as Dr. Weekes saw the fractures he knew how serious they were. He set the bones as carefully as possible but the outlook was poor. One leg seemed beyond saving.

News of the accident spread through the village. Rumour had it that Peter Pratt was losing a leg. He would never work again. It was the end of the family: his daughter in Hurst workhouse, he and his wife apart from each other in Cuckfield.

People rallied to their aid. Peter's master rode over from Hickstead Place. A subscription was raised. Contributions were generous. Mr. Campion had independently sent the family £1. He gave another £2. Rev. Carey Borrer included the family on his visiting list and gave what comfort he could.

Time proved the doctor's skill sufficient. The bones knit together and Peter was able to keep his home but he was so badly crippled he would never be fit for a hard day's work. Labouring was the only trade he knew and he could neither read nor write. There would be difficult times ahead. Somehow or other he would overcome them. His family was not going into any workhouse.

The workhouse was the future that Samuel Stevens saw for his own family. He had a daily struggle to meet his commitments. His children were young; the girls aged seven, five, three and two. Baby brother, Henry, was just eight months.

Samuel knew that raising them on his present income was a passport to perpetual poverty with the workhouse its crowning glory. His work as shoemaker had too many families dependent on it. His only alternative was to try for a better life in South Australia. He decided to ask the vestry to help him obtain places on an emigration ship through the Poor Law Commissioners' scheme. [6]

Samuel's request was considered at the August vestry meeting. The churchwardens and overseers were far too busy with the corn harvest on their farms to attend vestry meetings. The only members present were Rev. Tufnell and Henry Muzzell. To them fell the decision whether or not to use money from the poor-rate to defray emigration expenses.

The curate was always sensitive to the needs of his poorer parishioners. Henry knew the wisdom of deference to those who held the parish reins. The decision was unanimous. £19 should be set aside for emigration. The minute was entered in the book, signed by the curate and witnessed by Henry.

Next, the Sussex agent had to be contacted in Lewes to arrange the passage. The necessary documents were completed and signed by the curate, his busy churchwardens and overseers, and by Henry Muzzell as witness. In December, Samuel Stevens would sail south.

When the sailing date approached, the family set off for London. They had been freshly fitted out with clothes and basic necessities for the voyage; bedding, two wooden bowls, two platters and two quart (litre) jugs.

At the docks they found their ship, the Buckinghamshire. She towered above them, 1500 tons of Bombay built teak, sturdy enough to give everyone confidence. It was roomy aboard although with sleeping space restricted to 6 feet by 1½ feet (2 metres by 0.5 metres) per adult there would be little privacy. The emigrants set sail for Adelaide full of optimism.

The Poor Law Commissioners themselves were having to face the problem of finding sufficient money to meet commitments. They decided a new appraisal of land values was imperative in order to increase their income from parishes. They sent a directive to vestries informing them they were to have a survey undertaken for a map of their parish on which future rate assessments would be made. [7]

Hurst landowners and farmers were aghast. A new appraisal would affect not only the poor-rate and tithes payments but also the highway and county rates. All would rise. The map needed co-ordinated opposition.

The Commissioners named a London firm of cartographers, Dixon and Maitland. The vestry declared their preferred choice, local surveyor Mr. Muzzell who had knowledge of the area and would prepare an accurate map at much less cost. Mr. Campion and a group of landowners announced via the Brighton Gazette that, as owners of more than a quarter of the land in Hurst, they would undertake the survey.

The Commissioners would not listen. Mapping had to be done on their terms. As soon as the harvest was in, Dixon and Maitland went ahead.

By Christmas the map was ready. The vestry displayed it for inspection at the New Inn. People examined it closely. To their great satisfaction, they found appalling errors; surveying inaccuracies, no allowances for differences in land quality, and people's houses over rated. It was impossible to make a fair assessment with the Dixon map.

In January, the vestry formed their own committee to ensure an accurate assessment could be made. Henry Muzzell was instructed to correct the map so that it could be forwarded to the Tithes Commissioners for acceptance. Until then, no new poor-rate could be made.

In the meantime, an uneasy peace remained between the vestry and the Poor Law Commissioners. Eventually, one or the other would have to give ground.

1839: Rev. Borrer Finds His Church Burgled

One night during the following spring, a lady roused from her bed and paced the room unable to sleep. As she looked through the window, she noticed the glow of a light in the churchyard where all should be darkness. She was at once suspicious. She could only watch and notice as much as possible. [1]

The glow was now within the church. Somebody was inside. The light flickered, died away, flickered, first in one part of the church then another as if set on visiting every last corner: an evil spirit abroad in the depths of night.

At last all was dark. The lady shuddered and returned to her bed.

Next morning, she was up early to give the alarm. She was too late. Everybody knew! St. Lawrence Church had been burgled.

Interior of St. Lawrence Church

Intruders had picked the lock of the north door and violated every inch of the interior; sacrilegious robbers searching by the light of a tallow candle that dripped their progress from pew to pew. Yet not even the huge box-pew of Danny House rewarded them. All they gained throughout the church was a surplice and a pair of silver-mounted glasses.

The material loss was small but the effect on the parish was enormous. A vestry meeting was called for the Saturday to decide what should be done.

The meeting was well attended. Opinions and suggestions abounded. Policing was not a question of numerical strength; it was one of competency. The Watch was an archaic remnant of the past and must go. An active police officer would be far more effective than a dozen watchmen merely performing the duty of walking the rounds. The parish should be modernized to the standard achieved by London's Police Force. The vestry should engage a policeman of the London Establishment. [2]

The proposal was made and carried. The Night Watch would continue but the parish would indeed employ a real policeman. A committee of nine was formed to carry out the new policy within an expenses limit of £100.

Police Constable Streatfield was appointed. The parish was safe.

Henry Muzzell was too concerned with personal sadness to take much notice of church sacrilege. His wife had died. For a second time he was having to endure a time of grief on his own; himself, his work and the solace of his garden.

He tried not to let it affect his work. In his capacity as superintendent of the Allotment Society, he arranged the last day of August for the society's show. As usual, Landlord Thomas Smith was booked to provide the New Inn marquee.

On the 30th, it was erected and set out with tables ready for the exhibitors in the morning. [3]

Dawn saw grey skies and wet ground. Men arranged their displays to the drumming of heavy rain on the canvas. Water cascaded off the marquee onto puddles that spread steadily wider through the morning.

Henry arrived with Thomas Smith to begin judging. The produce was as good as ever – and making the correct decisions remained as hard as ever. Eventually they finished but the rain kept on. Unless there was a break in the clouds, there seemed little prospect of visitors.

A steady downpour continued throughout the afternoon. Hardly anyone braved the weather to admire the displays or purchase any of the vegetables. Just before five, the show closed and the exhibitors made their way to the Rectory Barn for their show dinner.

It was as satisfying and enjoyable a meal as ever. When the cloth was removed, they sat back ready for the speeches and the presentation of prizes.

First were the toasts; the loyal toast followed by that of Nathaniel Borrer their benefactor. The chairman then rose and declared he wished to propose the health of their indefatigable superintendent of the allotments. He raised his glass: 'Henry Muzzell.' The men raised their glasses: 'Henry Muzzell'. Despite his sadness, Henry felt a glow of pride. People were drinking his health. He had come a long way.

The men listened respectfully as Mr. Borrer expounded on how wonderful an example the allotments were of society knit together for the mutual advantage of all classes; how the rich were dependent on the labourer for the cultivation of the soil, and how the poorer man relied on his more blessed fellow-creatures for many comforts in life. Next, Henry Muzzell gave his report as superintendent. He thanked Mr. Streeter of Brighton for his gift of a wagon load of dung which would be shared among four allotment holders. He then had to announce a disciplinary measure. A member had broken one of the cardinal rules of the society; he had neglected to manure his ground. The inevitable outcome was that he now forfeited his allotment. Henry Muzzell sat down.

At last the curate could award the prizes. He enjoyed a special feeling of pleasure as winning men proudly accepted their premium from the East Sussex Association for Encouraging Habits of Industry among the Working Classes. What a good influence the association had.

William Bartley swept the board with his turnips winning first and second prizes plus the bonus of a leg of mutton, the gift of Mr. Borrer. Others of the gentry had also given generously to boost the cash prizes. Best potatoes gained an eight week old pig, best carrots a leg of beef, best onions a shoulder of mutton. Finally, every allotment holder received a small Dutch cheese, and each non-winning man was given a shilling for encouragement.

To finish the evening, there were songs for everyone until at seven o'clock the curate announced the ebbing of the last jug of elderberry wine. It was time for home.

John Marchant chaired the next village event, the Dahlia Show held in the garden of the New Inn. There were some fine displays. Pride of place went to the Danny House gardener, Mr. Leach. Apart from his roses and dahlias, he had been nurturing a new flower, Salvia Patens. He had brought a plant with him, slender hooded blooms in spikes of glorious blue. Nobody could fail to appreciate his delight. [4]

The show concluded with a New Inn dinner, everyone's delight. Before the food was produced, the 50 guests needed several minutes to stand and gaze at the table decorations, three candelabra with wonderful cut flower arrangements. The centre was of a goose, and the others of pheasants. When the candles were lit, the flicker of light and shadow on the petals gave a strangely life-like effect.

Landlord Thomas Smith then produced such a meal as only the New Inn could produce. The company settled to eating. After dinner, Mr. Marchant gave one of his popular jocular speeches leading to the toasts which were drunk with the usual cheer. Next, Mr. Bignall from Henfield entertained with songs. When the company joined voice for choruses, the candles flickered afresh and goose, pheasants and diners became livelier than ever; another evening of well mulled bonhomie.

The next day Mr. Marchant had to travel to Cuckfield for a Union Board meeting. They had to agree several alterations. The children's diet had been amended by Dr. Weekes. At breakfast, gruel and broth were to alternate instead of both being served and the supper gruel or broth was to be replaced by bread and cheese or butter. [5]

Dr. Weekes also pressed for the girls to be taken out of the house every day properly attended for exercise. On three days of the week, weather permitting, they would enjoy four miles of fresh air walking to Wolstonbury Hill and back.

The board also had to decide on a recommendation of the auditors who had inspected the accounts and decided a saving should be made at the Hurstperpoint house. There, the old paupers were accustomed to having a half-pint (¼l) of beer with their dinner. A saving of £12 a year could be made if the beer was withdrawn.

Mr. Marchant, as Hurst guardian, suggested they should not deprive the aged of so moderate an allowance. The board agreed and went on to praise Billy Heaver's governorship. No house was provisioned so cheaply or gave such general satisfaction as Hurst. The old folk could continue to enjoy their nightly beer.

Next on the agenda was an offer of employment for the 14 to 18 year old workhouse boys on the London and Brighton Railway which at last was under construction.

Each boy would be maintained and clothed, sick or well. All that the union board need supply was one pair of shoes and a change of linen. Work was available north of Cuckfield at Balcombe from where the railway was to follow a newly surveyed line through the Sussex Weald across empty heath and commons as if avoiding all habitation in its quest for a direct route to Brighton.

The boys would be in for tough work, rough quarters and boisterous companions in the navvies whose days of hard work were followed by evenings of hard drinking. Be that as it may, the responsibility of the board was to keep people independent. The rail-road was making that possible.

Edward Oram was in Cuckfield workhouse at that time but at 33 he did not qualify for the railway scheme. He shared a room with Thomas Tulley. Tulley had been there several months and because he could read and write he held an official position as porter. [6]

When work became available, Edward returned to independence in Hurst. His independence lasted about six weeks before he lost his work and had to return to the workhouse. He spent his final evening in the New Inn tap-room and spent the last of his money.

It was then that he decided to sell his round-frock. At first nobody was particularly interested. Edward persisted. At last, Peter Sayers gave him 4d. (2p) for it. Edward handed over the round-frock, drank the money and set off for Cuckfield.

On his arrival at the workhouse, the master called him over and asked about a round-frock which had gone missing from under the quilt of Thomas Tulley's bed.

Edward was honest enough to admit having taken it. He had simply put it on under his shirt, tucked the tail in his breeches and walked out.

Thomas Tulley was called. His concern was not so much about the way the frock had been stolen as in the steps which would be taken to regain it.

He and Edward walked back to Hurst and found Peter Sayers. The snag was that he had given the frock to his son out at Pyecombe. Off they went again and at last there it was, a bit the worse for wear with a hole in one of the gussets but definitely Thomas' frock.

They made their way back to the workhouse. Edward had to pay a penalty in imprisonment at Lewes. It was a short sentence but it gave him a prison record. He needed to be a lot more careful about people's possessions.

Edward served his sentence and was safely back in the village for the next scheduled celebratory occasion, the Royal Wedding of Her Majesty Queen Victoria and Prince Albert of Saxe Coburg at the end of February.

On Sunday the 9th of February, the morning sermon was preached in accordance with the Queen's Letter on behalf of the funds of the Society for Promoting the Building and Enlargement of Churches and Chapels. The congregation was pleased to contribute to such a worthy cause.

Soon afterwards, a parish subscription was raised so that a commemorative wedding-day gift could be made to every poor family in Hurst. It raised more than £13.

On the great day itself, church bells rang, Mr. Weekes' canon boomed and the parish celebrated. The gifts were distributed; a shilling (5p) to each family, sixpence (2½p) to every pauper in the workhouse and fourpence (2p) to the children at the National Schools. [8]

The Boys' School had attendances of over 80 at times although the girls seldom numbered more than 45. The children eagerly accepted their gifts.

Numbers were not everything. The mistress of the Girls' School may not have had so many scholars but she was considered an excellent lady who instilled all the right principles into the minds of her girls. She had a real influence on her charges.

At school on the Monday after the wedding, 11 of the girls each gave a penny (½p), 23 gave a halfpenny (¼p) and two gave a farthing ($^1/_8$ p) to the collection for building churches. It was done without curate Tufnell being at all aware of their intention. How uplifting for him when children should so spontaneously contribute in the way they did. [9]

Pupils at the Boys' School seemed to lack the high principles of the girls.

Edward Harmes had to consider financial matters when his mother passed away at Hatches. Could he keep the house? It was a hard decision.

Hatches had been his mother's home for almost 30 years. Since the loss of Wanbarrow Farm, it was the family's one piece of property. Edward was loath to let go but he had once raised a loan of £40 on the house in order to clear a debt. With interest, he now owed nearly £50. Selling Hatches was his only way to repay the money. There was no real alternative.

The house was put on the market. Nathaniel Borrer offered £400. The sale was made. Edward cleared the loan. The remaining cash could be used to set himself firmly on his feet. He may be landless but he was no longer tied to the vestry like brother Michael. It made a world of difference. [10]

There was a far larger debt facing the trustees of the new toll road to Cuckfield. In the four years of the road's existence, not one penny interest had been paid to investors. The total debt was £2731. £16 was borrowed for the erection of toll-gates but the year's takings at them were less than £15. [11]

When Dr. Weekes chaired the annual meeting of the toll road to the south of the church, he had to announce a further debt of £2000.

Dr. Weekes had worked hard promoting the roads and persuading the likes of Sir John Dodson to forward their promised investments. The vision of London/Brighton stage-coaches using the new Hurst roads in preference to the grinding climb of Clayton Hill had never materialized. It was small wonder that the doctor's beautiful new hotel with its capacious stabling had withered to a beer-house.

At Lewes, the magistrates held a special sessions for highways. There, the trustees of both roads sought financial help. Mr. Kinchin, the surveyor, explained how the poor state of repairs on the toll roads contrasted with the good state of parish financed roads. He costed repairs at £16 per mile. People opposing the application, claimed the roads had been a public nuisance ever since they were made. Some parts were so little used that grass grew on them. The magistrates concluded that £22 should finance necessary repairs. The doctor and Sir John would not see any return on their investments.

Another matter was coming to a head, the Tithes Map dispute. The vestry had maintained their refusal to pay Dixon and Maitland for the inaccurate map. Henry Muzzell had corrected the errors and the vestry's special committee had set a new rate at 1s. 0d. (5p) in the £. Samuel Goodman had lodged an appeal against it at the Cuckfield Petty Sessions.

The magistrates had decided the Goodman appeal should stand adjourned while solicitors tried to find a mutually acceptable position. The only common ground the solicitors could find was that a new map should be produced.

The vestry were delighted. They wrote to the Commissioners explaining how the mapping errors had necessitated the vestry setting their own assessments. They asked for a new map to be made. 14 ratepayers signed, each adding their rateable value (vestry version), from Mr. Campion's £455 to Henry Muzzell's £9.

A prompt reply arrived. If the vestry set their own assessment, the costs of any appeals against it would become the personal liability of the overseers as private people for ignoring advice provided by the Commissioners.

The vestry spread the message wide: the overseers were being threatened.

A ratepayers meeting was called. Neither the overseers nor the churchwardens attended but 40 supportive residents did. A resolution was proposed: only for appeals resulting from a rate based on the Dixon and Maitland map would the parish hold the overseers personally responsible. The 40 signatures were added, headed by Mr. Campion, through smaller landowners, tenant farmers, doctors, lawyers, shopkeepers and craftsmen to Henry French, the son who had refused to emigrate to New York.

Three days later, the churchwardens and overseers sent their own letter protesting that in conscience they could not accept the Dixon and Maitland map because it was unfair and incorrect. Also, from the resolution passed at the recent ratepayers' meeting, if they made a rate on the Dixon map they would incur the censure of the parish and be liable to the costs of appeals.

Everybody awaited the Commissioners' response.

It came, signed by just one official; enough to settle the issue. The map by Dixon and Maitland was the relevant document. Payment to them was to be made promptly to prevent further legal proceedings. [12]

The vestry bowed to pressure. Central authority was all powerful; the fact had to be accepted. The cartographers were paid. The only chance of respite lay in the result of the Goodman appeal.

When the court verdict was announced, the vestry reeled. The poor-rate was to be increased immediately to accord with the assessments of the Dixon and Maitland map and case costs of £113 were to be paid by Hurstperpoint.

Another vestry meeting was called. Where was the money to come from? Dr. Weekes supplied the answer: from the poor-rate. Agreement was unanimous. They had done their best but the Commissioners' Map was permanent. [13]

English Corney Goes to Market

At Horsham gaol, now used solely for debtors, the surgeon and chaplain had an extra problem pushed on their hands, and on everyone's hands, which made life even more depressing for the prisoners there.

By any standards their gaol routine was monotonous; distribution of the 2lbs (1kg) bread allowance to accompany anything they could afford to buy, workless hours in the yard until dusk, confinement to the day room until 9.00 p.m. and finally lock-up in single cells for the night.

The extra problem was the man delivered to the gaol one day in March. The chaplain recalled it as the 9th. The debtors recalled it as an unnecessary embarrassment, the start of an imposition that should never have been inflicted upon them.

The man had arrived in a weak state from Hoxton Asylum, an insane and penniless insolvent. Having neither means with which to buy nourishment nor mind to realize he needed it, he was given a daily ration of ½lb (¼kg) of meat. Adequately provisioned, he was left to wander the yard.

The case was highlighted when the visiting justices made their Easter report to the Lewes quarter sessions. It could not continue. The man was entirely misplaced. They were adamant relevant approaches should be made to obtain his release. Meanwhile, the people responsible for his removal to Horsham should be made to provide for him.

A letter requesting his release was sent to the Insolvent Debtors Court. The delayed reply was that the release could not be allowed. Parliament made no such provision; the law must take its course.

At the same time, the authorities responsible for the man's transfer were traced. It turned out to be the Cuckfield Union. The man was theirs, Luke Wickham of Hurstperpoint. Hapless Luke Wickham. It was now seven years since he had been taken from his farm.

The Union instructed Billy Heaver to reimburse Horsham and continue payments as long as needed. Luke remained in gaol, weak in both body and mind, a continuing embarrassment to everyone.

He was still there when the summer quarter sessions report was made. Again the justices demanded arrangements be made to ensure his return to a suitable place.

Cuckfield Union were instructed to arrange Luke's return to Hoxton Asylum. Cuckfield wrote to Hoxton. Hoxton considered the matter and replied that they could accommodate the man. Cuckfield informed Lewes and Lewes informed Horsham.

When sufficient letters had passed between everyone concerned, the doors of Horsham gaol opened. Out came Luke Wickham to be taken north back to Hoxton. It was the 25th of September; a happy day for the sane debtors, another non-day for Luke and economic news of yet another £3 lunatic expenses for Hurst vestry. [1]

Rev. J.C.F. Tufnell was also soon to move. He was to become rector of Edburton, the tiny hamlet tucked in the shadow of the Downs. [2]

The Allotment Society were keen to show their appreciation of the man who had worked so hard to obtain ground for them. At their show dinner they would have the ideal opportunity.

Show-day weather proved fine: so different from the downpour of the previous year. The show itself proved a special occasion for hay trusser James Hazelgrove whose exhibit for 'Best 3 Cabbages' was judged supreme. He became the proud recipient of a prize with an added bonus of 5s. 0d. (25p) that made memories of the snowy Christmas his family had spent separated in the Union workhouses seem part of a different life. Taking his place among the prize winners set the seal on James' allotment endeavours. [3]

Prize-giving was followed by the excitement of cricket until five o'clock, the time for an excellent tea provided by Mr. Borrer in the marquee erected on the spacious lawn in front of his mansion. The men settled to enjoy the food while their children watched wide-eyed as large slices of beef, veal and gammon bacon were handed round followed by portions of rich plum pudding.

The men ate heartily but there was still plenty left and Mr. Borrer then made the day complete by commanding the children be fed.

The children joined their fathers. Polite, anxious faces pleaded to be noticed. Eager hands stretched for the richness of plum pudding. Ecstatic thanks were breathed and the children feasted. Mr. Borrer and the curate felt quiet satisfaction, their benevolence was being appreciated.

With the food completed, it was time for healths and speeches. When they too were completed, Henry Muzzell rose to speak. He explained how, as superintendent of the society, he had a pleasing duty to perform. He, and everyone assembled, knew the day was a particularly special one for the allotment holders who, one and all, wished to mark the departure of the man who had done so much for them, their curate Rev. Tufnell. As a mark of their heartfelt appreciation, they had got up a subscription among themselves for a small gift which they now asked him to accept.

The curate accepted the gift and was taken aback – an inscribed silver plate. He read the inscription: 'Humbly presented by the tenants of the Hurst Allotment Gardens, to the Rev. J.C.F. Tufnell as a token of gratitude for his exertions in procuring for them land which has proved a source of great benefit to them and their families August 31st 1840.'

He said how he was utterly taken by surprise and knew not what to say. He then gave a most able address declaring the gift would go among the choicest of his furniture and he trusted that whenever it pleased God to remove him from this world, the gift might be handed down to his children and his children's children. The members clapped their benefactor and finished the evening with song and elderberry wine.

In November, the Rev. Shaw-Brooke made the long journey from Kent for his tithes dinner. Many people felt he was too frail to travel from Eltham and should give up his Hurst living. If he did so, Mr. Nathaniel Borrer would have the responsibility of appointing the next rector as he had purchased the patronage of Hurst from the Shaws. [4]

A hundred tithe payers sat down to the expectedly excellent dinner at the New Inn. Dinner was followed by the usual toasts being drunk, after which the Rev. Shaw-Brooke retired from the room.

Now, the evening became a ceremony to mark the curate's departure from the parish. Nathaniel Borrer stood to address the company. He thanked the curate for his multitudinous good works and begged him to accept a token of the parish's goodwill. Rev. Tufnell was handed two pairs of richly chased solid silver candlesticks with snuffers and tray to match. Overwhelmed, he thanked them for their kind generosity and gave an off-the-cuff address on the spiritual message of candles. At its conclusion he recommended to everyone his well known successor, their new 'curate elect'.

Rev. Tufnell sat down to exuberant applause, the new 'curate elect' rose to his feet – and there stood Nathaniel Borrer's son, Carey!

The Rev. Carey Borrer gave a few apposite words to draw the evening to a close and the tithe payers returned home satisfied that the new curate, born and bred in the parish, was the perfect antidote to their absentee rector.

Just after Christmas, dramatic news came from Eltham. The Rev. Shaw-Brooke had suffered a fatal stroke. Church people in Hurst were sorry to hear of his passing but their hearts lifted when his successor was announced. Their curate of so few weeks was now to be their rector. From an absentee pluralist to a son of the parish in one leap; they knew their youthful rector would have a closer feel for the village.

The next event at the New Inn, the graziers and butchers annual Friendly Dinner, was a time for serious farming talk and cheerful banter. Landlord Thomas Smith laid a good foundation to the evening with a sumptuous dinner that was accompanied by a wide ranging discussion on the breeding and feeding of cattle. [5]

After the dinner, the loyal toasts were made and after them the agricultural toasts. All were drunk 'three times three' in tradition's grand manner but none more so than the special one to the health of Hurst's champion, famed that evening for his achievements at Pakyns Manor not only in cattle breeding, where no one could match his attributes, but also in their feeding. Members raised their glasses and loudly acclaimed: 'Mr. Henry Bull!'

Mr. Bull replied as appropriately as he could to their kind sentiments although he lacked the easy flow of the curate. It was not that Mr. Bull doubted the graziers' sincerity but he was mindful how certain members when gathered together on such a cheerful and spirituous occasion had a propensity to enjoy their own brand of humour at another man's expense. Was he being credited with attributes beyond his capabilities?

What none of them could joke about was hydrophobia. Hydrophobia could destroy a man's prize herd. Recently, cattle had been affected in Clayton and on one of Mr. Campion's farms. Both occasions had followed the shooting of dogs suspected of being mad. Healthy cows had suddenly become unwell deteriorating rapidly, kicking out violently, head-butting the ground and attacking men and beasts. The only course had been to shoot the animals. Not even Mr. Bull could breed immunity to a mad dog's bite.

The wheelwright, English Corney, also had an interest in cattle. He was not so much interested in breeding as in selling on to other farmers. For him, cattle dealing was an important adjunct to his income. With four children to raise, every penny was needed. [6]

English did not have any cattle in Hurst itself. His favoured market was Guildford in Surrey, too far to drive home-grazed beasts. He had found Guildford a propitious market before and was confident of it being so again. He set out for the first sale in March, a long walk through Crawley and Charlwood but well worth it.

Early on market day, he arrived with his cattle, just two cows and two heifers. The place was filling steadily; it augured well for a quick sale.

English soon had a prospective buyer. The man was satisfied with the cattle and had just about clinched a deal when up stepped the constable to accuse English of having stolen the animals and that they were actually the property of Mr. William Brown at Charlwood.

English, 5ft. 4½ (1.6m) in his boots, was hemmed in and up against it. He made no attempt to refute the charge and was taken into custody. On the Monday, he was examined before a magistrate and committed to trial at the Newington Sessions. On Tuesday, he was placed at the bar. He pleaded: 'Guilty.'

It then came to light that at an earlier Guildford market there had been a sale which turned out to be of rustled cattle and that they too had come from Mr. Brown's Charlwood farm. A man of short stature had sold the cattle. English fitted the description. He was credited with both crimes.

Instead of walking home with gold sovereigns in his pocket, English was taken by coach to the Leviathan hulk at Portsmouth to await shipment for Van Diemen's Land, the beginning of a 15 years transportation sentence.

When Mrs. Corney heard of the arrest and sentence, she was speechless. How could her husband be guilty of crime? How would the family cope?

Mrs. Corney was a practical woman and did not waste time bemoaning her fate. She took in washing. English's brother helped financially and the family was able to keep free of the workhouse. At least mother and children were together, but any thought of seeing English again was a forlorn hope.

To Mrs. Corney, the Southern Continent seemed the end of the world. To Samuel Stevens settling in with his family it was the new beginning.

He wrote from South Australia full of praise for the life out there. They were now well settled in Adelaide.

The voyage out on the Buckinghamshire had been arduous for his young children but had been well worth it. He was now earning £3 a week as a shepherd. Labourers earned six shillings (30p) for a day's work, three times the Hurst wage. He had a new house of his own with an acre (0.4hectare) of land. His garden was providing good vegetables to go with beef and mutton a-plenty, whichever he chose to have. Bread, fresh butter, cheese, sugar, coffee, tea were there for everyone. Clothing was good too. Even though things had to be shipped out, they were still sold cheaper than in Hurst. Samuel's advice was to emigrate as soon as possible. He, his wife and the children were all happy, Australia was as fine a country as could be, better than England.

Adelaide, South Australia

For all that, he still yearned for news from friends and his old shoe-making mates. [7]

Peter Pratt Collects Mutton for His Family

At Mr. Campion's October Court Baron, manorial justice was being administered. It did not concern law breaking – just the Lord of the Manor securing his dues from the tenants.

Henry Hider and Dr. Richard Weekes were there to settle up for the sale of timber from their land.

Henry Muzzell had agreed which trees could be felled and that the wood was to be sold. As court beadle, he collected the dues, one third the value of the timber. Mr. Hider had £5 15s. 0d (£5.75) to pay on 18 oaks felled at Goddards Green while Dr. Weekes paid £6 3s. 0d (£6.15) on 16 mixed trees. [1]

Henry was hardly home from court when he went down with a fever. He knew nothing of what went on around him. Sir John Dodson received a letter from his Lewes agent explaining how Muzzell was so extremely ill that certain business could not be settled. Mr. Campion and the parish in general were also affected, such were the posts held by Henry. His recovery to full health would be a relief for them all.

At the workhouse there was drama that could easily have become disaster when the residents were roused from sleep by a cry of 'Fire!' They fled the house as hurriedly as their condition allowed. [3]

Smoke was seeping into the street from the pantry. Flames could be seen around the fireplace and a deal cupboard – threatening flames which had to be dealt with swiftly before they became engulfing fire.

Billy Heaver quickly organised the bigger children and the more able of his old paupers into a fire-fighting team. Buckets of water were passed hand to hand from the well to Billy Heaver at the pantry. He sloshed the water into the flames. They yellowed and wavered giving way to a widening patch of blackened boards spreading down the wall to the flooded floor.

When the fire was out, Mrs. Heaver inspected the cost to her pantry. Eight sacks of flour, a half-tub of butter, the bread store, the soup supply all ruined. She would be hard put to produce the breakfast gruel.

For Billy Heaver, there was relief that the fire had been noticed so quickly. As to its cause, he had no doubt. The pantry was the vestry room of pre-Union days. The fire-place had never been blocked and was still connected with the kitchen chimney. The kitchen copper had been alight all day. Soot must have caught fire and the flames spread into the unswept pantry chimney and out into the room. If the fire had caught hold, nothing would have saved the workhouse. To Billy Heaver, the breakfast difficulties were insignificant. The workhouse was safe.

Among the group of inmates powerless to help at the fire was Eliza Heaseman. Eliza was a strong 13 year old but had been blind most of her life, blindness said to result from parental neglect. She was a spirited girl of great determination who had been one of Mr. Bubb's students at the workhouse inspection which so amazed everyone just before Queen Victoria's coronation.

Eliza had an outstanding memory. She could recite from books the ordinary man had never heard of – or want to hear of – Crossman's Introduction, Gastrell's Institute, Pinnock's Catechism of Bible and Gospel History.

With her great store of Bible knowledge, Eliza was entrusted with teaching the younger ones in the school. Yet her greatest feat was in reading from the raised-type. Eliza certainly merited attention.

The plight of such a virtuous young girl doomed to a life in the workhouse stirred people's hearts. Some Hurst families were soliciting votes from subscribers to the School for the Indigent Blind at St. George's Field in London. The votes could help Eliza gain admission.

Her story was told in a printed appeal with a lithographic sketch showing her in the midst of her pupils. Copies could be obtained from the Rev. J.C.F. Tufnell at Edburton Rectory. All it needed was a shilling (5p) in a letter prepaid with one of the new adhesive penny postage stamps. The money would go to the Eliza Heaseman Fund.

The response was encouraging at first. Then complaints began about people sending their money but receiving no reply. Soon it was apparent that more letters were being unanswered. For the Rev. Tufnell this was terrible. He was dealing with all he received. Who was dealing with the rest?

Reason made it the postman. A trap was laid. Letters containing marked coins were sent. For each one, another letter informed Rev. Tufnell that money had been posted. It worked.

The postmaster now played his part in the plan and asked the postman for change for a sovereign. The change included marked coins. Eliza's fund could grow again.

The lithograph proved its worth. Subscribers to the School for the Blind were impressed by the young girl's achievements. She gained her place by almost 3000 votes.

The postman appeared at the next assizes to face a charge of theft. He had been well and truly caught out and knew there was little chance of release.

The man who prepared the trap explained how the marked coins had been sent. The coins were produced and identified. Defence counsel asked the witness to swear to the identity of them. He could not honestly do so – and the postman left court a free man. [4]

The Eliza Heaseman affair had been a non-event for Henry Muzzell. His fever had been really severe. He had done well to hold on to life. When he did regain enough strength to participate in village events, his first public duty was at the opening of the Library and Reading Society.

The rector took centre stage. He explained how the aims of the society included making knowledge available to all classes of the community, the mechanic and agricultural labourer as well as the more wealthy. It would promote unity and do much good in the parish.

The audience cheered his sentiments. Treasurer Henry Rowland gave his report and then the rector called upon secretary, Mr. Henry Muzzell, to read the Society's rules. Henry was working again. [5]

In March, the vestry reappointed him and shoemaker William Randell as collectors of land tax and assessed taxes. At the end of the month he was made collector of highway rates and church rates. In April they appointed him assistant overseer with all the authority and duties of a normal overseer in addition to which he was to continue collecting poor rates. For this his salary would be £25 per annum.

Henry could feel immense satisfaction and pride. He was now trusted, solely or in partnership, for the collection of virtually all parish taxes: a responsibility and reward for long years of unstinted service.

He had lost none of his acumen. He was an excellent organizer and had as keen a head as ever for figures. All his duties were attended to diligently. There were no bad debts. No one owed the parish a penny. Not until the end of May, when he was certain that everybody had paid their dues, did he allow himself a hard earned break away from the parish.

In Henry's absence, the vestry called a special Thursday meeting at the New Inn to discuss his future. It was well attended. As the room filled, so the level of noise increased. The buzz of conversation gripped everyone.

At the appointed time, the meeting was called to order. People were quiet. The chairman spoke in precise tones as he announced the single item of business: the parish vestry should accept the resolutions made at the previous Saturday's informal meeting. In particular, they should authorize the churchwardens' prompt action in employing the Brighton police to track down Henry Muzzell and an unknown amount of parish money. [6]

Henry Muzzell, 58 and of exemplary character, had gathered the taxes and run.

It was an indignant meeting. Angry, bemused officials feared the full extent of their losses. How much had he got away with? What made him do it? Had his illness affected his mind? Could he really be a fraudster after so many years service?

To more purpose, Mr. Ellis was asked to inspect the accounts and discover how much was missing. With his experience as vestry clerk he was best placed to assess the damage.

The other definite action was to thank Jeremiah Bartley for his quick response in setting off after Muzzell. Sadly he had failed. At a later date he would be repaid his expenses.

Sir John Dodson was informed in London by his Lewes agent. Muzzell had been unmasked as a rogue. Swindles had been found in his dealings but the cost need not be borne by Sir John. When money had been sent from Lewes for Muzzell to settle accounts, the man had had the audacity to obtain receipts and where possible persuade people that he should hold the money in safe keeping. However, those traders simple enough to be duped would have to suffer the loss themselves.

In all fairness, Henry had duped everyone including the lord of the manor. Mr. Campion had to find another £56 for assessed taxes which had gone into Henry's capacious pockets.

The vestry auctioned Muzzell's belongings. They sanctioned £3 expenses for Jeremiah Bartley going after him and £8 for the Worthing constable responding to a reported sighting there. They detailed William Randell to collect all poor-rate arrears and only to accept that a person had already paid if an official receipt could be produced.

When the 1841 census was taken, Henry Muzzell might never have existed. Also missing was strange Ann Grey. She had passed away during the winter. George Sayers of the George and Jesse syndicate had also gone. He had removed to a Portsmouth prison hulk having stolen a hen and a Locks Farm gander valued together at seven years transportation.

Mad Luke Wickham was remembered although his census abode was London's Hoxton asylum. An advertisement announced that, by direction of the Insolvent Court, a brick built tenement with outbuildings and five enclosures of land, in all about 12 acres (5 hectares), the estate of Luke Wickham, farmer of unsound mind, was to be auctioned on Thursday 24th June. The vestry's concern for his wife and children had lost priority to Poor Law accountancy. [7]

Hurst had increased by 40% since the 1831 census to 2118 inhabitants in 348 houses. 105 of those houses had been built during the last 10 years.

The property with most inhabitants by far was the workhouse crammed to the limits with 30 old men and 6 women mostly in their 70s and 80s and with 32 young boys and 27 girls aged from 14 down to 3. Matron Elizabeth Heaver certainly earned her money.

Old Isaac Sayers had made a move leaving his shared house in the north of the parish for one in the west at Sayers Common. There he had become a grandfather twice through his two daughters who remained with him because neither of them had a husband.

Down the Old Hollow by the church was Isaac's son, Isaac, who occupied one of Sir John Dodson's tastefully named Spring Garden cottages a few yards up from a stagnant pool fed by the cottage privies. William Bartley's rented cottage up by Church House was high enough to miss the worst of the pool's pollution.

Parish-clerk Richard Davey had his own freehold property near the church so at last qualified to vote for his M.P.

His near neighbour, Jeremiah Bartley, did too. He had made alterations to his property and opened it as a beer-house. With a feeling of great pride and family unity, he named it The Oak. Jeremiah was guaranteed trade because more than 70 of Hurst's residents were railroad navvies on the Brighton line, good business for any beer-house.

Michael Harmes now had one of the ex-Royal Oak cottages. His neighbours were George and Charity Rowland. George was nearing 80 and his months in the Horsham debtors' prison seemed like an episode of youth.

A hundred miles away from Hurst, in the Cold Dunghills area of Ipswich, a widow filled in her census schedule. She was Hannah Buckman, schoolmistress, and she had one daughter living with her, also Hannah, who was a shoebinder. She did not claim any affinity with Hurstperpoint. Not that the enumerator could be interested. She was just the next name, the next poverty stricken name and whether he transcribed her details correctly or no, the name went down and he moved on to the next.

The vestry had long forgotten Widow Buckman. They were fully occupied in making good the damage done by Henry Muzzell. Something they would never do again was to put all their eggs in one basket. William Randell would collect the highway-rates whilst a new assistant overseer would be appointed for poor-rates. Yet if Henry Muzzell could turn out such a fraudster how would they find anyone to trust?

They felt they did have such a man in Richard Davey. He already held office as parish-clerk and as deputy to Billy Heaver the registrar of births and deaths.

If ever there was an honest, upright man it was Richard Davey, ex-sergeant of Wellington's glorious army.

So Richard became assistant overseer at £20 per annum. To safeguard his integrity he had to give security of £300 with two backers. This time the vestry had a steadfast man.

The rector himself came in for praise from the archdeacon who highlighted the devotion to duty and zealous concern for the welfare of the parish exemplified by Rev. Carey Borrer. The archdeacon was sugaring the pill.

Earlier in the year, the rural dean had detailed 11 items in the church that needed improvement from relettering the creed on the eastern wall to repairing the belfry ceiling. Now the archdeacon was calling their venerated church of St. Lawrence a miserable piece of patchwork containing hardly anything worth preserving. It was not big enough for the growing parish and could not effectively be enlarged. The crux of his letter was they should build a new church. [8]

The Rev. Carey Borrer was determined to modernize his parish. He and the archdeacon had shared their views at private occasions. Both understood the importance of replacing the church with a larger, grander edifice more appropriate for his congregation to worship in. He knew some people would oppose him. He had every confidence in overcoming opposition. The biggest difficulty would be in financing the project. Where was the money to come from? Subscriptions from even the most supportive sources could never raise sufficient.

Peter Pratt would have been sympathetic to the rector's plight if only he had known of it. The source of money had been Peter's overwhelming worry ever since the awful accident with the timber wagon. He knew from bitter experience that subscriptions, however generous and well intentioned, provided nothing permanent. He had tried time and again to overcome his financial difficulties and he could find no solution. His lameness prevented him holding down work, his wife was ill and his daughter still fully dependent on him. Without income how was he to provide for them?

At last his family was in such desperate need that he went to nearby Seven Acre Field and killed a sheep. He struggled home with the carcass, cut it up as best he may and provided a decent meal for his family. [9]

He put the mutton pieces at various safe places around the house and buried the entrails in the garden. He planted some cabbages there and made sure nothing incriminating was left.

That Sunday, when butcher Samuel Beeching checked on his sheep he discovered one was missing. He looked for clues to its disappearance and found dried blood drips along the footpath and on a stile. He reported his loss to Police Constable Streatfield.

Constable Streatfield checked the field. True enough, there were blood drips and indistinct footprints. Where did they lead? Of the few cottages around, the most likely seemed that of Peter Pratt.

The constable returned to the village and collected James Gander, parish constable for the year. They paid Peter Pratt a visit.

P.C. Streatfield stated his business. Peter was agreeable to a search and invited them into the kitchen. He pointed out his cupboard saying they certainly had a leg of mutton.

Streatfield went to the cupboard. As well as a leg of mutton there was a pot of boiled bones, more than a leg's worth. He decided to widen his search. In the wash-house, there was more mutton in the meat-safe.

Peter did his best to keep relaxed. He took Streatfield upstairs to complete enquiries. He explained how his wife was ill, confined to bed. Their little daughter was looking after her.

It was difficult for Streatfield. Discretion dictated that Mrs. Pratt should not be disturbed. He concentrated on the other room. Nothing untoward was there. He and Peter returned to the kitchen.

Streatfield remained suspicious. Essential evidence could be hidden in the bedrooms. He sent James Gander to fetch a woman neighbour.

Peter went back upstairs. He and his daughter busied themselves seeing to his wife's needs. To Streatfield's ears she was receiving a lot of attention.

When Gander returned, Streatfield took the neighbour straight up to search Mrs. Pratt's room. Just her husband was with her. Their daughter was now in the second room. The neighbour made sure all was as it should be. Mrs. Pratt was not nursing mutton.

Constable Streatfield was still not satisfied. He determined to inspect the other room again. There, something caught his eye, a bulge in the bedding. The daughter explained how part of the old mattress got stuck all of a lump inside and would not shake out.

Streatfield handed the neighbour a knife and told her to cut the ticking. When she did so, he thrust his hands in and met obstruction. He pulled out mutton; two shoulders and six other pieces. Peter rushed from his wife's room and stumbled downstairs. Streatfield yelled for Gander to take him.

Peter was not trying escape; he was just a defeated father. He had known James Gander for many a year; they were both parish men. Peter explained the mutton to him: 'I bought it of a man privately but I don't know who he was.'

Streatfield came down with the meat. He told Gander to search the garden. The sheepskin should be obvious somewhere. Gander found some recently planted cabbages. The soil seemed very disturbed. He dug. No woolly sheepskin came to light but scattered in the ground were animal's entrails.

Peter and the mutton were taken away. His wife and daughter would have to see to themselves.

The next day, he was put before a J.P. His statement was simple: 'I've done things which I should not have done but I did it through want. I've nothing more to say only that my wife does not know anything about it.'

At the trial, P. C. Streatfield explained that when taking Pratt to Hurst they passed a stile with blood stains on it. He pointed them out and said: 'I suppose they came from the sheep.' The prisoner answered: 'I know. I did it. I hope you won't say anything about it for the sake of my family.'

A neighbour told how Pratt when taken away had said: 'I'm a done pin. I did what I ought not to. I was in want and I must stand the consequences.'

At the trial's end, the judge remarked that the police constable should not have asked the blood stain question in the way he did because it was very material to the case. He then asked the jury to consider their verdict.

They took little time to decide: guilty – with mercy recommended on account of the family. The defence counsel backed the plea by presenting a petition signed by several neighbours attesting to Peter's good character; he had acted out of desperation to provide food for his wife and child.

The judge accepted the jury's recommendation and declared that in setting sentence he took due account of the former good character of the prisoner; ten years transportation.

Peter Pratt shuddered.

He was taken to the Leviathan hulk. There they recorded his description: height 5ft 5½ins (1.7m), hair brown, eyes grey, nose prominent, mouth large, face thin, build slender. Peter Pratt: hollow cheeked and half starved.

The sympathetic neighbours of Hurstperpoint may have given Peter a good character but aboard the Leviathan he was on a par with the worst of convicts detailed to a ward on the bottom deck.

Work was at last assured him. His day started at 5.00 a.m. with the 'All Hands' signal to dress rapidly and lash hammocks. He then lined up ready for the ward to be unlocked for the march to the washing troughs. After that, came breakfast quickly followed by the morning session of ship cleansing; decks, poop and forecastle.

The official workday began at 7.30. Fit men were employed about the dockyard. Peter's lameness confined him to duties on ship – his world was small.

At noon was the hour break for dinner. Even then, time was not his own: the duty officer inspected bedding and clothing.

The working day ended at 5.30 p.m. The men lined up at the washing troughs, mustered to be counted for the 'All is Right' check, ate supper and began another hour of ship cleaning.

If Peter could keep a good conduct report for two years, he would qualify for 3d. (1p) a day earnings and the chance to progress to the middle deck and eventually to pride of place – the top deck reserved for the elite 'best behaved' prisoners.

He would need determination and strong staying powers to reach that goal. [10]

1841: Samuel Goodman Supports the Railway

In July 1841, part of the railway which George Stephensen had declared 'Impossible to be made', the London to Brighton line, opened for the conveyance of passengers, horses and carriages, and parcels. It began at London Bridge and terminated some 15 miles from the sea at a countryside station they named Haywards Heath. [1]

Between Haywards Heath and Brighton the passengers had to rely on the everyday horse-coach. Six crack coaches, including one of Mr. Goodman's, were ready to finish the journey in exactly two hours, thereby equalling the time taken for the train's 35 mile section.

The Campions were quick to try the train. They had already experienced the Greenwich Railway and now seized the chance to travel up to London and back. Mr. Campion felt his £8 was well spent. [2]

People were not flocking to try the new line. Tales of earth slips, burst steam pipes and a near collision were off-putting. Stage coaches maintained heavy bookings while trains ran almost empty. Perhaps the London Brighton Railway would not be the threat to horse transport that other railways had proved.

The first Hurst people to feel the effects of the railway were George and Elizabeth Lander. They lived at Hurst Wickham along the secluded lane that ran from Mr. Faithfull's house, past the Cophall stockings hedge and along to St. John's Common. [3]

Theirs was a lone house with only a farm barn as a neighbouring building. It was August harvest time. Mrs. Lander was up early to buy provisions; sugar, cheese and 1½ ounces (45 grams) of tea that would have to brew as many cups as possible. She came home and placed her basket on the kitchen table. It was almost eight o'clock, high time she was with her husband in the fields. She bolted the back-door, carefully locked the front door behind her, put the key in her pocket and set off.

About mid-morning, a visitor arrived at the house. Finding nobody at home, he proceeded to break in. Once safely out of sight of passers-by he could work more easily. The first obvious haul was the silver watch and the snuff-box beside it on the kitchen mantelpiece. A search of kitchen drawers brought a half-sovereign. A wooden box was more rewarding with a small bag full of cash. The basket of provisions and fresh bread from the pantry provided welcome food. There seemed little else worth having in the kitchen but on the stairs handrail were two strong calico shirts.

Upstairs by the bedroom was a pair of good half-boots. In the room was a box containing a pair of cord trousers, braces to hold them up, a flannel jacket, a hat, handkerchiefs and two round frocks. A chest was full of ladies-wear from gowns through to stays. A small metal box on the mantelpiece held more cash. In all, an opportune morning's work.

The intruder changed into a selection of George's clothes, bundled his own and everything else in a sheet, and got out. He set off north along the lane.

Some half-mile further on, Henry Steel was at work. About 11 o'clock, a stranger passed and bid him 'Good morning.' What took Henry's notice was a large white bundle over the man's shoulder. It was so cumbersome it was tied across his chest.

At midday, Elizabeth and George returned home. George was still by the barn when Elizabeth unlocked her front door and went indoors. The kitchen was in turmoil, the back-door bolt on the floor. She rushed back outside to George.

Cautiously they went in together. All was silent and very wrong: no tick of his watch, the drawers on the floor, the deal box emptied. Upstairs showed how thorough the robbery had been.

The immediate task was to try and get their things back. Thieves would be unlikely to head for the village. George turned north. Ten minutes away he met Henry Steel. Henry told of the stranger. The picture was clear. They knew who they were looking for. They hazarded a guess at the sort of place to make for, the new railway across at Haywards Heath. George was well into middle-age, almost 50. Henry was young enough to travel fast, he would pursue the man.

Henry made the best time he could to the station. There he told his story to railway-policeman Wright. On the ground outside the nearby beer-shop was a large white bundle. The pair waited patiently. At last two men left the beer-shop.

One walked over to the station steps and went up to the booking office. The other hoisted the white bundle onto his shoulder then he too walked towards the station. Railway-policeman Wright approached and advised him to hurry if he intended catching the train because it was just about to leave.

The man hurried to the steps and began mounting them. He was safely on railway property.

Wright followed and made his arrest. Mr. Savage, the superintendent of the railway-police, was called. He decided the second man should also be held. A very surprised passenger-to-be was prevented from boarding the train. He said his name was Shaw, he had a ticket for Reigate Road and had nothing whatsoever to do with any robbery.

Mr. Savage informed him why he was a suspect and how it would entail questioning before a J.P. next morning. He and the prime suspect, William Reeves, were taken into custody. There was little Reeves could do apart from accepting he should change back into the dirty garments found in the bundle of clothes. He maintained he had simply changed into clothing he found heaped in a lane and that the money was his own.

The following day, J. P. Cherry was able to dismiss Shaw. Reeves had to await trial.

Elizabeth Lander and Henry Steel travelled to Lewes to give evidence. It meant a night away from Hurst but they had the satisfaction of seeing justice done.

For William Reeves, it meant a berth in a prison hulk awaiting transportation to Australia for 15 years. For sceptics, the railway had proved itself the 'get-away' link with London.

The completion of the line did not take long. Its supporters commended the safety measures taken at the stations where the platforms were erected beside an extra loop of the track so that any 'runaway' engine or train would pass straight through on the main track. The company was also praised for the wonderful architecture of Brighton Terminus and the wise policy of not expending too much on intermediary station buildings.

Brighton Railway Station

In September, the railway was officially opened to Brighton. Hurst people went out to welcome the first train at Hassock's Gate Station. It was a fine day and all who could afford the time joined the crowd gathering where the ruler-straight track gave a grand view to the north. [4]

At last there was a steamy disturbance on the horizon – and suspense as the train drew steadily nearer in a swathe of smoke with ever growing noise above anyone's experience. Suddenly it was there, thundering through the station and away between steep banks to disappear in the tunnel beneath Clayton Hill.

The day was quiet again. The breeze drifted a familiar yet different smoke smell. It was a changed world; progress, with polluting noise, fumes and breathtaking speed. Older people sighed and the not-so-old wondered. Where was modern man bound?

If the first weekend of the new through service was anything to go by, modern man was bound for Brighton with trains carrying enough visitors to fill hotels and lodging houses. On the second Saturday, the 10.45 from London Bridge clouded the issue. It was a heavy train, a mixture of 1st and 2nd Class coaches, carriage-trucks and horse-boxes headed by a powerful six wheeled engine. [5]

The leading coaches were 1st Class with the centre enclosed but the front and back parts open. In the first coach sat Dr. Carpue, celebrated for his work as an anatomist, enjoying the comfort of padded seats and glass window protection from the elements. In the open part were his two servants intent on enjoying their excursion to the sea. John Hardy, M.P. for Bradford, and his son-in-law shared the next coach with two ladies.

Among the 2nd Class passengers further back, was one who took his rail travel seriously. He was intent on using his watch to time the train between stations and calculate its speed. He meticulously logged the 10.45's progress.

For some reason the train started nine minutes late. It lost more time when it had to be diverted to the up track for several miles because of an earth slip on one of the embankments.

Progress continued to be slow. Consistent rain had affected the bed of the track. With such a heavy train in those conditions the engine had difficulty achieving speeds much above 20 miles per hour.

At Horley, the half-way station, a four wheeled engine was backed onto the train to assist at the steeper gradients. John Hardy M.P. grunted approval; he had been calculating a late arrival of over half an hour – not at all palatable.

The second engine provided the crucial extra power. The speed reached 30 M.P.H. Lost time was gradually being made up. The dizzy heights of the Balcombe Valley Viaduct were safely crossed and the train approached the Copyhold Cutting outside Haywards Heath.

James Cory was on duty in the cutting. His job was straightforward but crucial.

If the line was clear he had to hold his right arm straight out from his body. To make the train slacken speed he had to put his hand straight above his head.

Because of the wet weather affecting the line, Cory signalled 'Slacken speed'. The driver of the leading engine decreased steam.

The sway of the train increased rapidly. The front coaches rocked violently spreading alarm among the passengers. Something was happening too quickly for them to register.

In no time, the first engine left the rails, dragging the other engine and leading coaches with it in a cacophony of clashing metal, snapping wood and escaping steam. There were scared screams, cries for help and the terrifying boom of a bursting boiler. The front three coaches, windows shattered, were tilted as if about to topple.

Mr. Hardy's son-in-law lowered himself from the window and helped the ladies out, their hat veils shredded by glass fragments.

Dr. Carpue lay injured in his compartment. His two servants had been thrown onto the track from their open section. Both were dead.

Two other doctors fortuitously on the train gave aid where they could. For passengers further back it was a horrifying experience but nothing worse.

The afternoon 'Up' train stopped as near the crash as possible. It returned to Brighton with those still willing to use the railway. Those who could not face doing so were taken by road to Cuckfield where post-chaises were hired to complete the journey.

The company was appalled. At the inquest, their solicitor, none other than George Faithfull's brother Hugh, said that any recommendations to improve safety would be carried out.

When questioned, the driver of the larger engine declared the Brighton Line's four wheel locos were top heavy with high boilers. As the engine swayed, so too did the water in the boiler thereby making the rocking motion increase until the engine capsized.

A recommendation was made: all four wheeled engines should be withdrawn.

Four wheeled engines were immediately taken out of service. Luggage-carriages were made obligatory, placed immediately behind the engine to protect passengers. The public could face the future with confidence – so claimed the company.

The press was scathing in its criticism. The new railway was a disaster. Safety had to be improved. Not only safety. Clayton Tunnel, lit only by oil lamps, was a terrifying subterranean experience for delicate ladies. It should be lit by gas like the Haywards Heath Tunnel. Yet even there during wet weather, water cascaded from the brickwork onto carriage roofs frightening every nervous passenger, particularly in the 2nd Class with no glass window protection. The Greenwich Railway provided leather blinds in 2nd Class. The Brighton Railway should do the same.

People were already writing to the Brighton papers expressing their views. Mr. Ellis wrote from Hurst. The Guardian, ever ready to castigate the railway, was pleased to print his letter.

Mr. Ellis was happy with the short time the journey took but the fares were too high. He was astonished that Hassock's Gate, the station for traffic from Lewes, Steyning, Henfield, Hurst and Ditchling, was designated a second-class station meaning that of 12 trains daily only six would stop. The last Hassock's Gate train from London was far too early. When the trains had terminated at Haywards Heath he had been able to make the most of his London day by remaining until 5.00 p.m. Now he would have to leave as early as 2.45 thus losing valuable business hours. No doubt experience would soon bring necessary changes. [6]

One change did occur. Hassock's Gate was upgraded to a first-class station so that all trains except the express stopped there.

By winter, there were complaints about the deterioration of the roads between Brighton and London. At places the horses had to slow almost to walking pace. In one instance men had to guide the 'fast' coach through the worst parts by lantern light. Another coach became entirely stuck in the mud and eventually arrived two hours late. [7]

On a bright Sunday morning, Samuel Goodman experienced the full power of the railway. The Times, his prize London coach on the direct Hickstead route, well horsed and popular, handled only by crack drivers, left Brighton empty – not a passenger was aboard. A lesser man might have wilted and adjusted his business to a 'Coach and Railway Office' ferrying passengers to and from the station like his rivals. Samuel Goodman refused to give up. [8]

In the new year, he put an advertisement in the Brighton Gazette:

'THE PROPRIETORS OF THE TIMES COACH BEG TO INFORM THEIR FRIENDS AND THE PUBLIC THAT IT WILL IN FUTURE LEAVE THE RED OFFICE EVERYDAY AT 12 O'CLOCK TO THE GOLDEN CROSS, CHARING CROSS AND BULL INN ALDGATE THROUGH CRAWLEY, REIGATE, SUTTON AND CLAPHAM. FROM GOLDEN CROSS AND BELLE SAUVAGE EVERYDAY AT 12 O'CLOCK, ELEPHANT AND CASTLE AT A ¼ PAST 12. FARE 20/- AND 8/- OUTSIDE.' [9]

The Times was still operating in April although not to every customer's satisfaction. A gentleman had booked two inside places from Brighton for the ease of access to his house in the West End. The coach had been fine but he had been charged an extra 13s. 4d. (67p) for luggage. He warned coach proprietors to reflect on the relative charges of coach and rail and whether the public would continue to favour the Times. [10]

That same month, the Royal Blue Vans begged to announce they were ceasing to run to London. All goods, merchandise and luggage was to go by train. Omnibuses would run from Kemp Town and Brunswick Terrace to convey passengers to Brighton Station. [11]

For the railway, it was confirmation that they were the way ahead. Their freight traffic rates were excellent. Shoreham Harbour imports of eggs, wine, dead poultry, walnuts, chestnuts, fruit and vegetables were conveyed to London Bridge cheaper and quicker than by any competitor. The Brighton Railway was the direct link between London and Paris: 2 hours by first-class train to Brighton, 7 hours on the General Steam Navigation Company packet from Brighton's Chain Pier to Dieppe and a diligence from there to Paris. The complete journey in only 21 hours for less than £3.

Samuel Goodman knew his coaching days were over. The railway had won.

1842: George Sayers Sails for Bermuda

Hurst farmers were not worried by the foreign produce imported at Shoreham. What concerned them was talk of the repeal of the Corn Laws. The Anti Corn Law League of northern industrialists was having too much influence in Parliament. Most farmers were convinced the league's sole purpose was to achieve unrealistically low bread prices to enable the industrialists to reduce their factory workers' wages. Press reports of military defeats in Afganistan and setbacks in opium shipments to China could be put to one side. The real threat was the end of the Corn Laws: it would mean vast imports of foreign grain – and that would mean the end of the home producer.

News of riots in Manchester heightened the tension. Employers had reacted to a slump in trade by reducing wages without waiting for cheaper bread. Protesting activists forced their way into cotton mills to take out the plugs from the steam boilers and stop machinery. More and more workers turned out to join the protest until mobs 5000 strong were on the streets.

Three magistrates had travelled to London by train to inform the Home Office. The cabinet met and ordered out the Grenadier Guards. Headed by their regimental band, they marched from Trafalgar Square up Regents Street and on towards Euston Station. Word spread among bystanders that the soldiers were marching against working men. Memories 20 years old arose: the Peterloo Massacre was about to be repeated. People groaned and hissed. Crowd taunts increased. 'Remember you are brothers,' became louder and more aggressive until the officer in charge ordered: 'Fix bayonets'. At Euston the Grenadiers boarded special trains to take them north.

Demonstrators across Lancashire and beyond were confronted. The soldiers dispersed the crowds and the mills reopened but discontent simmered among the workers.

To the Sussex farmers, the future strategy of the northern manufacturers was obvious: a greater resolve than ever to destroy the Corn Laws. The only way to counter it would be by determined corporate action.

A meeting was held at Steyning to support the Sussex Society for the Protection of Agriculture. William Marshall represented Hurst and became a committee member. They resolved to take every constitutional means to suppress the Anti Corn Law League and safeguard British wheat. A petition was sent to Sir Robert Peel calling on him to continue Parliament's protective Corn Laws. Without them the arable farmers' very livelihoods were in danger. [1]

George Sayers, serving his seven years for stealing the Locks Farm gander, had no knowledge of riots or farm problems but he had as great a concern for his future. He had left the cramped confines of the York hulk and was now across the Atlantic in the sunny Bermudas aboard an equally cramped prison hulk, the Dromedary. [2]

His years would be spent quarrying and cutting stone for the islands' fortifications. In the tropical heat he would sweat profusely so was issued with flannel shirt and drawers to absorb it. The uniform was light; white duck trousers, white duck working-frock emblazoned with his name and number and a wide straw hat as defence against the sun.

Work was tough but the men were suitably fed. Their diet included fresh beef and salt pork, vegetables, pea soup and best wheaten bread. At breakfast there was a pint (½ litre) of cocoa and at supper a pint of tea.

With the regime's current moderation in the observance of the strict rules, and a daily ration

Illustrated LondonNews 17-6-1848

264

of a ¼ pint (⅛ litre) of rum, George could feel his future lay in his own hands. If he did digress he knew the consequences; loss of pay, solitary confinement, heavy irons or a flogging strictly limited to 60 lashes.

Convict 9566 had seven years to serve. With good behaviour, and reasonable health avoiding the perils of yellow fever, he could see England again in 1849.

Hurst's one time lone rioter, Henry Henty, was also absent from the village but he was no further away than the Union Workhouse driven there by loss of work again. It was a quieter, mature Henry, as different as chalk and cheese from the 'Zip you up!' Henry of old.

When he and his wife were able to return home, the workhouse governor reported on Henry's behaviour. The report was good. The Cuckfield Union sent instructions to Billy Heaver as Hurst's relieving officer. He was to pay Henty 4s. 0d. (20p) in recognition of his good behaviour.

The medical officer of Cuckfield workhouse did recommend that one inmate, a woman with a bastard child, should leave the house on account of ill health and be granted out-relief. It was Mary Tugwell, the plague of Governor Kerby's life. Now that she was in continual poor health she would at last be free from the officials who had controlled so much of her life. Mary and her baby went – the governor's prayer times could proceed in peace. [3]

Dr. Weekes and Dr. Holman shared the medical contract for Hurst workhouse. An important duty was the administration of smallpox vaccination. New legislation allowed the service to be financed from the rates. The doctors had to attend at the workhouse on the first day of each month when anyone who wished could attend and be vaccinated. The following week the recipients had to attend for the doctors to ensure the treatment was successful. If it was, a certificate was issued. If not, the vaccination was repeated until it proved effectual. Each vaccination had to be recorded and annual figures were sent to the Poor Law Commissioners. None but the ignorant would fail to give their offspring protection against the perils of smallpox. 95 children were treated, 34 of them under three years old. [4]

The doctors also reported on the general state of the workhouse. Their report was critical. Sleeping quarters for the old were too crowded. The boys lacked sufficient beds but conditions for the girls were appalling, 12 beds for 37 girls. Even so, general health was tolerably good except for the infirmities and illness the old seemed to suffer once they were in the house. The doctors listed the presence of palsy, cancer, dropsy and the 'itch'. If any virulent disease were to appear the consequences could be fearful. [5]

One of the Poor Law's own Assistant Commissioners inspected the workhouse to determine how many inmates could be accepted. He considered it deficient in space, ventilation and facilities with the position of the privies in the centre of the premises affecting the atmosphere of the airing yards. [6]

The day room for the 34 old men was just 15 feet by 12 (5 metres by 4), its furniture four rows of seats. On fine days, the men could find sitting space on benches in their yard. In poor weather, they crowded every seat in the room and still some had no place.

Yet the old women had less. The workhouse entrance door from the street led straight into their day room. They slept in two small rooms, one of which had a sick inmate in it whose illness offended the air.

The inspector declared that he had carefully examined the place. 95 paupers there may be, but the accommodation was totally inadequate for the numbers. To back up his opinions, he included a plan of the ground floor complete with the men's Roman style two-seater privy.

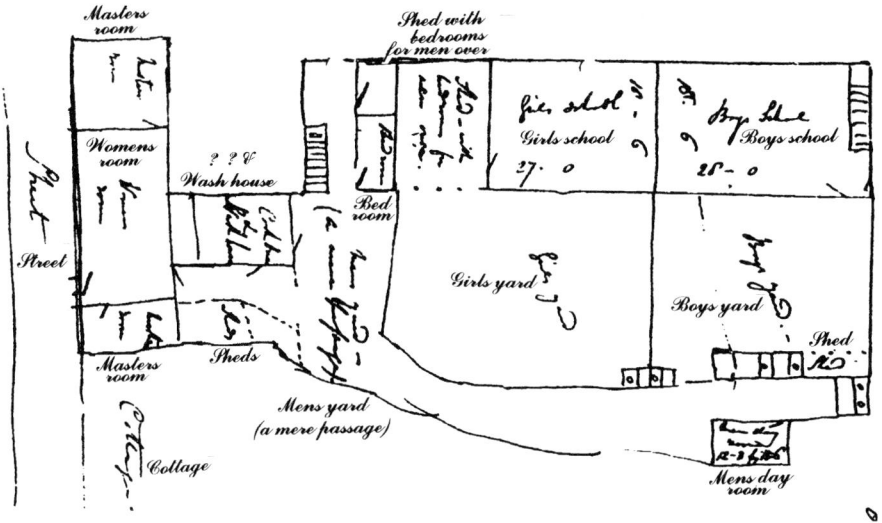

Ground floor plan of Hurstperpoint Workhouse.

Adam Adams, landlord of the White Horse, had plans for new public facilities. His was a grand idea. He owned a piece of land a quarter mile down the hill from his inn. He decided it should be landscaped and opened as the Chinese Gardens. The public would take their pleasure strolling among well tended lawns and flower beds or enjoy a boat on the lake. Genteel afternoon tea would be provided as befitted the class of society frequenting his gardens. Only on special celebratory occasions would alcoholic beverages appear. [7]

Hurst was quite a popular place for day trippers from Brighton. Adam Adams had planned his gardens for such a clientele. Sadly, the early summer had seen a minor fever epidemic in the village: expected visitors were keeping clear. And when the great day came for the Chinese Gardens to open, the heavens opened too which dampened the ardour of many, though not of Adam Adams. He was certain he had invested in a winner regardless of the wet beginning.

In the High Street, Henry King had an even safer investment, a coal merchant's business. He could neither read nor write but that was of little importance. He had his supplier, his customers, his horse and his cart. Coupled with his energy and enthusiasm his business was secure. When the day's work was done, he stabled his horse, gave it hay and water, and set off home. [8]

The stable was in a yard behind William Randell's shop, a quiet place for the horse and a quiet one for any person who found that the building was under repair and could not be locked.

Somebody did know the state of things. One night, Henry returned to the stable and discovered that some hay had gone – a good quarter of a truss missing. Three days later it happened again.

The next morning, Henry informed the police. Constable Streatfield went with him to inspect the premises. It was decided the constable should keep the place under surveillance by making a hide-out in the loft over the stable. There he could keep well hidden behind the straw and hay yet still be close enough to apprehend any intruder.

Saturday evening, he climbed the ladder, made a comfortable watch-place and settled himself for a long vigil.

About 11.00 p.m. there was movement in the yard. The stable was entered. For a time, quiet movements continued around the stall. They stopped. Next someone was at the ladder, climbing it to the loft. Whoever it was had been there before and knew the way around. The door above the yard opened. The constable could see a silhouette figure pushing hay from the loft. Quietly he edged himself from concealment.

'Halt!' he commanded. The intruder froze in surprise. The constable strode forward to make his arrest. It was easy: no attempt to flee, no desperate punch.

Down in the stable he could identify his man. It was Edward Oram, ex parish-boy, now 35 and in trouble again.

Charges were made. Edward stood trial accused of stealing 5 lbs. (2½kg) weight of hay from Henry King valued at 2d. (1p) and 5 lbs. weight of straw from William Randell also valued at 2d.

The trial was simple, there was no defence and the only thing in doubt was the severity of the punishment. Edward's record was taken into account which revealed the workhouse round-frock theft. He was sentenced to seven years transportation.

They put Edward aboard the Leviathan. There his spirits sank. Cuckfield Workhouse had been degrading but was as nothing compared with the prison hulk. Within months, his health deteriorated. He lacked the criminal's capacity for self preservation. Cooped in the insanitary conditions of the prison hulk, he caught a fever and died. No more would he drink at the White Horse and ruminate on suspicious card-playing visitors.

That winter saw more and more men out of work. Families were dispersed in the workhouses until both Cuckfield and Hurst were full, crowded to their limits. The Board decided the only solution was to amalgamate them in a new Union Workhouse at Cuckfield.

Hurst Vestry called a special meeting. Mr. Marchant explained the position. Increased population throughout the Union area made the establishment of larger facilities imperative.

The ratepayers then had their say. They had been obliged to fund improvements to the facilities and sanitation of Hurst workhouse, a total waste of money. It was regretful that having been put to so much expense they now had to pay yet again. If a new place was inevitable, the Board should promote the best interests of people by erecting a workhouse that ensured the health, comfort and advantage of all its inmates.

The parish conscience now at peace, the ratepayers resigned themselves to the inevitability of the building and awaited its construction.

In January, a group of men met to enjoy an event for which they had been waiting a long time, the seventh annual meeting of the curate's Society for Industry and Prudence designed to keep men free from any workhouse. It took place at the New Inn, the setting for so many celebrations.

First, Rev. Tufnell gave a glowing report. £700 had been deposited in the Brighton Savings Bank. The membership stood at 26; agricultural labourers, shoemakers, tailors, butchers, millers, carpenters, bricklayer and carrier. Under the rules of the society, a few had been required to leave because of marriage. It was now time for the awards promised by the generosity of the parish gentry to those who had saved for five years and remained single.

In turn, the four qualifying members marched proudly up to the curate to receive their award, a pair of high quality half-boots.

The previous year, half-boots had been awarded to 11 men, of whom six had since married. The remaining five were about to receive their second award: the choice of a set of six silver teaspoons or £1 5s. 0d. (£1.25) worth of clothing. In turn they stepped up to the curate. Only one had chosen clothes.

At last it was time to make the highest award to the men most steadfast in preparing themselves for marriage. They had been in the society from the start and had achieved seven years of saving. Their prudence would prove its value when in the due course of time they did marry. To each of those exemplary men, the curate was pleased to present an inscribed silver watch.

The watches were presented and admired, the recipients returned to their seats and members settled to an evening of song.

George Marchant Auctions More Building Plots

Hurst was on the verge of a great building venture. The vestry committee had agreed to the new parish church being built. Moreover, they had accepted a design by Mr. Charles Barry, the eminent architect of the new Houses of Parliament. [1]

Although the few objections made by local people were easily overcome, the rector's fears over fund raising proved correct. In the end, generous donations were made by Mr. Campion and the rector's father. The biggest contribution was to be £1700 from the church-rates.

The church-rate could not provide such a sum in a single year. An intermediary had to be found; someone with the well being of the parish at heart willing to loan a lump sum and be prepared to await its repayment over a number of years. [2]

In truth, someone with the parish interest at heart had already been found, Richard Weekes, doctor, land proprietor and the Brighton Patriot's 'Builder of hovels for the parish poor'.

Not even the most invective newsprint could throw such names at him now – unless they were privy to the business conditions of the loan. It would be 5% per annum over 17 years, the first repayment due after two years at £100 capital plus £85 interest. The doctor's outlay would eventually earn a profit of £765; parish interest at its best.

The rector obtained the bishop's sanction for St. Lawrence to be razed to the ground, and his blessing for services to be held in the school during rebuilding. The bishop stressed that his blessing covered only baptism, burial and normal worship. For marriages, the school had to be licensed. A licence was obtained.

The bells of St. Lawrence rang a final peal. A few of them would ring again from a shining new steeple. It was time for the old church to go.

First, the family monuments were removed with great care for they would adorn the walls of the new church. Once they were dismantled, a more aggressive approach was possible. Down came the stonework, destined for boundary walls or rough infill. Some of the arches would adorn Pakyns grounds. The font would have an agricultural use.

A novel but practical use was made of the smaller timber. Sticks and mementoes were fashioned and sold around the village. They were deemed acceptable in the better households, even gracing Danny House where Mr. Campion paid 10s. 0d. (50p) for his souvenirs of St. Lawrence. [3]

At the end of September, the corner stone of the new church was consecrated. The Bishop of Chichester conducted a service in the school before leading his congregation up the High Street to the churchyard. There the bishop blessed the stone, the school children sang a hymn, and all was ready for the builders. [4]

The school became the venue for the funeral service of Charity Rowland. She had suffered hardship throughout life; from her days of spinning for the linen weavers, of losing her husband to the debtors' prison and seeing her boys taken into the workhouse. Now her earthly life was over. She was laid to rest in the churchless churchyard.

A much happier event was the marriage of the rector's sister, Emily, a wonderful day for her and a celebration for the village. [5]

Early in the morning, workmen from Pakyns erected an evergreen arch outside the school. Village well-wishers lined the street in ample time for the wedding. The schoolchildren were marshalled at the arch. Each boy had a hat-band message: 'May happiness crown their union', and every child held a bunch of flowers.

The bridal party left Pakyns Manor and drove in five carriages down the High Street cheered by the onlookers. The boys raised their decorated caps to the bride as she stepped from her carriage and walked beneath the arch into the school.

When the happy couple re-emerged as Mr. and Mrs. Masters, the children showered them with flowers and followed the procession back up to Pakyns.

There at the main entrance, more than 100 tenants and traders had gathered. Each wore a white rosette. All joined in hearty cheers for the newly-weds. A band lined up and led the way to the house for the wedding breakfast.

Outside, the crowd again waited. The schoolchildren were given cake and beer. Tenants talked quietly among themselves, knowing that the spacious marquee erected for the day contained a dinner for them.

At last a four-horse carriage drew up at the door. The young couple appeared, stepped into the carriage and were away to their honeymoon.

Then the dinner was eaten. When the cloth had been removed, everyone received a bottle of wine. Mr. Bull gave the toasts: 'The Queen,' 'Mr. and Mrs. Masters,' and slowly through both families with a tune from the band between each toast.

Afterwards Nathan Stoner, the Hurst carrier, sang a song especially for the occasion and sang it again to please the happy guests. They now took over singing their favourites until six o'clock when Mr. Bull vacated the chair and led them to the front of the house. There, everybody sang 'God Save the Queen' and went quietly home.

By now dusk had fallen. The village became a twinkling show-ground of lamp-lit illuminations. Henry Pierce, the carpenter, created Cupid thrusting his arrow between two hearts; 'Happiness to Love' read his motto. Billy Heaver showed a flair for language, 'Amour et sympathie' and the united arms of the families. Grocer Mr. Wells had the Goddess of Love in a carriage drawn by doves. Throughout the High Street, the lights continued; a colourful finale to the festive day.

The school was also the venue for the third anniversary of the Hurstperpoint Missionary Society. It was a reserved occasion presided over by the rector. Members were going to hear about work in Africa, the land of lions and dark jungle where native men drummed hidden messages through the night. The members listened attentively as speakers told of the great work being done there by the Church of England. Intrepid missionaries were showing the African the way forward through faith to change from his heathen, savage ways to true enlightenment. The tribal African was learning not only how to behave in a civilized way but also how he should dress. More men were needed, and more funds to support the work.

Hurst people were not yet ready to become missionaries but they were willing to put their hands in their pockets to find something for the collection. Their thoughts were in the right place. [6]

In October, the Wesleyan Missionary Society met in their chapel by the Chinese Gardens. The chairman told how the society sent the word among the heathen in the remote parts of Africa and other quarters of the world so that the poor, dark and deluded creatures might be saved and brought back to the fold. He was followed by the Independent Minister of Henfield who reminded them how the society had always suffered sneers and scorn, and warned them how they were confronted by a different more powerful foe, the Popery of Rome. He then recounted the tale of the freed slaves in the West Indies who declared their simple-hearted faith: 'All given to God, hands no touch, heart no wish for it. Work for God first, den he help us.'

His listeners nodded their approval. They, too, contributed to a collection and showed that Wesleyans as much as anyone supported their missionaries in the wonderful work being done among the heathen races. [7]

In November, the Established Church held a meeting of a very different nature; the rector's annual New Inn dinner for his tithe-payers. The higher assessments imposed on them by the Commissioners' new map still grated. The 113 guests were far happier now they were being regaled with an excellent meal. They were as one that the very fact of having Rev. Borrer as their rector made a strong argument for continuing the good old custom of tithe and rent feasts. Nobody compared the amount of money spent on the dinner with the collection given to the Missionary Society. [8]

An even better celebration came at the end of the month with the Corn Market dinner, a convivial eat, drink and be merry evening shared by some 60 farmers and gentlemen with not a lady in sight. [9]

The market closed around four o'clock and people made their way to the New Inn to take their allotted places at the tables. In the chair was John Marchant, champion of so many village causes.

When all were assembled, they ate their way through a hearty meal and expounded the latest farming gossip. After the removal of the cloth, they settled down to drink healths and enjoy the evening.

First were the loyal toast and a patriotic rendering of 'Victoria, the Queen of the Sea'. Next they drank to the prosperity of the market and followed with a comic song, 'The Joys of Emigration'.

There were doctor jokes and political jokes about shirtless Chartists petitioning for the vote, and they had the comic story of the Irishman who began a letter to a friend but had to give up over spelling because his pen was so bad. Then they guffawed afresh as Mr. William Pike sang the tale of 'The Old Maid'.

Fourteen songs and a recitation later, the vice-chairman at last called the final toast: 'The health of the working man'. Well mellowed with wine, the farmers heartily concurred and agreed on the desirability of improving conditions for the men, of encouraging their skills and acknowledging their achievements. After all, the loyal labourer was well worth his keep.

On that happy note, the farmers went home to sleep off their Annual Market Dinner.

Christmas Day brought more cheer. The Brighton Herald rejoiced at the thought: joyous parties; turkey redolent in oyster sauce, the goose, the ham; the plum-puddings, mince pies, tarts and oranges; the wine and old ale; the games, the gambles and the never-to-be forgotten mistletoe.

The inmates of the workhouse, the old men and women together with the children, were having their own Christmas dinner to remember; beef, plum-pudding and good strong beer funded by a parish subscription. They had guests as well: a local magistrate, Colonel Elwood, with his wife and several of the neighbouring gentry there to witness the happy effects of their generosity.

At the end of the dinner one of the old men gave thanks for the meal. He read from the prepared speech that he had so carefully practised: 'Honoured Sir, I feel much gratified at being chosen by my fellow inmates to express upon the present occasion our heartfelt thanks to you and to our other benefactors for your repeated liberality to us at this season of the year. This is in all probability the last time that we shall any of us eat our Christmas dinner under this roof, and we beg respectfully to say that we are very sorry for it because we are treated here with such uniform kindness, the matron and her worthy husband do all in their power to make us comfortable, we have kind and daily intercourse with the inhabitants and are so much at home that we no doubt shall very much feel our removal to the new Union House at Cuckfield. We trust you and our benefactors may live long to enjoy the fruits of your benevolence in the gratitude of those who partake your bounty and that at the end you may attain everlasting happiness is the prayer of Honoured Sir, your most obedient humble and grateful servants, the inmates of Hurstperpoint Poor House.'

The colonel had the goodness to reply ensuring them that any humble efforts on his part were as gratifying to him as, he was glad to find, the results had been pleasing to them. He trusted they would find themselves as comfortable at Cuckfield as they were now and it would at all times afford him much pleasure to do everything in his power to promote their welfare and happiness.

The Agricultural Express felt that such an exhibition of spontaneous good feeling and sympathy between the rich and the poor must convey its own lessons to the heart.

That Christmas proved the last for John Marchant at Little Park. In February, there was sad news of his death. The November market dinner had been his final public engagement. There he had championed the local farmers. He had been an esteemed figure supporting many parish interests and was people's churchwarden to the end. His Home Field would still host village cricket. Memories of his batting prowess would continue. So too would the family secret, the crippling mortgage on John Marchant's land. [10]

His sons made the immediate future secure. Nathan, as heir, sorted out estate affairs with Edward Duke the Brighton solicitor. George, an auctioneer, advertised more building plots for sale. Whether or not Little Park kept the creditors at bay and its secret intact depended on the brothers' business acumen and the fortunes of the farming community. [11]

There was a secret the East Sussex Police needed to probe; the arrangements for a prize fight that was scheduled to take place somewhere within the area. They had been detailed to prevent the fight. The who, the when and the where they had to discover. Local constables would have to be on their toes. [12]

Between 300 and 400 enthusiasts did know the relevant information and they assembled ready for the fray in a field near the Friars Oak. The match was between Cane, from London, and 'Watercress' so dubbed from his trade cry on Brighton streets. The majority of the crowd were 'Watercress' supporters but a fair number were locals, there just for the fun of it.

The pair were well matched. For an hour and a half they went for each other urged on by eager spectators. The outcome remained in the balance.

Then came an unwanted interruption: police. Inspector Daws of the East Sussex Constabulary arrived with Colonel Elwood the magistrate and Hatfield the new Hurst policeman. With them in case of trouble was a contingent of special constables.

Colonel Elwood lost no time in addressing the crowd. With his military background he was well able to handle such a situation. He spoke briefly and with clarity. Nobody could fail to understand him, the fight was over and they were to disperse immediately.

Hoots and hisses rent the air. The fight had yet to be decided, their money was on it. The evening was not going to be spoilt by a handful of special constables.

Colonel Elwood read the riot act; no rabble was going to take liberties with him. No one moved. The combatants remained in the ring within a barrier of noisy supporters.

The colonel consulted with Inspector Daws. It was time for the police to act.

The inspector spoke to Constable Hatfield. With their special constables, they rushed the barrier, broke through and seized the combatants. After 90 minutes of intense slogging at each other, Cane and 'Watercress' had little resistance.

With the fighters under arrest, the police could allow mob bravado to evaporate as the crowd melted into the darkness. Constable Hatfield could feel satisfied with his night's work.

Fifty miles away at Portsmouth, an event was about to happen that Peter Pratt and his fellow convicts could quietly celebrate. Ever since the unfortunate mutton theft, his home had been the insanitary Leviathan. Now the admiralty had decided the hulk was no longer habitable even for convicts. Orders were issued for its replacement by the Sterling Castle.

The Sterling Castle was at Devonport, 150 miles west along the English Channel. Early in October, it was hauled off the dockyard and made ready for towing. [13]

Two steamships would tow the hulk. One of them, the Eclair, was still on her way from Portsmouth. By the time she arrived, southerly gales were whipping up the seas to such a state that towing was impossible. For a fortnight the ships were trapped.

As soon as the weather abated, lines were fastened and the tow began; a pair of modern steamships, paddles churning the waves, heading up Channel with the Sterling Castle bouncing in their wake.

They reached Portsmouth without mishap and the new hulk was manoeuvred to her permanent moorings. The Eclair set her paddles for the African coast.

Once the new hulk was provisioned, Peter Pratt limped aboard with his fellow convicts. Unfit for work in the colonies, he would complete his time on Stirling Castle as a 'best behaved' prisoner privileged with top deck accommodation. It was still a dismal home but it had to be better than the rotting Leviathan.

English Corney had by now served four years of his sentence in Van Diemen's Land. He was being a model prisoner and had completed his probationary period successfully. This meant that he could ask for his family to join him there.

Mrs. Corney was eager to go but her money as a washerwoman could never finance them. The vestry resolved that £70 should be offered towards the expenses. Mrs. Corney was delighted. When she told her brother-in-law, he explained how £70 was insufficient for a woman with six children. He wrote back for her asking £90. [14]

William Ellis took the chair at the meeting called to consider the request. They debated the implications and refused the extra £20. They also withdrew the original offer.

The decision was unpopular with more than just Mrs. Corney. A group of supporters decided to do something about it. They wrote to the vestry calling for a special meeting to consider the propriety of assisting Mrs. Corney.

The vestry acceded. A meeting was held and there the £70 offer was again made official. This time Mrs. Corney accepted.

Preparations went ahead. The Poor Law authorities were advised. Back came the ruling that because English Corney had deserted his family the Commissioners could not provide for such measures.

Cuckfield Union replied explaining that English had been maintaining his family and living with them until his arrest. The authorities saw no reason to change their decision. Mrs. Corney and her children would not be financed from poor-rate money. [15]

The vestry's reaction was to help the family move to Brighton – on the hill above the railway station where Mrs. Corney should be able to earn enough to keep her family out of the workhouse. The original intentions had been good. Somehow they had gone awry.

1845: Billy Heaver Climbs
the Social Ladder

When Kelly's 1845 Post Office Directory came out, Hurst had risen to market town status with a long street of clean, regular and respectable houses. It had attractive pleasure gardens with an excellent mineral spring, a pleasure fair every 1st of May, and total income tax assessed a little above £10,000. [1]

The town was on the Brighton railway, less than two miles from the Hassock's Gate station. It also had a thrice weekly passenger link with Brighton by Nathan Stoner's accommodation van housed in the spacious stables of the Lamb Beer House where Dr. Weekes had once fondly imagined the hustle and bustle of stage-coaches.

The National School for boys and girls was supported by subscription. It was common knowledge among many parishioners that Rev. Carey Borrer hoped public subscription would enable him to achieve his dream of a school run by clergy of the Church of England for boys from middle class families. At present it was just an idea. The new church was taking all available funds and his school could progress no further than a paragraph of hope in the Brighton papers.

The rector had sufficient call on his time dealing with daily worship. He had growing competition. Dissenting worshippers now had three chapels to choose from (Baptist, Wesleyan and Antinomian) all temporarily superior to the Established Church's place of worship (the schoolroom) although the new church should be the finest in the county when finished.

In the High Street, the workhouse was full to overflowing with a hundred inmates. Billy Heaver was still there with his wife as matron. He was steadily climbing the social ladder and gained a place in the directory as registrar of births and deaths. And there too, as assistant registrar, was Richard Davey.

George Batchelor, who had twice spent time in the workhouse, was now a trader in his own right. He would not remember the weeks his mother spent nursing her children while her husband tramped the London Docks looking for work, but he would remember his second experience under the reforming hand of the governor detailed to rehabilitate a young thief. The results had justified the means, for George now had his own shoemaker's shop. Even greater, he had a second entry as steward of the Wesleyan Chapel – a sinner saved indeed.

Another name from the old workhouse books was there as saddler and harness maker; Henry French, eldest son of 'parish-child' Henry who had emigrated to New York with the rest of his family in 1832.

Jeremiah Bartley, whose boyhood japes once saw him in the parish stocks, and Edward Harmes, one time debtor, both had a place as beer retailers. Michael Harmes did not appear but, being Michael, he would not go without a record in some form or other.

Dr. Richard Weekes continued as surgeon and physician. For instant service, there was Mr. Wyborn in his chemist's shop dispensing his own medicines or providing a patent bottle from the shelf. He stocked 'Blair's Gout and Rheumatic Pills', authentically amazing as witnessed by the gentleman regularly laid up several weeks each year, bled with leeches and with his foot wrapped in poultices. A single day of Thomas Wyburn's pills saw wonderful relief, the second day crutches discarded, the fourth a complete cure. All for 2s. 9d. (14p) a box, large – what value!

There, too, was Edward Dench who had transferred his business from Brighton. He was happy to fit that feature of superior residences, a water closet, to any house within 20 miles at no extra charge.

Tinman and brazier, stationer and bookseller, plumber, painter and glazier, pork-butcher, milkman, hairdresser, coal-dealer, watch and clock maker; all were at hand. Hurst was a modern, bustling community. Long gone were the days of grocer-cum-draper, the baker and the shoemaker.

Yet local-government was still the rector, the churchwardens and the overseers at the monthly vestry meeting. And winds from whatever quarter wafted farm-yard and privy smells so familiar that only the worst were noticed.

At last the day came for the new church to be consecrated by the Bishop of Chichester. Just one section awaited completion, the spire, so the tower stayed swathed in scaffolding. [2]

It was a truly magnificent building; a symbol of hope soaring heavenward. Within it, were light, symmetry and an aura of humble grandeur. Sculptures of their majesties Queen Victoria and Prince Albert on the chancel arch gazed benignly on those of the bishop and archdeacon set on pillars in the nave – all preserved for posterity. And outside in a hidden corner, near Mr. Campion's private door to his transept, a name was chiselled in clear block letters, M. HARMES 1845. Michael too was an indelible part of the church fabric.

Holy Trinity Church

The bishop and 70 invited clergymen assembled at the rector's home, Pakyns Manor, ready for the consecration service. From there they solemnly processed eastward to the church where churchwardens Mr. Beeching and Mr. Ellis waited at the great west door.

They greeted the bishop and conducted him to the altar. After him came a host of ecclesiastics, including Rev. Tufnell back for the day from Edburton, who were all shepherded into the confines of the chancel.

The barrel organ, temporarily housed in the side aisle, guided everyone through part of the 82nd psalm. The bishop then walked down to the chancel steps and disappeared through a doorway to reappear a few moments later at the stone pulpit set high by the chancel arch. From there he looked down upon the packed congregation and delivered a lengthy sermon. When he had finished, he consecrated the building. It was now Holy Trinity Church.

The next day, the Union Society held their 20th anniversary. They assembled at the New Inn ready to form up behind the Brighton Chain Pier Band. At 10.00

a.m. the band began. The society's 125 members marched cheerfully westward in holiday mood to Holy Trinity for their service. The rector had his turn in the high pulpit and reminded his listeners: 'Render therefore unto Caesar the things which are Caesar's and unto God the things which are God's,' after which the band marched them back along the High Street, straight past the New Inn and left into the Bowling Alley. There, dinner was awaiting them in the usual big marquee. After dinner, more pleasures were to come; the wine and toasts, the music and song to while away the hours to evening. [3]

In June, Holy Trinity witnessed its first baptism when the rector christened baby Isabella Emily and accepted her into the family of the Church. How satisfying for him to record the baptism as: 'The first in the newly built parish church', and what added pleasure for him and his wife in the baby being their own first child, Isabella Emily Borrer. [4]

The first wedding was as great a day for the bride and groom. Charlotte Austin, daughter of the excise officer, was marrying John Randell the shoemaker who, if he followed in his father's footsteps, would maintain a thriving family business. It was the new curate, not the rector, who had the pleasure of conducting Holy Trinity's first wedding.

But around the fields and gardens something was happening that gave nobody any pleasure. Potatoes were failing to mature. Healthy foliage withered, tubers proved unfit for food. Decayed plants spread a putrid stench in the air. Farmers were losing a cash crop; the gardening labourer a staple food. Everyone accepted that produce could vary with the year, but rotting potatoes were different. They belonged to newspaper stories, not Hurst's fields. [5]

Serious as the potato trouble was, Adam Adams did not let it distract him from his Chinese Gardens programme. He had planned a respite from the daily woes of old age for all those aged 70 or over who were still independent of the workhouse. They were invited to a special tea in the gardens. The gentlemen of the village who had subscribed to the occasion would have the pleasure of attending and quietly witnessing the old folk enjoy their unexpected treat. [6]

The weather proved beautiful. 35 guests assembled on the lawn. In the shade of the oak trees, a musician played as places were taken at tables set with antique china.

The rector gave a blessing and tea began; a tea including whipped cream with wine syllabubs and choice mixed liqueurs. The guests ate and drank with relish. After tea, the musician played for old time rustic dancing: great fun whether the guests could actively dance or simply sit and listen. In the background a fire-balloon tugged on its tether.

At the close of his day, Mr. Adams fired his prize marvel, the seven-pounder cannon purchased from Dr. Weekes, and released the fire-balloon.

In a gesture of genuine appreciation, one of the guests clambered onto his chair to propose a vote of thanks. The old folk waved their hats and bonnets aloft as they gave three hearty cheers for Mr. Adams before going happily home to their insanitary cottages.

For the old who did have to inhabit the workhouse, there was news that the new building in Cuckfield was ready. There was no ceremony, just the Union Board informing Hurst that their workhouse was to close and the inmates were being transferred. Billy and Elizabeth Heaver also had to leave. They moved to a terraced cottage beside the new church.

The vestry held a meeting to ensure that nothing belonging to the parish disappeared to Cuckfield. William Ellis had such long vestry experience he could safeguard parish property. The overseers were Henry Hider, son of the farmer who once lost his newly washed socks from the Cophall hedge, and Henry Rowland, the grocer on the old Royal Oak property who had enjoyed good business providing the workhouse groceries. He would have to be thankful for past trade. [7]

Early in the morning, the inmates began the move to Cuckfield. Hurst's old workhouse stood empty. In the new year it was put up for sale by auction under the hammer of George Marchant. By way of advertisement, an auction notice was pinned to the church door. [8]

Sale day came. Bidding began and the best offer was £650 by Hurst's Thomas Wadey, builder of the parish black hole.

Thomas Wadey was a man of skills. He straightway began his dream of converting the buildings to a row of cottages. The occupants could be confident of good workmanship. Thomas would enjoy a responsibility that went hand in hand with property ownership, that of voting for his Member of Parliament.

Property ownership caused an incident one Sunday as the congregation were arriving for morning service at Holy Trinity. Most people approached from the east. This meant walking past Mr. Campion's north transept door and along to the west door. It was accepted by everyone that only Mr. Campion's party used the transept entrance.

When Dr. Weekes arrived, he made straight for the transept. The door was abruptly shut in his face and locked. It was no accident. Dr. Weekes was being admonished. He felt offence keenly, but people were watching. Quietly he made his way to the west door with the general congregation. [9]

After the service, he and his nephew, Dr. Richard Weekes junior, reviewed the incident. No man could possess the right of entry at a church. There could not be exclusive use of a transept. It was time to voice a protest.

A small group met together. They compiled a letter to the bishop seeking to end the unprincipled privilege bestowed upon the lord of the manor.

Mr. Campion was informed. He read the letter. It was an infamous reflection on his character. He asked his solicitor to negotiate with the complainants. It did no good. Legal action would ensue.

The case was decided at the church consistory court. Was or was not Mr. Campion entitled to the transept? The Chancellor of the Diocese made a lengthy judgement and declared the transept to be Mr. Campion's legally and morally. By rights, Dr. Weekes and his associates should be made to pay all costs. In an endeavour to prevent ill feeling and rancour, both parties would be left to defray their own expenses.

Mr. Campion was satisfied. Dr. Weekes felt dirt rubbed in his face.

Two months later, came the anniversary of the consecration of the new church. The parish had been collecting money for the bells during the year. Those saved from the old church were added to by new ones cast at Whitechapel. There was now a full peal of eight bells hanging from a frame made by William Pierce the church organist/carpenter. One of his assistants had carefully carved a name into the frame, M. HARMES. Michael was now within the church as well as without.

At 9.00 a.m. the first peal heralded the annual service of the Union Benefit Society. Headed by their banners and a rhythmic band, the 160 members marched up the High Street, held their service and marched back again for their New Inn meal chaired this time by Nathan Marchant. With Nathan, conviviality was the order of the day and they spent a humorously happy afternoon.

The bell ringers too were in their element ringing a peal of grandsire triples. The air reverberated: 1000 changes, 2000, 3000 in unbroken rhythm and still on.

Parish clerk Richard Davey looked at the clock. Time for evening service: he must ring the bell to summon the worshippers as he did every day, morning and evening. Being the first church anniversary, it was even more important to let people know. He ordered the ringers to stop.

The bell ringers were stunned, bemused. The four thousandth change was almost there. Stop! Could he really mean it?

Richard could think of only one thing, ring the service bell. His military training and devotion to duty blanked his mind to all other considerations. The grandsire triples suddenly stopped. A lone bell sounded.

The ringers were upset, many villagers were upset. Clerk Richard Davey had been authoritarian and unquestionably wrong.

Rev. Borrer did his best to smooth ruffled feelings. He seemed to be spending half his time smoothing people's ruffled feelings. The promise of another peal in the near future calmed everyone; it would be a peal of Oxford treble bobs.

There were no ruffled feelings when Billy Heaver was appointed sidesman and assistant to the church wardens. No one questioned his integrity or that his progress from workhouse governor was thoroughly deserved. His election to a post of responsibility within the Holy Trinity hierarchy was the social seal of respectability. At his cottage beside the church he was well positioned to carry out his new duties whenever needed.

Billy Heaver had another role to play as relieving officer for the Cuckfield Union. He was ordered to attend at Brighton Town Hall to give evidence about the Corney family's settlement. Mrs. Corney had been obliged to seek relief from Brighton overseers or she and her children would starve. She had been taken before the magistrates where she had to disclose her husband's cattle dealing and transportation. Brighton had granted temporary relief but wanted the family removed.

Billy Heaver was put on oath. He had to accept that Hurst had been the Corneys' home for a number of years. Brighton's case was proved. The Corneys were returned to Hurst.

When they arrived, Richard Davey, in his role as assistant overseer, was there to accept them and sign the order acknowledging their safe delivery.

Arrival was one thing, being welcome another. The Commissioners had previously ruled English Corney to have deserted his wife so she no longer shared his settlement and had reverted to her Brighton one. The magistrates may have said the Corneys belonged to Hurst but the real authority lay with the quarter sessions at Lewes.

Hurst lodged an appeal. The case was adjourned, the start of protracted proceedings that continued from sessions to sessions. Until a judgement could be made, the Corneys were to remain in Hurst as temporary inhabitants.

1846: Jenny Lind Captivates Brighton

Hurst's farmers were angry. Prime Minister Peel had reneged on his election pledge and done the unforgivable. He had given in to the northern industrialists and repealed the Corn Laws. The newspapers may have quoted good reasons for Peel's change of heart but Sussex men knew the resulting flood of grain from overseas would ruin the markets. There would be no more money in wheat.

Suddenly, everybody knew there would be no money from Sussex potatoes either. Once again the air stank as healthy plants withered inexplicably and tubers decayed in the ground.

Letters to the papers expounded theories for the failure: electricity in the air; rain and windless warmth producing putridity; invasive microscopic yellow insects with horned heads and four golden stripes down the body. Whatever the reason, the result was the same, no potatoes. [1]

Reports from Ireland told of a summer morning when people woke to discover that their potato fields which had been green with promise in the evening were now black and rotting: a second year of blight – and this time destroying the entire crop; the year's staple food gone.

After the last year's disaster, they had managed to struggle through helped by imported maize, the sale of the family pig and a pittance earned on public works but how were they to survive the coming months?

People traipsed the towns searching for food and work. Hopelessly weighed under by malnourishment, they declared it was as good to die by the bayonet as by starvation. Reporters warned that unless the Government took measures to meet the emergency, law and order would not be respected.

When February papers highlighted the latest conditions, readers were horrified. Unknown places – Skibbereen, Kilrush, Ballycroy, Belmullet – widely spread across the far reaches of Ireland were calling the same lament.

No longer was it the clergyman being deprived of his tithes. It was hundreds of thousands of penniless, starving families forcibly ejected from their homes and left desolate by the roadside – their houses made roofless, doors torn from hinges. 'Famine fever' and starvation were being recorded at inquest after inquest.

Any lingering doubts were dispersed by graphic illustrations of wrecked streets, ragged beggars and decimated children. [2]

The Society of Friends responded by opening soup kitchens. An Irish Relief Fund received £2000 from Her Majesty Queen Victoria. Hurst people would do their part.

A subscription was opened. Rev. Borrer announced that Church offertories for the next two months would go to the Irish poor. Mr. Campion recorded his donation, £25 – almost a year's hunt subscription: the equivalent of 500 beggars knocking at his door. Once again, he had responded generously to the call for charity.

In August, Mr. Campion was able to put his money to a far happier purpose. He managed to buy tickets for his family to attend the musical extravaganza being presented at Brighton Town Hall. The Borrers, too, were going. They would hear the incomparable Jenny Lind, the famous Swedish Nightingale. Mademoiselle Lind had chosen Brighton as her first provincial venue after her London opera season. [3]

The best seats were expensive but well worth it, two guineas (£2.10) for a place in the concert room: far better than a five shilling (25p) seat in an adjoining room with no view of the singer or the orchestra. The event was a sell out. Nearly a thousand people would attend.

On the day of the concert, crowds gathered outside the town hall awaiting the star's arrival. They might not be able to hear her sing, but greet her they certainly would. At last, as the clock struck two, she was there, the one and only Jenny Lind: what a privilege to see her.

Those inside had a far greater privilege. They thrilled to her singing. It was exquisite with a captivating sweetness and purity of note. She dazzled and charmed her way with perfect execution in even the most difficult passages. The audience's enthusiastic applause was rewarded with encores that drew yet more ecstatic applause. Her final songs were two Swedish Melodies so beautifully rendered that everyone was in raptures. Jenny Lind had lived up to her reputation.

Mademoiselle Lind left the Town Hall, took tea at the Bedford Hotel and caught the 8 o'clock train back to London. Brighton had been conquered.

Two days later, the Campions and Borrers were in force at Coneyborough for the season's final South Saxon Archery meeting. It was a meeting of note: the Earls and Countesses of Chichester and of Sheffield with so many lords and ladies that the gentry of Hurst were well down the list. They all enjoyed an afternoon of archery, where each congratulated the other on their prowess with the bow, followed by an excellent dinner for nearly 150 guests. [4]

The next evening was the Grand Ball and Supper at the County Hall in Lewes. It lasted into the early hours of morning when dance weary guests entered their carriages and were driven home.

The August celebrations were not solely for the gentry. Adam Adams had taken great pains to book a special event. Mr. Batty's London Circus was touring Sussex. On Saturday the 28th it would arrive from Henfield. [5]

Two performances were advertised for the Archery Ground in the Chinese Gardens introducing the celebrated 'CHARIOTEERS OF THE HORATII' and 'THE MANDARINS OF CHINA'. Tickets for boxes cost 2s. 0d. (10p), the pit 1s. 0d. (5p) and the gallery 6d. (2½p) with the first performance at two o'clock and the evening one at seven. Entrance would be via the Pavilion Gate where a plan of the seating was available.

The circus arrived in a wonderful parade. At the head, a first rate band clad in aristocratic scarlet, then the performers and animals; a six-in-hand, 40 horses, ponies and two Syrian camels, such strange humped creatures. Anybody in ear shot just had to see the parade.

The huge tent was erected, tickets were sold and at two o'clock precisely the show began.

The ponies were amazing, completing their performance without a human in the ring. The clowns and acrobats were superb. The vaulters excelled themselves with one of them completing 18 and then 23 successive back somersaults. There was marvellous horsemanship, especially the Wild Indian sequence, but most amazing was the strong man who astonished everyone with his feats of strength. Finally, he stood on his head upon a single pole and rotated himself at speed as if he were a horizontal mill wheel. The ladies, the gentlemen, the children were all dumbfounded.

The evening performance was as good with one extra act. An unannounced performer, with great skill and utter silence, went among the benches and cut selected purses from ladies' dresses. Not until the circus was over did the unfortunate victims discover their loss.

Batty's circus moved on to Cuckfield. Police Inspector Flanagan went to the crowded evening show. Whilst most eyes were on the circus, the inspector's were on the look-out for the cutpurse. There was movement beneath the benches. Flanagan watched. A purse was cut. Flanagan moved to arrest his man. [6]

The prisoner was a circus hand, a new one, John Smith taken on at Henfield. He had a pair of sharp scissors, too much money in his pocket and no good reason for crawling around on his knees amongst ladies dresses: a fine finale by the inspector.

In September, Adam Adams celebrated the close of his Chinese Gardens season by holding a special dinner in the garden ballroom for 90 guests. They would dine on game-pie prepared by Mrs. Adams and baked by baker Small.

What that meant, the guests were about to discover.

In came Mr. Adams and his helpers with a giant pie 10 feet (3 metres) in circumference. Beneath its wide cap was a hundredweight (50kg) of rabbit, hare, pheasant, partridge, chicken, duck, geese, ham, beef, mutton and pork.

'Ooohs' and 'Aahs' of astonishment came from the delighted guests as they settled to the feast.

Game-pie was followed by a nine-foot (2½m) partner pie of fruit – all the fruits of the season; a night of unashamed gluttony. It would need well filled tankards to wash it all down – and brim full tankards they had.

Mr. George Marchant led the thanks and started in great good humour:

'Why are ladies like churches?' he joked.

The bloated guests held their breath for the answer:

'Because there is no living without them!'

The guests roared their approval. And so it continued; high mirth, toasts and song – a brilliant tribute to Mr. Adam Adams and his Chinese Gardens.

The annual corn market dinner in November suffered a fall in attendance. It was as excellent a dinner as ever and the entertainment as lively, yet less than 50 were there to enjoy it. Those present were sure the pressures of the time accounted for their colleagues staying at home.

The absence of Mr. Gravely was accepted as simple misfortune. He and some friends had stayed on after the previous week's market to sort out the wagers they had laid over the corn prices. The wagers had been in wine. By the time they had all been settled, the farmers were a bit unsteady.

Mr. Gravely got into the saddle all right for the ride home but outside Pakyns Manor his horse became frisky and threw him. His friends picked him up and took him to the Kings Head where he was left to sleep it off. The next day, the doctor was called. He diagnosed severe concussion. Mr. Gravely remained at the Kings Head.

There was no shortage of numbers at Adam Adams' Annual Ball at the Chinese Gardens. It took place soon after Christmas and proved a great success. Some 80 guests enjoyed their meal and at the appointed hour made ready to dance.

The ballroom decorations of evergreens and flowers were effective enough but Adam Adams had done more. He had copied royal fashion. In each corner of the room was a large Christmas Tree decorated with fruit and sweets. When the trees were lit up, the effect was wonderful.

In such a setting, the dancers could hardly fail to enjoy themselves, and so they did until five o'clock in the morning; a fine start to the year.

By April, dark clouds were hanging over the worshippers at Holy Trinity. The rector had refused their requests for a special vestry meeting to discuss several controversial church issues. At the annual Easter meeting for presenting the accounts and electing new churchwardens, the rector had to face his critics.

Dominant amongst the speakers was Dr. Richard Weekes. He denounced the unprecedented evil of over 200 church seats being allocated to only two people, the rector and the lord of the manor. Even worse was the locking of the transept door to the exclusion of several persons wishing to enter by it. Dr. Weekes waxed eloquent as he explained how respectable inhabitants had endeavoured in vain to end such an unchristian practice. His listeners applauded his sentiments.

The rector knew that much of the difficulty stemmed from his celebration of the Holy Eucharist after morning service every Sunday. He was convinced the real bone of contention was not the celebration itself but the money collection that preceded it. Those who objected to the weekly collection had become so stubborn that they were now threatening a complaint to the Bishop. It was a dilemma. Either the weekly Eucharist ceased, thus denying the whole essence of Pusey's tutelage at Oxford, or the threatened letter would probably materialize. The rector determined to stick to his guns.

The objectors were equally determined. Unless he relented his Puseyite ways they would leave the service at the end of the sermon. Nor would they be deterred by threats to take them before the Ecclesiastical Court on a charge of disturbing the Church.

When the meeting ended, rector and flock were as far apart as ever.

Rev. Borrer held his ground. His opponents held theirs and the complaint went forward: the rector was imposing erroneous innovations – would the bishop either stop the practice of weekly Holy Eucharist in Hurst or institute it throughout the diocese?

The bishop's ruling was eagerly awaited.

That Sunday, people attended morning service as usual. The time came for the sermon. Rev. Borrer preached and then began the offertory prayer. Next would be the collection. Up stood 200 of his congregation. They walked out. The rector calmly continued the celebration of Holy Eucharist.

The next Sunday, events took the same course; sermon, pre-collection exodus for the many and Holy Eucharist for the remainder. Guidance was needed before the split became a schism. [7]

The bishop's reply arrived that week outlining the way forward. He felt deep sorrow at the rift in Hurst parish. Changes were not always understood by everyone. Too many preferred to cling to old ways. He regretted that any worshipper disturbed others by leaving the service early. If he thought any good would result, he would admonish them. As it was, he would limit himself to prayer. The Sunday Service should be attended in full.

The following Sunday, Rev. Borrer's congregation, somewhat smaller, stayed beyond the sermon. After the offertory prayer, Billy Heaver conveyed the collection bowl with solemn discretion approaching only those who indicated they wished to give. Everyone celebrated the Holy Eucharist.

It was not the end of petitions in Hurst. George Faithfull was as devoted as ever to electoral reform. The Reformers of Hurst wanted equal electoral districts, household suffrage, voting by ballot and triennial Parliaments. They signed their petition and sent it to their favoured East Sussex M.P. for presentation to the House of Commons the following Tuesday night when electoral reform was to be debated. Mr. Faithfull still had an appetite for reorganizing Westminster. [8]

Parliament was more concerned with the threat of Chartist mobs on London streets. Hurst vestry could empathize: the problem of unruly youths had returned to their own streets. Each evening, young men and boys were loitering along the narrow pathways and passages forcing visitors into the road and in many instances grossly insulting them. So bad was the nuisance that there were continual complaints of ladies being annoyed on their way to and from church.

The tradesmen signed a memorandum to the magistrates alerting them to the unacceptable lack of police presence in Hurstperpoint village.

The magistrates felt unable to provide more police. Instead, they appointed one of the High Street shopkeepers to the post of parish constable. Saddle-maker Henry French was chosen. Henry French, son of a parish workhouse child: now to be accredited parish law keeper – another rung higher on the social ladder.

Henry was sworn in at the Cuckfield Petty Sessions and issued with an official staff and a set of handcuffs. Anti-social behaviour decreased rapidly.

While the tradesmen's troubles were appeased, the farmers' troubles continued. A cold, wet summer saw a disastrous harvest. Wind and rain battered the wheat in the fields, weeds grew rank, interludes of warm days resulted in grain germinating where it lay. When men managed to harvest the crop, it was too wet for milling.

Farmers bowed to the inevitable – American flour from Ohio shipped hundreds of miles down rivers to their sea ports, trans-shipped and carried thousands more miles across the Atlantic to arrive in Liverpool or London and rule the markets. Assailed on all sides, the farmers gritted their teeth and ploughed on. [9]

October brought cold winds followed by sharp frosts. Farm labourers were laid off early. The bad season had already meant less harvest income for them and their families: less opportunity to put money aside for the hard days of winter; a greater likelihood of falling foul of the workhouse.

There had been more illness than usual during the year. The Union Benefit Society had paid out £84 in sickness benefits. As a result, the dividend for members at the annual meeting was down to 7s. 0d. (35p). Only 118 were there to receive it. The Brighton Band led them up to the church and back down to the Bowling Alley for their dinner but the usual holiday atmosphere was missing. The society's officials knew their finances were in poor shape. Agricultural labourers were facing difficult times and needed all the support that could be given. Even so, dividends would have to remain low if the Union Society was to continue. [10]

The growing plight of aging parishioners was highlighted by a meeting advertised at the New Inn for tradesmen and agricultural workers interested in establishing a branch of the Brighton Provident Society. The rector explained how village Friendly Societies became unviable as members grew older and needed more assistance. When new membership income failed to balance expenditure, societies failed. The Brighton Provident Society offered security in sickness and old age because it was enrolled by Act of Parliament. [11]

Hurst's poor in general came under scrutiny when the vestry met to decide who should be excused payment of the church rate, now set at sixpence (2½p) in the £ plus the twopence (1p) to cover the Holy Trinity building repayments. It was decided that such money was beyond the pocket of 76 parishioners. The old names were still there; Isaac Sayers, Michael Harmes, Henry Henty, James Hazelgrove, John Talmey and William Bartley still caught in poverty's web. Others too had become entangled, game-keeper John Jupp and coal merchant Henry King among them. [12]

Several aged stalwarts of the parish had passed away. William Jenner at his farm behind the workhouse and George Rowland in his Royal Oak cottage were both in their eighties. Lame shoemaker John Henley had slipped back to the bottom of the heap finishing his days in Cuckfield workhouse. When he died, the vestry carried out their obligation to remove the body. He was carried home on a cart to be given a pauper burial in Hurst's own churchyard.

One death stunned everyone – Dr. Weekes, still in his sixties. People were in shock. Their doctor had gone.

Critics of his business transactions now remembered his medical skills and prompt response whenever anyone in sickness or injury needed him. The rector buried him and recalled his devoted attention to people of all classes both within and outside the parish.

The doctor's land and houses passed to his widow. For the land that was in Hurst Manor, she first had to pay Mr. Campion a heriot of one old pony. Her lord settled for £3. Widow Weekes could possess her inheritance.

The vestry tried to ensure an inheritance for Luke Wickam's family. Although Luke's insanity was incurable, people accepted that he was not a dangerous lunatic. First, the authorities were asked to allow his removal to a less expensive hospital. They insisted that he must remain at Hoxton. That ruling had to be accepted but there was the question of the money raised from the enforced sale of Luke's land in 1841. The vestry felt it should be available for his wife and children, yet for eight years it had all been held by the Insolvent Court. A resolution was made to claim it for the maintenance of the family.

Solicitor Kell saw to the paper work. The application went ahead. The authorities sent their reply. The money belonged to the Insolvent Court. It was for their designated use, not that of Hurst vestry. Once again, central authority was out-punching the parish.

Before the year was out, there was something out-punching everyone. Cholera was in the country again. Attacks were most frequent and virulent in low lying areas, especially in the neighbourhood of sewers and where there were large collections of refuse among human dwellings. Parishes were advised to set up committees to report on possible health hazards.

The vestry heeded the advice. Twelve sober and upright men were appointed as Hurst's committee. They included churchwardens Henry Beeching and Nathan Marchant, Baptist dissenter Henry Rowland, innkeeper Thomas Smith, farm steward Henry Bull and auctioneer George Marchant; respected parishioners all of them. They were to lose no time in splitting the parish into areas and completing their investigation as quickly as possible. People hoped one of the measures would be to install a few more public lamps in the streets. Valued visitors spending the season in Hurst had been complaining all too long about the dark state of the roads. [13]

A week later, the committee's printed report was to hand and ready for distribution to all householders who needed to update their sanitation. Somehow the healthy and invigorating market town of Kelly's Directory had lost its purity. [14]

There were certainly some unwholesome spots. Out at Sayers Common, Mrs. Weekes, widow of the old doctor, had inherited a stagnant pool of water at the front of four of her cottages. It was to be filled in and efficient drainage made for the privies. A quantity of exposed filth from a privy of Adam Adams was to be removed and not allowed to accumulate again. Jeremiah Bartley had to improve the state of The Oak's privy. The inspectors doubted it had ever been cleaned out.

Around the new church, the cottage drainage system was archaic. The landlord was Sir John Dodson: the likes of William Bartley the tenants. William's cottage had an open gutter drain leading to a blocked ditch in the bank that was meant to connect with a blocked ditch beside the road. The gutter had become nothing more than a sewage canal.

Just down the hill, were Sir John's Spring Garden Cottages, the home of the younger Isaac Sayers. There, the privies still drained into the stagnant water in the field beyond the cottages, an unfenced hazard for any small child. And the smell from it was still a constant annoyance that on hot days became an unbearable stench.

Across the other side of the road, the cottages had privies with neither drain nor cesspit. The effluent flowed straight across the backyards. Further down, from a privy lacking a door, the waste emptied straight into the road.

The High Street with The National School

Parts of the village were little better. Along the High Street, there were more blocked drains and overflowing cesspits. The privies along School Row were a disgrace and the well which the cottages and school shared was an open invitation to fever. Mr. Marshall the butcher had a dung heap right beside the road. Pig sties added to the filth. From Thomas Wadey's workhouse cottages, up the High Street and along to the church, people were told to clean sties and dig proper drains.

Hurst roads would remain as dark as ever but it would be a far healthier environment.

1849: William Bartley
Writes a Letter

George Sayers had been waiting for the year 1849 ever since his arrival in Bermuda for stealing the Locks Farm gander. Life on the prison hulks had been tough, especially during the hot months of summer with poor ventilation making conditions almost unbearable. George had managed to maintain reasonable health and he had wisely steered clear of trouble. At last his sentence was finished. He quitted the Dromedary hulk, marched aboard the Mariner and sailed east for home. [1]

Peter Pratt was half-way through his sentence on the Stirling Castle hulk in Portsmouth. The mutton theft had been his one mistake and he was doing his best to atone for it. He kept his copy book clean and gained consistently excellent behaviour reports. It proved a wise investment. With five years still to serve, Peter Pratt experienced the thrill of being set free. He hobbled home to his wife and daughter.

Everyone in Hurst, while not condoning his offence, had known it was committed because of a genuine need of food for his family. Now they would be able to welcome him back into the parish.

Peter Pratt chose not to test Hurst's hospitality. He found a house in nearby Keymer parish close to the railway and took his family there. It was a developing place able to provide a new beginning for the man content to earn an honest living. [2]

Others had their eyes set on Australia. Joseph and Charles Gander and their friend Thomas Glazebrook had been together at Sayers Common since childhood. The Gander brothers were both married, Joseph with two young children. Glazebrook was still single. In winter their outlook in Hurst seemed as bleak as ever and they decided the future lay overseas. They knew it was possible. All they need do was ask the vestry's help under the scheme for the Emigration of Poor People. They went ahead and applied.

At the vestry's February meeting, approval was given to provide clothes and provisions for the voyage; bedding, food utensils and a storage chest. Billy Heaver was instructed to compile an official list for Henry Rowland to supply up to £20 value. [3]

The families were fitted out. Passage was confirmed on the Scotia, due to sail for Sydney in early April. Never had Hurst organized such a rapid emigration.

The Scotia had docked at London in January from the magical Coromandel Coast of India with a cargo of cotton bales, indigo, wine, sugar and ivory gathered at Cuddalore, Pondicherry and Madras – the stuff of dreams. For the Gander brothers, their own dreams could come true; dreams of freedom from Sussex poverty, of independence and their own home in the land of opportunity. [4]

When they left Hurstperpoint, the Australia bound families did not ride high on the stage-coach seeing new views of Sussex as Mrs. Gorringe and her children had once done. The coach had disappeared; blown into history by the railway. Instead, in the early morning they set out by wagon to Hassock's Gate station where they boarded the 7.18 for London, the only morning train to cater for third-class passengers. And now, thanks to parliamentary legislation, even the third-class travellers had seats and a roof to their carriage. In bad weather, shutters could be closed across the glassless windows. Special louvered sections in the shutters would allow air and light. In such comfort they travelled to London.

The Scotia set sail and readers of the Lloyds London News waited for reports of the ship being sighted by incoming vessels.

More people were keen to emigrate. In May, Rev. Borrer chaired a vestry meeting to grant assistance for another four families seeking a new life in Canada; William and Sarah Steel with five children, Reuben Sayers with his wife Jane and their five, Stephen and Ann Simmonds with four including baby Joseph, and Elijah King with his wife and three year old daughter, both Harriett.

Richard Marchant proposed the motion, Henry Bull seconded it and the unanimous vote of the vestry (six men) set the seal for the largest ever exodus from Hurst. The fares out totalled £100. Parish donors subscribed £70 to the Hurstperpoint Emigration Account with the remainder from the Commissioners and Union Board.

The families left Hurst on the 5th July. Their ship, the 'Toronto' was a modern vessel, a 406 ton barque built the previous year in Sunderland.

There were new opportunities, too, for Mrs. Corney and her children. Husband English had continued as a model prisoner in Van Diemen's Land and had once more asked for his family to be allowed to join him.

Hurst and Brighton had been arguing at successive Lewes quarter sessions over Mrs. Corney's rightful place of abode. Hurst now took the initiative by failing to send a representative when the case came up yet again. Brighton consequently won and Hurst was left to deal with the family.

The vestry agreed to allow £25 to help Mrs. Corney and her five children sail south. She need no longer rue the day she had turned down £70 as insufficient. Experience taught hard lessons. She was happy to accept anything that could see her family reunited. A passage was booked for them on the William Jardine. Henry Rowland was asked to supply necessary articles in accordance with the Colonial and Emigration Office's list.

Finally the day came for the family to set sail from London bound for Van Diemen's Land and their grand reunion.

While the Scotia and Willam Jardine headed for the equator and the Southern Ocean, the Toronto sailed west across the Atlantic. On the 22nd August the Canada bound families stepped ashore at Quebec and were safely put aboard a steam boat with their luggage, two days provisions and fare paid up the St. Lawrence River to Montreal and a new life.

The Ganders and Glazebrook aboard the Scotia were also in safe hands. It was a long and tedious voyage but at last the ship berthed in Sydney. They too could begin their new life.

The voyage to Van Diemen's Land took three months. When the William Jardine docked in Hobart, the Corneys were together again after nine years of separation. For English Corney and his family it was a time of rejoicing.

For Hurst farmers, the future seemed more doubtful. The flood of imported wheat had destroyed prices. Crops were averaging barely 44 shillings (£2.20) per quarter (300 litres) – a fall of almost 25% in two years. It was scant encouragement to see an abundance of top quality wheat in fields when the cost of producing it meant farmers could never compete with imported grain. They knew their adjustment of the men's wage down to 10 shillings (50p) a week had been a realistic move: how else would money be found for wages, the rent, rates and taxes? [5]

They repudiated the Brighton Herald's claim that it was the farmers voiding their spleen on the labourers. Never was a newspaper so far from the truth. The price of the quartern loaf (4lbs/2kg) had already dropped from 11d. to 7½d. (5p to 3p). With cheaper bread, a family was much better off than in the days of a 12 shillings (60p) wage and a more expensive loaf. The men may grumble among themselves but their work depended on the farm being profitable. It was the farmer who bore the full brunt of low prices and it meant just one thing, men driven out of business. [6]

In the south of the parish, Mr. Davies decided to give up Randells Farm. In the west, Stroods was going. They were both well equipped. Besides the normal run of carts, wagons, ploughs and harrows, there was plenty of modern machinery. Stroods had its subsoil plough for better drainage and a mechanized winnower for the threshed grain. Randells, with its greater emphasis on dairy farming, had its calf weigher and a special chaff box for feedstuff. The equipment remained sound, but for some of the farmers it was time to quit. [7]

Times were even harder for the labourer. His working day remained long with money short – and the potato crop again failing.

The one new pleasure for the struggling labourer was the fish cart that did business in the High Street. Pulled by dogs, the narrow cart brought sea-food from Shoreham. A man's evening drink could now be followed by oysters.

Francis Richardson and William White were enjoying such an evening in September. They finished their beer at the New Inn and left for a pennyworth of oysters. 'Bogey' Lellcott was already at the cart tucking in and seemingly without a care for anyone. [8]

Francis bought his oysters and tried to get to the vinegar bottle. 'Bogey' was in the way and Francis made it clear that he should move. There were a few ripe words and talk of blows, whereupon 'Bogey' struck first. Francis went down and that was the end of his oysters. It cost him a morning's work and medicine.

Francis took 'Bogey' to the County Court and won £3 damages, enough for a real night out. It would run to more than New Inn beer and oysters.

Landlord Thomas Smith was expecting new neighbours for the New Inn. An advertisement had appeared in the papers announcing a school to be opened next door to him at the Mansion House after Christmas. It was intended for the benefit of the sons of tradesmen, farmers and clerks, and others in the middle classes offering them the advantages of a sound education by clergymen of the Church of England. The curriculum would include English, French and Latin; history, geography, writing and book-keeping; vocal music and mathematics, including navigation, surveying and the elements of natural philosophy. Nothing seemed to have been overlooked. Boys were to be provided with three pairs of shoes and a pair of slippers. Trousers and waistcoat were to be dark or there would be an extra charge for washing. Fees were 18 guineas per annum with four guineas for Greek if required. Day scholar terms could be obtained from the headmaster the

Rev. E.C. Lowe. The instigator of the new school was the Rev. Nathaniel Woodard who already had a college at Shoreham. It was just the type of school Rev. Carey Borrer had been hoping to start in the village. [9]

News of the impending school was received with horror by the members of Holy Trinity congregation who disliked Rev. Borrer's Puseyite ideas of worship. They were adamant the Shoreham College was a hotbed of Puseyism. The papers had been full of it.

They knew, too, that the rector favoured such an institution and was actually negotiating the sale of land at Cophall Farm for a permanent building. Such a school in the parish would only increase the threat to their faith. It was akin to Roman Catholicism, to the pope's insidious infiltration into Britain. Loyal parishioners were already composing a humble address to Her Majesty Queen Victoria asking her to preserve the faith pure and undefiled, free from the popish invasion which was planting Roman Catholic bishops in the kingdom. Rev. Woodard's misguided vision would be countered by concerted opposition. [10]

William Bartley felt a more personal and immediate threat, and he turned to Sir John Dodson:

> 'Hurstpurpoint Oct 11 1849
> Sir John
> I hope you will excuse the great liberty I take in writing to you respecting my rent. I have been a tenant of yours and the late Mrs. Marchant in one of the Church Cottages for 30 years and have Managed to pay my rent till lately. I am now one year in arrear £6 10s. 0d. in consequence of illness to myself and family. I have been laid up 2 or 3 months and lost one eye and then my children all had the typhus fever both of which have distressed me very much and on Monday last my wife had the misfortune to fall and broke both bones of her leg and the bone protruded through the skin – she is laid up and her loss to me and family is very great – would you kindly take my case into consideration and set me free and I hope my circumstances will improve and I shall be able to continu paying as I have done before as I do not wish to leave the house after living there so many years – and I have done little repairs such as whitewashing etc – I am the second son of the late Thos. Bartley of the Royal Oak Inn one of the old inhabitants of Hurst – if you have any doubts respecting my statement the Rev. C. H. Borrer or any gentleman in Hurst will verify it if you will kindly write to them – may I make bold to ask an answer to relieve my anxiety. I have a family of 9 children and my present wages is but 10s. 0d. per week – and I have 4 children entirely depending on me.
> I am your very Humble Servant Wllm Bartley.' [11]

Sir John was a feeling man and he let them remain – down the hill in a Spring Garden cottage where the cleansed stream was no longer such a hazard. There, Mrs. Bartley faced long months of painful recovery, dependent for everything on her family and the goodwill of friends.

In spite of his troubles, perhaps William could afford a wry smile. He had a landlord who did not throw him on the street, a benevolent 'squire' and a rector who would subscribe to winter needs. He had work and a productive allotment for his vegetables. Just up the road, there were good neighbours in sexton Richard Davey and his wife. On the other side of the church, were Billy and Elizabeth Heaver who had never refused to give help when times were bad. Opposite them was brother Jeremiah at the Oak Beerhouse. All could be relied upon when needed.

His children had the National School just a short walk through the High Street past their grandfather's ex-Royal Oak Inn, now Henry Rowland's shop with the chapel and the cottages where old Michael Harmes still lived as verbally adroit as ever. With education, the children should have greater opportunities in life. It was what William's grandmother had promised for him so many years ago.

A brighter future for his children? Time would tell.

And Today

Today, Wolstonbury Hill continues to watch over Hurstpierpoint. The flint diggers' way up the steep north face remains, together with gentle paths for the quieter walker. Flints still lie among the chalk debris. At the foot, Danny House stands serene amongst its lawns. No longer the seat of the lord of the manor, it continues as a quiet retreat for retirement.

Pakyns Manor has become a set of desirable country residences. The windmill went long ago, the site now lost in a cutting of the realigned London/Brighton Road.

Thomas Wadey's workhouse cottages on the Town Field have given way to a pair of modern buildings. The field remains, venue for the tennis club, the bowls club, a children's playground and the annual St. Lawrence Fair held July instead of May Day.

The Chinese Gardens are now houses but beyond the Old Hollow's one time hazards of unhygienic cess pond and door-less privy lies the village Farm Centre – haven for family visitors motoring up the old south toll-road.

The High Street stays as narrow as ever and squeezes by as best it may at Upper Trumpkins just as it did when Richard Pockney drove his cart. Village shops trade on with bright displays for 21st century needs. The White Horse and New Inn continue to provide welcome refreshment along with modern café and restaurants, while on the site of Thomas Bartley's Royal Oak stands the village grocery.

The National School where Henry Muzzell taught is now the theatre of the local dramatic society. The present school is a short way down Dr. Weekes' Cuckfield Road, just past his dream hotel, on a corner of Little Park Home Field. Much of that is now houses but enough remains for the school children's cricket to be played on the slopes familiar to John Marchant's team and for their fetes to be 'near enough' to the grand fete of Queen Victoria's coronation.

The once maligned 1850 School for Middle Classes thrives on the grounds of Cophall Farm – Nathanial Woodard's St. John's College with its wonderful chapel and playing fields.

Queen Victoria and her consort still gaze benignly from their niches high on the chancel arch of Holy Trinity Church. Campion and Borrer memorials grace the walls, and in the tower hangs the bell-ringers verse of 1832.

On the church wall outside, just west of the north porch, the diligent searcher may find the neatly chiselled carving: M. HARMES 1845. Michael and his wife share a table-tomb close by with his father, James. Dr. Weekes and George Faithfull M.P. (sometime antagonists) lie at peace along the east wall. William Bartley, too, has a stone, not far from his father's beside the Garden of Remembrance.

And Isaac Sayers, Elizabeth Dunton's baby child, old John Henley from the Union Workhouse and the unknown vagrant from the barn are all somewhere within the churchyard. Tread softly as you go.

1: 1806 – 'Royal Oak' Bill.

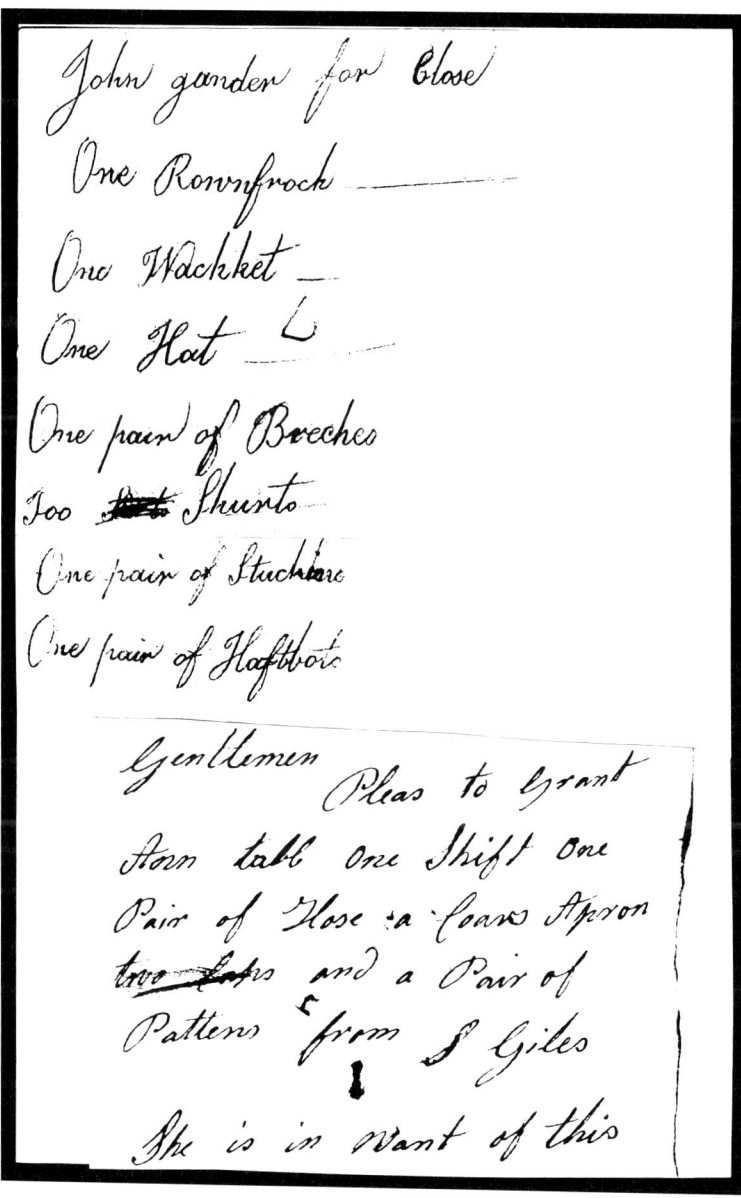

John gander for Close

One Rownfrock ———

One Wackket _

One Hat ___

One pair of Breeches

Too ~~Shut~~ Shurts ——

One pair of Stuchbare

One pair of Hafbote

Gentlemen Pleas to Grant

Ann tabt One Shift One

Pair of Hose a Coars Apron

~~two Laps~~ and a Pair of

Pattens from S Giles

She is in Want of this

2: Clothing Requests for a Boy and for a Girl.

Laxative bolus: bowel loosening medication within a large pill.
An Emetic: medicine to induce vomiting.
Febrifuge Julep: fever medication in a more palatable medicine.

3: 1806 – Doctor's Bill (with Journey Charges) for Hernia Truss, Medications, Treating a Fracture and Attending at Child-birth.

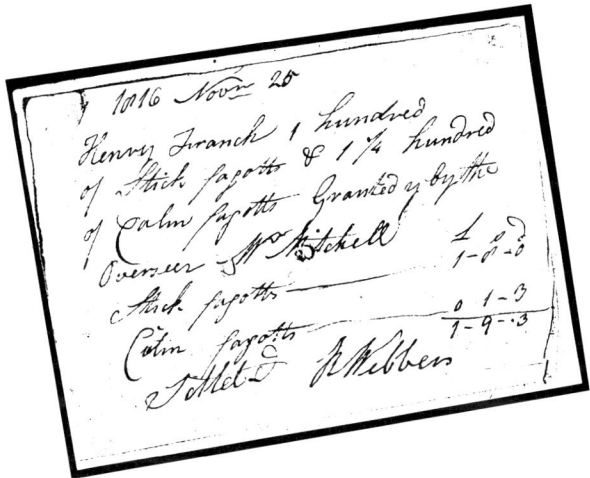

1816 Nov 20

Henry Franch 1 hundred
of Stick fagotts & 1¼ hundred
of Calm fagotts Granted by the
Overseer J^o Mitchell

Stick fagotts ——————
Calm fagotts ——————
Settled J. Kibben

1-0-0
0 1-3
1-9-3

(Recd) 22. 1822

Mr Chandler
              Please to mend
James Geere. Mathook.
              Wm Jenner

Octr 26. 1822

Mr Chandler
              Please to let Samuel
Geere have a new Spade
              Wm Jenner

4: 1816 & 1822 – Fuel Bill and Tool Orders to Blacksmith.

5: 1814 & 1830 – A Pair of School Bills by Henry Muzzell and Mrs Burry.

The Tender made by Mr. Jesse Gosling of
Hurstperpoint Grocer to supply the two Workhouses
of the Union with the undermentioned Grocery for
26 weeks from the 16th instant was accepted viz:

Best Third Cork Butter   7¼   per tb
Fine Gouda Cheese.   4½   per tb
Split Peas   ——   2.   per tb
Best Store Candles .   6d.   per tb
Best London Soap .   5¼   per tb
Prime Bacon . -— 5½   per tb
Prime Congou Tea —4/2   per tb
Raw Sugar . -— 6½   per tb
Oatmeal —— — 3.   per tb
Salt . —— .   1. 9   per Bushel

Mr. Barrowcliff that in the Opinion of this Meeting
Alteration is necessary in the mode of dieting the Child—
in Hurstperpoint Workhouse that instead of Broth or
Gruel and Bread for Breakfast as at present the
Broth or Gruel and Bread be served out separately
that for Supper Bread and Cheese or Bread and Butter
be substituted for Broth or Gruel And that on Satur—
the Dinner consist of Bread and Cheese or Bread and
Butter or other substantial Food instead of Soup as
hitherto.

6:   1842 – Workhouse Groceries Tender and Diet Order.

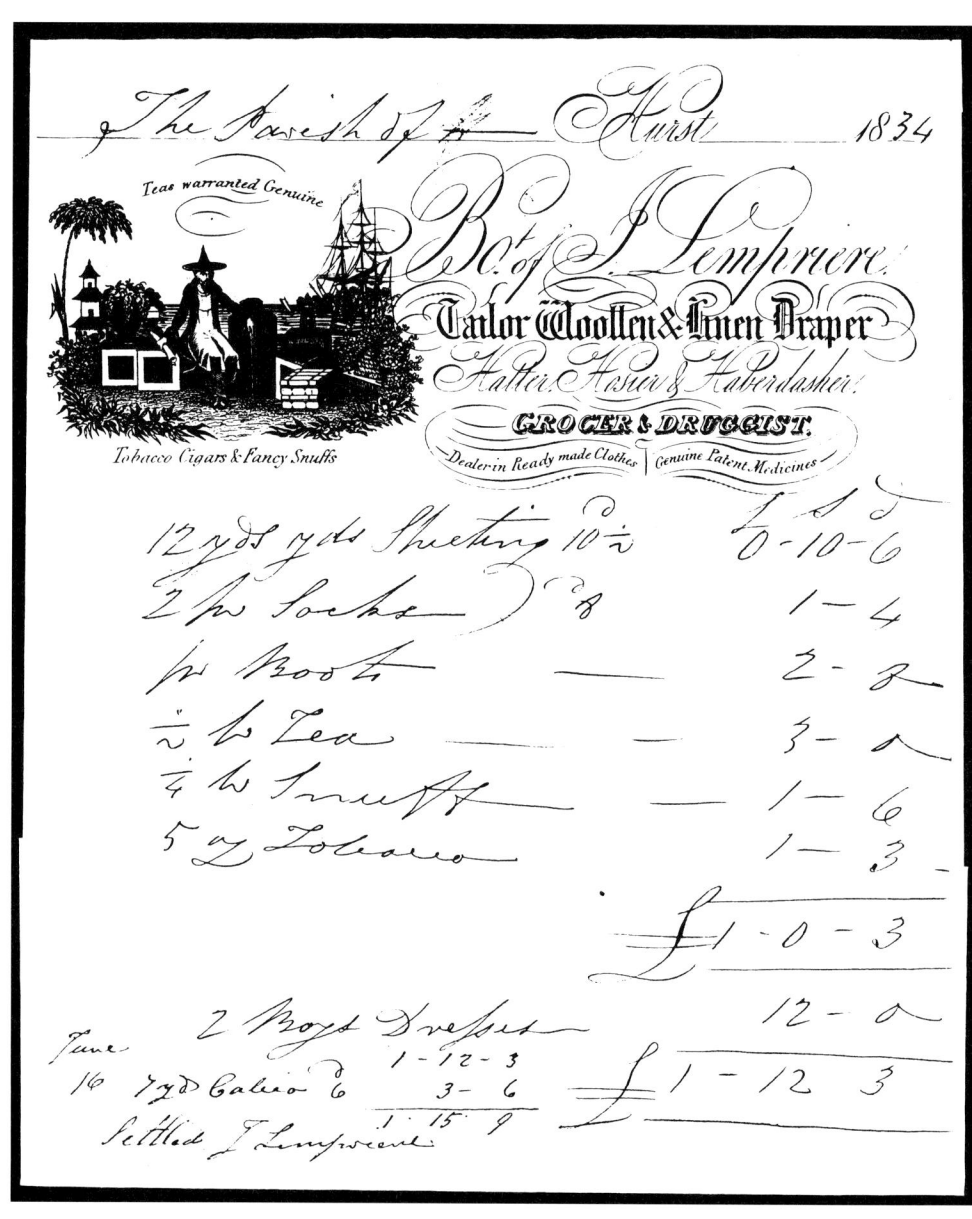

7:    1834 – 'Grocer & Druggist' Bill.

References

This code has been used where a number of references are from the same source. Otherwise the source is named in full.

CODE SOURCE

A West Sussex Record Office, Chichester. **

B East Sussex Record Office, Lewes.

C Public Records Office, Kew.

D Brighton Gazette Newspaper.

E Brighton Guardian Newspaper.

F Brighton Herald Newspaper.

G Brighton Patriot Newspaper.

H Lewes and Sussex County Advertiser Newspaper.

I Sussex Agricultural Express.

J A Medical Student at St. Thomas's Hospital, 1801-1802 The Weekes Family Letters by John M.T. Ford: London Wellcome Institute 1987.

K Lloyds Register, London.

L A Soldier in Wellington's Army: Sussex County Magazine, 1928.

M Sussex in Bygone Days.

N The Illustrated London News.

** All references for A '400' are 'PAR400' references;

James Fisher Map of Hurstpierpoint 1841

1: A ADD. MS. 17,683

The Village and The Gentry

1: H 27-1-1783
2: B LCG/3/EW
3: A MF 369
4: A 400/37/63-66
5: B DAN 2169
6: GENTLEMAN'S MAGAZINE 1806
7: A 400/7/24
8: A 400/4/91

The Workhouse and The Vestry Committee

1: A 400/12/2
2 & 5: A 400/12/1/1
3: A 400/31/58
4 & 8: A 400/31/59
6: A 400/12/1/5
7: A 400/37/73
9: A 400/31/71

Richard Pockney Buys a Horse

1, 3 & 4:
2: A 400/12/1/2
   A 400/12/1/1
5 & 6:
7: A 400/36/2
   B QO/EW/30
8: H 5-1-1795
9: A 400/13/1
10: H 28-1-1795
11: A R.S.R. PH 3/1

Thomas Godman's Children Go in the Workhouse

1: H 27-5-1793
2: A 400/37/19
3: A 400/31/64
4: A 400/31/75
5: A 400/31/60
6: A 400/12/1/1
7: B QO/EW/30
8: A 400/30/1
9: A 400/12/1/2

Mr. Markwick Reaps a Poor Harvest

1: A 400/31/60
2: A 400/31/62
3 & 8: A 400/31/63
4: A 400/31/64
5: H 20-2-1795
6: A 400/12/1/2, 31/63 & 37/33-62
7: A 400/12/1/2

Henry Beazley Joins the Navy

1: H 28-1-1793
2: H 5-12-1796 4 H 9-3-1795
3 ,5 & 6: A 400/31/69
7: A 400/31/72
8: A 400/31/71
9: A 400/12/1/4
10 & 11: A 400/12/1/5
12: GOODWOOD HOUSE

Hampton Weekes Attends Medical School

N.B. *J numbers are the **letter number** not the page number; i.e. 2 is letter number 2 (page 35 of Weekes Family Letters).*

1: J 2
2: J 19, 54, 56, 73, 85, 96, 109
3: A 400/12/1/6 & J 9, 13, 25, 88, 102, 103, 109
4: J 111
5: J 152
6: J 28, 31, 35, 40, 41, 43, 44
7: J 12, 14, 22, 34, 54, 111, 114, 116
8: J 17, 18, 34, 35, 36, 37, 38, 48, 54, 55, 60, 80, 96, 117
9: J 3, 21, 34, 39, 52, 64, 68, 772
10: J 70
11: J 18
12: J 45, 47, 73, 77, 81, 91, 95, 111
13: J 98

3: B WILLS, FISCHE 73
PG 245
4: B ADA 12
5: A 400/12/1/20
8: A 400/13/119
9: A 400/37/124
10: A 400/31/17

Mr. Marchant Promotes Cricket

1: D 14-7-1834
2: F 31-8-1833
3: A 400/37/123
4: B MOB 1002
5: E 18-9-1835
6: A 400/30/4 & 31/118

Mr. Faithfull Campaigns Again

1 & 4:
G 24-2-1835
2: E 14-1-1835
3: H 9-2-1835
5: A 400/31/119
6: C MH 12/12829
7: A 400/12/1/20
8: A G3/2A/1
9: G 26-3-1835

Mr. Marchant Hits Out

1: D 19-6-1835
2: D 24-7-1835
3: G 11-8-1835
4: E 22-7-1835
5: A 400/12/1/20
6: G 18-8-1835
7: G 15-9-1835
8: E 23-9-1835
11: BAXTER'S BRIGHTON DIRECTORY 1822

Samuel Goodman Meets The Marquis Of Worcester

1: D 22-7-1835
2: D 13 & 27-8 1835
3: G 15-9-1835
4: E 18-11-1835
5: E 18-11-1835
6: A 400/12/1/21
7: H 14-12-1835
8: N 21-2-1846

Edward Oram Enjoys an Evening Drink

1: M PG 167
2: B QO/EW/54
3 ,5, 8 &11:
A G3/1A/1
4: D 2-7-1835
6: G 13-10 1835
7: C MH 12/12824
9: G 8-3-1838 & D 17-3-1838
10: C MH 12/12832
12: D 24-8-1837
13: A G3/2A/1

Samuel Goodman Braves the Winter Snow

1: D 8-9-1836
2: B ADA 11
3: D 2-5-1836

4: D 8-12-1836
5: B MOB 1004
6: C MH 12 12381
7: G 27-12-1836
8, 9 & 11:
A ADD.MSS 17,735 1, 6, 12, 15, 19, 22, 23, 29-1 & 18-4-1837
10: C MH 12/12831

Dr. Weekes Builds a Grand Hotel

1: I 15-12-1838
2: D 14-2-1839
3: G MAY 1838
4: A ADDMS 17734 & E 11-9-1833
5, 6 & 7:
A ADDMS 17734

Peter Pratt Breaks his Leg

1: E 8-7-1838
2: I 14/21-7-1838
3: I 14-7-1838
4: I 25-9-1828
5: I 15-11-1838 & B DAN 497 30-11 & 1-12-1838
6: C MH 12 12831
7: A 400/12/1/21, C MH 12 12832 & H I 1-4-1837

Rev. Borrer Finds his Church Burgled

1: I 14-4-1839
2: B QAC/1/E1(32)
3: E 4-9-1839/D 19-9-1839
4: I 24-9-1839
5: A G3/1A/ 2
6: B QE/E/868
7, 8 & 9:
D 30-1, 13 & 20-2 1840
10: B ADA 12
11: D 27-2-1840
12: A G3/1A/2 & C MH 12/12832
13: E 2-12-1840

English Corney Goes to Market

1: D 2-7-1847
2: D 10-9-1840
3: I 12-11-1840
4: I 16-1-1841

Peter Pratt Collects Mutton for his Family

1: B ADA12 PG 123
2: A G3/1A/3
3: H 8-2-1841
4: I 27-3-1841 & D 29-4-1841
5: I 20-3-1841
6: A 400/12/4 & G3/1A/3
7: D 2-6-1841
8: A 400/12/4
9: B QO/EW/58 & I 3-7-1841
10 & 11:
N 21-2-1846

Samuel Goodman Supports the Railway

1: I 17-7-1841

2: B DAN 498
3: B QO/EW/57 & QR/ E/878
4: D 23-9-1841
5 & 6:
E 6-10 & 22-9 1841
7, 8 & 9:
D 25-11, 4-11-1841 & 20-1-1842
10, 11 & 12:
D 13-1, 14-4 & 14-7-1842

George Sayers Sails for Bermuda

1: D 15-2-1844 & H 16-3-1844
2: C HO8, 893
3: C MH 12/12832
4: A G3/1A/3
5 & 6:
C MH 12/12833
7: I 24-6-1846
8: B QO/EW/58

George Marchant Auctions more Building Plots

1: A 400/12/4
2: A 400/4/39
3: B DAN 499
4: I 7-10-1843
5: I 25-3-1844
6 & 12:
D 15-2 & 4-4 1844
7: D 14-10 1843
8: I 14-11-1843
9: I 28-11-1843
10: I 12-2-1844
11: B ADA 11
13: HAMPSHIRE TELEGRAPH 5, 12, 19 & 25-10-1844
14: A 400/12/4
15: C MH 12/12834

Billy Heaver Climbs the Social Ladder

1: KELLY, POST OFFICE DIRECTORY 1845
2 & 3:
I 31-5-1845
4: A BORRER DIARY MS
5: I 23-8 & 13-9 1845
6: I 30-8-1845
7 & 8:
A 400/12/1/4
9: B DAN 2171

Jenny Lind Captivates Brighton

1: I 18-7 & 15-8 1846
2: N 20-2-1847
3: E 24-8-1847
4: D 2-8-1847
5: H 24-8-1847
6: I 17-9 & 9-10-1847
7: E 21-6-1848
8: H 2-6-1848
9: F 1-9-1848
10: H 30-5-1848
11: H 5-12-1848
12: A 400/12/4

13: H 7-11-1848
14: A 400/13/3

William Bartley Writes a Letter

1: C HO/893
2: C HO/893
3: A 400/12/4 & C MH 12/12836
4: CUSTOMS BILL LONDON 'A' 1-1-1849
5: I 17-3-1849
6: F 24-8-1849
7: I 3-10 -1849
8: I 13-11-1849
9: E 6-2-1850
10: I 23-11-1850
11: B MOB 1072

Parish Vestry: bills; receipts; request notes

1: A 400/31/82
2: A 400/31/97 & 107
3: A 400/31/110
4: A/G3/1A/4
5: A 400/9/3/2
6: A/400/31/93 & 118
7: A 400/31/92

Money, Weights and Measures

It is impossible to make exact conversions every time. In money, one old penny (1d.) is a bit less than ½p, although one shilling (1s. 0d.) is exactly 5p. In weight, one old ounce (oz.) is 28.35 grams; one old pound (lb.) is 454 grams. In length, one inch (ins) is 25.4 millimetres, one yard (yd.) is 0.9144 metres ('exactly' says the dictionary!). In area, one acre is 0.405 hectares – but who can envisage a large area? Even harder is comparing old prices with today's: the 1790 farm-worker's weekly wage of 9 shillings (45p); a year's rent £2 10s. 0d. (£2.50); cheese 2¾d. per lb (about 2p per kg!); £12 to cross the Atlantic; a new church for £7000.

		'Old'		'New' Equivalents	
Money		¼d farthing (th as in 'the')			
		½d halfpenny ('hayp-nee')			
	penny	d.		2.4d = 1p	
	shilling	s.	12d. = 1s. 0d.	1s. 0d. = 5p	
	half-crown		2s. 6d.	2s. 6d. = 12.5p	
	crown		5s. 0d.	10s. 0d. = 50p	
	pound £		20s. = £1	20s. 0d. = £1	
	guinea		21s. = a guinea	guinea = £1.05	

4s. 8¾d. is read 'Four shillings and eightpence three-farthings'.
£3 10s. 6½d. is 'Three pounds, ten and sixpence hayp-nee.'
1s. 0d. is 'one shilling'.
7d. is 'sevenpence.'

Weight	ounce	oz.	16 ozs. = 1 lb.	1 oz. = 30 g	
	pound	lb.	14 lbs. = 1 st.	1 lb. = ½ kg	
	stone	st.	2 st. = 1 qr.	1 st. = 6 kg	
	quarter	qr.	4 qrs. = 1 cwt.	1 cwt. = 50 kg	
	hundredweight	cwt.	20 cwt. = 1 ton	1 (long) ton = 1.016 tonnes	

4lbs. 6ozs. is read: 'Four pounds six ounces.'

Length	inch	in.	12 ins. = 1 ft.	1in. = 25 mm	
	foot	ft.	3 feet = 1 yd.	1ft. = 0.3 m	
	yard	yd.	1760 yds. = 1 mile	1yd. = 0.9 m	
	mile	ml		1 mile = 1.6 km	

ell = 1¼ yds.= 1.1m A cloth measure in weaving & bleaching and making up into clothes.
2 ft. 6ins is : 'Two feet six inches.'

Liquid	pint	pt.	2 pt. = 1 qt.	1pt. = 0.5 litres	
	quart	qt.	4 qts. = 1 gal.	1qt. = 1.0 litres	
	gallon	gal.		1gal. = 4.5 litres	
Dry	quart	qt.	4 qts. = 1 gal.	1 quart = 1 litre	
	gallon	gal.	2 gals.= 1 peck	1 gallon = 4.5 litres	
	peck		4 pecks = 1 bush.		
	bushel	bush.	8 bush = 1 qr.	1 bushel = 36 litres	
	quarter	qr.	5 qrs. = 1 load.	27.5 bushels = 1 kilolitre	
Area	square yard	4840 sq yd.= 1 acre	1 sq yd. = 0.8 sq m		
	acre	640 acres = 1 sq ml	1 acre = 0.4 hectares (ha)		
			1 sq ml. = 259 hectares		

Sources

Libraries and Collections

◇ West Sussex County Record Office, Chichester

◇ East Sussex County Record Office, Lewes

◇ Kent County Record Office, Canterbury

◇ Suffolk County Record Office, Ipswich

◇ Hurstpierpoint Library

◇ Brighton Reference Library

◇ British Museum Library

◇ Hove Library

◇ National Newspaper Library, Colindale

◇ Public Records Office, Kew

Books

◇ *A Medical Student at St. Thomas's Hospital, 1801-1802 The Weekes Family Letters* by John M.T. Ford: London Wellcome Institute for the History of Medicine 1987

◇ *A Sussex Farmer.* William Wood: Jonathan Cape 1938

◇ *A Sussex Soldier of Wellington's Army. 1811-1815*: The Sussex County Magazine, 1928

◇ *Baxter's Brighton Directory, 1822.Kelly's Post Office Directory, 1845*

◇ *Slight Sketch of a Picture of Hurst by A Native of this Village.* W. Randell, 1825

◇ *Sussex in Bygone Days.* Nathaniel Paine Blaker; Combridges, Hove, 1919

Newspapers

◇ Brighton Gazette

◇ Brighton Guardian

◇ Brighton Herald

◇ Brighton Patriot

◇ Hampshire Telegraph

◇ The True Sun

◇ Lewes and Sussex County Advertiser

◇ Sussex Agricultural Express

◇ The Illustrated London News

Index

The index is of people, places and selected items – e.g. food. It records first relevant appearance in each chapter. Surnames are in **bold** print; place names within Hurstpierpoint Parish are in *italics*; other Sussex place names are underlined; seas and foreign places are in Capitals.

A

Adams 205, 206, 266, 279, 285

Adelaide 231, 245

Afganistan 263

Africa 271

Agricultural Association 223

Albourne 59, 95, 112, 156

Aldgate 262

allotment 202, 213, 223, 235, 242, 297

Althorp 177, 189

America 70, 73, 167

animal 2, 12, 37, 47, 124, 129, 151, 223, 244, 252, 286

Antinomian 276

Antwerp 226

apprentice 6, 78, 83, 98, 100

archery 152, 225, 285

Ardingly 10

army 29, 41, 69, 82

arson 158

Arundel 13

assizes 45, 59, 76, 148, 158, 161,

asylum 33, 54, 173, 250

Atlantic 73, 143, 167, 264, 289

Attree 53

auction 61, 146, 168, 190, 225, 250, 280

Austin 279

B

Australia 148, 158, 231, 245, 258, 292

bailiff 17, 89, 94, 146, 203

Balcombe 236

balloon 39, 133, 229, 279

band 171, 196, 201, 270, 278, 289

bank 268

Barcombe 9, 23

Bartley 4, 16, 33, 44, 54, 61, 75, 82, 94, 100, 151, 160, 182, 190, 213, 223, 235, 250, 277, 289, 297

Bath 138

Battle 15, 31, 43

Batty 285

Bay of Biscay 60

beadle 103, 127, 145, 247

Beard 4

Beazley 30

Beeching 252, 278, 290

Belfast 225

Belgium 73

bell ringers 36, 45, 127, 169, 281

Bermuda 264, 292

Bethlehem Hospital 54

Bexhill 133

Bignall 44, 59, 236

Bingham 166

bird 2, 35, 124, 160, 207

Birmingham 166, 226

Blackfriars 68

blacksmith 4, 14, 42, 115, 118, 180

blindness 248

Bodle 7, 48, 53

Bolney 156

Bombay 231

Bonaparte 41, 59, 69, 73

Borrer 1, 6, 16, 17, 36, 41, 50, 87, 94, 110, 124, 127, 155, 174, 180, 187, 202, 213, 225, 229, 235, 242, 252, 271, 276, 284, 293

Botten 129

Bowling Alley 5, 91, 180, 279, 289

Bramber 46, 169

Brenchley 82

bricklayer 13, 98, 104, 197, 268

Brighton 18, 41, 72, 78, 88, 95, 101, 103, 111, 116, 127, 150, 155, 196, 200, 206, 256, 266, 275, 277, 285

Bristol 59, 138

Brixton 130

Brooker 207

Brussels 227

Bubb 211

Buckman 78, 97, 134, 162, 251

Bull 94, 184, 229, 244, 270, 290, 293

Burchett 17, 52

Burdett 177

Burry 141

Burt 161

Burtenshaw 6, 13

butcher 5, 10, 116, 190, 252, 268, 277, 291

C

Cain 166

Campion 1, 6, 16, 20, 28, 33, 37, 42, 50, 61, 66, 89, 113, 129, 145, 151, 155, 159, 167, 174, 181, 186, 192, 197, 205, 230, 239, 244, 247, 256, 269, 278, 284

Canada 293

Cane 274

Canterbury 83

Carlisle 166

Carpenter 30

carpenter 1, 25, 78, 104, 205, 268, 271, 281

Carpue 259

carriage 68, 144, 164, 216, 225, 259, 270

carrier 39, 102, 268, 270

cart 11, 39, 47, 59, 90, 93, 102, 138, 140, 183, 267, 289, 295

cattle 47, 150, 244

census 34, 61, 159, 250

Chailey 186

Chain Pier 262, 278

Chalcroft 116